Interpreting Educational Research

An Introduction for Consumers
of Research

Daniel R. Hittleman
Alan J. Simon
Queens College of the City University of New York

Merrill, an imprint of
Macmillan Publishing Company
New York

Maxwell Macmillan Canada
Toronto

Maxwell Macmillan International
New York Oxford Singapore Sydney

Cover art by Marsha McDevitt
Editor: Linda A. Sullivan
Production Editor: Constantina Geldis
Cover Designer: Cathleen Norz
Production Buyer: Pamela D. Bennett

This book was set in Caledonia and was printed and bound by
R. R. Donnelley & Sons Company. The cover was printed by New England
Book Components.

Macmillan Publishing Company
866 Third Avenue
New York, NY 10022

Macmillan Publishing Company is part of the
Maxwell Communication Group of Companies.

Maxwell Macmillan Canada, Inc.
1200 Eglinton Avenue East, Suite 200
Don Mills, Ontario M3C 3N1

Library of Congress Cataloging-in-Publication Data

Hittleman, Daniel R.
    Interpreting educational research : an introduction for consumers
of research / Daniel R. Hittleman, Alan J. Simon.
        p.   cm.
    Includes index.
    ISBN 0-675-21261-8
    1. Education—Research.   2. Research—Methodology.
3. Education—Research—Evaluation.   I. Simon, Alan J.   II. Title.
LB1028.H537   1992
370′.7′8—dc20   91-21421
                                                                                      CIP

Printing: 2 3 4 5 6 7 8 9   Year: 4 5

To Carol and Carole
With our love

Preface

We intend this text for use in introductory research courses in which students are prepared as consumers rather than as producers of research. We provide preservice and inservice teachers with basic knowledge and the skills for reading, interpreting, and evaluating both quantitative and qualitative educational research so that they can make instructional decisions based upon those research results. This knowledge base will also be useful for teachers who will collaborate in research projects and act as classroom teacher researchers; however, that is not our principal concern. In addition, our text provides a guide for composing action reviews of research.

Through directed activities, which we base on current whole-language theories and practices for reading and writing content area discourse, we guide readers to independence in the use of techniques for reading, interpreting, evaluating, and writing about educational research. We approach the evaluation of educational research from the point of view that teachers become research consumers by understanding the underlying methodological and procedural assumptions used by educators who are research producers. In essence, we guide teachers to research literacy by having them learn to think as researcher producers.

ORGANIZATION

The text is organized into eleven chapters and two appendices. In Chapters 1, 2, and 3, we lead the reader to an understanding of research designs and the general procedures used by research producers, and we provide a plan for reading research reports. In Chapters 4 through 9, we present extended discussions of the different aspects of research design and methodology and we present illustrations of the manner in which research producers present their findings in research reports. In Chapters 10 and 11, we provide information about reading and writing reviews of research and about sources for locating research reports. In the appendices, we have included five complete research reports for additional study and analysis. A glossary of key terms is also provided.

For each chapter, we begin with a graphical overview of the content in addition to focus questions so readers can attend to the key ideas of the chapter and the interrelationships portrayed in the structured overview. In the main body of the chapters we have placed techniques for reading, interpreting, and writing about the portions of the research methodology. In the activities section at the end of each chapter, we present ways for the reader to gain greater understanding of the key concepts and proficiency in applying the evaluative techniques. For each of these activities, we provide feedback, in which we give readers samples of how we respond to our own students' work.

A list of special features follows:

- The material is conceptualized for consumers of educational research.
- Preservice and inservice teachers learn to read and write about educational research in a nonthreatening, supportive manner. A step-by-step process leads teachers to an ability to understand and use research reports.
- Information about and strategies for reading both quantitative and qualitative (ethnographic or naturalistic) research are included.
- The chapters begin with a structured overview of the content.
- Specific strategies that have proved effective for the reading of texts for typical content areas and the writing of content area–related expository prose are applied to the reading of research reports and writing of research reviews.
- Ample practice is provided for developing each reader's skills in evaluating educational research.
- All forms of research are illustrated with current original research reports.
- Readers get an understanding about both integrative reviews and meta-analyses and guidance in the preparation of action-integrative reviews.
- A glossary contains the definitions of all key terms presented in the text.
- The appendices contain whole research reports for additional practice and supplementary information for the students.

ACKNOWLEDGMENTS

No book is ever done without the input and assistance of others, and we are indebted for the help and assistance of many people. We are grateful for the encouragement and support of our colleagues at Queens College/CUNY and the comments and reactions of students who read preliminary drafts of the book. We are appreciative of the critical comments of David Bills, University of Iowa; David Bloome, University of Massachusetts—Amherst; Richard Burnett, University of Missouri—St. Louis; Karen Ford, University of North Texas; John Guthrie, California State University—Hayward; Glen Hymel, Loyola University; Barbara Lezar, Loyola Marymount University; Glenn Mitchell, University of Massachusetts—Boston; and Paul Westmeyer, University of Texas—San Antonio. Also, we appreciate the critical review of a preliminary draft by the late John Kron, Edinboro University of Pennsylvania. Although we have taken their comments under advisement and made efforts to attend to their concerns, we ultimately are responsible for the contents of the text. We also are extremely grateful for the help and assistance of the editorial staff at Merrill, an imprint of Macmillan Publishing Company: Linda Sullivan, Connie Geldis, Dave Faherty, and Russ Maselli.

Brief Contents

Contents

Figures and Tables

FIGURES

TABLES

1 The Research Process

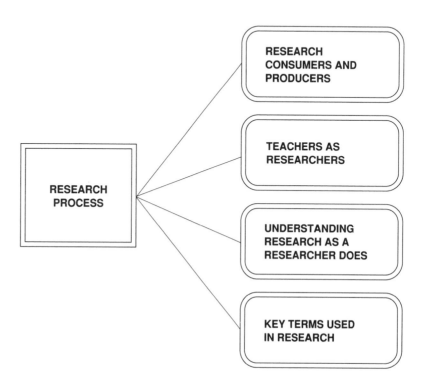

FOCUS QUESTIONS

1. Why do educators conduct research?
2. What is the distinction between research consumers and research producers?
3. What does it mean to understand research like a research producer?
4. What are some key terms about educational research?

Teachers at all levels continually make decisions about instructional activities such as curriculum selection, teaching techniques, classroom management, and student learning. They base these decisions on their experiences, other teachers' experiences, and their understanding of accumulated knowledge about education. Much of the knowledge

why would teachers be interested?

about teaching and learning comes from educational researchers who seek answers to educational questions or try to clarify some existing educational issue. One sign of a productive profession such as education is the systematic attempt by its researchers and practitioners to examine the knowledge base upon which the profession functions. For the purposes of this book, the systematic attempt to examine a knowledge base is called research.

Research is the systematic attempt to (a) collect information about an identified problem or question, (b) analyze that information, and (c) apply the evidence thus derived to confirm or disconfirm some prior prediction or statement about that problem. The research process follows the principles of the scientific method. Educational research is not unique within the total research community; it is the application of some generally accepted systematic procedures to examining the knowledge base of education. Akin to educational research is educational evaluation, the use of research techniques to judge the effectiveness of existing, in-place programs of instruction. For the general purposes of this book, educational evaluation is considered a subarea of educational research.

Five characteristics seem indicative of a profession whose members research its knowledge base (Berliner, 1987). First, professionals work at verifying ideas and practices believed to be effective. Often teachers read about a "new" teaching technique in a professional journal and say, "We've known that all along!" As professionals, however, teachers cannot rely entirely on a commonsense approach; intuition needs to be supported and substantiated through research.

Second, professionals work at discovering new ideas and practices. The need for new ideas and practices is almost self-evident but is exemplified by one new idea that was researched and is now being used in schools: the application of students' self-regulated learning to improving classroom practice (Corno, 1987).

Third, professionals clarify ideas that are designed to simplify teaching. This is illustrated by the application of research results about collaborative learning procedures in elementary and high schools (Cooperative Learning, 1989–1990).

Fourth, although professional educators try to simplify teaching, they often express ideas that may complicate everyone's teaching. An example of this effect is the growing body of research findings indicating how the learning of many students with disabling conditions is improved in mainstream classes as opposed to self-contained classes (Leinhardt & Pallay, 1982; Madden & Slavin, 1983).

Fifth, professionals discover ideas and practices that are counterintuitive. For example, many educators assume that grouping in self-contained classes according to students' ability permits students to work more effectively with peers and to have instruction adapted to their performance level. Regarding mastery learning, however, research evidence does not seem to support this contention. Instead, it shows that students may achieve more when they are in classes of mixed ability for most of the day. Cross-grade assignments also may increase students' achievement. Limited grouping of students at the same level seems effective only when it is done for specific skill instruction (Slavin, 1987a–c).

RESEARCH CONSUMERS AND PRODUCERS

audience for book

This book is intended for research consumers—the people who read, interpret, and apply the information systematically collected and examined (researched) by others. Like research producers, research consumers are interested in answering educationally related questions; however, they do so by reading and applying research producers' results, rather than by conducting research.

Research consumers need to read research with a mindset similar to that of research producers—similar, but not the same. Research producers need certain skills to put different phases of educational research into operation. They need technical competence in applying research strategies. Research consumers, on the other hand, need to understand decisions facing research producers, possible alternatives they may consider at those decision points, and implications of researchers' results and conclusions. Also, they need a means of judging the adequacy of research producers' work.

We believe a research consumer can more fully understand educational research by reading research as a research producer does. The research consumer reads research by reconstructing the researcher's message and constructing a meaning from the information on the page—much as students reconstruct a message during a class lecture and then construct its meaning for themselves. The reader may create meanings different from those intended by the writer (as may a listener in response to a speaker). Research consumers reach understanding by reconstructing the ideas of researcher producers as well as by constructing meanings of their own. A consumer's understanding is constructed from that person's prior knowledge and prior experiences, combined with that person's maturity and his or her proficiency in manipulating research ideas.

TEACHERS AS RESEARCHERS

Although the concept of teachers as researchers is not new, our understanding of how important it is for classroom teachers to collaborate with research producers and to produce research themselves has been increasing (Olson, 1990; Santa, 1988). This text is not intended to create research producers. Even so, the mindset of "reading research as a researcher" presented here, and the ideas about research methods and research evaluation presented in subsequent chapters (especially those about qualitative research and action research methodology) will provide teachers with the background knowledge and understanding they need to participate in such research projects.

It is especially important that classroom teachers collaborate with researchers when changes in curriculum and instructional procedures are being reevaluated. Curriculum and instructional leadership should not be expected to come solely from university research centers and state and federal agencies; instead, teachers are being called upon to participate in research that will significantly affect what happens in the classroom. Collaborating in this research

(1) reduces the gap between research findings and classroom practice, (2) creates a problem solving mindset that helps teachers when they consider other classroom dilemmas, (3) improves teachers' instructional decision making processes, (4) increases the professional status of teachers, (5) helps empower teachers to influence their own profession at classroom, district, state, and national levels, and (6) offers the overriding and ultimate advantage of providing the potential for improving the educational process for children. (Olson, 1990, pp. 17–18)

UNDERSTANDING RESEARCH FROM THE PERSPECTIVE OF A RESEARCHER

Research producers present the results of their research in reports. (The specific form of those reports is discussed in Chapter 3.) To comprehend a research report fully, the research consumer must understand research producers' processes in conceptualizing, developing, implementing, and reporting research. To illustrate the process, the way one research team might develop a project is described below. Although the process is presented linearly for illustrative purposes, research consumers should realize that the process actually may not unfold in such a clear sequence. The researchers may start and stop several times, reject questions and possible solutions, and encounter many pitfalls.

The researchers select a problem area and specify research questions.

From personal experience, professional readings, or discussions with colleagues, our hypothetical research team selects a problem area for study. For example, thoughts arise about the writing performance of middle school students who are learning disabled. (The differing and often confusing definitions of learning disability will be disregarded here.) These thoughts flow from an array of concerns, a few of which follow.

First, many students with learning disabilities are mainstreamed for particular academic classes. Second, writing skill has increasingly become an issue in the teaching and learning of content areas other than language or communication arts. Third, different writing skills may be needed in different content areas (e.g., science, social studies, mathematics, or technology).

The researchers are concerned about the use to which the answers of these questions might be put. These concerns lead to other questions. Are the answers to be applicable only to the students in one specific school, grade level, or class? Are the answers to be used for the students in an entire district, state, region, or nation? Should the writing of students with learning disabilities be compared with that of students who do not have such disabilities?

The next set of concerns deals with the teaching and learning of writing. The researchers wish to know: What is the writing performance of the students with learning disabilities and how does it compare with that of students without disabilities? Also, what can be done to help the students with disabilities write effectively in the content areas? Of equal importance to the researchers is: Are these question interrelated or can any one of them be answered without answering the others?

(The question "Why do students with learning disabilities write the way they do?" is also of concern. However, seeking answers to it moves the researchers away from a primary concern with instruction.)

The researchers examine and search data bases to review existing research results and define terms.

At this point, the researchers try to find out what other researchers have done to answer these or similar questions. By consulting books, educational encyclopedias, professional journals, and electronic data bases, the researchers gain insights about what others have done and what conclusions were drawn from their research. The researchers know their work is based on certain assumptions, one of which is that it will add to the body of educational knowledge. Their aim is to help other researchers and practitioners reach some agreement about the controversy surrounding the teaching of writing to students with learning disabilities.

After reviewing the material from these sources, the researchers conclude that the meaning of certain terms requires clarification. For example, they realize several terms are defined differently by different researchers: learning disability, language arts, communication arts, content area classes, writing, composing, mainstreaming, and regular education. The researchers select an accepted definition or create new ones to enhance communication with other researchers and users of the research.

The researchers formulate researchable questions.

Now they return to the questions about the teaching and learning of writing. A decision must be made about answering one or more of them. They decide to answer three questions and must now determine whether those questions need to be answered in a specific order. The answer is yes, because the answer to the question "What can be done to help students with learning disabilities write effectively in the content areas?" presupposes answers to the others. So, the researchers decide first to answer the questions "What is the writing performance of students with learning disabilities?" and "How does that performance compare with that of students without learning disabilities?" (a question of major concern since the researchers wish to examine the writing of students with learning disabilities in mainstream classes).

The researchers select research designs.

The researchers now have three studies. (It is possible for the researchers to conduct these three studies as one, but this is not done here so that the three different research plans can be highlighted.) For each, they need a different research plan, or design. **Research designs** are methods for answering questions. Just as skilled craftspeople and artisans have several methods for manipulating their raw material, so do researchers. Some research designs are more appropriate or effective for answering certain questions. Also, more than one plan may be appropriate or effective for answering a particular question.

In the first study, the researchers want to describe the writing performance of students with learning disabilities. The description is to be in statistical and in nonstatistical form (see **statistics** in Glossary). They decide on several activities. They decide to describe the students' processes for beginning a writing task, their topics and organization of ideas, the maturity of their vocabulary and sentence structure, the grammatical form of their works, and the physical aspects of their writing.

To compare the writing of students with learning disabilities to that of students who do not have such disabilities in a second study, the researchers will collect the same data from both groups. They plan a statistical and nonstatistical comparison of the two types of students.

For the third study, the researchers will seek to answer "What can be done to help students with learning disabilities write effectively in the content areas?" To answer this question, the researchers set up one or more instructional programs and look at them singly and in combination to see which has the greatest effect (or any effect) on the writing performance of these students.

The researchers determine the research method.

Each of the three plans has both common and unique aspects. The common aspects include efforts the researchers must make to determine (a) where and when the research is to occur, (b) with whom specifically the research will be done, (c) with what device students' characteristics and their writing will be assessed, and (d) what statistical methods will be used in describing, comparing, and analyzing the data.

INTERPRETING EDUCATIONAL RESEARCH

In selecting a location, the researchers think about conducting the studies in a special site such as a college educational clinic or in a middle school classroom. Both have advantages and disadvantages. An educational clinic allows the researchers better control of the data collection environment and the opportunity to make unobtrusive observations and recordings. However, the setting is not educationally natural, since the students need to be brought to it under special circumstances. A classroom lets the researchers observe and collect data in the setting where the students usually learn and work. However, a classroom has distractions that might influence the data collection and the students' performances in ways the researchers may not recognize. After weighing the pros and cons, the researchers decide to conduct all three studies in middle school classrooms, fully aware that they must make some effort to reduce or eliminate the possible influence of certain distractions.

The researchers describe and select the students to be used in the study.

The researchers are interested in doing the study with middle school students. The specific students for the study are selected with consideration for the researchers being able to pass on the results to others in similar urban centers. They select a middle school affiliated with their college because its total student population reflects the same range of ability and performance test scores and demographic characteristics of the county as a whole. All students classified as learning disabled in grades five through eight, in both mainstreamed and self-contained classes, are included.

The researchers must describe the students for others, and so they collect relevant data normally found in students' permanent records —information such as age, sex, grade level, educational history, and attendance.

The researchers select tests to score students' writing.

The researchers also begin to document the students' writing performance. To do this, samples of the students' writing in content area classes are obtained and scored by some accepted system. The researchers have the option to use one or more achievement tests or a scoring system known as holistic scoring.

The researchers conduct the study.

The researchers now have enough information to answer the first question, "What is the writing performance of the students with learning disabilities?" To answer the second question, "How does the writing performance of students with learning disabilities compare with that of students without learning disabilities?" the researchers collect the same data about students who do not have learning disabilities. Because it is impractical to collect data about all such students in the middle school, the researchers decide to randomly select a portion of the students without learning disabilities at each grade level.

As the researchers proceed, another question arises. The researchers want to know, "Are teachers using any instructional strategies and techniques that seem to enhance the learning of students who are learning disabled?" To answer this question, they set up a series of classroom observations and teacher interviews. They wish to determine possible answers to this question by collecting information about what occurs in classrooms while teaching and learning are happening. As they collect this information, they sort it and seek out patterns of teacher–learner interactions.

To answer their last question, "What can be done to help students with learning disabilities write effectively in the content areas?" the researchers select and prepare instructional activities and collect additional data. Using the information gleaned from other research, from professional sources, and from their classroom observations and teacher interviews, the researchers create or select three instructional programs that have shown promise for teaching students who are learning disabled. The researchers' question now becomes "Which of these instructional programs help the students who are learning disabled write effectively in content area classes?" or "Which of the programs causes the students to write effectively?" The researchers decide how long (for how many days, weeks, or months) the instructional program will last and who will do the actual teaching. They plan to have all content teachers in the middle school participate in a special eight-week after school workshop about implementing one of the instructional programs. The teachers are to use the techniques for the 12 weeks following the workshop.

Additional data about students' writing performance are collected during and after the instructional programs. The researchers now conduct the studies.

The researchers analyze the data and determine implications of the research.

After conducting the study and collecting the data, the researchers analyze the data using appropriate statistical and nonstatistical methods. Then, they determine what implications the results have for other researchers and teachers.

The researchers publish their results.

After conducting its research, the team produces a written report. For example, after beginning activities to answer their third question, the researchers describe (a) their reason for conducting the study; (b) the conclusions they and others have made about previous research; (c) the steps they took to select the students, the writing scoring procedure, and the instructional activities; (d) the in-service workshop, the instructional programs, and the way they were used in the content area classes; and (e) the statistical and nonstatistical results.

KEY TERMS USED IN RESEARCH

Most key research terms are defined as they occur in this book. A few, however, are introduced now because they underpin most of the discussions. Additional information about these and other key terms occurs elsewhere. The glossary contains all key terms discussed in this book.

Variable. In the broadest sense, a variable is anything in a research situation that varies. It can be a human characteristic (of students or teachers) or it can be a characteristic of classrooms, groups, schools and school districts, instructional materials, and so on. These characteristics are called variables, and they can be measured. Educationally relevant traits of humans, among many, include age, intelligence, reading scores, learning style, level of motivation, sensitivity to noise, and ethnicity. Educationally relevant nonhuman characteristics include, among many, the size of print in textbooks, the number of times an event occurs, the location of schools, the economic status of families, and students' attendance records.

Research design. The research design is the plan used to study an educational problem or question. In the example of the research team, three broad designs were discussed: descriptive, comparative, and causative. **Descriptive research** provides information about one or more variables. **Comparative research** provides an explanation about the extent of a relationship between two or more variables. **Causative,** or experimental, **research** provides information about how one or more variables influence another variable.

Hypothesis. A hypothesis is a tentative statement about how two or more variables are related.

In current practice, many researchers convey the relationship as a statement of purpose, a question, or a prediction. For the causation design above, the researchers' question "Which of two instructional programs helps students with learning disabilities write effectively in content area classes?" could be in these forms:

Directional hypothesis: There will be a change in the way students with learning disabilities in middle schools write after receiving effective writing instruction in content area classes.

Prediction: Instructional program A will produce a greater change in the way students with learning disabilities in middle schools write in content area classes than will program B.

Statement of purpose: The purpose of the study is to determine whether either of two instructional programs helps students with learning disabilities in middle schools to improve their writing.

Question: Which of the two programs causes students with learning disabilities in middle schools to write more effectively?

implicit hypothesis

Subjects. The subjects are the particular individuals used in the research. One group of subjects in the above designs consisted of all students classified as learning disabled in grades five through eight in mainstreamed and self-contained classes in an urban middle school. In the comparative and causation designs, the researchers also used as their subjects a small group of students who were not learning disabled. They randomly selected a portion of the students without learning disabilities at each grade level. This selected group is a **sample** of all the students without learning disabilities in the school. The **population** is the larger group with which the researchers think their results can be used. They are interested in being able to pass on the results about students with and without learning disabilities in middle school to other educators in other urban centers.

Generalizability. When research producers' results can be extended to other groups (for example, to other students with and without learning disabilities in urban centers), these results are said to have **generalizability.** That means, a research consumer in a different urban center can have confidence in applying the team's research results because they are applicable to middle school students with learning disabilities in urban centers.

OVERVIEW

The ideas in this book are organized to reflect the phases of research as research producers would go through them. In Table 1.1, the phases of research undertaken by the research team in the example is linked to the information in later chapters.

ACTIVITIES

Each chapter has an activities section in which the book's readers are asked to apply the chapter's content. Two sources of feedback are available to the reader. The first consists of the authors' ideas imme-

Table 1.1 Overview of the Research Process

The Research Team's Activity	Phases of Research
Selecting a problem area; specifying research questions and defining terms	Reading and Evaluating Introductory Sections: Abstract, Background, and Purpose, Chapter 4
Searching data bases	Locating Information about Research Reports, Chapter 11
Selecting research designs	Research Designs, Chapter 2
Describing and selecting subjects	Reading and Evaluating Subject Selections, Chapter 5
Selecting tests and materials	Reading and Evaluating Instrumentation Sections, Chapter 6
Conducting the study	Reading and Evaluating Procedure Sections, Chapter 7
Analyzing the data	Reading and Interpreting Results Sections, Chapter 8
Determining implications of the research	Reading and Evaluating Discussion Sections, Chapter 9
Reporting the results	Reading and Evaluating Research Reports, Chapter 3; Reading and Interpreting Reviews of Research, Chapter 10

diately following the activities. The second consists of the course instructor's feedback.

1. Write a summary of the key ideas found in the chapter. The focus questions at the chapter beginning should be used as a guide to structure your summary.
2. Using Table 1.1 as a guide, read the research report "The Role of Underlining and Annotating in Remembering Textual Information" by Nist & Hogrebe (1987) on pp. 12–22. As you read the report, locate the particular sections in which information is given. Do not be concerned about fully understanding the report.

Nist, S. L., & Hogrebe, M. C. (1987). The role of underlining and annotating in remembering textual information. *Reading Research and Instruction, 27,* 12–25.

The Role of Underlining and Annotating in Remembering Textual Information

Sherrie L. Nist
University of Georgia

Mark C. Hogrebe
National College of Education
St. Louis, Missouri

ABSTRACT

(1) The purpose of this study was to explore opposing theoretical viewpoints as they relate to and attempt to explain the effects of text underlining. The subjects were 67 provisionally admitted freshmen who were randomly assigned to one of four experimenter-generated underlining or underlining and annotating conditions, or a fifth group who generated their own text marking. During two sessions, all subjects took a test of prior knowledge, read the assigned passage, and took a 24 item multiple-choice test consisting of 12 high relevant and 12 low relevant questions. Data analysis supported the von Restorff effect as a theoretical explanation of text underlining since subjects in the high relevant groups answered more high relevant items correctly, while subjects in the low relevant groups answered more low relevant items correctly. Subjects who generated their own underlining did not perform significantly better than those who were given experimenter-generated marking. Additionally, prior knowledge was not significantly related to the three dependent measures.

(2) The major purpose of this study was to investigate opposing theoretical viewpoints as they relate to and attempt to explain text underlining. While underlining is perhaps the most widely used of all study strategies (Anderson & Armbruster, 1984), it has not been researched very extensively. One possible explanation for this dilemma is that the process is extremely complex and convoluted, hence difficult to explore. Perhaps this is why the extant research offers little insight into the role that text marking plays in remembering important textual information.

(3) The majority of the available research focuses on two major areas: (1) comparing subject-generated underlining with researcher-generated underlining (Cashen & Leicht, 1970; Fowler & Barker, 1974; Glynn & Divesta, 1979; Hartley, Bartlett, & Branth-

waite, 1980; Rickards & August, 1975; Schnell & Rocchio, 1975; Smart & Bruning, 1973) and (2) comparing underlining with other study strategies (Hoon, 1974; Idstein & Jenkins, 1972; Johnson & Wen, 1976; Kulhavy, Dyer, & Silver, 1975; Stordahl & Christensen, 1956). However, as Hartley et al. (1980) correctly point out, it is very difficult, if not impossible, to compare the results of these studies. Of primary consideration is the fact that the number of studies is small. Additionally, passage length, age and ability levels of subjects, length of retention time, and the amount of detail given in the studies themselves varied to the point that about the only safe conclusion we can draw is that underlining is not detrimental.

(4) There is some evidence to suggest that students who generate their own underlin-

ing experience increased recall over those who simply interact with experimenter-generated underlining (Bobrow & Bower, 1963; Rickards & August, 1975; Schnell & Rocchio, 1975; Smart & Bruning, 1973). Greater recall for student-generated underlining is generally attributed to the levels of processing theory (Craik & Tulving, 1978) which states that information which is processed at deeper levels through elaboration is ultimately remembered better. However, the depth of processing explanation is valid only if students are indeed interacting with text while they are underlining actively, hence using underlining as an encoding device at the time of input. If they are using underlining merely as a concentration technique, leading to subsequent over-underlining, random underlining, or sparse underlining, student-generated text marking would appear to be of little value.

(5) A seemingly opposing theoretical explanation of why underlining may be effective (or ineffective) is due to what is called the von Restorff effect (Wallace, 1965). The major tenet of this theory is that when an item is isolated against a homogeneous background, increased recall of that item occurs. In the case of underlining, we assume that if text information is underlined or in some way marked, students will tend to study and remember that information better than non-underlined information. Carrying this logic a step further, if students underlined important information (key ideas, examples, application of theories, etc.), and subsequently studied said information, they should remember it and perform well on exams. If, however, they underlined unimportant information (insignificant details, repetitive text, etc.) they would tend to study this underlined information and subsequently exhibit poor test performance. It seems that the pay-off comes when students use text markings, whether theirs or someone else's, as a means of reviewing, rehearsing, and preparing for exams at the time of output. Therefore, while the act of underlining may increase performance, it does not

necessarily have to. If such is the case, it should make little difference in a controlled research study as to whether the researcher or the subject generates the underlining since the bigger pay-off comes during direct interaction with the underlined material at the time of studying (output), not in the act of underlining itself (input). Moreover, while the depth of processing theory explains increased performance for those who underline by focusing on what occurs during input (the act of underlining itself), the von Restorff effect is more concerned with what occurs at output (studying).

(6) In a study examining the von Restorff effect, Cashen & Leicht (1970) found a significant effect for information that had been researcher underlined, supporting the major tenet of the isolation theory. While some problems with this study are quite apparent (i.e., different passages were used with different groups without checking for prior knowledge) and the information is sketchy in parts (there was no information given on passage length or on how to determine which information to underline), it offers some support for the speculation that what occurs at output has more to do with test performance than what goes on at input. Since we were working with a very specialized group of freshmen students (those who were required to enroll in a study strategies course due to a combination of Scholastic Aptitude Test scores and high school grade point averages), coupled with the fact that past research has shown prior knowledge to be an important factor in performance (Anderson & Pearson, 1985), we were concerned about the prior knowledge factor. If, for example, as Wilson and Anderson (1986) suggest, "Prior knowledge must be ranked as a potent determiner of performance" (p. 32), we would expect that students who had considerably more background on the topic of colonization would do better on the dependent measure no matter what the condition. Additionally, we could locate no empirical underlining study which had been conducted after 1980, an interesting finding

in itself, and one which may explain why no previous research had considered the importance that prior knowledge plays in underlining.

(7) We considered two final factors in this investigation. The first was the issue of passage length. One of the problems in synthesizing the results of the extant research is that they are very difficult to compare. Passage length ranged from 300 words (Hartley, Bartlett, & Branthwaite, 1980) to 6,000 words (Idstein & Jenkins, 1972), to others which gave passage descriptions that were so vague that they were of little use (i.e., 100 sentences or four paragraphs). The problem in comparing what it takes to process 300 words differs considerably from what it takes to process 6,000 words. Since we attempted to make the reading and learning tasks appropriate for the time constraints, we decided on a passage between 2,000 and 2,500 words. The average reading rate of our subjects was a little over 220 words per minute, which would permit 20 minutes of reading, 20 minutes for studying, and then the 10 minute review during the following session. We also felt that using longer passages would provide more generalizable results since college students are expected to read and synthesize large amounts of text.

(8) The final factor that concerned us was that of text annotation. Text annotation consists of making marginal notes which cover key concepts, noting potential test items, using a symbol system such as a star for important information, an "ex." for example, and so forth. Annotations are similar to and serve the same purposes as marginal glosses (Singer & Donlan, 1985). Though the idea of glossing is an old technique, virtually no research exists to confirm whether or not it is any more effective than underlining alone. Our purpose for adding the annotation variable was to determine if the presence of researcher-generated annotating added anything to the subjects' performance. This factor, like prior knowledge, has been totally ignored in previous research.

PURPOSES

(9) The present study was designed to answer the following research questions. One of the questions is concerned with the issue of input and two with the issue of output.

1. Is the amount of prior knowledge significantly related to expert, alternative, or total scores?
2. Does researcher-generated underlining influence the information on which subjects concentrate during test preparation? (output question)
3. Do the performances of subjects who read text material which is either underlined or underlined and annotated differ significantly on multiple-choice questions? (output question)
4. Do the performances of subjects who read text material that has been underlined and annotated differ significantly from the performances of subjects who generate their own underlining? (input question)

METHOD

(10) *Subjects*

The 67 subjects in this study were drawn from the freshmen population who were required to enroll in a study strategies course at a large Southern university. The mean Scholastic Aptitude Test-Verbal score was 390; the mean high school grade point average was 2.7. Though all subjects were provisionally admitted to the university, they possessed intact reading skills (no decoding or severe comprehension problems), but they were generally deficient in processing lengthy text and in their use of study strategies. A series of state-mandated and program tests placed all subjects in an upper level reading/study strategies course.

(11) *Instruments*

The passage was a 2,200 word excerpt from an American government text (Burns, Peltason, & Cronin, 1978) which focused on the colonization of Anglo-America. This freshman level text was representative of textbooks designed for such courses.

⑫   Since we were interested in knowing the extent to which subjects use text marking as a method of test preparation, we marked the passage four different ways. To accomplish this task, three experts in reading/studying considered to be mature readers (Smith, 1982), were instructed to independently read, underline, and annotate the passage as though they would be responsible for taking a multiple-choice exam over the material. Information that was marked by two out of the three readers was used to determine the expert underlining and underlining and annotating conditions for Groups 1 and 2 respectively. Information that was underlined by only one reader or by no reader was used to determine alternative underlining and underlining and annotating conditions for Groups 3 and 4 respectively. The following paragraph serves as an example of the underlining for the expert group; the alternative group's paragraph had the opposite information underlined.

⑬   The first permanent settlements from which distinctive American culture traits evolved were the English Jamestown Colony, established in 1607, and the French settlement at Quebec, established in 1608. Soon following was the Plymouth Colony (English, 1620) and later settlements in New York (Dutch, 1625). Germans and Scandinavians also made their appearance, but it was above all others the English cultural imprint that was the most profound and lasting on the new continent. The English came in greater numbers and, over all, exercised the greatest control in the development process. English dominance should not preclude recognition of the value of native American, African, Asian, or other European peoples (the French in Quebec) to American culture.

⑭   From the expert marking, four forms of the passage were devised. Those in Group 1 (EU) received the passage with information marked that was deemed important by the panel of experts; Group 2 (EUA) received the passage with the same underlining as Group 1 but with appropriate accompanying annotation. Group 3 (AU) received the passage with alternative information underlined. Alternative information was defined as that which was underlined by only one or none of the experts.

⑮   Group 4 (AUA) received the same underlining as Group 3 but with accompanying annotation. Group 5 (SGU), the self-generated group, received the passage with no underlining or annotating and were instructed to generate their own.

For the present study, text aid referred to the two conditions of underlining and underlining and annotating. Marking referred to whether the text aid emphasized material marked by the experts or the alternative markings.

⑯   To determine if prior knowledge influenced test performance, a ten-item multiple-choice test was developed. Similar to past studies which have investigated the relationship between prior knowledge and comprehension (i.e., Lipson, 1982), we developed a test which contained items that examined subjects' general knowledge on the topic of Anglo-American colonization. The two items which follow are representative of the questions which were asked about the colonization of Anglo-America:

1. Jamestown was established in the early
   a. 1400's.
   b. 1500's.
   c. 1600's.
   d. 1700's.
2. The first country to establish a permanent colony in Anglo-America was
   a. Spain.
   b. England.
   c. Portugal.
   d. France.

(17)   Finally, based on the text excerpt, a multiple-choice test was constructed. The test, administered to all groups, consisted of a total of 24 items, 12 of which were drawn from the information marked by the experts given to Groups 1 and 2, and 12 of which were drawn from the alternative information given to Groups 3 and 4. Questions one and two below are examples of items drawn from the expert underlining. These items tend to cover the major ideas presented in the chapter. Items three and four are examples of alternative items and tend to cover less important details in the chapter.

1. Differences between Northern and Southern colonies arose over issues such as
   a. tariffs and slaves.
   b. farming and slaves.
   c. tariffs and farming.
   d. cotton and tobacco.
2. What was the major European motivating force which caused colonization?
   a. expansionism
   b. political unrest
   c. social strife
   d. positive economy
3. Which of the following caused small numbers of people to move inland?
   a. fur trading
   b. cotton farming
   c. lumbering
   d. industrial growth
4. The most distinctive culture was formed in the
   a. lower St. Lawrence.
   b. Ohio Valley.
   c. Midwest.
   d. isolated Appalachians.

Procedures

(18) The study was carried out in two sessions. During the first session, as subjects were randomly assigned to one of the five conditions and each was given a folder which contained the ten-item test of prior knowledge, a set of directions for completing the task, and the appropriate passage. Subjects in the four researcher-generated underlining and underlining and annotating groups were given the following directions:

> Remove the "Anglo-America" chapter from your folder. Read and study it in preparation for a multiple-choice test which you will be given during tomorrow's class. You will have the remainder of the period to read and study the article. Do not make any marks on the article itself. Any notes or comments should be made on a separate piece of paper. At the end of the period, return your article and any notes you may have made to the folder and give it to the instructor.

(19)   Those subjects in Group 5, self-generation, were encouraged to underline and/or mark the passage in any way that would aid in the learning the information, but they were given no instructions as to how to interact with the material or clues about what information was important.

   In Session 2, which occurred the following day, all subjects were given their folders from the previous day and were permitted ten minutes for review. They then took the 24-item multiple-choice test. Subjects were given no time constraints, but all completed the test within 35 minutes.

(20)   Both the prior knowledge test and the test covering the text selection were scored by giving one point for each correct answer. Product-moment correlations were computed to determine the relationship between prior knowledge and expert, alternative, and total scores. Because we were interested in determining if subjects did, indeed, concentrate on researcher-generated marking when preparing for the multiple-choice test covering the "Anglo-America" expert, three raw scores were computed: an expert score (number correct out of 12), an alternative score (number correct out of 12), and the total score (number correct out of 24).

(21)   Because of unequal cell sizes, a weighted means analysis of variance was performed

for the expert, alternative, and total scores (Myers, 1979 p. 116). A Dunnett test (Myers, 1979, p. 300) was used to compare the SGU group mean with the mean of each of the researcher-generated conditions.

RESULTS

(22) *Question 1*. Is the amount of prior knowledge significantly related to the expert, alternative, or total scores? The product-moment correlations of prior knowledge with expert, alternative, and total scores were respectively, $r = .10$, $r = .19$, $r = .19$. These coefficients were not significantly different from zero.

(23) *Question 2*. Does researcher-generated marking influence the information on which subjects concentrate during test preparation? (output) The means and standard deviations of the five conditions are reported in Table 1. Because of unequal cell sizes, a weighted means analysis of variance (Myers, 1979, 116) was performed for the three dependent variables. These results are reported in Tables 2, 3, and 4 respectively. The main effect for marking was significant,

$F (1, 49) = 13.56$, $p < .01$ when the dependent measure was the expert marking score. The main effect for the marking was also significant, $F (1, 49) = 6.98$, $p < .05$ when the dependent measure was the alternative marking score. There was no main effect for marking when the total score was used as the dependent measure, $F (1, 49) = .12$, $p < .05$.

(24) *Question 3*. Do the performances of students who read text material which is either underlined or underlined and annotated differ significantly on multiple-choice questions? (output) The main effect for text aid and all interactions between text aid and marking were not significant for the three dependent measures. In other words, nothing was significantly added to performance for subjects who received passages that were both underlined and annotated over subjects who received passages that were only underlined.

(25) *Question 4*. Do the performances of students who read text material that has been underlined and annotated differ significantly from the performances of subjects who gen-

Table 1   Means and Standard Deviations for Multiple-Choice Test Scores

	Total Score		Expert Score		Alt. Score	
	M	SD	M	SD	M	SD
Expert Underlining Only (n = 14)	14.57	3.01	8.07	1.59	6.50	1.79
Expert Underlining & Annotation (n = 12)	15.00	3.49	8.75	2.22	6.25	.05
Alternative Underlining Only (n = 13)	13.54	5.78	5.92	2.40	7.62	3.55
Alternative Underlining & Annotation (n = 14)	15.29	2.64	6.71	1.90	8.57	1.45
Self-generated No Underlining or Annotation (n = 13)	16.23	2.01	8.08	1.61	8.15	1.46

Table 2   Weighted Means Analysis of Variance for the Expert Score

Source	df	SS	MS	F
Text Aid	1	.5401	.5401	1.673
Marking	1	4.377	4.377	13.558**
Interaction	1	.0031	.0031	.01
Error	49		.3228	

**p < .01

erated their own underlining? (input) A Dunnett test (Myers, 1979, p. 33) was used to compare the student-generated underlining group with each of the four experimenter-generated groups. This test was employed in order to keep the alpha level of .05 constant for the family of comparisons defined by each dependent variable. For each dependent variable, the mean of the SGU group did not differ significantly from the most disparate mean of the four experimenter-generated conditions.

DISCUSSION AND RECOMMENDATIONS

(26) This study sought to examine both the role of depth of processing (input) and the von Restorff effect (output) as they related to text marking. Also considered was the effect that prior knowledge had on subjects' ability to recall text information.

(27)   Prior knowledge was not significantly related to the number of questions answered correctly. The mean prior knowledge score

was 4.27 out of 10 questions with a standard deviation of 1.6. While the lack of relationship between prior knowledge and the comprehension scores may initially seem strange, it is a frequent occurrence in research which is conducted on developmental college students (i.e., Alvermann & Hague, 1986; Simpson, Hayes, Stahl, & Weaver, 1987). This rather low mean prior knowledge score, together with the small standard deviation suggested that subjects in the sample had relatively weak schema on the colonization of Anglo-America. We assume, as others whose research has resulted in similar findings, that the nonsignificance and little variability on the prior knowledge variable stems partially from the fact that there was also little variation in verbal abilities of these subjects as measured by SATV scores.

(28)   The results of the present study suggested that when text material was underlined or underlined and annotated, subjects directed their attention to the information emphasized by these text aids, supporting

Table 3   Weighted Means Analysis of Variance for the Alternative Score

Source	df	SS	MS	F
Text Aid	1	.1246	.1246	.29
Marking	1	2.953	2.9533	6.976**
Interaction	1	.3636	.3636	.86
Error	49		.4233	

**p < .05

Table 4 Weighted Means Analysis of Variance for the Total Score

Source	df	SS	MS	F
Text Aid	1	1.1836	1.1836	1.00
Marking	1	.1396	.1396	.12
Interaction	1	.4346	.4346	.36
Error	49		1.1892	

the operation of the von Restorff effect. Subjects in Groups 1 and 2 who read and studied the passage which had information emphasized deemed as important by the experts correctly answered more expert questions than subjects who read the passage in which alternative information was emphasized. Likewise, subjects who read and studied the passage in which alternative information was emphasized correctly answered more alternative questions than students who read the passage with emphasis on expert material. These results suggested that text material which had been marked by the researchers, regardless of the quality of that marking, had a rather strong influence on directing the reader's attention to certain parts of the text. The emphasized information appeared to be learned more thoroughly, in that performances on questions covering the emphasized text were significantly better than on questions covering the unemphasized portions of the passage. This finding, like that of Cashen and Leicht (1970), was particularly interesting because it indicated that the reader's attention was influenced more by the author's marking than by what were, in reality, the more or less important parts of the passage. It also suggested that studying the underlined information was more important to increasing test performance than the actual act of underlining and thus supports the idea that what occurs at output has a greater influence on test performance than what occurs at input. The isolation effect was a rather strong one. Eta-squared, which is a measure of the amount of variance in the dependent variable accounted for by the treatment variable, was .21 for the score on the expert questions and .12 for the score on the alternative questions. Rosenthal and Rubin (1982) offered a way of interpreting the effect of a treatment called the "binomial effect size display" (BESD). An eta-squared of .21 indicated that 73% of the subjects in the EU and EUA groups performed above the median score on the expert questions, while only 27% of the subjects in the AU and AUA groups performed above the median score on the expert questions. Similarly, when the score on the alternative questions was used as the dependent variable, an eta-squared of .12 indicated that 67% of the subjects in the AU and AUA groups performed above the median, compared to 33% of the subjects in the EU and EUA groups.

(29) Annotation of the passage did not increase test performance over underlining alone. Researcher supplied underlining was sufficient in directing students' attention to the expert or alternative material. This finding, however, does not offer any insight into how student-generated annotation might improve understanding and recall. The results of the analyses in which the performances of the SGU group were compared to the performances of the text aid-marking groups suggested that when underlining and annotating were not supplied, subjects were able to answer as many questions correctly as the subjects in the four researcher-generated groups, albeit not significantly more. This finding seems to suggest that students

in the SGU group attempted to remember as much of the passage as they could, with little discrimination about the importance level of the information. The significant results for marking discussed previously suggested that students in the researcher-generated groups directed their attention toward the underlined and annotated information. Since there were no significant differences on the dependent variables between the SGU group and the other four groups, the results indicated that subjects who were allowed to use their own reading and marking techniques appeared not to be able to make clear distinctions between important and unimportant information at the time of input. Additionally, these results differ from the bulk of previous research which found that subjects who generated their own underlining outperformed those who received researcher-generated underlining and also questions the depth of processing theory as an explanation of why underlining is effective. Evidently subjects in the SGU group did a fairly effective, but perhaps inefficient, job of learning both key ideas and less important details because the performances of subjects in conditions which emphasized either expert or alternative material were no better than the performances of the SGU group.

(30) The results of this investigation indicated that researcher-generated underlining and annotating had an effect of directing subjects' attention and were equally effective as student-generated underlining. These results certainly question the depth of processing theory which several past researchers have used to explain the results in their underlining studies. However, experimenter-supplied markings place substantially different demands on the reader than do reader-generated markings. Experimenter-generated marking greatly reduces the number of decisions for the reader as to what is important and, in a sense, makes the task reader's task easier. The present study offers no insight about the processes that subjects in the SGU group employed in deciding what they should remember. However, it appears that the SGU group may have adopted a "remember all" strategy, thus allocating their mental resources inefficiently. This speculation is supported by the fact that many of the questions taken from the alternative marking dealt with minute details which instructors would not normally ask students. Yet subjects in the SGU answered this type of question with the same degree of accuracy as the AU and AUA groups, indicating that at least part of their studying was over relatively unimportant information.

(31) Alternatively we might also speculate that the cognitive demands go considerably deeper than that. Since the expert markings tended to focus more on key ideas and the alternative underlining focused more on unimportant details, further investigations need to examine how underlining one over the other influences performances. It could be that underlining disproportionate numbers of key ideas over details leads to more effective and efficient performance; the opposite may also be true.

(32) Additionally, subsequent research needs to focus on the strategies students use in making decisions about what is important and what should be marked. The results of the present study do suggest that students tend to focus on and learn what is marked, whether the information is important or not, and lends credence to the von Restorff effect as an explanation of why underlining can be a successful strategy. The results also indicate that what goes on at output, the studying at rehearsal, is perhaps more important than the act of underlining itself. While the underlining in this study was experimenter-generated, it is safe to generalize that when individuals do their own underlining they also tend to learn that which they underline or in some other way mark.

(33) Finally, we believe that the effect that annotation plays in increasing performance deserves further investigation. Studies which train students how to underline and annotate may clarify the role annotation

plays. We feel that subject-generated annotation may lead to deeper levels of processing since it does require active involvement on the part of the reader whereas underlining alone does not necessarily require such involvement.

Anderson, T. H., & Armbruster, B. B. (1984). Studying. In P. D. Pearson (Ed.), *Handbook of reading research* (pp. 657–679). New York: Longman.

Anderson, R. C., & Pearson, P. D. (1984) A schema-theoretic view of basic processes in reading comprehension. In P. D. Pearson (Ed.), *Handbook of reading research* (pp. 255–291). New York: Longman.

Bobrow, S. A., & Bower, G. H. (1963). Comprehension and recall of sentences. *Journal of Experimental Psychology, 80,* 455–461.

Burns, J. M., Peltason, J. W., & Cronin, T. E. (1978). *Government by the people.* Englewood Cliffs, NJ: Prentice-Hall.

Cashen, V. A., & Leicht, K. L. (1970). Role of the isolation effect in a formal educational setting. *Journal of Educational Psychology, 61,* 484–486.

Craik, F. I. M., & Tulving, E. (1975). Depth of processing and the retention of words in episodic memory. *Journal of Experimental Psychology: General, 104,* 268–294.

Crouse, J. H., & Idstein, P. (1972). Effects of encoding cues on prose learning. *Journal of Educational Psychology, 63,* 309–313.

Fowler, R. L., & Baker, A. S. (1974). Effectiveness of highlighting for retention of text material. *Journal of Applied Psychology, 59,* 358–364.

Glynn, S. M., & DiVesta, F. J. (1979). Control of prose processing via instructional and typographical cues. *Journal of Educational Psychology, 71,* 595–603.

Hague, S. A., & Alverman, D. E. (1986). *Comprehension of counter-intuitive science text: The effects of text structure and activation of prior knowledge.* Paper presented at the annual meeting of the American Reading Forum, Sarasota, Florida.

Hartley, J., Bartlett, S., & Branthwaite, A. (1980). Underlining can make a difference: Sometimes. *Journal of Educational Research, 73,* 218–224.

Hoon, P. W. (1974). Efficacy of three common study methods. *Psychological Reports, 3,* 1057–1058.

Idstein, P., & Jenkins, J. R. (1972). Underlining versus repetitive reading. *Journal of Educational Research, 65,* 321–323.

Johnson, D., & Wen, S. (1976). Effects of correct and extraneous markings under time limits on reading comprehension. *Psychology in the Schools, 13,* 454–456.

Kulhavy, R. W., Dyer, J. W., & Silver, L. (1975). The effect of notetaking and test expectancy on the learning of text material. *Journal of Educational Research, 68,* 363–365.

Lipson, M. Y. (1982). Learning new information from text: The role of prior knowledge and reading ability. *Journal of Reading Behavior, 14,* 243–262.

Myers, J. L. (1979). *Fundamentals of experimental design (3rd ed.).* Boston: Allyn & Bacon.

Rickards, J. P., & August, G. J. (1975). Generative underlining strategies in prose recall. *Journal of Educational Psychology, 67,* 860–865.

Rosenthal, R., & Rubin, D. B. (1982). A simple, general purpose display of magnitude of experimental effect. *Journal of Educational Psychology, 74,* 166–169.

Schnell, T. R., & Rocchio, D. (1975). A comparison of underlining strategies for improving reading comprehension and retention. In G. H. McNinch & W. D. Miller (Eds.), *Reading: Convention and inquiry.* Twenty-fourth Yearbook of the National Reading Conference.

Simpson, M. L., (1987). *Training college students to use writing as a means of independent learning.* Paper presented at

the Annual Meeting of the American Educational Research Association, Washington, DC.

Singer, H., & Donlan, D. (1985). *Reading
and learning from text.* Hillsdale, NJ:
Lawrence Erlbaum Associates.

Smart, K. L., & Bruning, J. L. (1973). *An
examination of the practical importance
of the von Restorff effect.* Paper presented at the annual meeting of the
American Psychological Association,
Montreal, Canada.

Smith, S. L. (1982). Learning strategies of
mature college learners. *Journal of Reading, 26,* 5–12.

Stordahl, K. E., & Christensen, C. M.

(1956). The effects of study techniques
on comprehension and retention. *Journal of Educational Research, 49,* 561–
570.

Wallace, W. P. (1965). Review of the historical, empirical, and theoretical status
of the von Restorff phenomenon. *Psychological Bulletin, 63,* 410–424.

Wilson, P. T. & Anderson, R. C. (1986).
What they don't know will hurt them:
The role of prior knowledge in comprehension. In J. Orasanu (Ed.), *Reading
comprehension: From research to practice,* (pp. 31–48). Hillsdale, NJ: Lawrence Erlbaum Associates.

FEEDBACK

Activity 1: Chapter Summary

For what reasons do educators conduct research?

Educators produce research to verify the effectiveness of teaching and
learning ideas and practices already in use, to discover new ideas and
practices, to develop practices that simplify people's lives, to introduce
practices that complicate people's lives, and to discover counterintuitive practices.

*What is the distinction between research consumers and research pro-
ducers?*

Research producers need technical competence in applying research
strategies—the procedures for conceptualizing, developing, implementing, and reporting research. Research consumers need skills in
understanding how researchers undertake research and in reading,
interpreting, and applying others' research results.

What does it mean to understand research like a research producer?

To understand research like a research producer means understanding
research with the mindset of a research producer. To do that, research
consumers need to understand (a) the research process and the decisions facing research producers, (b) the possible alternatives research
producers consider at those decision points, and (c) the implications
of the research producers' results and conclusions.

What are some key educational research terms?

Key research terms are (a) variable—anything in a research situation that can vary; (b) design—the plan or type of research; (c) hypothesis—a tentative statement about two or more variables; (d) subjects—the people used in the study; and (e) generalizability—being able to apply the results from one study with students not used in the study.

Activity 2: Locating Sections in the Research Report by Nist & Hogrebe (1987) (See pp. 12–22.)

Paragraph 1: The abstract, a summary of the entire research report.

Paragraphs 2–8: A statement about the researchers' purpose, why they are doing the research, and what others have found in answering related questions.

Paragraph 9: The research questions that the researchers set out to answer.

Paragraph 10: A description of the people used in the study.

Paragraphs 11–17: A description of the materials and tests used in the study.

Paragraphs 18–21: A discussion of the steps taken by the researchers to complete the study.

Paragraphs 22–25: An explanation of the results of the study. The statistical data are found in Tables 1, 2, and 3.

Paragraphs 26–29: A summary of the purpose and results of the study with ideas about what might have caused the results.

Paragraphs 30–33: The researchers' ideas about how the results can be used for instructional purposes and other research.

The reference section contains all the other research the authors referred to in their report.

2 Research Designs

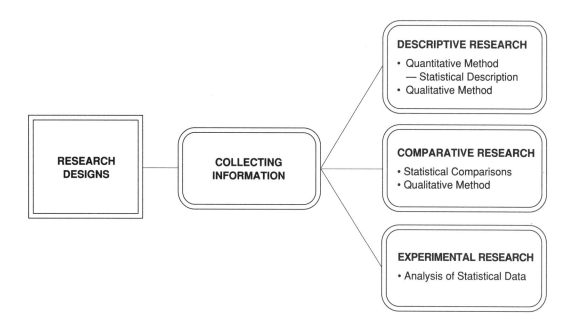

DESCRIPTIVE RESEARCH
- Quantitative Method
  — Statistical Description
- Qualitative Method

COMPARATIVE RESEARCH
- Statistical Comparisons
- Qualitative Method

EXPERIMENTAL RESEARCH
- Analysis of Statistical Data

FOCUS QUESTIONS

1. What are the designs used to conduct research?
2. What are the methods used to organize research projects?
3. What are the instruments used to collect data?
4. What are descriptive, comparative, and experimental research?
5. What distinguishes the three types of research designs from each other?
6. What are central tendency and variability and how are they measured?
7. How are data analyzed in each of the three types of research designs?

When researchers pose questions about educational problems, there are concomitant connections to one or more plans for obtaining answers. The plans, or **research designs**, structure researchers' methods for answering their questions and conducting studies. The three basic research purposes are to describe, to compare, and to attribute causality.

In **descriptive research**, the researchers' purpose is to create accurate pictures of one or more variables. They seek to answer questions about a variable's status. In **comparative research**, researchers' purpose is to examine the descriptions of two or more variables and make decisions about their differences or relationships. In research to attribute causality, or **experimental research**, the researchers' purpose is to draw conclusions about the influence of one or more variables in making changes to another variable. They seek to answer **if . . . then** questions: If they do something, then what change will occur in a particular variable?

Experimental research lets researchers establish the influence, or effect, of one variable on another. Descriptive and comparative research may show status, patterns, and associations among variables, but studies of this type cannot be used to say that one variable or combination of variables *does* cause a change in, or influence, another variable. Only when researchers follow the plan for attributing causality can they establish that a particular variable was the reason for a change in another. Causation research is different from the other research types, and this distinction cannot be over-stressed (Borg & Gall, 1983).

COLLECTING INFORMATION

Information, or data, for all three types of research is collected from direct observation, tests, and surveys (questionnaires and interviews). Researchers refer to these data collection devices and procedures as **instruments**. (The criteria for determining whether particular instruments collect information accurately are discussed in Chapter 6, Reading and Evaluating Instrumentation Sections.)

Researchers usually record direct observation with an observation form, which may consist of questions about the subject's actions or categories of actions. For example, the observer may collect information in response to set questions—"With which children did the target subject play during free play?" or "Which child started the play?" Or, the observer might tally the subject's actions during a specified time according to some predetermined categories: Subject started play with others, Others' play with subject, Self-initiated lone play, Fringe observer to others' play.

Test information includes scores from standardized **norm-referenced tests** such as the Wechsler Intelligence Scale for Children—Revised (Wechsler, 1974), the Metropolitan Achievement Tests (Balow, Farr, Hogan, & Prescott, 1985), the Comprehensive Test of Basic Skills (Comprehensive, 1988), the Boehm Test of Basic Concepts (Boehm, 1971), or the Woodcock Reading Mastery Tests (Woodcock, 1973). The scores also may be from standardized **criterion-referenced tests** such as the PRI/Reading Systems or the Life Skills Tests of Functional Competencies in Reading and Mathematics. Competency tests also might be created by a researcher or teacher for determining learning style, reading interest, or outcomes of instruction. Some tests are given individually, others are administered to groups.

Questionnaires require the respondent either to write answers to questions about a topic or to answer orally. The answer form may be structured in that there are fixed choices, or the form may be open in that respondents can use their own words. When the respondent answers orally and the researcher records the answers, researchers consider the instrument to be an **interview**. In interviews, researchers may obtain responses to structured or open-ended questions. Interviews differ from questionnaires in that the researchers can modify the data collection situation to fit the respondent's replies. For example, additional information can be solicited or a question can be rephrased. In addition, researchers use surveys to collect information from files such as subjects' permanent school records.

DESCRIPTIVE RESEARCH

Descriptive research is used when researchers want to show the status of one or more variables. Researchers use it to answer the question "What exists?" This question can be answered in one of two ways—using quantitative method or qualitative method.

Quantitative Method

The **quantitative descriptive research method** is a procedure involving the assignment of numerical values to variables. For example, Figure 2.1 contains partial results from a questionnaire used in a descriptive study

> to determine whether parents participated actively in their learning disabled child's educational program, how they perceived their role, and whether they thought integrated education programs were having a beneficial effect on their child. (Abramson, Willson, Yoshida, & Hagerty, 1983, p. 185)

These researchers collected general demographic data and parent's perceptions about five areas: their relationship with school personnel, their child's academic performance, whether their child was called pejorative names, their child's social–emotional reactions, and their feelings about the quality of their child's schooling.

Another research team might wish to know "What is the average intelligence of students in gifted programs in a particular county or state?" They would collect and tabulate data and find the average intelligence score of students in gifted programs to be 129. Still another team affiliated with a county library system might wish to know "What

1. Is the person filling out the questionnaire the:

    a. male parent or guardian   4   (9.3%)

    b. female parent or guardian   32   (74.42%)

    c. both parents or guardians   7   (16.28%)

7. Do you participate in school activities and/or meetings that are intended to make you familiar with your child's education?

    a. I participate a great deal   9   (20.93%)

    b. I participate a little   14   (32.56%)

    c. I have not participated   13   (30.23%)

    d. I have not been asked to participate   7   (16.28%)

13. How confident are you that your child's teachers are improving his/her academic and/or social abilities?

    a. very confident   19   (44.19%)

    b. moderately confident   14   (32.56%)

    c. less than confident   5   (11.63%)

    d. not at all confident   3   (6.98%)

    e. uncertain   2   (4.65%)

32. What type of classroom do you think your child would do best in academically?

    a. a class with other children who have disabilities   9   (20.93%)

    b. a class with children who do not have disabilities   5   (11.63%)

    c. some classes with nondisabled children and some with disabled children   19   (44.19%)

    d. uncertain   10   (23.26%)

Figure 2.1 A sample questionnaire. (From Abrahamson, Willson, Yoshida, & Hagerty, 1983, pp. 186–190.)

is the average (arithmetic mean) reading achievement test score of a sample of beginning sixth grade students using the public libraries in three local communities?" They collect and tabulate the data and find the average achievement test grade equivalent score to be 6.2.

However, having these two bits of information (average intelligence and average reading achievement score) does not allow the separate teams of researchers to create accurate pictures of the subjects. Average scores may give a limited picture because we know that not everyone had an intelligence score of 129, and not all sixth grade students in each community had scores of 6.2. Also, anyone who observes gifted students and sixth grade students sees that they differ in many ways other than intelligence or reading performance: personality, preferences and interests, and learning style to name a few.

Two premises, then, underlie quantitative researchers' collection of descriptive information. First, they should collect and average information for several relevant variables. For the sixth grade students, other variables relevant to library usage might be age, sex, intelligence, ethnicity, reading interest and preference, proximity of home to the library, and frequency of library usage. Second, after determining the average score for each variable, researchers should determine the extent to which the subjects' scores for each variable cluster near or spread away from the average score. Two patterns of clustering are common: (a) a clustering of scores around the mean and (b) a clustering of scores either above or below the mean. The reporting of this clustering or spreading gives a picture of the subjects' similarity or dissimilarity.

Statistical Descriptions of Data

After researchers collect data, they tally them. Figure 2.1 contains the number of responses for each answer and the percentage of the total group they represent. From these data, it is possible to get a sense of how most parents responded and whether their responses agreed.

However, most researchers following quantitative procedures use other descriptive measures of data, which are central tendency and variability. Although two common measures of central tendency researchers use in research reports are the mean and median, the mean is the measure of central tendency they most often use. The measure of variability most often used is the standard deviation. The following discussion is only an introduction to these measures. Chapter 8, Reading and Interpreting Results Sections, contains additional information about statistics and criteria for determining whether researchers' use of the mean, median, standard deviation, and other statistics is appropriate. Understanding the concepts of central tendency and variability is essential to understanding quantitative research designs.

Both the mean and median give researchers—producers and consumers—a sense of the middle or average score for a variable. The **mean** is an arithmetical average—one adds up individual scores and divides by the number of scores. The **median** is the middle score of a group of scores. The mean and median may not be the same for a particular group of scores. For example, the middle score of the following groups is the same (25), but the means of the two groups are different—the first is 33.57 and the second is 40.85.

10, 15, 20, 25, 40, 50, 75

4, 17, 24, 25, 26, 91, 99

INTERPRETING EDUCATIONAL RESEARCH

The **standard deviation (SD)** is used with the mean to show how the other scores are distributed around the mean. The use of the SD lets research producers and consumers see how homogeneous (alike) or heterogeneous (varied) a group is. For example, grade equivalent scores from a mathematics achievement test for a group of seventh grade students might have a mean of 7.4 (which represents the fourth month of the seventh school year) and a SD of 2 months. In this class, most students (approximately two-thirds) have grade equivalent scores between 7.2 and 7.6. In another group with the same mean (7.4) but a SD of 8 months, two-thirds of the students would have scores between 6.6 and 8.2. The first group would be more homogeneous in their mathematics performance than would be the second.

Table 2.1 shows an example of mean and standard deviation reporting. The table reports information from an investigation about reading and recall from four types of passages by undergraduate students in an education course (Shanahan & Kamil, 1982). The four passages were (a) cloze (systematic word deletion) test with all sentences in sequential order; (b) cloze test with sentences scrambled; (c) intact passage with sequential sentences; and (d) intact passage with scrambled sentences. The table gives the number of subjects (n), mean scores (M), and standard deviations (SD) for three sets of scores: percent of correct cloze reading test scores, average completion time, and percent of accuracy in recall ideas. It shows that for the first type of passage—cloze reading of a passage with the sentences in sequential order—the 20 students had an average of 48.55% of the items correct. The SD was 14.37, which means the scores of about two-thirds of the students clustered between 34.18% and 62.92%. The students completed the passage in an average time of 11.60 minutes, and about two-thirds of them finished in times between 8.45 and 14.75 minutes. The students had average recall accuracy scores of 20.30%, and about two-thirds of the students' recall scores were between 11.04% and 29.56%. (No cloze scores are possible for intact passages.)

Table 2.1 Example of Mean and Standard Deviation Reporting: Mean Percentage and Standard Deviation of Cloze and Recall Performance and Reading Times, and Standard Deviations, for Four Passage Types

Passage Type	n	Cloze (% correct)		Time (minutes)		Recall (%)	
		M	SD	M	SD	M	SD
Cloze—sequential	20	48.55	14.37	11.60	3.15	20.30	9.26
Cloze—scrambled	20	46.35	9.74	13.90	4.97	13.25	10.22
Intact—sequential	20			6.85	4.62	31.10	13.77
Intact—scrambled	20			7.20	3.32	23.95	10.03

Source: Adapted from Shanahan and Kamil (1982).

Qualitative research method is a term used for a broad range of research strategies that have roots in the field research of anthropology and sociology (Bogdan & Biklen, 1982; Firestone, 1987; Guthrie & Hall, 1984; Jacob, 1987, 1988; Lincoln & Guba, 1985; Smith, 1987; Smith & Heshusius, 1986; Van Maanen, Dabbs, & Faulkner, 1982; and Wilson, 1977). A term closely associated with qualitative research is **ethnographic research**. Some researchers distinguish between the two terms; others consider ethnography a type of qualitative research method. For the purposes of this text, the term ethnography is used solely for the type of research undertaken by anthropologists studying whole cultures. It is not used for the work of researchers from education, psychology, and social science who borrow the term but not the underlying theoretical framework of anthropological ethnography (Jacob, 1989).

ethnography vs. qual. research

The term qualitative research method can be best understood by noting the characteristics of qualitative research, which has several distinct features (Bogdan & Biklen, 1982; Firestone, 1987; Guthrie & Hall, 1984; Jacob, 1987, 1988; Lincoln & Guba, 1985; Smith, 1987; Smith & Heshusius, 1986; Van Maanen, Dabbs, & Faulkner, 1982; and Wilson, 1977). First, researchers collect data within the natural setting of the information, and the key data collection instruments are the researchers themselves. This means that researchers wishing to study educational questions must collect relevant information at the data source through direct observation and personal interviews. The methods for data collection include participant observing, interviewing, reading diaries, scanning records and files, using checklists, and conducting case studies. The basic premise for collecting data in natural settings is that people do not act in isolation. Their behavior and actions occur in specific social contexts or situations, and therefore these behaviors and actions must be studied in their natural settings. Researchers must become part of the natural setting and function as participant observers: In educational environments, students and teachers must accept qualitative researchers as regular members of the classrooms and not just as observers.

It is on the point of **participant observation** that some researchers distinguish between qualitative and ethnographic research. If researchers do not collect data in natural settings as members of the total group, the research may be considered by some researchers as qualitative but not ethnographic. To them, ethnographic research requires researchers to be fully integrated members of the educational environment. This distinction has been called the "insider and outsider perspective" (Van Mannen, Dabbs, & Faulkner, 1982, p. 17). The insider becomes part of the group and tries to detail what the members of the group know and how this knowledge guides their behavior. The outsider remains separate and tries to describe aspects of the social situation about which the groups' members may be unaware. Rarely, however, do participant observers function as pure outsiders or insiders.

The second major feature of qualitative research is that the data are verbal, not numerical. Although qualitative researchers may use checklists to count occurrences of educational events, behaviors, and activities, they count (quantify) to note trends and not to present pictures of averages.

Third, qualitative researchers are concerned with the process of an activity rather than only the outcomes from that activity. In educational settings, qualitative researchers look at instructional activities within the total context of classrooms and schools. Instead of noting only whether the students increased their test scores, they want to describe the interactions occurring during instruction.

Fourth, qualitative researchers *analyze* the data verbally rather than statistically. The outcomes of much qualitative research are the generation of research questions and conjectures, not the verification of predicted relationships or outcomes. This feature is crucial to the usefulness of qualitative research. Because some qualitative research is descriptive, many of its data collection procedures are similar to those found in quantitative descriptive research. A distinguishing feature between the two is that qualitative research seeks to identify logical patterns within and among aspects of the research setting. To some researchers, especially those who hold to a strong belief in quantitative analysis, qualitative analyses may seem to lack objectivity. Nevertheless, qualitative researchers contribute by identifying and interpreting patterns of human responses by means of their knowledge, experiences, and theoretical orientations to education.

An illustrative qualitative research study involved a field investigation of classroom management from the perspective of high school students (Allen, 1986). The study was based on the assumption "that classroom contexts interact with students' agenda and result in variations in students' perspectives of the management of the classroom" (p. 438). Data were gathered (a) from the students' perspective, (b) from different classroom management situations, (c) by uncovering the students' agendas, and (d) by analyzing the underlying theoretical constructs. To become part of the groups, the researcher enrolled in a ninth grade schedule so that he could learn about the students' perspective by taking the role of a student. He wished to gain the students' confidence, so he asked the teachers to treat him like any other student. After the classes began, he avoided contact with the teachers. The researcher attended four morning classes each day and did not volunteer information about himself to the students until they questioned him. Then, he emphasized his student role, deemphasized that of being a researcher, and participated in classwork, activities, tests, and homework assignments. During class he took observational notes under the guise of taking class notes.

In sum, qualitative research views "classroom behavior in the larger

context of cultural standards and patterns of behavior, goals of partic-
ipants, behavior settings, and social influences beyond the classroom.
The implications are significant for our understanding of education"
(Jacob, 1987, p. 38).

COMPARATIVE RESEARCH

Comparative research lets researchers examine relationships including
similarities or differences among several variables. These variables
might represent characteristics of the same group of subjects or those
of separate groups. That is, researchers might compare the writing
performance and self-concept of members of a single group of subjects,
or they might compare the writing performance and self-concept of
two groups. Comparative research is more common than is pure descriptive research, but comparative research depends on knowledge
generated from descriptive research. All researchers use descriptive
data. Quantitative researchers apply statistical procedures to answer
questions about similarities, differences, and relationships among variables, whereas qualitative researchers apply verbal analyses to answer
similar questions.

Also, researchers can use the comparative data to make predictions.
When researchers find two variables that are strongly related, they
can use one variable to predict the occurrence of the other. They
cannot, however, use relationship information to show that one variable
is the *cause* of a change in another.

For example, a group of researchers conducted a comparative study
of Israeli preschool, remedial, and elementary school teachers' teaching
performance. They found consistent differences among the three
groups of teachers in affective variables but not in direct, actual teaching behavior. The preschool teachers were seen to be the most flexible,
democratic, and expressive in warmth (Babad, Bernieri, & Rosenthal,
1987). The essential aspect to this comparative research is that researchers made no attempt to determine causality. In fact, the researchers state "the results provide no hint as to what might have
caused the observed pattern" (p. 414).

Statistical Comparisons of Data

After researchers following a quantitative procedure collect data, they
calculate measures of central tendency (the mean) and variability (the
standard deviation) as they do in descriptive research. These measures
by themselves, however, do not provide evidence of difference or
relationship. One or more statistical procedures can be used to determine whether differences exist between or among groups. Many of
statistical procedures used in comparative research are similar to those
used in experimental research. Research consumers must realize that
statistical procedures are tools for answering research questions; they
are not the research. They help researchers determine whether an

apparent difference or relationship is large enough to be considered real. They also help researchers determine the extent to which they can be confident about their research conclusions. (Chapter 8, Reading and Interpreting Results Sections, contains an extended discussion about the research reality, or significance, of differences and relationships.)

statistical detectability

One statistical procedure used in descriptive research is Chi square. Table 2.2 contains an example of a Chi square analysis. The information is from a study that examined how teachers responded when students made miscues (deviant oral reading responses) (Lass, 1984). Two types of miscues ([a] attempted pronunciation of word even when wrong and [b] refused or hesitated response) were compared to two types of teacher responses ([a] supplied word and [b] all other kinds of responses). The analysis showed that teachers who dealt with unattempted miscues supplied words more often than they used all other responses combined.

A statistical procedure used extensively in comparative research is **correlation**. Correlations show whether two or more variables have a systematic relationship of occurrence. That is, they help researchers answer questions about the scores: Do high scores for one variable occur with high scores of another (a *positive* relationship)? or Do high scores for one variable occur with low scores of the other variable (a *negative* relationship)? The occurrence of low scores for one variable with low scores of another is also an example of a positive relationship.

Table 2.3 shows an example of correlation reporting. The table contains information from a study about the relationships between topic-specific background knowledge and measures of total writing quality (Langer, 1984). It shows the obtained relationships among four ways of evaluating students' writing: (a) teachers' marks, (b) a measure of coherence, (c) counting the words and clauses, and (d) a holistic scoring method. The relationship between the holistic scoring method

Table 2.2   Example of Chi Square Reporting: Attempted Miscues vs. Refusals/Hesitations and Teacher Response

| | Miscues | | | | |
| | Attempts | | Refusals/ Hesitations | | Raw Total |
	EO[a]	AO	EO	AO	
Teacher response Supplies word	105.5	93	13.5	26	119
All other	237.5	250	30.5	18	268
Column total		343		44	387

[a]EO = Expected occurrences; AO = Actual occurrences
χ^2 = 19.83 with one degree of freedom (p > .001)

Source: Adapted from Lass (1984).

Table 2.3 Example of Correlation Reporting: Relationships among Writing Measures

	Correlations (n of papers)		
	Teacher's Mark	Coherence	Words/Clause
Holistic score	.44[a] (57)	.06 (99)	.25 (96)
Teacher's mark		.27 (22)	−.15 (20)
Coherence			−.10 (96)

[a]$p < .01$

Source: Adapted from Langer (1984).

and the teachers' marks is positive and significant—high coherence scores were given to the work of the same students who received high teacher marks. On the other hand, the relationship between coherence and the number of words and clauses, which is negative, was not significant. Therefore, the relationship between these two scoring methods can be said to be unrelated. (A detailed explanation of significance is in Chapter 8, Reading and Interpreting Results Sections.)

Researchers also use correlations in comparative studies to make predictions. Researchers can predict the existence or occurrence of one variable when a strong relationship has been established between that variable and another. For example, the high positive correlation shown in Table 2.3 between the holistic scoring method and teachers' marks of students' papers might be used to make this prediction: Students' writing that receives high scores through holistic scoring procedures most likely will receive high marks from teachers. Holistic scoring is not the cause of students receiving high marks from teachers. Whatever characteristics make students' writing receive high scores in one scoring method probably are responsible for high scores in the other, but the research data reported in Table 2.3 give no inkling what that third, causative variable is. Thus, researchers' use of one variable as a predictor of another variable or event is not justification for considering the first variable as a causative factor.

Qualitative Method

In comparative studies, qualitative method researchers use verbal procedures similar to those discussed in the previous section on qualitative descriptive research methods. Qualitative researchers make verbal comparisons to explain similarities and differences; they do not just describe events or activities. Since qualitative method researchers are concerned with verbally comparing and contrasting what they are observing, they create patterns, meanings, and definitions of the ongoing processes and moods of various events, activities, and human interactions.

An extended discussion of comparative research procedures is provided in Chapter 7, Reading and Evaluating Procedure Sections.

INTERPRETING EDUCATIONAL RESEARCH

In experimental research, researchers set out to answer questions about causation. They wish to attribute the change in one variable to the effect of one or more other variables. For example, one group of researchers (Team A) may be concerned with finding answers to questions such as "Will students who receive one type of reading aid (text with focusing questions interspersed every three paragraphs) have better comprehension than students who have a second reading aid (text with key ideas underlined)?" Another research team (Team B) may want to know "Will students who are taught to use calculators for solving mathematical problems do better on final tests than students who do not receive that instruction?"

The influencing variable—the one to which researchers wish to attribute causation—is called the independent variable. **Independent variables** are measurable human and nonhuman characteristics. For example, age (years or months), intelligence (average, above average, superior), sensitivity to noise (high or low), intensity of light (high or low), frequency of an occurrence (never, sometimes, often), and teaching style (democratic, autonomous), to name a few, can be independent variables. Sometimes the independent variable is called the experimental variable. When the independent variable is an activity of the researcher, it is called a treatment variable. Researchers manipulate all independent variables. If the independent variable is a treatment, researchers can study the effects of two or more activities. If the independent variable is not an activity, researchers can subcategorize it. In the questions of teams A and B above, the treatment, or activity, in Team A's research is type of reading aid (focus questions or underlining). Team B's treatment is type of mathematics instruction (with calculator or without calculator). When characteristics such as age or intelligence are used as independent variables, researchers can subcategorize them (for example, 6-year-olds, 8-year-olds; average, above average intelligence).

The acted upon variable—the one being studied for possible change—is called the **dependent variable**. Not all human characteristics can be used as dependent variables. Reading ability is something that researchers might wish to change, as is degree of self-concept, or teachers' comprehension-questioning behavior. Something such as age, obviously, cannot be a dependent variable, because individuals' ages are not subject to modification—people will mature according to their biological clocks. The dependent variable for Team A (above) is comprehension performance and for Team B is problem-solving performance on tests.

An example of the attribution of causality is found in the research of a team that studied fifth graders. They wanted to find out whether classroom discussion resulted in greater science vocabulary learning than did individual work and, if it did, whether just listening to a discussion or actively participating in it produced the greater effect (Stahl & Clark, 1987). They found that "students in the discussion classes performed better on two measures of concept and vocabulary learning than students who simply read the target passages and took the tests" (p. 551). In this study, method of teaching (listening or participating) was the independent variable or treatment; learning (concept and vocabulary terms) was the dependent variable.

The following is an example of the attribution of causality in a study without a treatment. A team of researchers studied the effect of the gender of a story's main character (independent variable) on fifth-grade boys' and girls' reading interest and comprehension (dependent variables) for mystery, adventure, and humorous stories (Bleakly, Westerberg, & Hopkins, 1988). Here, differences in children's interest and comprehension (dependent variables) changed as a result of a story character's gender. However, the researchers did not engage in an activity, or treatment.

Researchers can study the individual or combined effect of several independent variables on a dependent variable, or one independent variable and its effect on two or more dependent variables. An example of experimental research in which two independent variables were examined set out

> to identify the relative contribution of the nature of instruction and the frequency of encounters in bringing about word knowledge proficiency. (McKeown, Beck, Omanson, & Pople, 1985, p. 525)

In this study, the two independent variables were (a) the type of vocabulary instruction (treatment activity) and (b) the frequency of vocabulary instruction.

Researchers can use one independent variable with more than one dependent variable. An example of such a study is the one about story character gender (above) (Bleakley, Westerberg, & Hopkins, 1988). A study in which one independent variable was examined for its effect on several dependent variables set out to determine whether

> text explicitness would enhance children's *silent reading rates, their ratings of story interest, their abilities to recall stories and answer questions about them*, and *ratings of their overall understanding of stories* [italics added to identify the dependent variables] (Sundbye, 1987, p. 86).

Both sets of researchers can conclude that something (type and frequency of vocabulary instruction or text explicitness) caused a change in something else (students' word knowledge or students' reaction to stories). Researchers can make these conclusions because they make decisions about the control of variables that are not of concern in descriptive or comparative research. **Control** means the researchers used procedures to limit or account for the possible influence of variables not being studied. They use these controls before the research is done (a priori). The control of these **extraneous variables** can be done in one or more ways. Two ways to develop control in experimental studies are presented below. (Extended discussions of these and other ways to control extraneous variables are in Chapters 5, Reading and Evaluating Subject Sections, and 7, Reading and Evaluating Procedure Sections.)

In the study about story character gender and students' story interest and comprehension (Bleakley, Westerberg, & Hopkins, 1988), a variable that might possibly affect students' reading interest is reading ability. The researchers controlled for the possible effect of students' reading ability by dividing them into three groups based on the results of a standardized reading test. This way, the researchers saw whether students at different levels of reading ability responded differently on measures of interest and comprehension. Although the researchers in the study about science vocabulary learning (Stahl & Clark, 1987) used students with similar achievement scores, other variables might have accounted for learning. To control for the possible effect of such things as students' interest, learning style, and science ability, and possible researchers bias in selecting the subjects, researchers used randomization to group the subjects in the treatment groups (those to whom the independent variables were applied). **Randomization** is an unbiased, systematic selection or assignment of subjects. When they use randomization, researchers assume that most human characteristics are evenly distributed among the groups.

In the above illustrations, researchers had the opportunity to manipulate the independent variable before doing the research. Sometimes, however, researchers want answers to questions but cannot manipulate the independent variable for practical or ethical reasons. They realize a condition exists and are unsure about what might have been its cause. For example, researchers might be interested in why some children develop autistic tendencies after birth. They question whether prenatal conditions might account for the development of the autistic tendencies. In such a case, it would be unethical to create an experimental study in which researchers manipulate the prenatal environment. But, by starting with the effect (children with autistic tendencies) and identifying possible causes (nutrition, mother's age, ingestion of abusive substances, illness), researchers can try to establish a cause–effect relationship. This ex post facto (after the fact) research is called **causal–comparative research**.

The name causal–comparative research can be confusing when discussing experimental research. This type of research is comparative because researchers compare possible independent variables to see which variable, if any, has a strong relationship with the already known outcome. It is more than comparative research because the data analysis procedures do more than compare or correlate; the researchers analyze data with the purpose of establishing causality. Since researchers cannot establish a cause–effect relationship experimentally, they do so rationally. They take already intact groups—mothers whose children show autistic tendencies and mothers with children who do not —and compare them statistically under controlled conditions. The groups already differ on the independent and dependent variables. The researchers do not induce differences; they seek to identify one or more preexisting conditions (independent variables) in one group that exist to a lesser degree in the other. When researchers identify one or more conditions, they can attribute causality; however, this attribution may be less strong than in an experimental design where the researchers can control all of the variables.

An illustration of causal–comparative research in education is shown in a study about reading comprehension and creativity in the use of English by blacks (DeLain, Pearson, & Anderson, 1985). The research team

> explored the hypothesis that the rich and varied experience of black youth with figurative language outside school would enhance their understanding of figurative language in school texts. Results confirmed that for black students, "sounding" skill, as well as general verbal ability, has a direct influence on figurative language comprehension. Black language ability influences figurative language comprehension indirectly through its effect on sounding skill. For white students, only general verbal ability affects figurative language comprehension. (p. 155)

In this exploratory study, the independent variables, "sounding" or "playing the dozens" and general verbal ability, already existed and varied within and between black and white students. The researchers could not manipulate the variables, nor could they teach the ritual-insult verbal play in a school setting. Also, differences in the dependent variable, understanding figurative language, existed. The researchers, in an ex post facto study, examined the possible causative linkage. They used causal–comparative research to draw conclusions about the positive influence of black youths' ability to "sound" and their ability to understand school-based figurative language.

A limitation of causal–comparative research is that researchers cannot have the same assurance as they do in experimental research about the cause–effect linkage. Often, and whenever possible, causal–comparative results need to be confirmed by experimental research. Causal–comparative research also lacks other controls used by researchers in experimental research. Randomization of subjects among treatments or the creation of closely comparable groups is usually not possible. Also, researchers cannot control the quality of students' previous experiences that relate to the independent variable. And, the people selected for the study may differ on some other variable that the researchers did not consider. These limitations show up in causal–comparative research as an estimate of unaccounted-for influence. When there is a large unaccounted-for influence, researchers

Seldom can do Experimental ed. research

INTERPRETING EDUCATIONAL RESEARCH

must seek and test other independent variables for the possible cause of a recognized result.

Analysis of Experimental Statistical Data

After data are collected in experimental studies, measures of central tendency (means) and variability (standard deviations) are created. This descriptive information forms the basis of other statistical procedures. When researchers conduct simple one-variable studies, they use a common statistical procedure known as the *t*-test. The ***t-test*** is used to determine whether the difference between the means of two groups on a dependent variable is significant: that is, whether the examined results could have happened by chance or whether the researchers can reliably attribute the difference to the influence of the independent variable.

But, as discussed previously, single-variable studies provide limited insight about educational questions. Multiple-variable research requires the calculation of many *t*-tests, which is awkward, possibly misleading, and limiting since the interaction among multiple variables cannot be shown by *t*-tests. To overcome this limitation, researchers use the **analysis of variance** (**ANOVA**). Results of an ANOVA are reported in **F-ratios**. ANOVAs are used to determine whether differences can be attributed to one or a combination of independent variables.

Table 2.4 contains a common form for reporting ANOVA results. The information is taken from a study about the effect of three different

Table 2.4   Reporting of ANOVA Results: Summary Table for Three-Way Analysis of Variance

Source of variation	df	SS[a]	MS[a]	F
Format of text	2	313.01	156.51	9.751[b]
Students' grade	1	141.67	141.67	8.827[c]
Students' comprehension	1	447.32	447.34	27.871[b]
Format × grade	2	20.88	10.44	0.650
Format × comprehension	2	93.69	46.85	2.919
Grade × comprehension	1	52.74	52.74	3.286
Format × grade × comprehension	2	133.81	66.91	4.169[d]
Within cells (error)	120	1926.58	16.05	
Total	131	3129.72		

[a]MS = Mean square; SS = Sum of the square
[b]$p < .001$
[c]$p < .01$
[d]$p < .05$

Source: Adapted from Radebaugh (1983).

sentence organizations during cloze tests on fourth and fifth grade readers. The results show that there were differences in results based on (a) the type of sentence organization (format of text). (b) the students' grade level, and (c) the comprehension ability of the students (students' comprehension). The results also indicated that particular types of organization were most effective at certain grade levels with students of specific ability (Format × Grade × Comprehension.)

SUMMARY

What are the designs used to conduct research?

Three types of designs, or plans, for conducting research have the purposes of (a) description, (b) comparison, and (c) attribution of causality.

What instruments are used to collect data?

Data are collected with instruments, which are direct observation forms, tests, and surveys (questionnaires and interviews).

What are descriptive, comparative and experimental research and what distinguishes the three types of research designs from each other?

Descriptive research is done to answer questions about a variable's status. Comparative research is done to make decisions about two or more variables' differences or relationships. Experimental research is done to draw conclusions about the cause–effect relationship between two or more variables. Descriptive and comparative research may reveal status, patterns, and associations among variables, but only experimental research can be used to attribute causality.

What are central tendency and variability and how are they measured?

Central tendency is the middle score or average in a group of scores. The middle score is called the median; the arithmetic average score is called the mean. Variability is the extent to which other scores in the group cluster about or spread from the mean. The variability is usually reported as the standard deviation (SD).

How are data analyzed in each of the three types of research designs?

In descriptive research, information most often is described with means and standard deviations. In comparative research, in addition to the descriptive measures of data, two common statistical procedures are the correlation and Chi square. In experimental research common statistical procedures are the *t*-test and analysis of variance (ANOVA).

ACTIVITIES

Effective learning can be gained from the following activities when they are done with another class student. This *peer interacting* can follow a simple format:

INTERPRETING EDUCATIONAL RESEARCH

a. Each student reads a passage and then does an accompanying activity.
b. Each student explains to the other what the response to that activity is and why that response is chosen.
c. The students' responses are compared with the authors' feedback.
d. If there are differences between peer responses or between peer responses and the authors' feedback, students should refer to the text or the course instructor for verification.

Activity 1

For each of the research purposes, questions, and hypotheses listed below, indicate (a) the type of research design (descriptive, comparative, experimental, causal–comparative), and (b) the research variables. For experimental or causal–comparative designs, differentiate between the independent and dependent variables. *Note*: Some of the studies have more than one research purpose.

1. The study was designed to focus on the general question What do teachers mean when they identify work-related factors as sources of stress? (Blase, 1986, p. 14)
2. Two fundamental questions about problem-solving instruction need to be addressed: "What does it look like?" and "Is it different from basic skills instruction?" This study examined these questions by describing the instructional conditions and arrangements set up by nine seventh-grade mathematics teachers for a six-day unit of their own design on problem solving. These data are then compared to similar descriptions of the basic skills instruction of the same teachers. (Burns & Lash, 1986, p. 394)
3. This study investigated the effects of microcomputer use on preschoolers' knowledge of basic reading readiness concepts and on their attitudes toward the microcomputer. There were two major purposes. The first was to compare prereading skills of children who had been randomly assigned to the following three groups: (a) an "adult-assisted" group who used the microcomputer in the presence of an adult who assumed a teacher role; (b) an "adult-unassisted" group who used the microcomputer on their own after being given only minimal instructions from an adult; and (c) a control group who did not use the microcomputer at all. The study's second purpose was to investigate the effects of the treatment variable on the children's attitude toward the microcomputer. (Goodwin, Goodwin, Nansel, & Helm, 1986, pp. 349–350)
4. The researchers hypothesized that classroom intellectual composition positively affects the student's academic achievement. (Dar & Resh, 1986, p. 360)
5. The hypotheses of the study were that, regarding one wage earner from each household in a small town (a) higher levels of education

will be associated with higher volumes of certain (but not all) content of reading than lower levels of education; and (b) occupational category will be associated with different volumes of certain (but not all) content for reading. (Guthrie, Seifert, & Kirsch, 1986, p. 152)

Activity 2

Using a research report of your own choosing or one from Appendix B, (a) locate the research hypothesis, purpose, or question; (b) indicate the research design; and (c) identify the research variables. For experimental or causal–comparative research, indicate the independent and dependent variables.

FEEDBACK

Activity 1

1. This was descriptive research. Data were being collected that described what teachers indicate as the sources of stress (the research variable). No causality was presumed.

2. The study had two parts. Part one was descriptive. The researchers were collecting data about the research variable "teachers' problem solving instruction." No causality was being attributed to their instruction or as a result of their instruction. Part two was comparative. The teachers' instruction was being compared to the teachers' description of "basic skills instruction" (a second research variable). Again, no causality was presumed.

3. The study had two parts. Part one was comparative. In it the research variable, "prereading skills," was compared between three groups. No causality was presumed in the comparison, only differences in skills. Part two was experimental. The effect of the instructional groupings (the treatment or independent variable) on children's attitudes toward the microcomputer (the dependent variable) was examined. Causality *was* presumed—the instructional groupings would cause a change in attitudes.

4. The study was experimental. The independent (experimental or variable) was "classroom intellectual composition" and the dependent variable was "student's academic achievement." Causality *was* presumed—classroom composition would cause differences in academic achievement.

5. The study was causal–comparative because both the independent variables, "higher levels of education" and "occupational category," were in existence prior to the study. The dependent variable in both parts of the study was "content of reading." Causality *was* presumed—level of education and occupational category would cause differences in reading content.

3

Reading and Evaluating Research Reports

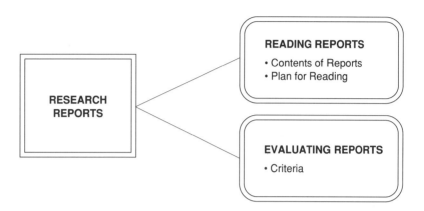

FOCUS QUESTIONS

1. What are the major sections of research reports?
2. What is an effective strategy for reading research reports?
3. What are the criteria for evaluating the quality and appropriateness of research reports?

Research consumers read research reports to increase their general knowledge about educational practice, to acquire knowledge that they can apply in professional practices, and to gain insights about effective instructional procedures that they can use in classrooms.

A **research report** is not research. Research is conducted by systematically collecting information about an identified problem or question, analyzing the data, and, on the basis of the evidence, confirming or disconfirming a prior prediction or statement. A research report is a summary of researchers' activities and results. Research consumers can judge the effectiveness of research producers and the appropriateness of their results only by reading and evaluating research reports.

Research reports are pictures of research: They are representations of what researchers have done and how they wish to present their research procedures to the public. Four pictures of research, are possible: (a) good research methodology, well reported; (b) good research methodology, poorly reported; (c) poor research methodology, well reported; and (d) poor research methodology, poorly reported. Research consumers' ability will be tested in identifying the second and third pictures. In situation (b), researchers might have conducted appropriate research and reported it inappropriately; in situation (c), they might have conducted inappropriate research and dressed it in the garb of an appropriate research report.

This chapter explains the contents of research reports, presents models of well-written research reports, demonstrates effective report-reading procedures for research consumers, and lists questions for evaluating the quality of research reports. These evaluative questions form the bases for discussions in succeeding chapters about reading and analyzing research methods.

READING RESEARCH REPORTS

Content of Research Reports

Research reports contain information related to research producers' questions and their research activities. This information is organized to show researchers' efforts in

Selecting a problem area

Specifying research questions

Describing subjects

Describing instruments

Explaining procedures and treatments (if appropriate)

Presenting results based on data analyses

Discussing implications

The information is generally organized into sections with headings such as Background or Literature Review; Purpose, Questions, or Hypothesis; Method, including Subjects, Instruments, and Procedure; Results; Discussion; and References.

A **background section** contains (a) an explanation of the researcher's problem area, (b) its educational importance, (c) summaries of other researchers' results that are related to the problem (called a literature review), and (d) strengths from the related research that were used and weaknesses or limitations that were changed. The background section is often preceded by an **abstract**, a summary of the report. Researchers usually omit the literature review from the abstract.

A **purpose section** contains the specific goal or goals of the research project. These can be expressed as a statement of purpose, as questions, or as hypotheses. The following is an example from a report in which both a purpose and specific questions are expressed.

> The purpose of the present study was to investigate the effects on children from lower socioeconomic backgrounds of one-to-one readings in school settings that encouraged interaction between the teacher and child. Specifically, the study was designed to answer the following questions:
>
> 1. Do frequent one-to-one story readings at school increase the number of questions and comments children make about stories?
> 2. Do frequent one-to-one story readings at school increase the type and complexity of questions and comments made about stories?
> 3. Do repeated readings of the same story elicit different types of questions and comments than a series of readings of unrepeated books? (Morrow, 1988, p. 95)

From reading the purpose section, research consumers can identify and classify the type of research and the research variables (independent and dependent when appropriate). In the above example, the word *effect* in the purpose statement and the word *increase* in questions 1 and 2 are clues to the type of research method followed—in this case, experimental research. In questions (Q) 1 and 2, the independent variables were "one-to-one story readings." The dependent variables were "the number of questions and comments children make" (Q1) and "the type and complexity of children's questions and comments" (Q2). In question 3, the independent variable was "readings" (repeated or unrepeated), and the dependent variable was children's questions and comments. The following is an example in which a hypothesis is stated. Notice how the researcher predicted the expected results.

> It was hypothesized that teachers and students in Choctaw intercultural classrooms using a switchboard participation structure, when compared to similar Anglo-American classes, would show differences in the behaviors examined in the study. It was further hypothesized that observed differences in the Choctaw student behavior would be in the direction of decreased classroom participation and increased violations of the turn-taking rules of switchboard participation. (Greenbaum, 1985, p. 105)

Sometimes, researchers (as the ones quoted above) do not place their purpose, questions, or hypotheses in a section with a separate heading. In such cases, they include this information in the background section, most often in the section's last paragraph.

The **method sections** of research reports usually contain several subsections. These are Subjects, Instruments, and Procedure.

The **subjects section** contains a description of the individuals included in the study, giving general information about such factors as age, sex, grade level, intellectual and academic abilities, and socioeconomic levels. It also contains the number of subjects and an account of how the subjects were selected and assigned to groups. The following is a typical subject section.

Subjects

The subjects for this study were 75 second graders from a public school located in a moderate-sized Southern city. These students were placed in their respective classrooms by homogeneous grouping procedures. This grouping procedure was based on the use of the Stanford Diagnostic Reading Test, the Ginn 720 Basic Skills Test, and the Louisiana Basic Skills Testing Program. Testing and grouping assignments were conducted by the various classroom teachers and administrators in the school system.

Subjects were drawn from three of five second-grade classrooms located within this school. The three classrooms that were selected for use during data collection were those that had been designated as the average or above-average classes. Subjects participating in this study were randomly assigned to one of three instructional groups, traditional basal lesson, the Reconciled Reading Lesson, or the List-Group-Label lesson. (Thames & Readence, 1988, pp. 3–4)

The **instruments section** contains a description of the data collection instruments: observation forms, standardized and researcher-made tests, and surveys. When instruments are standardized tests, researchers usually assume the readers' familiarity with them and do little more than name them. (In Chapter 6, Instrumentation, is an explanation of how readers can obtain information about unfamiliar standardized tests.) When instruments are less well known, researchers describe or give examples of them and give evidence of their effectiveness. If tests other than standardized tests were administered, researchers explain the testing circumstances and the qualifications or training of the test givers and provide information about the test and how it was constructed. If observations or surveys were used, researchers relate how they were done and how the observers or interviewers were trained.

The following is a typical instruments section, which explains in detail how the researchers developed one instrument, a questionnaire, and refers to two standardized tests.

Instruments

A parent questionnaire, standardized intelligence test, and standardized reading subtest were used to examine the research question.

Parent Questionnaire. A parent questionnaire was developed to examine the four written language areas. All items on the questionnaire were validated by a panel of nine expert judges who had previous experience in helping young children develop reading capabilities. During the validation process, all panel members were provided 21 cluster headings (i.e., Listening Activities Involving Recitation) which represented groupings of questions related to each of the four areas. Panel members were required to sort the cluster headings under the four major construct headings (or an additional heading identified as "Other"). Panel members also performed a sorting task involving the individual questionnaire items (i.e., While reading a story to your child, to what extent have you—or other members of your family—had your child repeat sentences that you just read?) and 21 cluster headings. Members read each questionnaire item and matched the question content to the appropriate cluster heading. An additional agreement was required by panel members before individual questions were placed within clusters under major constructs.

The final questionnaire was composed of 24 descriptive questions and 245 quantitative questions that were divided into the four major constructs (i.e., Concepts About Print, Print in the Environment, Invented Spelling, Story Recall). Each construct represented a macroview of many different types of opportunities related to each of the four areas. Items within each construct had been investigated in previous research . . . and found to be important to the development of written language. Data for the quantitative sections was recorded as parents responded to a five-point Likert scale (i.e., Never, Seldom, Sometimes, Often, and Very Often) estimating the degree to which specific experiences were provided in the home environment. Reliability coefficients of .89 to .97 (Cronbach's alpha) were estimated when the questionnaire was administered to the mothers.

Test Administration. All 125 potentially gifted children were administered the Stanford-Binet Intelligence Test and Letter-Word Identification subtest from the Woodcock-Johnson Psycho-Educational Battery by certified examiners.

Administration and Scoring of Parent Questionnaire. Mothers of identified accelerated readers and nonreaders were contacted by telephone once they had received notification regarding eligibility (or non-eligibility) of their children for the preschool gifted program. Dates were scheduled for one examiner to administer the parent questionnaire to mothers in the home. All questions were read to the mothers and responses were recorded by the examiner.

The questionnaire responses were scored by assigning a value (i.e., 1, 2, 3, 4, or 5) to each item based upon the degree to which the child was demonstrating the behavior in the home (i.e., Never = 1; Seldom = 2; Sometimes = 3; Often = 4; Very Often = 5). All items for each questionnaire construct were totaled and a mean score was calculated for each of the four constructs. (Burns & Collins, 1987, pp. 241–243)

A **procedure section**, a subsection of the method section, contains a detailed explanation of how researchers conducted their study. In descriptive and comparative studies, researchers explain how data were collected and analyzed. In experimental studies, researchers also describe the treatments and how they were administered. If special instructional materials were prepared for the study, they are described and often sample portions are included.

The following example is a typical methods section. It is taken from an experimental study about the activation of students' background knowledge during reading assessment.

MATERIALS

Materials for this study were drawn from the Primary, Elementary, and Advanced levels of the research edition (a preliminary version developed for field review and comment) of the Metropolitan Achievement Test (1985). In order to investigate the types of background knowledge students activate in response to adjunct questions used on comprehension tests, we randomly selected three purpose questions from each of the three test levels. When we examined these questions in relation to their passages, we determined that they required students to infer answers by integrating information across sentences and paragraphs. Each question was removed and attached to an unlined 3″ × 5″ (7.5 cm × 12.5 cm) card. Three stimulus questions seemed an appropriate number for providing adequate content variability, but not too many to promote fatigue among the younger students participating in the study. Table 1 presents the purpose questions used with the three grade levels.

INTERVIEW PROCEDURES

Interview procedures were first piloted with a group of 10th-grade students not participating in the study. We followed a semi-structured interview guide containing the major questions to be asked and specifying the types of follow-up questions to be used. However, we adjusted question phrasing and pacing according to the responses of individual students. The order of presentation of the three questions was counterbalanced at each grade level.

Each participant was individually interviewed in a quiet location. Interviews were audiotaped and usually lasted approximately 15 minutes—roughly 5 minutes per purpose question. Students were in-

Table 1 Purpose Questions Used in the Interviews

Grade 1
1. How can you cross a street safely?
2. Why did the neighbors plant trees?
3. What was Tom's joke?

Grade 6
4. Why would people eat weeds?
5. How does this writer get away from the city?
6. Why was Socrates important?

Grade 10
7. How good were Jules Verne's predictions?
8. Why doesn't Philip have friends?
9. How are these scientists trying to read your mind?

Note: These questions were selected from the Primary, Intermediate, and Advanced levels of the research edition of the *Metropolitan Achievement Tests* (1985).

formed that their task was not to read the passages or answer the test items, but instead to "guess" about passage content. Students were briefly shown a copy of the test booklet appropriate for their grade level, and were informed of the general nature and function of purpose questions; that is, they were told that purpose questions had been added to this new test to help test-takers begin thinking about the passages before they read them. Next, students were shown both a purpose question isolated on a card, and the corresponding test page. We briefly pointed to the prepassage location of the question and explained that the isolated

Table 2 Sample Transcript of a 10th-Grade Interview

Researcher (R):	O.K. That's pretty good. Now let's do another question. Would you please read this question, and then tell me what you think the story is going to be about.
Student (S):	How are (*pause*) these scientists trying to read your mind?
R:	Right. How are these scientists trying to read your mind? What do you think the passage is going to be about?
S:	(1) About some scientists who are reading/ or (2) trying to read your mind./
R:	O.K. Can you tell me some more?
S:	Well, it's about (3) mind readers (4) who are some scientist people (5) who work in laboratories / and (6) read minds and things. (*pause*) (7) I guess I don't really know./
R:	O.K. That's good. Try thinking about some more things.
S:	(8) They are mind readers (9) who read minds./
R:	O.K. Now think about if you were taking a reading test and the passage had this question in front of it . . . what would the passage be about?
S:	Well, it would be about (10) some men who made up ways to read / (*pause*) (11) they read minds, (12) get into your head / and (13) find out about you, (14) about the way you think / and (15) what you think about / and like that. And it would tell you about (16) how they could do it / and (17) could not do it / and (18) why it's illegal (19) for all of us to do it / but (20) the Government can. / And (21) names / and (22) the men who are doing it / and (23) why./
R:	Tell me some more . . .
S:	(24) So they can find out things about it./ (25) My aunt had mind readers./
R:	She did?
S:	Yeah. (26) She said they attached some little dart / or (27) something to her head (28) when she was in the hospital / and then (29) she had it (30) even after it was paid for . . . (*etc.*)

Note: (#) marks the beginning of a coded predicate proposition marks the close of a coded proposition, or separates connectives not coded (*and, but, or,* etc.)

purpose question had been cut from a similar test booklet. After this brief exposure to the context in which the purpose question was used, the booklet was removed and the students' attention was focused on the isolated question.

Respondents were asked to read each purpose question and make predictions about the passage that accompanied it in the test booklet. Pilot interviews indicated that a number of first-grade children needed help in reading the selected purpose questions, so we supplied unknown words when necessary. Sixth- and 10th-grade students, however, were asked to read the questions on their own. For all grade levels, we avoided supplying any substantive information about the purpose questions, and instead used neutral elaboration probes (Gordon, 1980) to encourage students to make predictions and extend their responses.

When participants had completed their responses to this initial prediction task, we used two other types of probing questions. Students were asked to put themselves in the position of a test-taker and to describe what they would "try to find out" during reading if they had encountered that purpose question on a test. Finally, they were asked to assume a test-taking perspective and to guess about the content of the questions that might appear at the end of each test passage. These two interview questions were included to encourage students to use their knowledge of test-taking to provide a context for understanding the nature of the interview task, and for activating background knowledge related to the purpose questions. The transcript presented in Table 2 [on p. 49] illustrates the questions used to elicit student predictions. (From Rowe & Rayford, 1987, pp. 164–165. Reprinted with permission of D.W. Rowe and the International Reading Association.)

The **Results section** contains the outcomes of the researchers' data analyses. This section contains not only the numerical results (often presented in tables and charts) but an explanation of the significance of those results. To many research consumers, results sections are confusing because of the statistical information. (The next subsection of this chapter, A Plan for Reading Reports, explains how these sections can be read. In Chapter 8, Results and Statistical Procedures, is a discussion about how to judge researchers' presentations of data analyses.)

The following example is a typical results section. It is from an experimental study about the effects of preteaching different levels of vocabulary with two different instructional methods on students' comprehension of basal stories (Wixson, 1986). Notice that the results of the statistical analysis were reported as part of the commentary and in tables and graphs. The analyses for teaching method and comprehension were reported separately. The two teaching methods were "definition" and "example." The two comprehension testing procedures were "recall" and "questions." The results indicated that (a) the level of vocabulary taught had an effect on both word knowledge and text comprehension and (b) the questions for evaluating students' story comprehension were a more sensitive measure of their comprehension than was a recall procedure.

RESULTS

The data were analyzed using repeated-measures analysis of covariance (ANCOVA) procedures with word level (central/noncentral), method of instruction (dictionary/concept), and story (*King/Cave*), as the between-subjects factors, and response level (central/noncentral) obtained for each of the dependent measures as the within-subjects factor. Separate analyses were conducted for each of the vocabulary and comprehension measures. Follow-up tests using one-way tests of simple main effects were performed only for the interactions that were free of story effects. Interactions involving story effects were not pursued. Achievement was the covariate in each of these analyses. The means and standard deviations for the vocabulary and comprehension measures are presented in Tables 1 and 2.

Vocabulary Measures

Definition. The results of the ANCOVA for the definition measure indicated significant main effects for method. $F(1, 111) = 4.45$, $p < .05$; word level, $F(1, 111) = 8.98$, $p < .01$; story, $F(1, 111) = 11.84$, $p < .001$; and response level, $F(1, 112) = 4.81$, $p < .05$. The following interaction effects were also statistically significant: Method × Story, $F(1, 111) = 5.86$, $p < .05$; Story × Response Level, $F(1, 112) = 20.45$, $p < .0001$; and Word Level × Response Level, $F(1, 112) = 46.95$, $p < .0001$. All other interactions were nonsignificant ($p > .05$ for all).

The most interesting result was the significant Word Level × Response Level interaction effect (see Figure 1). Follow-up tests using simple main effects indicated that subjects who received instruction on central vocabulary words performed better on the definition items for central vocabulary than for noncentral vocabulary, $F(1, 112) = 10.85$,

Table 1   Means (and Standard Deviations) for Vocabulary Measures by Word Level, Method, and Story

Group[a]	Definition Measure		Example Measure	
	Central	Noncentral	Central	Noncentral
Central Words				
Definition				
King	2.5(.64)	3.1(1.2)	2.6(1.6)	2.3(1.1)
Cave	4.3(1.1)	3.0(1.4)	2.6(1.5)	3.1(1.2)
Concept				
King	3.5(1.2)	3.2(1.2)	3.1(1.4)	2.9(.70)
Cave	4.0(1.2)	2.9(1.2)	2.8(1.1)	2.6(.99)
Noncentral Words				
Definition				
King	2.3(.82)	3.5(.74)	1.9(1.1)	2.6(.83)
Cave	3.6(1.1)	4.0(.93)	1.9(1.1)	3.3(1.3)
Concept				
King	2.5(.92)	4.4(1.1)	2.1(1.4)	4.1(1.1)
Cave	3.3(1.2)	4.3(.88)	2.3(1.4)	3.6(1.2)

Note: Range of possible scores is 0.5.
[a] = 15 for each group.

Table 2 Means (and Standard Deviations) for Comprehension Measures by Word Level, Method, and Story

Group[a]	Recall Measure		Question Measure	
	Central[c]	Noncentral[d]	Central	Noncentral
Central Words				
Definition				
King	4.4(2.9)	6.9(4.0)	3.2(1.7)	2.5(.74)
Cave	10.5(3.4)	7.7(3.3)	3.3(1.5)	3.6(1.1)
Concept				
King	5.1(2.8)	5.3(3.1)	3.4(.91)	2.7(1.1)
Cave	9.5(4.8)	5.9(3.3)	3.5(1.3)	2.5(1.3)
Noncentral Words				
Definition				
King	3.1(2.4)	4.7(4.5)	2.7(1.4)	2.6(.83)
Cave	9.4(5.0)	6.8(4.4)	2.3(1.2)	3.7(.82)
Concept				
King	3.0(2.4)	5.1(4.8)	3.2(1.1)	2.9(.64)
Cave	10.0(6.4)	7.3(7.9)	2.9(.80)	3.3(1.4)

[a] = 15 for each group.
[b]Range of possible scores is 0-5
[c]Range of possible scores. *King*, 0-44, *Cave*, 0-59
[d]Range of possible scores. *King*, 0-89, *Cave*, 0-88

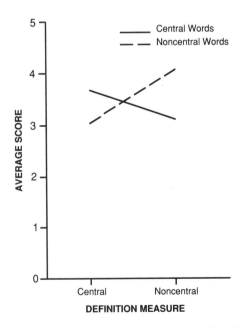

Figure 1 Word level by response level interaction effect for definition measure.

$p = .001$; and subjects who received instruction on noncentral vocabulary words performed better on definition items for noncentral than for central vocabulary. $F(1, 112) = 40.90$, $p < .0001$. In addition, the subjects who were taught the central vocabulary words learned more central definitions than the subjects who were taught the noncentral words, $F(1, 111) = 6.46$, $p < .01$; whereas the subjects who were taught the noncentral words learned more noncentral definitions than those who were taught the central words, $F(1, 111) = 44.56$, $p < .0001$.

Example. The results of the ANCOVA of the example measure indicated main effects for method, $F(1, 111) = 8.64$, $p < .01$, and response level, $F(1, 112) = 23.53$, $p < .0001$, but no main effects for either word level or story ($p > .05$ for all). The results also indicated a significant Method × Story × Response Level interaction effect, $F(1, 112) = 4.62$, $p < .05$. As with the definition measure, the most interesting finding was the significant Word Level × Response Level interaction. $F(1. 112) = 27.23$, $p < .0001$ (see Figure 2). All other interactions were nonsignificant ($p > .05$ for all).

Follow-up tests to the Word Level × Response Level interaction indicated that the subjects who received instruction on the central words performed in a similar manner on both central and noncentral example items ($p > .05$), whereas the subjects who received instruction on the noncentral words performed better on the noncentral than the central example items. $F(1, 112) = 50.69$, $p < .0001$. Follow-up tests also indicated that the subjects who were taught central vocabulary words

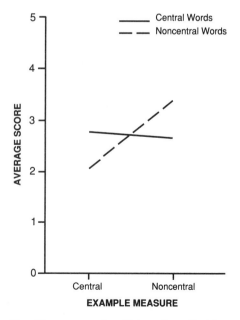

Figure 2 Word level by response level interaction effect for example measure.

answered correctly more central example items than the subjects who were taught the noncentral words, $F(1, 111) = 4.02$, $p < .05$, whereas the subjects who were taught the noncentral words answered more noncentral example items correctly than those who were taught central words, $F(1, 111) = 18.48$, $p < .0001$.

Comprehension Measures

Recall. The results of the ANCOVA for the recall measure indicated significant main effects for story, $F(1, 111) = 30.51$, $p < .0001$, and response level, $F(1, 112) = 5.05$, $p < .05$. In addition, there was a significant Story × Response Level interaction effect, $F(1, 112) = 61.46$, $p < .0001$. All remaining effects for this analysis were nonsignificant ($p > .05$ for all).

Questions. The results of the ANCOVA for the comprehension questions indicated no main effects (p > .05 for all). However, there were several statistically significant interaction effects: Method × Response Level. $F(1, 112) = 6.29$. $p = .01$. Story × Response Level. $F(1. 112) = 9.30$, $p < .01$; and Method × Story × Response Level. $F(1, 112) = 4.41$, $p < .05$. As in the analyses of the definition and the example measures, there was also a significant Word Level × Response Level interaction effect. $F(1, 112) = 11.95$. $p < .001$ (see Figure 3). All remaining interactions were nonsignificant ($p > .05$ for all).

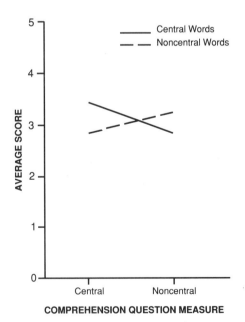

Figure 3 Word level by response level interaction effect for comprehension question measure

INTERPRETING EDUCATIONAL RESEARCH

Follow-up tests to the significant Word Level × Response Level interaction indicated that the subjects who received instruction on central words understood ideas related to the central vocabulary better than ideas related to the noncentral vocabulary. $F(1, 112) = 9.41$. $p < .01$, whereas the subjects who received instruction on the noncentral words performed in a similar manner on both central and noncentral comprehension items ($p > .05$). The follow-up tests also indicated that the subjects who were taught the noncentral words understood ideas related to the noncentral words better than subjects who were taught the central words. $F(1, 111) = 6.76$, $p < .01$, but there was no difference between subjects taught central and those taught noncentral words in their understanding of ideas related to central words ($p > .05$). Thus, although instruction on noncentral words served to improve the understanding of the noncentral ideas, the effects of the central vocabulary instruction were less clear. It appears that some of the subjects who received the noncentral vocabulary instruction were able to understand the central ideas without instruction on the central vocabulary. This variability accounts for the nonsignificant results obtained in the comparisons.

> *Non-parametric tests.* As a check on the generalizability of the word level effect across words, the Mann-Whitney U procedure was applied to the measures for which the Word Level × Response Level interaction effects were significant. Specifically, the interaction between the word level treatment (central and noncentral) and the responses to the items for central and noncentral words (response level) were tested for the definition, example, and comprehension question measures, with words treated as a random effect. The results of these tests were as follows: definition, $U = 2.5$, $p < .001$; example, $U = 4.5$, $p < .001$: comprehension questions. $U = 18$. $p < .01$. These results indicate that the effects of the word level treatment were generalizable across words. (From Wixson, 1986, pp. 323–324. Reprinted with permission of K. K. Wixson and the International Reading Association.)

A **conclusions** or discussion **section** contains the researchers' ideas about the educational implications of the research results: how the results can be used in school settings or what additional research may be called for. Often this explanation is prefaced with a brief summary of the research results. When researchers obtain unusual or unexpected results, they discuss possible reasons for these results.

The following example is a typical conclusions section. It is from a descriptive study about teachers' perspectives on effective school leadership (Blase, 1987). The first three paragraphs contain a summary of the results. The next two paragraphs contain the researcher's conclusions about those results, and the final part contains his ideas about what activities should be in programs to train school leaders.

SUMMARY AND CONCLUSIONS

Data from the research discussed above point out that nine task-related factors and five consideration-related factors represent, from the perspectives of the teachers studied, the major dimensions of effective high school leadership. In addition, the data indicate that such factors have, in varying degrees, dramatic effects on teachers and their relationships with significant others. Along these lines, it was discovered that leadership factors affected teacher motivation, involvement, and morale and, in general, enhanced the possibility of productive interactions between teachers and others. At a more abstract level, effective leadership was linked to the development of productive social and cultural structures in schools.

Throughout this article, it has been emphasized that the leadership factors described seemed to be highly interdependent. In their discussions of individual effective school principals, teachers voluntarily described (that is, without direct questioning by the researcher) all leadership factors identified here and did so in such a way as to suggest the interdependence of these factors. As one teacher explained, for example, "They're not going to be available [accessibility] if they don't have skill and knowledge [knowledge] and truly care about helping teachers with problems [support]."

Data related to teachers' perceptions of ineffective school principals—who were viewed as being inaccessible, inconsistent, lacking knowledge, indecisive, lacking follow-through, unsupportive, authoritarian, political, and practicing favoritism—indirectly substantiates the importance of the factors discussed in this article. To be sure, the extent to which teachers consider each of the leadership factors identified as essential to effective, school-based leadership can be expected to vary from one school to another.

It has been suggested throughout this article that factors associated with effective school leadership influence the social (behavioral) and cultural (values, norms) structures of schools. In summarizing the impact of effective school principals, Tables 1 and 2 highlight this point. Beyond this, however, the study data point to the conclusion that dramatic changes in the sociocultural context of schools can be expected as a result of changes in leadership. This conclusion is supported by two dimensions of the research data. First, as teachers described responses to various principals at other schools in which they had worked, they explained that their attitudes and behaviors tended to change significantly in response to changes in leadership. Second, examination of data drawn from teachers regarding the high school that was the site for this research again indicated important changes in culture. When teachers' perspectives were compared for each of the four principals at the school since 1974, significant shifts in the teachers' perspective, and thus school culture, were apparent.

Broadly speaking, effective school principals appeared to contribute to school cultures viewed as associative; such cultures were described as cohesive: Interactions between principals and teachers and between teachers and others were viewed as cooperative, empathetic, supportive, respectful, equitable, and productive. In contrast, ineffective school principals tended to create cultures viewed as dissociative; these cultures were seen as fragmented: Interactions between principals and teachers and between teachers and others were defined as distant, uncaring, nonsupportive, conflictive, inequitable, and in many ways nonproductive (Blase, in press). The terms *associative* and *dissociative* are used to capture the general impact of effective and ineffective leadership on the school. These terms are considered primitive concepts; their value is primarily heuristic and sensitizing (Bacharach & Lawler, 1982).

IMPLICATIONS

The overall pattern observed in the data stresses the importance of leadership competencies (related to working with people) in contrast to administrative competencies (associated with the technical aspects of work, e.g., scheduling, bookkeeping, budgeting). To illustrate, it was evident that personal qualities (e.g., honesty, security, compassion, respect for others) and competencies (e.g., listening skills, feedback skills, analytical and conceptual skills, problem-solving skills, and knowledge of curriculum) were perceived as essential to effective school leadership. Unfortunately, however, most university-level training programs tend to emphasize knowledge and skill in the administrative than the leadership dimensions. The present data suggest that such an emphasis may be misguided.

A broader training agenda, one that emphasizes those competencies directly affecting teachers' performance and the "everyday" sociocultural dynamics of schools (some of which have been described in this report), would seem useful. Among other things, training in communication, conflict management, problem solving, team development, and interpersonal and group dynamics would be helpful. Training experiences designed to increase self-awareness of an individual's values, beliefs, and behavior would also be relevant.

In addition, school officials should undoubtedly give much greater attention to "people-related competencies" in the selection, placement, and ongoing evaluation of school principals. Clearly, the use of instruments that measure knowledge of the interpersonal dimensions (for example, the *Relationship Inventory* [Barrett-Lennard, 1962]) could provide useful data. The services of principals' assessment centers should also be investigated. Needless to say, regular and systematic feedback from teachers and others with whom principals work would be invaluable.

In terms of research, Sergiovanni & Corbally (1984) have written:

> The real value of leadership rests with the "meanings" which actions import to others than in the actions themselves. A complete rendering of leadership requires that we move beyond the obvious to the subtle, beyond the immediate to the long range, beyond actions to meanings, beyond viewing organizations and groups within social systems to cultural entities. (p. 106)

The study reported here has attempted to understand meanings teachers have attributed to effective school leadership. This, of course, is only one perspective. Other qualitative studies focusing on how students, parents, superintendents, and school board members perceive effective principals would be helpful. Such studies would furnish data to help elaborate, interpret, and undoubtedly contradict some of the findings presented in this article. (From Blase, 1987, pp. 606–608. Copyright 1987 by the American Educational Research Association. Reprinted by permission of the publisher.)

A **reference section** contains an alphabetical listing of the books, journal articles, other research reports, instructional materials, and instruments cited in the report. Sometimes, researchers follow the reference section with appendices that contain examples of instruments or special materials.

A Plan for Reading Reports

In most research reports, researchers use common terms and organize their ideas similarly. Research consumers, therefore, can read most reports using a basic plan, which has three phases: prereading, reading, and postreading. In the first phase, research consumers determine what they know about the topic before reading and set purposes for reading the report. In the second phase, consumers systematically read parts of the report according their own purposes. In the last phase, they confirm whether their purposes have been met and learning has occurred.

The reading plan is illustrated with two model research reports. For the first report of comparative-predictive research (Hoover-Dempsey, Bassler, & Brissie, 1987) on pp. 59–73, the reading plan is fully explained with reference to the report's labeled sections. For the second one of experimental research (Pomplun, 1988) on pp. 76–86, the sections are labeled, but the reading plan is only outlined.

Using the Reading Plan with a Research Report: Guided Reading

First Phase: Previewing and Predicting the Research Report
The aim of this phase is to determine why you will read the report and what kinds of knowledge or information it presents. It is like a reconnaissance mission to find out what you know about the topic and to predict whether the report meets your intended purpose. It also is a time to determine whether the report is written as a standard research report.

1. Using the research report "Parent Involvement: Contributions of Teacher Efficacy, School Socioeconomic Status, and Other School Characteristics" (pp. 59–73), answer the question "Why am I reading this report—to gain knowledge, to apply the knowledge, or to implement an instructional practice?" For this demonstration, we

(Text continued on p. 73)

Hoover-Dempsey, K. V., Bassler, O. C., & Brissie, J. S. (1987). Parent involvement: Contributions of teacher efficacy, school socioeconomic status, and other school characteristics. *American Educational Research Journal, 24*(3), 417–435. Copyright 1987 by the American Educational Research Association. Reprinted by permission of the publisher.

① Parent Involvement: Contributions of Teacher Efficacy, School Socioeconomic Status, and Other School Characteristics

② Kathleen V. Hoover-Dempsey, Otto C. Bassler, and Jane S. Brissie
Peabody College of Vanderbilt University

③ The study tested the hypothesis that varying levels of parent involvement would be related to variations in qualities of school settings, specifically school socioeconomic status, teacher degree level, grade level, class size, teachers' sense of efficacy, principal perceptions of teacher efficacy, organizational rigidity, and instructional coordination. Teacher (n = 1,003) and principal (n = 66) reports and perceptions of the variables of interest were assessed in a sample of 66 elementary schools distributed across a large mid-Southern state. Stepwise multiple regression analyses revealed that various combinations of the predictors accounted for significant portions of the variance in all parent involvement outcomes: parent conferences (52%), parent volunteers (27%), parent home tutoring (24%), parent involvement in home instruction programs (22%), and teacher perception of parent support (41%). **Variables most consistently involved in outcomes were teacher efficacy and school socioeconomic status.** Results are discussed with reference to parent-teacher role complementarity and implications for increasing productive interconnections between parents and schools.

④ Families and schools are inevitably related as they respond to the legal mandate that children be educated. The nature of family-school relationships varies across individual children, families, schools, and communities as participants seek to implement the most satisfactory educational program within the confines of community expectations. Many parents and educators, and a host of theorists and researchers, have asserted the value of positive, communicative home-school relationships if children are to receive maximum benefit from their education. Polls of public opinion reported by Gallup (1986), for example, have shown that parents want more contact with schools. Studies of teacher opinion have consistently reflected positive views of active parental involvement in children's education (Cutright, 1984; Moles, 1982; National Education Association, 1981).

Despite the value placed on improved parent-teacher relations, however, the literature also suggests the difficulty of achieving this goal. For example, Cutright's (1984) survey of parents, teachers, and administrators revealed support for increased parent participation but agreement that actual parent involvement is usually quite low (see also Epstein, 1984). Depressed levels of parent-teacher communication, presumed to reflect detachment between school and home, have been reported (e.g., Powell, 1978), as have distrustful and negative relationships between teachers and parents (Lightfoot, 1981; Vernberg & Medway, 1981).

There is, nonetheless, a body of theoretical and empirical work asserting significant benefits to increased parent-teacher involvement. Building on a framework of relevant theory and empiricism, **we hypothesized that varying levels of teacher involvement with parents would be related to variations in selected qualities of school settings.**

⑤ LITERATURE REVIEW

Empirical work supporting the wisdom of teacher-parent interaction gained recognition when studies of early intervention efforts begun in the 1960s suggested benefits to children from parents' involvement in their schooling. Bronfenbrenner (1974), for example, concluded that parent involvement was critical to the success of educational programs for children. Although the strength of the data base supporting this conclusion has been questioned (e.g., Gray, Ramsey, & Klaus, 1982), the theme was subsequently echoed with reference to many educational programs (e.g., Hess & Holloway, 1984; Lazar, Hubbell, Murray, Rosche, & Royce, 1977; Phi Delta Kappa, 1980). Among the benefits suggested were improved student achievement, improved student behavior, lower student absenteeism, more positive student attitudes toward school, and improved homework habits. Theoretical constructions of home-school relationships also asserted the benefits of increased parent involvement in educational practice (e.g., Hobbs, Dokecki, Hoover-Dempsey, Moroney, Shayne, & Weeks, 1984; Laosa, 1983). Hobbs et al., for example, suggested that school recognition of family strengths is integral to the development of sound educational programs for children.

From parents' perspectives, however, several factors may mitigate against productive involvement in school: lack of time, minimal opportunities for involvement, and indifferent or antagonistic attitudes on the part of school personnel (Becker & Epstein, 1982a; Hobbs et al., 1984; Lightfoot, 1978; Lortie, 1975; Moles, 1982). Teachers may hesitate to involve parents because of the time investment required for productive parent participation, the absence of external rewards for efforts to involve parents, and problems with low commitment or skills on the part of parents (Epstein & Becker, 1982; Moles). Teachers may fear parents (Epstein & Becker), perhaps because of perceptions that parents question teachers' professional competence (Power, 1985) or blame them for children's problems (Vernberg & Medway, 1981).

Despite the evidence of conflicting roles (Lightfoot, 1978, 1981) and arms-length relationships between many schools and families, the necessity of overcoming the tenuous quality of home-school relationships has been made clear by many observers (e.g., Bronfenbrenner, 1979; Hess & Holloway, 1984; Hobbs et al., 1984; Lightfoot, 1981). In these views, avenues for productive interaction must be implemented if schools, families, and communities are to be strengthened rather than weakened as effective contributors to children's development.

Thus, investigators have examined variables associated with parent involvement practices in schools. Unfortunately, attempts to discern factors implicated in variations in parent involvement have produced few consistent findings.

The factor examined most frequently has been school socioeconomic status (SES) (e.g., Corwin & Wagenaar, 1976; Herman & Yeh, 1983). This literature leads to the conclusion that family SES plays a role in parent-teacher relations, but the general direction of its influence is difficult to discern. Teacher characteristics such as level of education and efficacy have also been examined. Higher levels of education have been associated with more positive attitudes toward parent involvement (Becker & Epstein, 1982b), but also with fewer parent contacts and more disputes (Corwin & Wagenaar, 1976). Ashton, Webb, and Doda (1983) examined teacher efficacy and suggested that low levels of efficacy may be causal in reducing teacher-parent contact; Dembo and Gibson (1985) asserted that lowered levels of parent-teacher contact may be due to the frustration and inefficacy resulting from teachers' reactions to characteristics of low-achieving students' parents.

Other school-based variables have also been examined. Lower grade levels have been associated with teachers' use of more parent involvement strategies; larger class sizes have been associated with more teacher efforts to involve parents (Becker & Epstein, 1982b). Corwin and Wagenaar (1976) assessed school formalization (social distancing characterized by rules and controls) and centralization (stratification and hierarchical structuring) and found that teachers in more formalized and centralized schools reported fewer parent contacts. Becker and Epstein (1982b) included school "professional climate"—defined as principal's support of teacher-parent involvement techniques and colleagues' parent involvement practices—as a predictor of parent involvement outcomes, but found few significant relationships.

Despite the paucity of compelling empirical work in the area, there is a theoretical basis for assuming that variables characterizing schools as settings—as specific organizational contexts for the work of teaching —are implicated in the behavior of individual teachers. Lewin (1951), for example, pointed to the intimate relationship between the individual and setting as central to understanding the behavior of individuals. Settings have qualities and sets of expectations that influence behavior (Barker, 1968) and must be examined if individual action is to be fully understood. Berger and Luckman (1966) asserted the primary role of social processes in individual constructions of appropriate roles and behavior. These constructions are built out of interactions with others in the setting, and are the product—at least in part—of expectations that are characteristic of the setting or environment. The products of person-environment interactions—although dynamic and changing in nature—are manifested both in characteristics of individual interactions with the environment and in qualities characteristic of interactions between people in the environment.

⑥ **PURPOSE**

Building on these findings, we investigated levels of teacher-reported parent involvement and variations in selected qualities of school settings. Our purpose was to examine the relative contribution of variables identified in the literature as potentially important to parents' involvement in their children's education.

We hypothesized that levels of parent involvement in activities commonly undertaken in elementary schools would be related to a set of organizational qualities characterizing the school. In doing so, we emphasized the *school's* contribution to levels of parent involvement. We also assumed that organizational conditions—manifested both in district policy decisions and school-level leadership and staff interaction—are strongly implicated in the extent to which parents are asked (implicitly and explicitly) to participate and in the extent to which they choose to participate. Because previous theoretical work and research have not addressed the relative strength of these potential contributors to variations in parent involvement, we made no hierarchical predictions concerning the order of importance of the variables entered.

⑦ **PREDICTOR VARIABLES**

Four predictor variables were related to factors influenced primarily by district level policies. *Average socioeconomic status of families* served by the school is a function at least in part of district-level decisions concerning school boundaries. It was included in the analysis because of its empirically established relationship—albeit in mixed directions—with variations in parent involvement in elementary schools (Becker & Epstein, 1982b; Corwin & Wagenaar, 1976; Epstein & Becker, 1982; Herman & Yeh, 1983; Powell, 1978). *Average degree level* of teachers in a school is a function of district policies concerning employment, as well as principal attitudes toward the importance of advanced degrees and his or her efforts to recruit teachers with advanced degrees to the school. Teachers with more academic knowledge might be expected to have more resources at their disposal and more confidence in their own competence in relating to parents (e.g., Becker & Epstein, 1982b). On the other hand, more education may increase teachers' autonomy and cause them to withdraw from parents (e.g., Corwin & Wagenaar, 1976). *Grade level* distribution in a school is usually a function of district-level organizational decisions. These decisions would not be expected to affect levels of parent involvement directly, but grade-level configuration may be influential in a school's general efforts if teachers in lower grades involve parents more frequently than upper grade teachers do (e.g., Becker & Epstein, 1982b). Thus, a school organized to include more primary grades might be expected to reflect higher levels of parent involvement than schools with more upper grade classes. The final variable in this group, *average class size*, is frequently a function of district level decisions concerning enrollment levels and staffing patterns in individual schools. Logic would indicate that teachers in schools with smaller classes would have more time for parent involvement efforts, but there is empirical evidence to suggest that teachers who have larger classes may be more motivated to seek parent contact and assistance (Becker & Epstein, 1982b).

The second set of variables included in this analysis was related to the organizational qualities of the school created primarily by the interaction and attitudes of teachers and principal. Though we believe that these qualities reflect the contributions of individuals to the environment—and though we agree that each is influenced by district level conditions and policies—they are also a function of interactions between individuals in the school setting itself.

Teacher efficacy was defined as teachers' beliefs that they are effective in teaching, that the children they teach can learn, and that there is a body of professional knowledge available to them when they need assistance. Based on Bandura's (1977) conceptions of generalized outcome expectancy and personal or self-efficacy, several researchers have suggested that teachers' sense of efficacy is positively related to educational outcomes (Ashton et al. 1983; Dembo & Gibson, 1985; Denham & Michael, 1981; Gibson & Dembo, 1984). We hypothesized that teachers' beliefs about their efficacy, combined within schools to create a sense of efficacy characterizing the school, would be related to the confidence and effort teachers bring to parent involvement. High efficacy schools, thus, would likely show higher rates of parent involvement. Our decision to construe teacher efficacy, generally considered a person variable, as a school characteristic was based on the theoretical work cited earlier concerning the influence of settings on individual behavior and suggestions implicit in some teacher efficacy (e.g., Denham & Michael; Gibson & Dembo) and school effectiveness literature (e.g., Brookover, Schweitzer, Schneider, Beady, Flood, & Weisenbaker, 1978) that specific qualities of individual schools as settings influence the efficacy of teachers in the school.

Principal's perceptions of teachers' efficacy was included as a related contributor to parent involvement. The principal's perceptions of teachers' efficacy is likely a function of personal disposition to believe in teachers' (potential) effectiveness and evaluation of the level of efficacy actually characterizing the group. We hypothesized that higher levels of parent involvement would be associated with higher principal perceptions of teacher efficacy. The hypothesis follows findings concerning the central role of principal leadership, support, and expectations in several dimensions of school effectiveness (Phi Delta Kappa, 1980) and suggestions that principal expectations may be specifically implicated in teacher efficacy (Denham & Michael, 1981).

Organizational rigidity was defined as the extent to which teachers perceive their school as requiring strict adherence to rules and regulations. Corwin and Wagenaar's (1976) findings indicated a relationship between school formalization and centralization and amount of teacher-reported contact with parents. Following their findings, we hypothesized that higher teacher perceptions of organizational rigidity would be associated with lower levels of parent involvement. The final variable in this group was *instructional coordination*. When teachers have a clear sense of the relationship between the activities and curricular goals of different grade levels, their schools should be characterized by increased concern for student acquisition of specific skills and concurrently higher incentive to ask for parents' help in ensuring the acquisition of skills when necessary. Our hypothesis that higher levels of instructional coordination would be associated with more parent involvement was based also on general findings concerning the potentially critical role of instructional coordination in school excellence (Phi Delta Kappa, 1980).

(8)   **CRITERION VARIABLES**

Because our interest was in components of parent-teacher interaction across a variety of elementary schools, we selected five indicators of involvement common to most elementary programs: *parent–teacher conferences*, parent involvement in classroom *volunteer* work, parent involvement in *"tutoring"* at home (assisting with homework, drill, etc.), and parent involvement in carrying out *home instruction* programs designed or suggested by teachers to supplement regular classroom instruction. In addition, we examined the teacher perceptions of *support from parents*.

(9)   **DESIGN AND PROCEDURES**
(10) *Sample*

Eight school districts whose superintendents agreed to encourage the participation of all elementary teachers and principals in the district were included in the study. The districts represented different regions of a large, mid-Southern state; they served urban, suburban, and rural populations. Schools within the districts varied by size and SES of families served. The 78 schools in these districts that included grades K-4 were initially included in the study. Teachers in all of these schools participated in the study, but principals from 12 of the schools chose not to participate themselves. The sample used for this particular study included the 66 schools with participating principals. The number of teachers in participating schools ranged from 6 to 43; the total number of teachers who participated in the study was 1,003. The average rate of teacher participation per school was 69%.

(11) *Procedures*

The investigators contacted all elementary school principals in each participating district and explained the purposes of the study. Principals were asked to complete a School Information Questionnaire and a Principal Opinion Questionnaire and to distribute materials to all teachers at a faculty meeting. At that time, each teacher was given a packet containing a letter explaining study purposes, procedures, and methods used to protect teacher anonymity; a Teacher Information Questionnaire; a Teacher Opinion Questionnaire; and an envelope for returning the materials to the researchers. Participation was voluntary. Teachers were asked to return the materials within 1 week—completed or not completed—in a sealed envelope to a central collection point at the school. Sealed envelopes were mailed to the investigators. Principal questionnaires were also returned by mail directly to the investigators.

(12) *Instrumentation*

Data for the study were gathered from (a) information provided by teachers on aspects of their background, classroom conditions, and parent involvement (Teacher Information Questionnaire); (b) information provided by principals on selected school conditions (School Information Questionnaire); (c) teacher and principal responses to questionnaires designed to assess their perceptions of selected school variables (Teacher Opinion Questionnaire; Principal Opinion Questionnaire).

The questionnaires to assess teachers' and principals' perceptions of the variables of interest were constructed by the investigators after consulting the instrumentation of others who had examined similar factors. The Teacher Opinion Questionnaire consisted of 164 items, constructed mostly with five-point Likert scale responses ranging from strongly agree to strongly disagree, or from almost always to almost never. Both negatively and positively worded items were used throughout the instrument to avoid generalized response patterns. After a preliminary version of the instrument was pretested on a separate teacher population, resulting in alphas on scale scores ranging from .63 to .77, final adjustments to the questionnaire were made. Similar procedures were used to construct the Principal Opinion Questionnaire. Information on all variables included in the study is presented in Tables 1 and 2.

⑬ **RESULTS**

Table 3 presents the means, standard deviations, and intercorrelations for the predictor variables and the parent involvement

⑭ **Table 1   Criterion Variables**

Variable	Source	Definition
Parent-teacher conferences	Teacher Information Questionnaire	Average number of students whose parents attended parent-teacher conferences during the year (indivdual teacher's estimate of the number divided by number of students in the class; resulting averages summed and divided by number of participating teachers in the school).
Parent volunteers	Teacher Information Questionnaire	Average number of students whose parents did volunteer work in the classroom during the year (school average score derived as above).
Parent tutoring	Teacher Information Questionnaire	Average number of students whose parents regularly spent time with them in school-related tasks (e.g., homework) at home (school average score derived as above).
Parent home instruction	Teacher Information Questionnaire	Average number of students whose parents provided home instruction on a plan devised by the teacher during the year (school average score derived as above).
Parent support	Teacher Opinion Questionnaire	Teacher response to the questionnaire item: "Most of my students' parents support the things I do" (5-point Likert scale, strongly agree to strongly disagree); (school average derived by summing individual teacher scores and dividing by number of participating teachers in the school).

Table 2 Predictor Variables

Variable	Source	Definition	Number of Items	Alpha
Average socioeconomic status of families served by school (SES)	School Information Questionnaire	Number of students not qualifying for free lunch divided by the number of students in school.	NA	NA
Teacher degree level	Teacher Information Questionnaire	Average of teacher degree levels (1 = Bachelors, 2 = Masters, 3 = Masters + 30 hours, 4 = Doctorate)	NA	NA
Grade level distribution	School Information Questionnaire	Average of grade levels in school	NA	NA
Average class size	Teacher information Questionnaire	Number of students in participating classes (K–4) divided by the number of K–4 classes.	NA	NA
Teacher efficacy	Teacher Opinion Questionnaire	Teachers' certainty that their instructional skills are effective; sample item: I feel that I am making a significant difference in the lives of my students.	11	.87
Organizational rigidity	Teacher Opinion Questionnaire	The freedom, or lack thereof, that teachers have to take instructional action; sample item: I have to follow rules at this school that conflict with my best professional judgment.	8	.75
Principal perception of teacher efficacy	Principal Opinion Questionnaire	Principal certainty that teachers have skills necessary to produce desired changes in students; sample item: I believe that student learning is linked directly to teachers' efforts and skills.	3	.69
Instructional coordination	Teacher Opinion Questionnaire	Levels of curriculum coordination between grade levels in school; sample item: I know exactly what is covered by teachers in the grade level above me and below me.	9	.69

criterion variables. Intercorrelations between criterion variables were all significant ($p < .05$). Teacher efficacy scores were significantly correlated with all five criterion variables, most notably perceptions of parent support ($r = .60$; $p < .0005$) variables, most notably perceptions of parent support ($r = .60$; $p < .0005$) and parent-teacher conferences ($r = .49$; $p < .0005$). School SES also recorded significant correlations

Table 3 Intercorrelation Matrix, Means, Standard Deviations: All Variables

	Parent/ Teacher Conferences	Parent Volunteers	Parent Home Tutoring	Parent Home Instruction	Support from Parents	Teacher Efficacy	Instructional Coordination	Organizational Rigidity	Principal Perceptions of Teacher Efficacy	School SES	Average Class Size	Average Teacher Degree Level	School Grade Levels
Parent/teacher conferences	1												
Parent volunteers	.44	1											
Parent home tutoring	.29	.26	1										
Parent home instruction	.34	.24	.39	1									
Support from parents	.40	.45	.39	.23	1								
Teacher efficacy	.49	.40	.42	.34	.60	1							
Instructional coordination	.30	.33	.28	.33	.39	.45	1						
Organizational rigidity	-.03	.10	.20	.20	.13	.12	.30	1					
Principal perceptions of teacher efficacy	.30	.22	.37	.36	.18	.29	.08	.10	1				
School SES	.53	.42	.24	.24	.35	.21	.19	.11	.20	1			
Average class size	.03	-.05	-.03	-.06	.02	-.13	-.09	.17	.05	.23	1		
Average teacher degree level	.46	.14	.12	.25	.28	.18	.25	-.15	-.05	.23	-.06	1	
School grade levels	.13	-.15	.05	.02	.01	-.02	-.13	-.01	.02	.19	.09	.18	1
$\bar{X}$	.56	.11	.45	.12	3.04	16.96	13.98	18.79	8.25	.59	23.58	1.39	2.59
SD	.20	.07	.10	.07	.29	2.11	1.12	1.17	2.11	.22	2.61	.22	.81

with all criterion variables, especially parent-teacher conferences ($r = .53; p < .0005$) and parent volunteers ($r = .42; p < .0005$). Instructional coordination was significantly associated with all criterion variables, most strongly with perceptions of parent support ($r = .39, p < .01$). Principal perceptions of teacher efficacy were significantly correlated with four criterion measures, the highest being parent tutoring ($r = .37, p < .005$) and parent home instruction ($r = .36; p < .005$). Teachers' average degree level recorded significant correlations with three criterion variables, most notably parent-teacher conferences ($r = .46; p < .0005$). Schools with higher efficacy, higher SES, higher instructional coordination, higher principal perceptions of teacher efficacy, and higher average degree levels were schools with higher rates of parent involvement.

Stepwise multiple regressions using SPSS New Regression (Hull & Nie, 1981) were conducted to examine the relationships between the predictor variables and the five parent involvement measures (Table 4). With parent-teacher conferences as the criterion, SES, degree level, and teacher efficacy accounted for 52% of the variance ($R(3.60) = .72, p < .0001$). Schools with higher average family SES, higher average teacher degree level, and higher teacher perceptions of efficacy reported more parent participation in conferences.

Parent involvement in classroom volunteer work was predicted by school SES and teacher efficacy, which together accounted for 27% of the variance ($R(2.62) = .52, p < .0001$). Schools with higher average SES and higher teacher efficacy reported more parents as volunteers in the school.

With parent involvement in tutoring as the criterion measure, teacher efficacy and principal perceptions of teacher efficacy emerged as significant predictors, accounting for 24% of the variance ($R(2.61) = .49, p < .0002$). Schools in which teachers and principals reported higher perceptions of teacher efficacy reported more parents in-

volved in helping their children with school-related skill development at home (homework, etc.).

Parent involvement in carrying out home instructional programs was predicted by principal perceptions of teacher efficacy and instructional coordination, which accounted for 22% of the variance ($R(2.61) = .47, p < .0005$). These results suggest that more parents were involved in carrying out home instructional programs for their children in schools where principals had higher perceptions of teacher efficacy and teachers perceived a higher level of coordination in the overall instructional program of the school.

Two variables were significant in predicting teacher perceptions of support from parents: Teacher efficacy and SES accounted for 41% of the variance ($R(2.62) = .64, p < .0001$). Schools with greater teacher perceptions of parent support were schools with higher average SES levels and higher teacher efficacy scores.

(16) **DISCUSSION**

Our model effectively identified some important contributors to different manifestations of parent involvement. In various combinations, the predictors contributed significantly to each indicator of parent involvement. **The two predictors most consistently involved in outcomes were teacher efficacy and school SES. Higher average levels of teacher efficacy were associated with higher levels of four parent involvement outcomes; higher levels of school SES were associated with three types of parent involvement. Other variables implicated in some outcomes were principal perceptions of teacher efficacy, instructional coordination, and average teacher degree level.** Organizational rigidity, average class size, and grade level did not contribute significantly to any outcome.

(17) *Teacher Efficacy and School SES*

The strongest and most intriguing results are those related to the potential role of teacher

Table 4 Regression Summaries for Predictors with Parent Involvement Criterion Variables

	Parent/Teacher Conferences		Parent Volunteers		Parent Home Tutoring		Parent Home Instruction		Support from Parents	
	Beta	t	Beta	t	Beta	t	Beta	t	Beta	t
School SES	.379	4.03***	.350	3.16**	.118	1.02	.124	1.06	.232	2.33**
Average class size	.006	.063	-.094	-.829	.001	.007	-.043	-.380	.044	.427
Average teacher degree level	.308	3.30**	-.004	-.032	.077	.674	-.210	1.82	.138	1.38
School grade levels	.009	.095	-.214	-1.98	.052	.467	.051	.446	-.025	-.253
Teacher efficacy	.355	3.83***	.322	2.91**	.344	2.95**	.138	1.05	.552	5.54***
Principal perceptions of teacher efficacy	.160	1.69	.063	.549	.265	2.28*	.334	2.95**	-.036	-.344
Instructional coordination	-.007	-.066	.146	1.20	.133	1.06	.304	2.69**	.121	1.10
Organizational rigidity	-.069	-.746	.028	.250	.134	1.20	.090	.755	.039	.396

* = $p < .05$.
** = $p < .01$.
*** = $p < .001$.

efficacy in parent involvement in conferences, volunteering, home tutoring, and teacher perceptions of parent support. We defined efficacy as including teachers' beliefs that they can teach, that their students can learn, and that they can access a body of professional knowledge when they need it. **Although the correlational and cross-sectional qualities of the design make causal conclusions impossible, teacher efficacy could contribute to higher rates of parent participation in several ways.**

Efficacy as manifested by confidence in one's teaching and instructional program, for example, implies a sense of professionalism and security in the teaching role. Such confidence would logically enhance teachers' efforts to discuss their teaching program and goals with parents, for example, during conferences. As parents receive useful information from teachers—and as parents are invited to ask questions and contribute information, rather than listen only—they are likely to feel that participation is productive and worth its cost in time. An efficacious teacher, sure of his or her teaching abilities, also likely conveys a sense that requests for parent help are a complement to the teaching program, not a sign of teaching inadequacy. Higher teacher efficacy may also work to increase teachers' and parents' sense of role differentiation and complementarity (cf., Lightfoot, 1978), thus minimizing perceptions of threat to role or expertise that may attend parent-teacher interaction.

That school SES was significant in predicting three outcomes (parent conferences, volunteering, and teacher perceptions of parent support) is not surprising. That SES was *not* significantly implicated in the two home-based indicators of parent involvement is interesting, however, as is the failure of the bivariate correlation between teacher efficacy and SES to reach significance. This indicates that the variables functioned independently to at least some extent.

There are several possible explanations for the positive contribution of school SES

to some outcomes. For example, higher SES parents, realizing the importance of education for their children *and* feeling confident of their right to be involved in the school, may take a more active role than their lower SES counterparts in supporting school programs. Schools with higher average SES may also be characterized by parents who view themselves as partners with teachers rather than inferiors or subordinates (Lightfoot, 1981). Higher SES parents may also feel greater confidence in the value of their contributions to the school. It is also possible, of course, that higher SES schools attract teachers who are higher in efficacy and more effective in involving parents. The failure of SES to enter the tutoring and home instruction predictions suggests differential operation of the variable across outcomes, but the correlational nature of the design precludes any causal conclusions.

(18) *Other Predictors*

When parent-teacher conferences served as the dependent variable, the most important predictors of outcome—SES and teacher efficacy—were joined by average teacher degree level. **This suggests that schools where more teachers have acquired advanced degrees may evidence more eagerness for instructionally relevant information from parents. Teachers with advanced degrees may also be more sensitive to theoretical linkages between home and school (Becker & Epstein, 1982a). The correlational nature of the findings also suggests that teachers who report more parent participation in conferences may also be more active in earning advanced degrees.**

When parent involvement in home tutoring served as the criterion, teacher efficacy and principal perceptions of teacher efficacy were significant contributors; SES did not enter this equation. The potential role of teacher efficacy in the outcome seems straightforward: **When teachers perceive themselves and their students as capable, they may be more likely to encourage parents' involvement with their children at** home as a means of increasing student achievement. Epstein (1984), for example, noted that when teachers make frequent requests for parent help, parents are more likely to believe that they *should* help at home. The role of principal perceptions of teacher efficacy in this outcome is interesting. Principals who see their teachers as high in efficacy may convey this idea to *both* teachers and parents, enabling more positive perceptions and expectations for an active role for each in the learning of students.

When parent involvement in programs of home instruction served as the dependent variable, principal perceptions of teacher efficacy and teachers' perceptions of instructional coordination in the school were significant predictors. The role of instructional coordination seems logical: **As teachers and principal work to ensure smooth flow of instruction within and between grades, teachers likely have a better sense of specific areas in which parents might profitably undertake home instruction.** The importance of principal perceptions of teacher efficacy may be related to the fact that developing even brief programs of home instruction is usually beyond the expectations of normal classroom teaching. If teachers prepare for and invite this kind of participation, they may need the support and recognition of the principal—reflected here in his or her higher assessment of efficacy—that their efforts are noticed and valued. Williams's (1981) report that principals tend to value parent participation in home-based learning activities and Denham and Michael's (1981) observation that high principal expectations may promote greater efficacy and expectations on the part of teachers may also be implicated here.

Three variables failed to predict any outcome. Grade level may have been too restricted in range (K-4) to emerge as significant, as may class size ($X = 23.58$, $SD = 2.61$). The failure of organizational rigidity to predict any outcome is more difficult to explain. It may be that the moderate mean score for this sample (18.79, out of a possible 32.0) and relatively restricted range ($SD = 1.18$) operated to diminish any unique contribution to parent involvement outcomes across schools.

CONCLUSION

Hobbs et al. (1984) and Bronfenbrenner (1979) have suggested that relationships between schools and families must be improved if children's education is to be optimized. Hobbs et al. spoke of developing shared responsibility between school and home, and Bronfenbrenner pointed to the need to develop the school's interconnections with other settings in the society. Both have suggested that families and schools must engage in frequent, confident, and complementary transactions if each institution is to contribute all it can to the socialization and education of children.

Although our correlational findings do not permit conclusions of a causal nature, they do suggest potentially fruitful points of entry into the task of developing shared responsibility between school and home. The finding that teacher efficacy is significantly implicated in several indices of parent involvement provides support, albeit indirect, for the importance of role clarity and complementarity in developing productive home-school relationships. Teacher efficacy, by definition, implies a clear, proactive, and strong conceptualization of the teaching role. As teachers grow in efficacy and clarity of role conceptualization, it seems likely that some areas of ambiguity and overlap between parent and teacher roles, as identified by Lightfoot (1978, 1981), for example, could be brought into sharper focus and resolution. This implies, of course, that teachers and parents must interact and communicate clearly as areas of complementary functions are identified. Although there is evidence that this effort in itself may pose a serious challenge in many schools (Lightfoot, 1981), it would seem an important part of any process focused on improving the content and goal-orientation of parent-teacher relationships.

The importance of principal efforts to increase teacher efficacy as a means of improving parent-teacher relations is also implied by these findings. While Ashton et al. (1983) suggested that parent-teacher interactions influence teacher efficacy, our results suggest that the influence may flow in the opposite direction as well. If the finding that teacher efficacy is an important contributor to parent involvement is replicated in other work, it would seem incumbent upon schools interested in increasing the productivity of home-school relations to encourage and build teachers' sense of efficacy. There are obviously many benefits to improved teacher efficacy (Ashton et al., 1983), but the potential for positively influencing levels of parent involvement in a variety of educationally productive activities seems a very important addition to the set of anticipated outcomes. The critical role of the principal in this effort is suggested by our findings concerning principal perceptions of teacher efficacy and is supported by literature (Phi Delta Kappa, 1980) pointing to the centrality of principals in creating conditions conducive to school excellence. Many such principal activities (e.g., buffering, evaluation, support for skill development, and teacher collaboration) are quite logically related to the development of any "baseline" sense of efficacy individual teachers bring to a school.

Although teacher efficacy and school SES were both implicated in school-based parent involvement outcomes, the fact that this particular combination was *not* involved in reported rates of home-based parent involvement suggests that increased efforts to improve shared responsibility between home and schools serving predominantly low-income families might well focus on specific, task-related parent-child involvement at home. This suggestion does not imply that efforts to involve lower SES families in school-based activities should be abandoned, however, for shared responsibility

on even a limited basis seems unlikely to come to fruition if parents do not enter the school setting.

Our correlational and cross-sectional design does not permit definitive statements about these suggestions. Future work should address these limitations and other aspects of this exploratory study. For example, our parent involvement outcomes were measured through teachers' reports of parent activities for students in their classroom. While the variability in outcomes across our sample of schools suggests the soundness of the estimates derived by this process, future work should include measurement of parents' reports of their involvement or other, more objective means of assessing participation. Further, as implied by Laosa's (1983) analysis, assessing discrete aspects of SES (parental education, employment, etc.) rather than global indicators might shed more light on the role and functioning of SES in parent-teacher relations. Finally, our measures of some school-level variables focused on assessing teacher and principal perceptions; behaviorally based data to validate the perceptual information would add strength to future work.

Nonetheless, our findings suggest intriguing and potentially powerful relationships between levels of parent involvement in elementary schools and selected qualities of teachers and schools as work places. Several of these qualities are dynamic and subject to change in schools concerned about improving the education of the children and families they serve. Exploration of such changes holds the promise of creating new paths to improved school-family relationships. They should be pursued.

(20)

REFERENCES

Ashton, P. T., Webb, R. B., & Doda, N. (1983). *A study of teachers' sense of efficacy: Final report, executive summary.* Gainesville, FL: University of Florida.

Bandura, A. (1977). Self-efficacy: Toward a unifying theory of behavioral change. *Psychological Review, 84,* 191–215.

Barker, R. (1968). *Ecological psychology.* Palo Alto, CA: Stanford University Press.

Becker, H. J., & Epstein, J. L. (1982a). *Influences on teachers' use of parent involvement at home* (Report No. 324). Baltimore, MD: Johns Hopkins University.

Becker, H. J., & Epstein, J. L. (1982b). Parent involvement: A survey of teacher practices. *Elementary School Journal, 83,* 85–102.

Berger, P. L., & Luckman, T. (1966). *The social construction of reality.* New York: Doubleday.

Bronfenbrenner, U. (1974). *Is early intervention effective? A report on longitudinal evaluations of preschool programs* (Vol. II). Washington, DC: U.S. Department of Health, Education and Welfare.

Bronfenbrenner, U. (1979). *The ecology of human development: Experiments by nature and design.* Cambridge, MA: Harvard University Press.

Brookover, W. B., Schweitzer, J. H., Schneider, J. M., Beady, C. H., Flood, P. K., & Weisenbaker, J. M. (1978). Elementary school social climate and school achievement. *American Educational Research Journal, 15,* 301–318.

Corwin, R. G., & Wagenaar, T. C. (1976). Boundary interaction between service organizations and their publics: A study of teacher-parent relationships. *Social Forces, 55,* 471–492.

Cutright, M. (1984, November). How wide open is the door to parent involvement in the schools? *PTA Today,* 10–11.

Dembo, M. H., & Gibson, S. (1985). Teachers' sense of efficacy: An important factor in school achievement. *The Elementary School Journal, 86,* 173–184.

Denham, C. H., & Michael, J. J. (1981). Teacher sense of efficacy: A definition of the construct and model for further research. *Educational Research Quarterly, 6,* 39–63.

Epstein, J. L. (1984). School policy and parent involvement: Research results. *Educational Horizons, 62,* 70–72.

Epstein, J. L., & Becker, H. J. (1982). Teacher's reported practices of parent involvement: Problems and possibilities. *Elementary School Journal, 83,* 103–113.

Gallup, G. H. (1986). The 18th annual Gallup Poll of the public's attitude toward the public schools. *Phi Delta Kappan, 68,* 43–59.

Gibson, S., & Dembo, M. H. (1984). Teacher efficacy: A construct validation. *Journal of Educational Psychology, 76,* 569–582.

Gray, S. W., Ramsey, B. K., & Klaus, R. A. (1982). *From 3 to 20: The early training project.* Baltimore, MD: University Park Press.

Herman, J. L., & Yeh, J. P. (1983). Some effects of parent involvement in schools. *The Urban Review, 15,* 11–17.

Hess, R. D., & Holloway, S. D. (1984). Family and school as educational institutions. In R. D. Parke, R. M. Emde, H. P. McAdoo, & G. P. Sackett (Eds.), *Review of child development research: Vol. 7. The family* (pp. 179–222). Chicago: University of Chicago Press.

Hobbs, N., Dokecki, P. R., Hoover-Dempsey, K. V., Moroney, R. M., Shayne, M. W., & Weeks, K. H. (1984). *Strengthening families.* San Francisco: Jossey-Bass.

Hull, C. H., & Nie, N. H. (1981). *SPSS Update 7–9.* New York: McGraw-Hill.

Laosa, L. M. (1983). School, occupation, culture, and family: The impact of parental schooling on the parent-child relationship. In I. E. Siegel & L. M. Laosa (Eds.), *Changing families* (pp. 79–135). New York: Plenum.

Lazar, I., Hubbell, V. R., Murray, H., Rosche, M., & Royce, J. (1977). *The persistence of preschool effects: A long-term follow-up of fourteen infant and pre-*

school experiments. Ithaca, NY: Cornell University.

Lewin, K. (1951). *Field theory in social science*. New York: Harper.

Lightfoot, S. L. (1978). *Worlds apart: Relationships between families and schools*. New York: Basic Books.

Lightfoot, S. L. (1981). Toward conflict and resolution: Relationships between families and schools. *Theory Into Practice, 20*, 97–103.

Lortie, D. C. (1975). *School teacher*. Chicago: University of Chicago Press.

Moles, O. C. (1982). Synthesis of recent research on parent participation in children's education. *Educational Leadership, 40*, 44–47.

National Education Association. (1981). *Nationwide teacher opinion poll*. Washington, DC: Author.

Phi Delta Kappa. (1980). *Why do some urban schools succeed?* Bloomington, IN: Author.

Powell, D. R. (1978). Correlates of parent-teacher communication frequency and diversity. *Journal of Educational Research, 71*, 333–341.

Power, T. J. (1985). Perceptions of competence: How parents and teachers view each other. *Psychology in the Schools, 22*, 68–78.

Vernberg, E. M., & Medway, F. J. (1981). Teacher and parent causal perceptions of school problems. *American Educational Research Journal, 18*, 29–37.

Williams, D. I. (1981). *Final interim report: Southwest Parent Education Resource Center*. Austin, TX: Southwest Educational Development Laboratory.

will assume that you desire additional general information about factors that can predict effective parent involvement in their children's learning.

2. Read the report title ① and the first sentence of the abstract ③.
3. Answer the question "Will reading this report meet my purpose?"

The answer is yes, because the study looked at factors that predict levels of parents' involvement in several school-related qualities.

4. Answer the question "What do I know about the topic?"

On a sheet of paper or in the margin next to the report, list what you already know about factors related to parental involvement. Start with those listed in the abstract's first sentence: socioeconomic status, teacher's degrees, grade level, class size, and so on. What others can you add?

5. Read each of the headings and subheadings ⑤ through ⑬ and ⑯ through ⑲, and answer, "Is the report organized using typical section headings?"

The answer is yes: literature review ⑤, purpose ⑥, design and procedures ⑨, sample ⑩, procedures ⑪, instrumentation ⑫, results ⑬, discussion ⑯, conclusion ⑲. The researchers have used additional headings and subheadings. Two, predictor variables ⑦ and criterion variables ⑧, are important because they help you identify the research design (predictive research), and they might signal information that is unfamiliar to you. Using the context of this report, answer, "What do you think criterion variables are?"

Second Phase: Reading the Research Report
The aim of this phase is to find information suggested by your purpose for reading and to confirm or modify your list of known information. Your purpose determines whether you read the entire report or only select sections.

6. As you read the report, keep alert to two things: (a) your purpose is to obtain information about factors predicting parents' involvement in their children's learning, and (b) some factors will add to your list and some will modify or contradict items on your list of factors related to parental involvement. As you read, note that key information regarding the purpose has been **highlighted**.

7. Read the research report sections in the following order (note that several sections have been intentionally omitted from the list):

> Abstract ③
>
> Introduction/background ④ (the opening, unheaded section)
>
> Purpose ⑥
>
> Sample ⑩
>
> Discussion (all subsections) ⑯ ⑰ ⑱
>
> Conclusion ⑲

You will not read the remaining section now—literature review ⑤, predictor variables ⑦, criterion variables ⑧, Procedures ⑪, Instrumentation ⑫, results ⑬, and tables 1 and 2 ⑭ and ⑮—because the information to meet your reading purpose can be obtained in the previously listed sections.

Third Phase: Confirming Predictions and Knowledge
The goals of this phase are to verify that the purpose has been met and to immediately recall key information. You should now decide which information that supports the researchers' purpose and adds to your knowledge base.

8. Refer to the list you made during the first phase of report reading and revise it by adding new information or deleting inappropriate information. Answer the question "Were the subjects similar to

those in my own school situation so that the results can be applied there?"

9. Write a short (2–3 sentence) statement that applies to your purpose for reading the report and contains the report's key points. (The statement should contain information from the highlighted text in the report.)

Using the Reading Plan with a Research Report: Independent Reading

Using the report of experimental research, "Retention: The Earlier, the Better?" (Pomplun, 1988), on pp. 76–86, apply the reading plan procedures.

First Phase: Previewing and Predicting the Research Report
Set purpose and identify known information about the topic. Determine which sections are to be read.

Suggested purpose: Reading to identify a possible effective instructional practice.

Suggested sections to be read: ①, ③ paragraphs 1 and 12, ⑤, ⑨ and ⑭.

Second Phase: Reading the Research Report
Read the report and identify key information. Note the researchers' use of organizational signals: "in summary," "after the first," "the conclusion" and "at the primary level," and "at the intermediate level."

Third Phase: Confirming Predictions and Knowledge
Verify that your purpose has been met and recall key information. If purpose has not been met or if additional information needs to be identified, select sections to be read or reread.

Suggested sections as sources of key information: ②, ③ paragraph 12, ⑭ paragraphs 31, 32, 37, and 38.

Suggested sections to be read additionally (if needed): ⑥, ⑧, and ⑨.

EVALUATING RESEARCH REPORTS

Informed consumers effectively compare and shop in a store for products by using a set of criteria. Research consumers can "shop" among research reports to identify well-written reports of appropriate methodology. You have already taken the first step in being a research

(Text continued on p. 86)

Pomplun, M. (1988). Retention: The earlier, the better? *Journal of Educational Research, 81,* 281–286. Reprinted with permission of the Helen Dwight Reid Educational Foundation. Published by Heldref Publications, Washington, D.C. Copyright © 1988.

(1)

Retention: The Earlier, the Better?

Mark Pomplun
Citrus County Schools

(2)

ABSTRACT

The hypothesis that there is a trend of decreasing effectiveness for grade retention at successively higher grades was tested in this study. We used measures of self-concept, motivation, teacher, student, and parent attitudes; and reading, language, and mathematics achievement to compare primary, intermediate, and secondary retainees with borderline and regular students. The data collected over a 2-year period showed significant academic improvements for primary and intermediate retainees but not for secondary retainees. Whereas parent, teacher, and student attitude scales also showed the decreasing effectiveness of retention at higher grades, self-concept and motivation results were inconsistent. All results, however, supported the effectiveness of retention at the primary level especially in comparison to the secondary level.

(3)

[1] Whereas the promotion–retention controversy has taken place since the early 1900s (Keyes, 1911), professionals still are undecided about the issue (Medway, 1986). This is in spite of minimum competency policies (Haney & Madaus, 1978) that contain provisions for automatic retention that have resulted in the retention of more than 30% of certain grade levels in Virginia (Owens & Ranick, 1977) and Washington, DC (CBS, 1981).

[2] A pivotal article in retention research was Jackson's (1975) review of 44 studies, and his conclusion that "the accumulated research evidence is so poor that valid inferences cannot be drawn concerning the relative benefits of these two options" (Jackson, 1975, p. 627). Jackson's finding that most of the retention research suffered from inadequate experimental design ignored the difference between basic and applied educational research (Ausubel, 1953) with applied "research performed in relation to the actual problems . . . under the conditions in which they are to be found in practice" (Ausubel, 1953, p. 6). As a result, Jackson's grouping of research by design has proved

unfruitful as demonstrated by the date of the last random assignment of students into promotion-retention groups (Cook, 1941).

[3] This study employed the nonequivalent group design of the untreated control group with pretest and posttest (Cook & Campbell, 1979) for the investigation of the effectiveness of retention across grade levels. The specific expectation was that the beneficial effects of retention in achievement, self-concept, attitude, and motivation would decrease as the students' grade levels increased. Grade level was represented by three groups, one from Grades one and two, another from Grades three and four, and one from Grades seven and eight. In order to increase the validity of the findings, two control groups were used, one consisting of students who were considered for retention but were promoted, and another group of students who were regularly promoted.

[4] A review of retention promotion research revealed that studies that found academic benefits for retention were mainly in the primary grades (Scott & Ames, 1969; Chase, 1968; Reinherz & Griffin, 1970). These analyses were supported by studies

that have included all grade levels but have found academic benefits chiefly in the primary grades (McAfee, 1981; Kerzner, 1982; Leggett, 1982).

[5] Additionally, past studies that have emphasized the absence of negative personal and social adjustment effects (Chansky, 1964; Scott & Ames, 1969; Finlayson, 1975) have studied primary grade students. In contrast, researchers' study of retention at progressively higher grade levels indicated that academic benefits decreased (Farley, 1936; Coffield & Bloomers, 1956; Worth, 1960; Wolf, 1965; Muessen, 1954) and the negative effects of retention on personal and social adjustment increased (Morrison & Perry, 1956; Bedoian, 1954; Anfinson, 1941; Sandin, 1944; White & Howard, 1973).

[6] Research from higher grade levels suggested, however, that retention does not increase academic achievement for most students. Beginning at the fourth-grade level, studies have found either no significant difference between retention and promotion (Farley, 1936) or differences favoring promotion (Worth, 1960; Farley, 1936; Wolf, 1965; Kamii & Weikart, 1963; Muessen, 1954; Holmes & Matthews, 1984). Worth (1960) found a decrease in the effectiveness of retention at the fourth-grade level. Both Wolf (1965) and Muessen (1954) found that although 20% of sixth- and eighth-grade retainees benefited, 60% of the retainees made no significant progress and 20% decreased in academic achievement.

[7] Whereas the academic effects on retainees appeared to develop over grades from positive to negative, research on the personal and social adjustment of retainees suggested negative effects from retention at the higher grades.

[8] Although Scott and Ames (1969) described behavioral gains favoring first-grade retainees, Chansky (1964) and Finlayson (1975) detected no difference at this grade level between groups of retained and promoted students in personal adjustment. In third grade, however, Coffield and Bloom-

ers (1956) discovered a small difference in personal and social adjustment favoring promoted over nonpromoted students in the third grade. Morrison and Perry (1956) found increasing nonacceptance of overage students in the fourth, fifth, and sixth grades, and both Godfrey (1972) and White and Howard (1973) discovered sixth-grade overage students scoring lower than regularly promoted students on measures of self-concept. Anfinson (1941) concluded that those regularly promoted at the seventh-grade level scored significantly higher on personal and social adjustment than overage students. Sandin (1944) extended this trend to the eighth grade where nonpromoted students scored lower on social and personal adjustment and also displayed more behavior problems than regularly promoted students.

[9] Although the majority of research has been conducted on the academic and emotional consequences of retention, some studies have explored motivational effects. The two most cited proponents of retention as a method to increase motivation (Viele, 1966; Ebel, 1980) present no research on the question. In contrast, there is evidence that threats of punishment, as opposed to praise, do not increase achievement in the laboratory (Dici, 1975) or in the classroom (Otto & Melby, 1935). It should be noted that the above studies used achievement levels to measure motivation. Whereas few have studied student motivation, several researchers have investigated parent, student, and teacher attitudes on retention.

[10] Past studies of parent attitudes toward retention at the primary grade level indicated that the majority felt it was helpful (Finlayson, 1975; Chase, 1968; Scott & Ames, 1969; Byrnes & Yamamoto, 1986). Sandoval and Hughes (1981) found that students who benefited the most from retention on the first-grade level had parents who viewed the retention decision favorably and who were most involved in the school. Reinherz and Griffin (1970) found that parents of retained second and third graders were less

hopeful and positive than first graders' parents.

[11] Also, teachers at the primary grades were positive toward retention (Finlayson, 1977; Chase, 1968; Horn, 1976; Scott & Ames, 1969) whereas Sandoval and Hughes (1981) found teachers' confidence in the retention decision a crucial factor in the students' academic progress. Results from student attitude scales indicated that retained students also viewed retention at the primary grades as more desirable but still a negative experience (Brynes & Yamamoto, 1985) and even more negative at the upper-grade levels (Sandin, 1944).

[12] Three expectations were derived from the preceding research review and were tested in the following study: (a) academic benefits of retention will decrease as grade level increases; (b) self-concept and motivation of retainees will decrease in comparison with regular and borderline students as grade level increases; and (c) teacher, student, and parent perceptions of retention as a beneficial alternative will decrease with increasing grade level.

(4)   **METHOD**
(5) *Subjects*

[13] Students from first, second, third, fourth, seventh, and eighth grades from a semirural area of west central Florida participated in the study over a period of 2 years. The school district followed state and county education guidelines that mandated retention of students who lacked minimal skills (Citrus County, 1983). Subjects were grouped into three levels by grade: primary (first and second), intermediate (third and fourth), and secondary (seventh and eighth). At each level, primary, intermediate, and secondary, there were three groups of students: retained, who were retained after the first year of the study; borderline, who were on retention lists in the spring of the first year but eventually passed on to the next grade; and regular students, who were nei-

ther retained nor on the retention lists in the spring of the first school year.

[14] After the first year, the students who were retained in their respective grade levels were matched with borderline and regular students for gender, grade, age, self-concept, and motivation. Although this matching was completed, the groups were still considered to be non-equivalent and to represent different populations because the decision process of student retention (or for this study, the assignment of a student to the treatment group) involved not only student characteristics but also teacher, parent, and administrative considerations. As such, the selection of the retainee group involved sociological and social psychological variables that resulted in this group being different from the borderline and regular groups in more ways than the matched variables.

[15] At the conclusion of the second year, the primary level had 22 students in each group and the intermediate level finished with 15 students in each group. Due to moving, illness, and changing schools, the secondary level had 10 students in each group.

[16] Table 1 shows the means and standard deviations of each of the three groups' age, self-concept, and motivation in the fall of the first year of the study at each of the three levels. Each level's groups had the same number of boys and girls and total students at each grade level.

(6) *Instruments*

[17] The Self-Concept and Motivation Inventory (SCAMIN) was used to measure self-concept and motivation (Milchus, Farrah, & Reitz, 1968). Reviewers in the area of self-concept measurement considered this instrument as adequate if used in research for group changes over time (Goodwin & Driscoll, 1980). Another consideration in its selection was the three forms for use from first through eighth grades: the Early Elementary Form (Grades

Table 1   Means and Standard Deviations for Group Characteristics at Each Level

	Group					
	Retain		Border		Regular	
Factor	M	SD	M	SD	M	SD
Primary (N = 22)						
Age	6–10	8	7–1	8	6–8	9
Self-concept	48	5	49	6	49	4
Motivation	43	8	43	8	45	5
Intermediate (N = 15)						
Age	9–3	9	9–10	10	9–2	12
Self-concept	101	9	104	7	98	8
Motivation	85	11	85	10	87	13
Secondary (N = 10)						
Age	13–1	8	13–0	12	12–10	9
Self-concept	125	11	126	9	126	11
Motivation	110	11	105	11	106	13

1 to 3), reliability of .77, the Later Elementary Form (Grades 3 to 6), reliability of .83, and the Secondary Form (Grades 7 and 8), reliability of .83 (Milchus, Farrah, & Reitz, 1968).

[18] The Comprehensive Tests of Basic Skills (CTBS) (CTB/McGraw-Hill, 1972, Forms S and T; 1982 Forms U and V) are norm-referenced group achievement tests measuring skills in reading, language, and mathematics. The CTBS/S was administered for the measurements of spring 1983, and the CTBS/U was used for the spring of 1984. The average correlation across grade levels for the CTBS/S and CTBS/U was .80 and KR-20 reliabilities ranged from .88 to .97 (CTB/McGraw-Hill, 1982(b)).

[19] Scales were developed to measure individual student, teacher, and parent attitudes about the effects of retention. Although the scales had 16 questions for the students and 11 questions for the parents and teachers, 60% of the items were iden-tical across all forms. The scales measured perceived achievement progress, motivation, peer relations, and satisfaction during the repeated year.

⑧ *Procedure*

[20] In the fall of 1982, several thousand students in grades one through four, and seven and eight were administered the SCAMIN. During the spring of 1983, teacher recommendations were used to construct lists of students who were in danger of failure. Late in the spring of 1983, using the lists constructed, several hundred students were administered the SCAMIN for the second time. In the summer of 1983, the list of students who had been retained were matched with borderline students who had not failed, and with regular students. In the fall of 1983, and the spring of 1984, all students in the retained, borderline, and regular groups were administered the SCAMIN

for the third and fourth times, while relevant CTBS scores for all these students were obtained from 1983 and 1984 and converted to normal curve equivalent standard scores (Fagan & Horst, 1976).

[21] In conjunction with the above, the scales developed to measure student, teacher, and parent attitudes were administered in the spring of 1984. Only students at the relevant grade levels who were retained (approximately 150 students), and their teachers and parents were administered the scales by district school personnel. Because this latter group contained only retained students, no matching or attendance for 2 years was necessary, and as a result, this analysis had more students at each level than the other measures.

[22] The scales were administered in an informal manner with any unknown words clarified to ensure that all students, especially the younger children, understood. The respondents chose one of three answers, which represented negative to positive attitudes. The three-step answer format was chosen to ensure understanding by the younger students. Answers were subsequently scored from 1 to 3, with the higher score representing more positive attitudes toward the retention experience. All questions, 11 on the parent and teacher form and 15 on the student form, were summed on each side for the unit of data analysis.

⑨ *Design and Analysis*

[23] This study's design and data analysis were based on the use of an untreated control group with pretest and posttest. Because the groups differed on sociological and social psychological variables and because no available covariate or combination of covariates contained all the relevant information used in the selection of subjects into groups, the data analysis for achievement, self-concept, and motivation scores used gain-score ANOVA (Kenny, 1975; Huitema, 1980). The gain-score analysis was accomplished and presented at the time by treat-

ment interaction effect in the repeated measures ANOVA (Cook & Campbell, 1979).

⑩ **RESULTS**

⑪ *Academic Achievement*

[24] The structure of the two-factor repeated measures ANOVA is demonstrated in Table 2 by the results for reading at the primary level. The time (T) by group (G) interaction effect is of primary interest in this study. Because of the dependent nature of the measures and the partial matching of subjects, conservative critical F values were used in significance testing.

[25] The results of the group by time analyses are displayed in Table 3. As shown, the interaction effects are significant at the primary and intermediate level for reading, language, and mathematics.

[26] From visual inspection of the achievement means for the primary, intermediate, and secondary levels, the nature of the interaction effect is clear. At the primary level (Table 4), whereas the retainee group showed noteworthy increases in every achievement area, the borderline group showed a marked decrease in the reading area and slight decreases in the mathematics and language areas that produced a disordinal interaction for the retainee and borderline groups. Cook and Campbell

Table 2 Summary ANOVA for Two-Factor Repeated Measures Design at Primary Level for Reading

Source	df	SS	MS	F
Independent	65	2,878,963		
Group (G)	2	959,963	479,982	15.76
S(G)	63	1,919,000	30,460	
Dependent	66	848,669		
Time (T)	1	14,177	14,177	2.45
T × G	2	469,640	234,820	40.55
S(G) × T	63	364,852	5,791	
Total	131	3,727,631	28,455	

Table 3   Results Summary

Level and Subject	Critical F	df	F	PDVE[a]
Primary				
Reading	4.32	1, 21	40.55	55
Language	4.32	1, 21	5.71	15
Mathematics	4.32	1, 21	16.41	18
Intermediate				
Reading	4.60	1, 14	6.67	22
Language	4.60	1, 14	6.42	23
Mathematics	4.60	1, 14	5.67	21
Secondary				
Reading	5.12	1, 9	1.52	10
Language	5.12	1, 9	1.59	10
Mathematics	5.12	1, 9	3.19	19

[a]PDVE = Percentage of dependent variance explained.

(1979) regard this outcome as one of the most interpretable from this type of design. This same disordinal interaction was present at the intermediate level (Table 4), where the borderline groups' decreases and the increases of the retainee group were similar to their primary counterparts but less in magnitude. In contrast at the secondary level (Table 4), the changes in achievement for the retainee group were indistinguishable from those of the borderline group in every achievement area.

⑫ *Self-Concept and Motivation*

[27] A 4 × 3 analysis of variance for repeated measures performed on the self-con-

Table 4   CTBS Means and Standard Deviations

CTBS Subtests	Year	Group					
		Retainee		Border		Regular	
		M	SD	M	SD	M	SD
		Primary (N = 22)					
Reading	83	38.69	13.44	48.17	9.57	68.99	10.77
	84	53.38	17.33	39.43	14.46	56.82	12.57
Language	83	49.56	17.74	49.60	11.56	67.64	12.69
	84	61.37	20.01	42.80	15.33	69.09	15.51
Math	83	44.91	20.42	49.57	18.50	69.24	16.77
	84	64.32	24.33	46.49	19.24	58.12	15.84
		Intermediate (N = 15)					
Reading	83	44.03	13.14	42.41	12.61	65.20	9.77
	84	48.45	9.09	33.74	10.96	58.47	9.05
Language	83	42.88	10.22	40.41	10.94	63.97	11.66
	84	52.29	9.48	40.13	9.66	59.29	15.18
Math	83	45.26	10.41	48.68	12.60	66.93	12.23
	84	54.79	21.12	40.81	12.89	61.08	10.33
		Secondary (N = 10)					
Reading	83	38.71	11.26	37.33	9.03	44.13	9.03
	84	42.34	11.77	34.91	8.14	41.30	12.34
Language	83	31.45	13.71	37.30	8.11	48.70	9.96
	84	35.46	7.61	31.19	10.25	46.87	8.97
Math	83	35.20	12.61	42.60	11.24	46.35	7.99
	84	43.22	8.04	39.01	8.28	41.53	9.60

cept scores from each level revealed no significant effects at the primary or secondary levels, but there was a significant main effect [F (.05; 1, 14) = 4.60] for time at the intermediate level. This effect was due to the decreasing scores in self-concept for all groups over the 2-year period. This decline in self-concept also was present at the secondary level, but not significantly, and accounted for about 10% of the dependent variance at both levels.

[28] A 4 × 3 analysis of variance for repeated measures performed on the motivation scores from each level revealed no significant interaction effects at the primary, intermediate, or secondary levels. At the primary and intermediate levels, however, the retainee groups showed motivation increases in comparison to the borderline group at the beginning of their retainee year, but they were not significantly different at the end of the second year.

⑬ *Attitude Scales*

[29] Table 5 presents the means and standard deviations for the parent, teacher, and student attitude scales for the three grade levels with higher numbers representing more positive attitudes toward the year of retention.

[30] A one-way analysis of variance was conducted on these attitude scale responses. Both the teacher, $F(2, 158) = 13.34$, $p <$ .01, and student, $F(2, 125) = 13.57$, $p <$ .01, responses for the three grade-level groups were significantly different at the .01

level and the parents' $F(2, 75) = 2.91$, $p <$ .06 at the .10 level. Consequently, the Fisher LSD test was conducted to determine the nature of the significant differences. Parent ratings for secondary students were significantly lower (less positive) than either their intermediate or primary counterparts ratings. For teacher ratings, those at every grade level were significantly different than those at the other levels, with the most positive for the lower grades and the most negative for the higher grades. For student ratings, those of primary students were significantly higher (more positive) than either intermediate or secondary students.

⑭   **DISCUSSION**

[31] The results indicated that the expected trend of decreasing benefits for retained students as grade level increased was confirmed by reading, language, and mathematics scores, and by parent, teacher, and student attitudes, but not by student self-ratings in self-concept and motivation.

[32] The expected trend in achievement areas was shown not only by statistically significant results but also by the size of effects as measured by percentage of variance explained. At the primary level, the Group × Time interaction effect explained 55% of the dependent variance in reading, 15% in language, and 17% in mathematics. At the intermediate level, the Group × Time interaction effect explained 22% of the de-

Table 5   Means and Standard Deviations for Attitude Scales

| | Grade Level | | | | | |
| | Primary | | Intermediate | | Secondary | |
Group	M	SD	M	SD	M	SD
Parent	26.50	2.43	25.87	2.80	24.36	3.56
Teacher	24.32	3.95	22.22	3.34	20.19	5.00
Student	38.45	3.88	35.27	4.21	34.14	3.58

pendent variance in reading, 23% in language and 21% in mathematics. In contrast, at the secondary level the Group × Time interaction effect explained only 10% of the dependent variance in reading, 10% in language, and 19% in mathematics.

[33] At the primary level, regular students showed stable achievement, self-concept, and motivation levels over the 2-year period. The borderline students exhibited stable self-concepts, along with temporary decreases at the beginning of the second year in motivation and at the end of the second year in achievement areas. Students who were retained, in contrast, showed increases in all achievement areas, a stable self-concept, and a temporary increase in motivation at the beginning of their retained year. These students also rated their retained year in significantly more positive terms than did retained students at the intermediate and secondary levels. Teachers and parents of students at the primary level also rated the retention experience in significantly more positive terms than did teachers and parents of students in later grades.

[34] At the intermediate level, regular students continued to manifest stable achievement and motivation levels. The borderline students displayed decreased achievement in reading, mathematics, and stable motivation. Students who were retained, in contrast, showed increased achievement in every area and an increase in motivation. All students, however, displayed a significant decrease in self-concept over the 2 years.

[35] This decrease in self-concept for students also was shown at the secondary level, but, at the same time, students exhibited stable achievement and motivation levels. The retained students displayed no significant achievement gains and insignificant decreases in self-concept and motivation. These students also rated their retained year in significantly less positive terms than did their primary level counterparts. Teachers and parents of retained students at this level

rated the students' experience in significantly more negative terms than did parents and teachers at both the primary and intermediate levels.

[36] An ever-present problem in the use of nonequivalent group designs was the threat to the validity of the findings. Fortunately, the disordinal interaction pattern reduced the usual threats such as selection maturation, regression to the mean, and instrumentation. The threat of possible selection maturation effects was reduced by the disordinal interaction because few growth rates or maturation patterns can be described in terms of trends that meet and cross over, and because students were matched for maturation relevant variables like age, sex, grade, and self-concept. Inspection of the data and the disordinal interaction ruled out most problems of scaling and ceiling or floor effects. The disordinal interaction outcome also left a regression to the mean effect less plausible. Although the retained groups did move to the mean, in most cases they ended higher than the mean, whereas the border group moved away from the mean. The above considerations lend extra credence to the findings of the quasi-experimental design.

[37] Whereas these results clearly show decreasing academic benefits for retention at later grades, the data appear inconsistent for self-concept and motivation. The self-concept and motivation data did not show the expected trend. Although the groups were similar in their reported self-concepts over the 2 years, at the intermediate and secondary levels all groups showed a consistent decrease in self-concept during this period. Although this finding conflicts with the reported lower personal and social adjustment of overage students at the secondary level (Anfinson, 1941; Sandin, 1944), the present study specifically examined self-concept of currently retained students who were not overage compared with the borderline and regular students (Table 1). The present findings for student motivation also showed few changes for any group over the

2 years. Although fluctuations were noted during the 2-year period, at the end of the second year the groups were not significantly different.

[38] In summary, the present findings suggest that retention as an educationally effective alternative decreases in utility as grade level increases. Parents, teachers, and students agree on these findings that also are supported by student achievement test scores. These findings supported the literature reviewed in this paper for achievement but not for personal and social adjustment. The results certainly suggest that further research is needed to ensure that student achievement is helped by retention and that we as educators are not wasting our tax dollars on retention at the higher grade levels.

(15) **REFERENCES**

Anfinson, R. D. (1941). School progress and pupil adjustment. *The Elementary School Journal, 41*, 507–514.

Ausubel, D. (1953). The nature of educational research. In H. S. Broudy, R. H. Ennis, & L. I. Krimerman. *Philosophy of educational research* (pp. 79–86). New York: John Wiley & Sons Inc.

Bedoian, V. H. (1954). Social acceptability and social rejection of the underage, at-age, and overage pupils in the sixth grade. *Journal of Educational Research, 47*, 513–520.

Byrnes, D., & Yamamoto, K. (1985). An inside look at academic retention in the elementary school. *Education, 106*, 208–214.

Byrnes, D., & Yamamoto, K. (1986). Views on grade repetition. *Journal of Research and Development in Education, 20*(1), 14–20.

CBS Evening News with Bob Schieffer. (1981, December 26).

Chansky, N. M. (1964). Progress of promoted and repeating Grade 1 failures.

Journal of Experimental Education, 32(3), 225–237.

Chase, J. A. (1968). A study of the impact of grade retention on primary school children. *Journal of Psychology, 70*, 169–177.

Citrus County Pupil Progression Plan. (1983). Inverness, Florida: Citrus County Schools.

Coffield, W. H., & Bloomers, P. (1956). Effects of nonpromotion on educational achievement in the elementary school. *Journal of Educational Psychology, 47*, 235–250.

Cook, T. D., & Campbell, D. T. (1979). *Quasi-Experimentation*. Boston: Houghton Mifflin Company.

Cook, W. (1941). Some effects of the maintenance of high standards of promotion. *Elementary School Journal, 41*, 430–437.

CTB/McGraw-Hill. (1972). *Comprehensive Test of Basic Skills, Forms S and T*. Monterey, CA: CTB/McGraw-Hill Inc.

CTB/McGraw-Hill. (1982). *Comprehensive Test of Basic Skills, Forms U and V*. Preliminary Technical Report. Monterey, CA: CTB/McGraw-Hill Inc.

Dici, E. L. (1975). *Intrinsic motivation*. New York: Plemure Press.

Ebel, R. L. (1980). The failure of schools without failure. *Phi Delta Kappan, 61*, 386–388.

Fagan, B. M., & Horst, D. P. (1976). *Types of test scores*. ESEA Title I Evaluation and Reporting System, Technical Paper No. 8, October.

Farley, E. S. (1936). Regarding repeaters. *The Nation's Schools, 18*(4), 37–39.

Finlayson, H. J. (1975). *The effect of nonpromotion upon the self-concept of pupils in primary grades*. October, (ERIC Document Reproduction Service No. ED 155–556).

Godfrey, E. (1972). The tragedy of failure. *The Education Digest, 37*(5), 34–35.

Goodwin, W. L., & Driscoll, L. A. (1980). *Handbook for measurement and evalu-*

ation in early childhood education. San Francisco: Jossey-Bass.

Haney, W., & Madaus, G. (1978). Making sense of the competency testing movement. *Harvard Educational Review*, 48(4), 462–484.

Holmes, C. T., & Matthews, K. M. (1984). The effects of nonpromotion on elementary and junior high school pupils: A meta-analysis. *Review of Educational Research*, 45(2), 225–236.

Huitema, B. (1980). *The analysis of covariance and alternatives*. New York: John Wiley & Sons.

Jackson, G. (1975). The research evidence on the effects of grade retention. *Review of Educational Research*, 45,(4), 613–635.

Kamaii, C. K., & Weikart, D. P. (1963). Marks, achievement, and intelligence of seventh graders who were retained (nonpromotion) once in elementary school. *Journal of Educational Research*, 56, 452–489.

Kenny, D. A. (1975). A quasi-experimental approach to assessing treatment effects in the nonequivalent control group design. *Psychological Bulletin*, 82, 345–362.

Kerzner, R. (1982). *The effect of retention on achievement*. May, (ERIC Document Reproduction Service No. ED 216 309).

Keyes, H. C. (1911). Progress through the grades of city schools, (Contributions to Education, No. 4). New York: Bureau of Publication, Teachers College, Columbia University.

Leggett, P. B. (1982). *Student characteristics and official school nonpromotion*. Unpublished doctoral dissertation, University of Florida.

Lindelow, J. (1982). Synthesis of research on grade retention and social promotion. *Educational Leadership*, 39(6), 471–473.

McAfee, J. K. (1981). *Towards a theory of promotion: Does retaining students really work?* April (ERIC Document Reproduction Service No. ED 204 871).

Medway, F. J. (1986). Grade retention. In T. R. Kratochwill (Ed.). *Advances in school psychology*, (Vol. 5). Hillsdale, NJ: Lawrence Erlbaum Associates.

Milchus, N. J., Farrah, G. A., & Reitz, W. (1968). *The self-concept and motivation inventory: What face would you wear?* SCAMIN Manual of Interpretation. Dearborn Heights, Michigan: Person-O-Metrics.

Morrison, I. E., & Perry, I. F. (1956). Acceptance of overage children by classmates. *Elementary School Journal*, 56(5), 217–220.

Muessen, E. J. (1954). *A determination of the effect of retardation on students*. Unpublished doctoral dissertation, University of Michigan.

Otto, H. J., & Melby, E. D. (1935). An attempt to evaluate the threat of failure as a factor in achievement. *The Elementary School Journal*, 35, 588–596.

Owens, S., & Ranick, D. L. (1977). The Greenville program: A common sense approach to basics. *Phi Delta Kappan*, 58, 531–533.

Reinherz, H., & Griffin, C. L. (1970). The second time around. *The School Counselor*, 17, 213–218.

Sandin, A. A. (1944). Social and emotional adjustments of regularly promoted and nonpromoted pupils. *Child Development Monographs, No. 32*, New York: Bureau of Publications, Teachers College, Columbia University.

Sandoval, J., & Hughes, G. (1981). *Success in nonpromoted first-grade children*. June (ERIC Document Reproduction Service No. ED 212 371).

Scott, B. A., & Ames, L. B. (1969). Improved academic, personal, and social adjustment in selected primary school repeaters. *Elementary School Journal*, 69, 431–438.

Viele, J. A. (1966). Does the no-failure plan work? *The Grade School Teacher*, June, 34–35.

White, K., & Howard, J. L. (1973). Failure

to be promoted and self-concept among elementary school children. *Elementary School Guidance and Counseling, 7*(3), 182–187.

Wolf, J. M. (1965). Syndrome of spring: So-cial promotions. *Elementary School Journal, 65,* 208–216.

Worth, W. H. (1960). Promotion or non-promotion? *Educational Administration and Supervision, 1*(46), 16–26.

consumer: learning to read research reports like a research producer. The second step is using the questions in Figure 3.1 to evaluate research reports.

The questions are about each of the major aspects of research reports. At this point in your learning, you should not be expected to answer all the questions appropriately. Because the content and length of research reports are often determined by the editors of the journals or books in which the reports appear, your determinations as a research consumer about the appropriateness and adequacy of the information in a report will necessarily be subjective. Remember that these subjective decisions change as you gain increased understanding of research methods and research reporting, and as you gain more experiences in reading and evaluating research reports and writing about them. Your work with this text is a beginning step in acquiring understanding and experiences.

The questions presented here provide an overview of the discussions in later chapters. The major headings within Figure 3.1 represent common, major headings found in research reports published in professional journals. As you can see reviewing the previously cited reports, researchers modify these major headings to fit their purposes and to highlight particular information. Research reports in other sources—books, encyclopedias, newspapers, and popular magazines—may have different organizations and formats. Some of these variations are discussed in later chapters.

ACTIVITY

Select a research report from the Appendix or from a professional journal. With a partner, another student in the class, read the research

QUESTIONS FOR EVALUATING RESEARCH REPORTS

ABSTRACT

Organization: Is information about the major aspects of the research—purpose, subjects, instruments, procedures/treatment, results—included?

Style: Is the abstract brief and clearly written?

INTRODUCTORY SECTION

Problem area: Are the problem area and its educational importance explained?

Related literature: Are research studies related to the problem area presented? Has the related research been evaluated and critiqued? Does the intended research logically extend the information gained from the related research?

Hypothesis(es), purpose(s), question(s): Is there a purpose that can be studied in an unbiased manner? Are the research variables (independent and dependent, when appropriate) easily identified from the hypothesis, question, or purpose statement? Are key terms or variables operationally defined?

METHOD SECTION

Subjects: Are target populations and subjects, sampling and selection procedures, and group sizes clearly described? Are these appropriate for the research design?

Instruments: What instruments are used in the study? Are they appropriate for the design of the study? Are the instruments valid for collecting data on the variables in the study and are reliability estimates given for each instrument? Are researcher-made instruments included (or at least samples of the instrument items)? Is information about the development of these instruments presented? Are the instruments appropriate for use with the target population and the research subjects? Collection procedures clearly described?

Procedures: Are the research design and data collection procedures clearly described? Is the research design appropriate to the researcher's purpose? Can the study be replicated from the information provided?

Qualitative method: Has the researcher's presence influenced the behavior of the subjects?

Treatment: Are experimental procedures fully explained? Are examples of special materials included?

Research validity: Are the procedures free from the influence of extraneous variables? Does the study contain any threats to its internal and external validity?

RESULTS SECTION

Data analysis: Are the statistical procedures for data analysis clearly described and are they appropriate for the type of quantitative research design?

Significance: Are statistical significance levels indicated? Does the research have practical significance?

Qualitative research: Are the processes for organizing data, identifying patterns, and synthesizing key ideas as hypotheses and research questions clearly described?

DISCUSSION SECTION

Discussion (conclusions, recommendations): Are the conclusions related to answering the research question(s) and are they appropriate to the results? Is the report free from inappropriate generalizations and implications? If inappropriate, are suggestions for additional research provided?

Figure 3.1 Questions for evaluating research reports.

report. Use the peer-interacting procedure discussed in the Activities section of Chapter 2 and the Research Report Reading Plan discussed in this chapter. You and your partner should take turns explaining the reason for selecting sections to be read and the location of key information. Discuss differences you may have about these choices.

4 Reading and Evaluating Introductory Sections: Abstract, Background, and Purpose

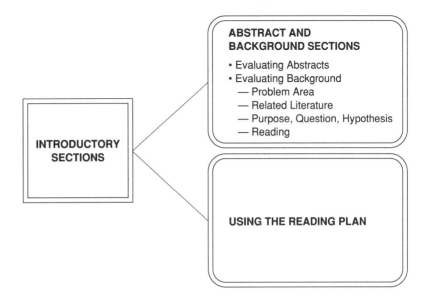

INTRODUCTORY SECTIONS

ABSTRACT AND BACKGROUND SECTIONS

• Evaluating Abstracts
• Evaluating Background
  — Problem Area
  — Related Literature
  — Purpose, Question, Hypothesis
  — Reading

USING THE READING PLAN

FOCUS QUESTIONS

1. What information should research consumers get from the abstract and background sections of a research report?
2. What criteria are used to evaluate abstracts?
3. What criteria are used to evaluate background sections?
4. What is the plan for reading abstracts and background sections?

In the background section, a researcher introduces readers to the problem area and its educational importance. Researchers also provide brief summaries of other researchers' results that are related to the problem area. The part with these summaries is called the **literature review,** and in it researchers indicate strengths from the related research that were used in their study and weaknesses or limitations that were changed. In many professional journals, the background section is preceded by an abstract, a summary of the report. Most often, researchers omit the literature review from an abstract.

THE ABSTRACT AND BACKGROUND SECTIONS

In the plan for reading research reports discussed in Chapter 3, the abstract and background sections are read first. From these sections, research consumers should be able to answer

What are the researchers' issues and concerns?

What have other researchers found out about these issues?

What question(s) did the researchers try to answer?

What kind of research was conducted by the researchers and what were the independent and dependent variables?

Are the researchers' issues and concerns relevant to me as a professional or to my teaching situation?

The questions for evaluating Abstract and Background Sections (taken from Figure 3.1, p. 87) are

---

QUESTIONS FOR EVALUATING ABSTRACT AND BACKGROUND SECTIONS OF RESEARCH REPORTS

ABSTRACT

Organization: Is information about the major aspects of the research—purpose, subjects, instruments, procedures/treatment, findings—included?

Style: Is the abstract brief and clearly written?

INTRODUCTORY SECTION

Problem area: Are the problem area and its educational importance explained?

Related literature: Are research studies related to the problem area presented? Has the related research been evaluated and critiqued? Does the intended research logically extend the information gained from the related research?

Hypothesis(es), purpose(s), question(s): Can the purpose be studied in an unbiased manner? Are the research variables (independent and dependent) easily identified from the hypothesis, question, or purpose statement? Are key terms or variables operationally defined?

Evaluating Abstracts

Most abstracts are written in a particular style and manner that facilitates readers' attempts to ascertain whether the research is appropriate for their purposes as consumers. Abstracts contain information about purpose, subjects, instruments, procedure (and treatment when applicable), findings, and conclusions.

Abstracts are usually short, containing 100 to 200 words, and are set in special type or indented to distinguish them from the main body of the research report. Some journals do not require abstracts: The decision is set by the journal editors and advisory boards. Some publications, such as *Psychological Abstracts* and *Current Index to Journals in Education* (CIJE), contain short abstracts that do not have the style and content of journal abstracts. Other publications, such as *Dissertation Abstracts International,* have abstracts 600 to 800 words long that contain more information than journal abstracts. A discussion of these publications and samples of their abstract forms are found in Chapter 11, Locating Information About Research Reports, pp. 297–314.

The following abstract from a report entitled "Cognitive and Affective Effects of Various Types of Microcomputer Use by Preschoolers" illustrates this style. The types of information are highlighted in the margin. For this demonstration, you should read the abstract for the purpose of finding out whether computers are an effective instructional activity in preschooler's education.

[Purpose]

[Subjects]
[Treatment]

[Materials]

[Instruments]

[Statistical analysis]

[Results]

An experimental study was conducted to investigate the effects of microcomputer use on preschoolers' knowledge of prereading concepts, and on their attitudes toward the microcomputer. After stratification by age and sex, 77 preschoolers were randomly assigned to three treatment conditions: (a) adult-assisted microcomputer instruction; (b) adult-unassisted microcomputer use; and (c) no microcomputer use (control condition). Children in the first two groups were given three 20-min. individual sessions on the microcomputer. The software programs used were designed to teach reading readiness concepts and were typical commercial programs available for this age group. A cognitive test was administered as a pretest and posttest and an attitudinal interview was administered post-study only. The cognitive data were analyzed with a multivariate analysis of covariance (MANCOVA). There were no significant treatment effects. The attitudinal data analysis revealed significantly greater interest in the microcomputer among the control-group children; however, that group's interest declined significantly after they were given post-study, 20-min. orientations to the microcomputer. (From Goodwin, Goodwin, Nansel, & Helm, 1986, p. 348)

Evaluative question: Are the major aspects of the research—purpose, subjects, instruments, procedures/treatment, findings—included?

As shown by the margin annotations, the abstract contains information about the major aspects of research.

Evaluative question: Is the abstract brief and clearly written?

In the example, the researchers have used only terms that a knowledgeable research consumer would be expected to know. Technical terms used in the abstract that are explained in this textbook are: *stratification, randomly, control, pretest, posttest, multivariate (MANCOVA)*, and *covariance*. Also, the abstract presents the information about the research aspects without unnecessary information.

Researchers sometimes omit specific information and merely refer to the type of information included in the full research report. Such a tactic does not provide report readers with a complete summary and hinders their understanding of the research because the specific details of the research report are omitted. Statements that illustrate this weakness in abstracts are "The study examined various instructional techniques," "The results are presented," and "The implications of the results are given."

Evaluating Background Sections

Background sections contain three major kinds of information. The first is the problem area and its educational importance. The second is related literature. The third is the research purpose, question, or hypothesis.

The Problem Area

In Chapter 1, five characteristics of a profession and its members were enumerated. Briefly, they were (a) to verify existing ideas and practices, (b) to discover new ideas and practices, (c) to clarify and expand information about ideas and practices, (d) to express ideas that complicate educational practice, and (e) to discover ideas and practices that are counterintuitive. Researchers try to justify the importance of their research in light of these aspects of professional activity. For example, in a descriptive study to determine what children's literature experts suggested for poetry instruction and what teaching procedures were included in basal teacher's manuals, the researcher indicated that

> Basal readers represent one source where teachers can find poetry to share with children. For some teachers, the basal reader is the sole source used in the teaching of poetry. The teacher manuals accompanying basal readers offer detailed guidance in the teaching of poems presented in the student texts. The methodology of teachers who rely on these manuals may be strongly influenced by the suggested teaching procedures. Because of the potential impact of basals on poetry instruction, it is important to examine the suggested pedagogical procedures in basal reader manuals to determine whether they reflect what is known about teaching poetry from research and expert opinion. (Shapiro, 1985, p. 369)

Related Literature

Researchers also need to examine what others have found to be important. By reviewing relevant research, researchers gain insights about the problem area that should then influence their research questions and methods. During this phase of research, research producers act as consumers. They critically analyze research using questions similar to those in Table 1.1, p. 11. As a result of their evaluation, they can:

Extend knowledge about a problem area. This can be done because the researchers see a next step in answering questions about the problem. For example, after reviewing research about parents who read aloud to their children, one group of researchers realized no one had described the views of those parents, so their research was concerned with identifying what parents thought about reading to their children (Manning, Manning, & Cody, 1988).

Change or revise knowledge about a problem area. This can be done because the researchers see weaknesses or limitations in other researchers' attempts to answer questions about the problem area. For example, after reviewing research about oral reading cue strategies of better and poor readers, a researcher identified several limitations with those studies and made modifications in materials that were used, the reading task assigned to the students, and the number and type of errors evaluated (Fleisher, 1988).

Replicate the study. Sometimes researchers wish to redo the research of others. **Replication** means repeating an investigation of a previous study's purpose, question, or hypothesis.

Researchers can replicate research in several ways. First, they can use the same method with different subjects. In this case, the researchers keep the original purpose, method, and data analysis procedure. The subjects have the same characteristics as the original subjects, but they are different people. For example, one team of researchers replicated a study looking at the effect on learning disabled and slowly developing readers of two instructional programs designed to teach the students how to detect their own errors (Pascarella, Pflaum, Bryan, & Pearl, 1983). In the original study, conducted by two members of the same research team, the subjects were individual students. In the replication, data were analyzed for both individual students and groups because the researchers felt that working with individuals overlooked the "potential interdependencies among individual [student] observations within the same reading group" (p. 270).

Second, in a procedure known as **cross validation**, the researchers use the same purpose, method, and data analysis procedure to investigate subjects from a different population. For example, if the subjects in an original study were second and third graders, a different target population might be high school students.

Third, in a procedure known as **validity generalization**, the researchers use the same purpose, method, and data analysis procedure, but they use subjects from a unique population. For example, if the subjects in an original study were suburban students with hearing impairment, a different population might be rural students with vision impairment.

Fourth, researchers can reanalyze other researchers' data. In this case, no new study is undertaken. For example, after reviewing research about students' silent reading, a team of researchers indicated that the results of one study in particular did not warrant certain conclusions, so they reanalyzed the data presented by the original researchers (Wilkinson, Wardrop, & Anderson, 1988).

Purpose, Question, Hypothesis

Most examples so far in this text have shown researchers stating their research aims as purposes or questions. This has been done because current practice in research journals is to use this form. Journal editors as well as authorities on effective reading practice feel that readers of research get a better mindset from purposes and questions than they do from hypotheses. Nevertheless, research reports are often written with traditional hypotheses.

A **hypothesis** is a conjectural statement of the relationship between the research variables. It is created after researchers have examined the related literature but before they undertake the study. It is "a tentative explanation for certain behaviors, phenomena, or events that have occurred or will occur. A hypothesis states the researcher's expectations concerning the relationship between the variables in the research problem" (Gay, 1987, p. 53).

One way to state a hypothesis is as a **nondirectional** (or *two-tailed*) **research hypothesis**, which is a statement of the specific relationship or effect among variables. Researchers use this form when they have strong evidence from examining previous research that a relationship or effect exists, but the evidence does not provide them with indications about the nature or direction (positive or negative) of the relationship or influence. The following, taken from a study about the connection between computer technology and reading comprehension, are examples of nondirectional research hypotheses stated to show that differences will exist between variables. Note that the researchers do not state how—positively or negatively—using a computer to mediate manipulations of the text (the independent variable) will influence reading comprehension (the dependent variable).

1. The comprehension of intermediate-grade readers reading expository texts will be affected by using a computer to mediate manipulations of the text.
2. Comprehension of expository text will be affected by varying control of textual manipulations from the reader to the computer program. (Reinking & Schreiner, 1985, p. 540)

If the researchers' evidence supports a statement of the specific way one variable will affect another, then the research hypothesis is stated as a **directional** (or *one-tailed*) **hypothesis**. The following example contains two directional research hypotheses from a study about the effects of teacher expectations and student behavior.

> The first hypothesis under investigation was that adults who are deliberate and more reserved would be more likely to adopt a task-oriented approach than would adults who are impulsive and highly sociable. Thus the reserved, deliberate adults would make more attempts to structure the task for the child, would more often redirect the child's attention to the task, and would make fewer task irrelevant comments to the child than would the sociable, impulsive adult. In addition, [the second hypothesis was that] compared with inexperienced teachers, experienced teachers are more likely to be task oriented. (Osborne, 1985, p. 80)

In this example, the researcher predicted that teachers' temperament factors (the independent variable) would have a direct effect on how they structure children's tasks (the dependent variable). Not only was an effect predicted, but the specific way the teachers would structure the task was predicted. The research predicted that teachers with reserved, deliberate temperaments would be *more directive* and offer *fewer irrelevant comments*. The second prediction was that teachers' experience (the independent variable) would affect task orientation (the dependent variable) and that experienced teachers would *more likely* be task oriented.

Another form of stating the hypothesis is the null hypothesis. In contrast to the research hypothesis (directional and nondirectional), the null hypothesis is used exclusively as an aid to statistical analysis and is rarely used in research reports.

Reading Background Sections

The following, a typical background section, is taken from a report entitled "Cognitive and Affective Effects of Various Types of Microcomputer Use by Preschoolers." Key information in this background section is annotated.

Cognitive and Affective Effects of Various Types of Microcomputer Use By Preschoolers

[Background] [1] Microcomputer acquisition by elementary and secondary schools in the 1980s has been dramatic (Center for Social Organization of Schools,

1983; Magarell, 1982). Not surprisingly, preschools and day care centers likewise have become entranced with this new technology. An estimated 25% of licensed preschools in the country now have microcomputers, and all preschools are predicted to have access to them by 1989 (Chin, 1984).

[2] Much has been written about actual and potential uses of microcomputers with young children, but there is a dearth of sound research-based information on the cognitive and affective effects of such use. Most published literature consists of unsupported claims about a myriad positive effects, such as acquiring programming abilities; recognizing letters and numbers; learning spatial and relational concepts; developing creative-thinking, problem-solving, decision-making, and logical-thinking abilities; encouraging autonomy, social interaction skills, and cooperation; and fostering fine-motor skills and eye-hand cooperation. A considerably smaller proportion of the literature raises concerns about whether or not preschoolers have the requisite skills to use microcomputers beneficially, and about issues such as the quality of available software and the inadequate preparation of teachers on computers. [See Goodwin, Goodwin, & Garel (in press) for a review of this "unsupported claims" literature.]

[Related literature]   [3] The few completed research studies on microcomputer use by preschoolers (3–5-year-olds) have tended to use descriptive or pre-experimental designs. Generally small increases in cognitive skills or knowledge specific to certain software programs have been reported (Hungate, 1982; Keller & Shanahan, 1983; Piestrup, 1982; Prinz, Nelson, & Stedt, 1982; Smithy-Willis, Riley, & Smith, 1982), as well as sex differences in children's preferences for problem-solving versus "drill and practice" types of software (Swigger, Campbell, & Swigger, 1983). Using a true-experimental design, Chatman, Love-Clark, and Ash (1984) found that the presence versus absence of "touch-tone feedback" to correct and incorrect responses had no significant effect on preschoolers' ability to perform a specific task learned on the microcomputer.

[4] Given the great attention paid to microcomputers by parents, preschool administrators, and teachers, the paucity of relevant experimental studies is unfortunate. This study investigated the effects of microcomputer use on preschoolers' knowledge of basic reading-readiness concepts and on their attitudes toward the microcomputer. There

[Purposes]   were two major purposes. The first was to compare pre-reading skills of children who had been randomly assigned to the following three groups: (a) an "adult-assisted" group who used the microcomputer with an adult present who assumed a teacher role; (b) an "adult-unassisted" group who used the microcomputer on their own after being given only minimal instructions from an adult; and (c) a control group who did not use the microcomputer at all. The three levels of the treatment variable were chosen after reviewing the available software for the 3–5 age group. Instructions provided with many programs specified that children should be given only minimal adult assistance; in other cases, no instructions concerning appropriate adult and child roles were given. The relative effectiveness of the adult-assisted and -unassisted conditions has such obvious implications for effective use of microcomputers in preschools that both conditions were incorporated into the design.

[5] The study's second purpose was to investigate the effects of the treatment variable on the children's attitudes toward the microcomputer. "Attitudes" was operationally defined as the children's rank-order preferences for the microcomputer as compared to toys and to books. (From Goodwin, Goodwin, Nansel, & Helm, 1986. Copyright 1986 by the American Educational Research Association. Reprinted by permission of the publisher.)

Evaluative question: Are the problem area and its educational importance explained?

In the example, the researchers succinctly presented the importance of the problem area. Although paragraph 1 is short, the researchers indicated the importance of computers to preschool programs and substantiated their claims with references.

Evaluative questions: Are research studies related to the problem area presented? Has the related research been evaluated and critiqued? Does the intended research logically extend the information from the related research?

In paragraphs 2 and 3, the researchers provided a summary of relevant research results and indicated what they feel are limitations of those findings. The researchers indicated how the research team addressed concerns about what they believed are unsupported claims of previous research and lack of experimental control. In paragraphs 4 and 5, the researchers indicated their two major purposes. What research consumers need to determine is: Did the purposes provide means for overcoming the indicated limitations of the previous research? This question can be answered in relation to the next evaluative question.

Evaluative questions: Is there a purpose that can be studied in an unbiased manner? Are the research variables (independent and dependent) easily identified from the hypothesis, question, or purpose? Are key terms or variables operationally defined?

The first research purpose in the example was to conduct a comparative study of the prereading skills (the research variable) among four groups of preschool children (subjects). For this purpose, the researchers collected data to examine their claim that statements in the related literature about preschoolers not having requisite computer skills were unsupported. The second purpose was to do an experimental study looking at the effect of computer instruction (independent variable—three treatment conditions and a control) on the children's attitudes toward computers (dependent variable). It was possible to conduct comparative and experimental studies without bias; the only way research consumers can be confident that no bias was introduced would be to evaluate the method section (this is discussed in the next four chapters). No terms needed special definitions.

USING THE RESEARCH READING PLAN WITH ABSTRACTS AND BACKGROUND SECTIONS

By using the research reading plan (see Figure 3.1, p. 87) for the initial reading of abstracts and background sections, research consumers can efficiently seek out information in a particular order. The abstract and background sections ("The Child's Developing Sense of Theme as a Response to Literature by Lehr, 1988) on pp. 99–101, from a research report about children's sense of theme in literature, contain highlighted numerals to illustrate the suggested order of reading. For this demonstration, you should read the report for the purpose of gaining knowledge about how children understand themes in children's literature.

READING THE ABSTRACT AND BACKGROUND SECTION

The title is read to gain a broad overview of the research topic. ①

The first sentence of the abstract is read to gain a general understanding of the researcher's concern. ②

The paragraph containing the researchers' research purposes, questions, or hypotheses is read to gain a specific understanding of the research. This information is usually found at the end of the background section. ③

From reading ①, ②, and ③, research consumers can determine that the purpose (gaining knowledge) will be met by reading the report. In the margin of this text or on a piece of paper, note what you already know about the topic.

The remainder of the abstract is read to gain a sense of the subjects, research methodology, and findings. ④

The remainder of the background section is read to understand what other researchers know about young children's response to literature (paragraphs 1 and 2), a definition of "theme" (paragraph 3), and some results and limitations of other researchers (paragraphs 4, 5, 6, 7, and 8). ⑤

Lehr, S. (1988). The child's developing sense of theme as a response to literature. *Reading Research Quarterly*, 23, 337–357. Reprinted with permission of S. Lehr and the International Reading Association.

①
The Child's Developing Sense of Theme as a Response to Literature

Susan Lehr
Skidmore College

②
④ The purpose of this study was to characterize the nature of the child's sense of theme in narratives as it develops across three age levels, and to determine the role of familiarity with literature in that development. Kindergarten, second-, and fourth-grade students were given a literature inventory. High- and low-exposure groups were then chosen from the 10 highest- and 10 lowest-scoring students in each grade, for a total of 60 subjects. Children listened to a series of three realistic fiction and three folktale books; two of the three books in each genre shared a common theme, as judged by university students. The author then interviewed the children individually, asking them to identify books with similar themes and to state the themes. Interview transcripts were analyzed, and thematic statements were rated for congruence with text and level of abstraction. Ability to identify theme appears to develop early; kindergarten children were able to identify thematically matched books for 80% of the realistic books and 35% of the folktales. Children's ability to generate thematic statements correlated highly with exposure to literature; those in the low-exposure group frequently gave responses that were too concrete or too vague. Kindergarten children most often gave responses that differed from adult choices but were congruent with the text, suggesting that the child's perspective of meaning differs from that of the adult. Kindergarten children were able to summarize stories and to consider the reactions of characters. Second- and fourth-grade children were able to analyze and make generalizations about the stories.

⑤ [1] Evidence from main idea research using expository passages has suggested that young children can *recognize* main ideas, but lack the ability to generate main idea statements (Baumann, 1981; Dunn, Matthews, & Bieger, 1979; Otto & Barrett, 1968; Taylor, 1980; Tierney, Bridge, & Cera, 1978–1979). However, expository text is structurally quite different from narrative (Meyer, 1977), and less frequently encountered by young children (Baker & Stein, 1981; Baumann, 1981).

[2] Studies of children's ability to generate meaning from narrative passages have shown that elementary age children have the ability to interpret themes in narrative text (Brown, Smiley, Day, Townsend, & Lawton, 1977; Christie & Schumacher, 1975; Danner, 1976; Meyer, 1977; Waters, 1978). Less is known about children's ability to generate thematic statements, or about the role of narrative literature in the child's developing sense of theme.

[3] The term *theme* has been defined by Lukens (1982) as "the idea that holds the story together, such as a comment about either society, human nature, or the human condition. It is the main idea or central meaning of a piece of writing" (p. 101). Huck, Hepler, and Hickman (1987) write that "the theme of a book reveals the author's purpose in writing the story," and that "theme provides a dimension to the story that goes beyond the action of the plot" (p.

19). Thus, a theme is an abstraction and can link stories and ideas in general terms without including specific elements of plot.

[4] Because a child's initial book encounters typically include illustrated storybooks and nursery rhymes, a child's sense of theme may develop from his or her earliest encounters with narrative. When an adult reads a story to a young child, how does the child perceive the meaning of the story, and how is that meaning generated? Applebee (1978) found that in telling their own stories, children 2–5 years old did not typically generate a thematic center or clear focus. However, other results have been found in studies with slightly older children. Korman (1945, cited in Yendovitskayz, 1971) studied the narrative recall of 4- to 6-year-old children in the Soviet Union and found that the material was related in a logical sequence and that certain episodes containing lower-level information were deleted in the retellings, particularly those not pertinent to the theme of the story. To extend this work, Christie and Schumacher (1975) tested kindergarten, second-, and fifth-grade children, and corroborated that the kindergarten child is more capable of "abstracting and producing relevant thematic information than has previously been assumed."

[5] In most studies of children's ability to generate meaning from narrative passages (Brown, Smiley, Day, Townsend, & Lawton, 1977; Christie & Schumacher, 1975; Danner, 1976; Meyer, 1977; Waters, 1978), researchers have not clearly distinguished between identifying theme and generating statements of theme. Children were not specifically asked to generate thematic statements, and results were based on analyses of children's retellings of stories. Moreover, in these studies none of the stories used were natural texts. In the passages used, story elements were often manipulated or deleted, and some of the passages included intrusive elements that students were forced to ignore. Some of the passages were too short to develop a meaningful context or were of low interest. And, in some studies, simplified texts were used for all ages tested. None of the studies used book-length texts with extended plot, setting, and characterization and with multiple themes.

[6] In addition, in most studies, prepared or audiotaped passages were presented in lieu of real books with pictures. It could be argued that these were unnatural book sharing experiences for the children tested, and that, as a result, the researchers were unable to elicit natural responses. Huck, Hepler, and Hickman point out that the picture book "conveys its message through two media, the art of illustrating and the art of writing. In a well-designed book in which the total format reflects the meaning of the story, both the illustrations and text must bear the burden of narration" (1987, p. 197). Thus, as Cochran-Smith argues, "it seems problematic to separate text and pictures, rather than to treat them as integral parts of the beginning reading/comprehension process" (1984, p. 11). Because of this interdependency, texts from picture books may "suffer a loss of meaning and significance when separated and displayed" (Marantz, 1977, p. 148).

[7] Siegel (1983) asked fourth-grade children to read books and draw sketches of what the books meant. The nature of sketching, according to Siegel, allowed a reader to reconsider the initial meaning-world and allowed the student to engage in signification rather than mere representation. That is, students related what was read to the specific context and moved from perception to interpretation. Children independently linked pictorial and written symbols in order to achieve clarity and organize ideas. Many of the written conventions used by the children were meaningful only in light of the context. Thus, one of Siegel's major findings was that interpretations by children cannot be explained in terms of reader and text alone, but instead require a consideration of the total reading event.

[8] Also, a child's initial book encounters are typically interactive in nature (Cazden, 1966). Flood (1977) has found that interaction during, before, and after the book sharing ex-

perience can elicit a high range of response from children. As children grow older, the book-sharing experience changes from home to school; however, one component remains: Pictures are shared during read-aloud experiences with picture books. To strip the context of pictures changes the quality of the interaction. None of the studies to date have been conducted in naturalistic settings where children are allowed to see and touch the actual books as they are read aloud.

③ [9] The major purpose of this study was to characterize the nature of the child's sense of theme in narratives as it develops across three age levels, and to determine the role of literature in that development. In particular, I wanted to explore in a naturalistic setting how young children learn to represent meaning in their encounters with books, and to describe how familiarity with high-quality literature might affect a child's developing sense of theme.

SUMMARY

The background section contains an introduction to the researchers' problem area and the educational importance they place on their study. Researchers also provide a brief literature review of other researchers' results that are related to their problem area. Researchers usually indicate strengths from the related research that were used in their study and weaknesses or limitations that were changed. Based upon an examination of the related literature, a researcher determines whether to develop a new study, replicate, or repeat, a study. It is common to find the researchers' purposes at the end of this section. Some research reports contain traditional hypotheses, which often are stated as directional or nondirectional research hypotheses. Nondirectional hypotheses are statements that a possible influence exists but the researcher does not indicate whether it is a positive or negative influence. Directional hypotheses contain statements of the specific way one variable will affect another. In many professional journals, the background section is preceded by an abstract, a summary of the report.

Ability Grouping and Student Friendships

Maureen T. Hallinan
University of Notre Dame

Aage B. Sørensen
Harvard University

This study examines the effects of membership in the same ability group on student friendships. We argue that assignment to the same instructional group increases opportunities for student interaction, underscores student similarities, and produces new similarities, and that these factors foster friendship. The relationship between grouping and friendship is examined in a longitudinal data set containing information on students in 110 reading groups in 32 classrooms of fourth, fifth, and sixth grades. The results show that the density of best friend choices within ability groups increases over time, the overlap between ability groups and cliques increases over time, and membership in the same ability group has a positive effect on the probability that a student will choose a peer as best friend.

[1] An extensive number of research studies have examined the effects of ability grouping on students' academic achievement. In contrast, little attention has been paid to the effects of ability grouping on children's social relationships. This is unfortunate since the development of students' social skills is an important dimension of schooling and the organization of students for instruction is likely to have an impact on this development. This paper aims to enhance understanding of the process of friendship formation in the classroom by examining how grouping children by ability for instructional purposes affects their friendship choices.

ABILITY GROUPING AND FRIENDSHIP FORMATION

[2] Grouping students for instruction is likely to affect student friendships in a number of ways. The most fundamental way is by constraining students' proximity and limiting their interactions. Instructional grouping facilitates interaction among students assigned to the same group and hinders it among students in different groups, at least for the duration of an instructional period. Face-to-face interaction is believed to have a positive effect on friendship (Hinde, 1979; Homans, 1950; Newcomb, 1961), and empirical studies demonstrate this positive relationship in classrooms (e.g., Byrne, 1961; Eder, 1975). Thus, ability grouping is likely to promote the formation of friendships within groups by increasing student interaction within ability groups and decreasing it across groups.

[3] Propinquity is a necessary but not a sufficient condition for interpersonal attraction. Once opportunities for interaction are provided, characteristics of individuals become bases for attraction. One of the strongest determinants of positive sentiment is similarity. Ability grouping brings together students who are similar in academic ability or achievement. In some classrooms where achievement is related to social class or ethnicity, grouping also clusters students by these background characteristics. Being assigned to the same group makes students' common traits more obvious. Ability grouping also creates expectations on the part of

students and presumably teachers for similar student performance within a group, which may lead students to behave more like each other than they would if they had not been grouped together.

[4] Ability grouping not only underscores existing similarities among students; it also fosters the development of new similarities. Students assigned to the same ability group engage in the same learning tasks, use the same materials, and are exposed to the same pace of instruction. Sharing the same learning environment creates new similarities among group members in attitudes, values, norms, and behaviors. These new similarities, in addition to those that existed before the students were grouped together, are the basis for friendship formation among students assigned to the same group.

[5] The amount of time students spend in ability groups clearly determines the magnitude of the effect of grouping on friendship. In early elementary grades, students are grouped primarily for reading but are also frequently grouped for mathematics and occasionally for other subjects. Group membership is often identical across curricula. The more time students spend together in the same instructional groups, the greater are the constraints placed on their interaction patterns and the more time there is for the social and psychological processes that foster friendship within groups to occur. Since ability groups generally are stable over a school year (Hallinan & Sørensen, 1983), the effects of grouping are expected to be cumulative over time with a denser within-group friendship network occurring at the end of the school year than at the beginning.

[6] This study tests the hypothesis that membership in the same ability group has a positive effect on the choice of a peer as close friend for elementary school children. The relationship between grouping and friendship is studied by examining the density of the friendship network in ability groups over the school year, by looking at change in the overlap between ability groups and cliques over the year, and by determining the effects of membership in the same ability group on the probability that a student selects a classmate as a close friend. The predictions are that ability group density and the overlap between ability groups and friendship cliques will increase over time and that membership in the same ability group will have a positive effect on a student's choosing a classmate as best friend.

ACTIVITIES

Use the research reading plan and the evaluation criteria on p. 98 to read and evaluate the abstracts and background sections on pp. 102–106.

Scruggs, T. E., Mastropieri, M. A., Levin, J. R., & Gaffney, J. S. (1985). Facilitating the acquisition of science facts in learning disabled students. *American Educational Research Journal, 22,* 575–586. Copyright 1985 by the American Educational Research Association. Reprinted by permission of the publisher.

Facilitating the Acquisition of Science Facts in Learning Disabled Students

Thomas E. Scruggs
Margo A. Mastropieri
Utah State University

Joel R. Levin
University of Wisconsin

Janet S. Gaffney
Arizona State University

Fifty-six learning disabled students were presented materials describing minerals of North America. For each mineral, the students had to learn three associated attributes: the mineral's hardness level, its color, and its common use. The students were randomly assigned to four different methods of study. The two principal conditions were direct instruction, where students were taught eight minerals according to the basic principles of direct instruction (in particular, student participation with repeated drill and practice), and mnemonic instruction, where students were shown thematic illustrations that integrated each of the eight minerals and its attributes. Also included were a reduced-list direct-instruction condition, where students were required to learn only half the number of minerals (i.e., four minerals) in the same amount of allotted time as in the other conditions, and a free-study condition, where students were instructed to learn the eight minerals however they wished. The results supported previous findings that learning was superior in the mnemonic instruction condition. In addition (a) mnemonically instructed students learned as much about eight minerals in the same amount of time that direct-instruction students learned about four minerals; and (b) direct instruction per se did not facilitate students' learning relative to free study. Implications of the results for handicapped learners are discussed.

[1] Mnemonic (memory-enhancing) strategy instruction has recently been found to result in dramatic increases in learning and retention for learning disabled (LD) and educable mentally retarded (EMR) students when compared with more traditional instructional approaches (Mastropieri, Scruggs, & Levin, 1985, in press; Mastropieri, Scruggs, Levin, Gaffney, & McLoone, 1985; Scruggs, Mastropieri, & Levin, 1985). Because learning and retention of factual information remain major problems in the education of these mildly handicapped learners (Worden, 1983), research efforts to improve their memory performance would

seem to be of critical importance (see Levin, 1981).

[2] A mnemonic strategy that has been extremely effective in helping students to recall factual information is the *keyword method* (Atkinson, 1975). The keyword method incorporates the "three R's" of associative mnemonic techniques (Levin, 1983). First, it has a *recoding* component, where an unfamiliar term is transformed into a concrete, familiar word that sounds like a salient part of the to-be-learned term. In a vocabulary-learning context, for example, the new vocabulary item *viaduct* could be transformed into the keyword *duck*. Second,

the keyword method invokes its *relating* component, where the keyword is linked to a desired response via an interactive episode. For *viaduct*, meaning *bridge*, a duck could be pictured waddling across a bridge. Finally, the third component of the method provides the learner with a systematic means of *retrieving* the meaning of the new vocabulary word. In the present example, to retrieve the meaning of *viaduct*, the learner is led directly from the stimulus (*viaduct*) to the keyword (*duck*) to the interactive picture (a duck crossing a bridge) to the correct response (*bridge*).

[3] Mastropieri, Scruggs, Levin, Gaffney, and McLoone (1985) successfully used the keyword method to teach LD junior high school students a set of 14 new vocabulary words. In comparison to a direct-instruction approach that is generally recommended for such students (Engelmann, Osborn, & Hanner, 1978), mnemonic instruction resulted in a substantially higher level of vocabulary learning. Scruggs et al. (1985) obtained similar results in a study where EMR junior high school students learned the definitions of vocabulary words according to *both* instructional methods, in a within-subjects crossover design. Of particular relevance to this study, however, is that the keyword method can be extended to a variety of curriculum domains, as well as combined with other mnemonic techniques, to become a potentially versatile learning strategy (see Levin, 1985a).

[4] For instance, Mastropieri, Scruggs, and Levin (1985) taught Moh's Hardness-of-Minerals Scale (Bishop, Lewis, & Sutherland, 1976) to ninth-grade LD students according to a combined keyword-"pegword" mnemonic strategy. With the pegword method, the numbers 1–10 are recoded as familiar rhyming words (e.g., *1* is *bun*, *2* is *shoe*, *3* is *tree*, etc.). Mnemonically instructed students were provided with interactive illustrations of keywords for the minerals and pegwords for their associated hardness levels. For example, the keyword for *apatite* was *ape*, and the pegword for its

associated hardness level of 5 was *hive*. The interactive illustration consisted of an ape stirring up a hive full of bees. Again, note that when learners are asked for the hardness level of *apatite*, "apatite" should trigger the keyword *ape*, which should remind them of the picture of the ape and the beehive. From this picture, they should be able to retrieve the correct hardness level of 5 (from *hive*). In the Mastropieri, Scruggs, and Levin (1985) investigation, mnemonically instructed students recalled over twice as many minerals as students who either received "direct-questioning" instruction (basically a repeated question-and-answer procedure) or were allowed to study the minerals on their own ("free study").

[5] Inasmuch as the direct-questioning condition of that investigation did not conform exactly to the essential elements of direct instruction (Rosenshine, 1979), two experiments were conducted to compare mnemonic instruction with direct instruction as more precisely defined in terms of the following components: rapid pace, interaction with the experimenter, and direct questioning and feedback (Mastropieri, Scruggs, & Levin, in press). In the first experiment, procedures were employed with LD adolescents, whereas in the second experiment the subjects were EMR adolescents. In both experiments students in the mnemonic condition substantially outperformed students in the direct-instruction condition.

[6] Although such results are promising, several unanswered questions remain. First, it is important to determine whether mnemonic instruction will facilitate students' ability to associate multiple attributes of a term or concept with each other. In the present context, in addition to learning the hardness level of a particular mineral, can students simultaneously learn other attributes of the mineral, such as its color and common use? The learning of multiple attributes is thought to have strong implications in many content areas. For example, in geography students are required to learn

multiple features of states and countries, in history they learn multiple causes of an event or multiple facts about a famous person, and in biology they learn multiple functions of systems and organs. This learning of multiple attributes is thought to constitute an important aspect of concept learning (e.g., Klausmeier, 1976). Although recent evidence suggests that mnemonic techniques *do* lend themselves to the simultaneous acquisition of multiple attributes in nonhandicapped learners (e.g., Levin, Shriberg, & Berry, 1983; McCormick & Levin, 1984), whether or not similar benefits will be realized in an LD population remains to be seen. Such was the primary focus of the present study.

[7] Second, because a free-study control group was not employed in the Mastropieri, Scruggs, and Levin (in press) study, an evaluation of direct instruction per se could not be made. All that could be concluded was that mnemonic instruction led to a higher level of performance than direct instruction. A second purpose of the present study, therefore, was to determine whether the efficacy of direct instruction could be substantiated in this content domain. It is one thing to expect direct instruction to be effective, and yet quite another to demonstrate it empirically.

[8] Finally, the inclusion of a second direct-instruction condition permitted a sup-plementary gauge of the relative efficacy of that approach. In particular, some would argue that learning much information in a limited time (here, three attributes for each of eight minerals in about 7 minutes) is not conducive to the power of direct instruction. Consequently, a direct-instruction condition was included in which students were given the same amount of time as in the other conditions, but they were presented only four of the eight minerals to learn ("reduced-list" direct instruction). If more extensive practice with fewer items is necessary for direct instruction to be effective in this context, then the reduced-list version of direct instruction constitutes an interesting baseline against which to assess the tradeoffs associated with the other forms of instruction. That is, what are the relative "costs" incurred in each of those conditions by having to learn twice as many items in the same amount of time?[1]

[9] In summary, this study was designed to address the above concerns by (a) requiring that two additional mineral attributes (color and common use) be learned along with the hardness-level information; (b) incorporating a free-study control condition; and (c) including a direct-instruction condition in which students had to learn only half the information presented in the other conditions.

FEEDBACK

Hallinan & Sørenson (1985)

Abstract

The abstract contains information about the major aspects of the research. It contains the purpose and directional hypothesis, the subjects, and the results. It does not, however, contain specific subject characteristics and information about what instruments were used to measure friendship.

Background

The background section identifies the problem area and indicates the importance of grouping students and the development of their friendships. Related literature is cited, but there is no critical analysis of the research methodology used in those studies. Although they do not state it explicitly, the researchers (in paragraphs 3, 4, and 5) imply three conditions that may not have been addressed in the related literature: (a) previous similarity, (b) new similarities, and (c) time. The research hypotheses (paragraph 6) are clear and the independent variables (group membership and time) and the dependent variable (friendship) are easily identified.

Scruggs, Mastropieri, Levin, & Gaffney, 1985

Abstract

Information about the major aspects of the research are presented. In comparison to the previous abstract, this one contains extensive information especially about the treatment procedures.

Background

The problem area and the importance of the treatment variable as a teaching method are stated. The previous literature is reviewed and the researchers' involvement in previously studying the topic is explained. The questions still unanswered by their and others' research are listed (beginning with paragraph 6). However, the specific research purposes are not listed separately at the end of the section; they are embedded within separate paragraphs. Of the three purposes, only one is clearly identified: by the words "a second purpose of the present study" (paragraph 7). The first purpose is found by the words "such was the primary focus of the present study" (paragraph 6), but the reader must go back to previous sentences to actually find the purpose. There is no direct clue to the third purpose (paragraph 8). The research variables, therefore, are not easily identified.

5

Reading and Evaluating Subject Sections

FOCUS QUESTIONS

1. What are populations and target populations?
2. What are samples and subjects?
3. What considerations should researchers have about subject selection?
4. What criteria should be used to evaluate subject sections?
5. What considerations should researchers have about sample size?

In subject sections, which are subsections within larger sections called method sections, researchers describe the individuals, objects, or events used in their studies. In most cases, researchers wish to apply the answers to research questions to others in addition to their subjects. The hypothetical research team discussed in Chapter 1 were concerned about the extent to which their results could be applied. They were concerned about questions such as: Are the answers applicable only to the students in one specific school, grade level, or class? Are the answers to be used for the students in an entire district, state, region, or nation? Of course, subjects can be others besides students: Subjects can be teachers, principals, parents, nonschool age individuals (preschoolers or adults), or entire groups (e.g., classes, schools, or teams), and so on.

Subjects can also be nonhuman. For example, subjects can be groups of textbooks or groups of classrooms (the physical aspect of the rooms without consideration for the people in them). In such cases, researchers may be interested in studying the physical characteristics of the books or rooms. In this text, the discussion focuses on human subjects;

nevertheless, the same principles of subject selection apply equally to human and nonhuman subjects. Research consumers can use the same criteria for judging the appropriateness of nonhuman subjects as they use for judging the appropriateness of human subjects.

The larger groups of subjects to whom researchers wish to apply their results constitute **populations**, which are groups of individuals or objects having at least one characteristics that distinguishes them from other groups. Populations can be any size and can include subjects from any place in the world. For example, a population of human subjects could be "students with learning disabilities," or "fourth grade students," or "beginning teachers." In these cases, the populations are large and include people with many additional characteristics, or variables. The existence of these other variables makes it unlikely that the population will be fully homogeneous and that the research answers are equally applicable to all. "Seventh grade social studies textbooks" is an example of a nonhuman subject population. Researchers, therefore, narrow the range of the population by including several distinguishing variables. This results in the defining of a **target population**, which is the specific group to which the researchers would like to apply their findings. It is from target populations that researchers select **samples**, which become the subjects of their studies.

Subject sections contain relevant information about the sample and how it was selected. Subject information might include age, gender, ethnicity (e.g., Black, Hispanic, Native American), ability levels (e.g., mental maturity or intelligence), academic performance (e.g., test scores), learning characteristics, affect (e.g., emotional stability, attitudes, interests, or self-concept), and geographic location (e.g., New York State, Chicago, rural/suburban, Australian). Subject selection information should include the number of subjects, procedures for identifying subjects, methods of actual subject selection, and, in the case of experimental research, steps for assigning subjects to groups or treatments. From a subject section, research consumers should be able to answer

What was the intended target population?

Who were the subjects?

How were the subjects selected and did the researchers show bias in their sampling procedures?

Were the subjects truly representative of the target population?

How were the subjects assigned to groups or treatments in experimental research?

Will the research results be applicable to my teaching situation and the students I teach (am I part of the target population? Are my students part of the target population)?

Subject sections should be evaluated using the following questions, which are from Figure 3.1 p. 87.

Evaluating Subject Sections

Are target populations and subjects, sampling and selection procedures, and group sizes clearly described?

Are these appropriate for the research design?

CONSIDERATIONS IN SUBJECT SELECTION

In subject sections, researchers should provide information about (a) the target populations, (b) the sampling processes, and (c) the sample sizes.

Target Populations

Answers to researchers' questions should be applicable to individuals other than those included in the study. The group to which they wish to apply their results is the target population. When researchers can apply their results to the target population, the results are considered to be **generalizable**. An example of how a researcher identified target populations within larger populations is found in a comparative study entitled "Concepts of Reading and Writing Among Low-Literate Adults" (Fagan, 1988). The researcher's purpose was to provide information about the perceptions of reading and writing held by low-functioning adults (the population). The subjects were selected from target populations. In the following portion of the subject section, the number of subjects is indicated along with descriptions of the target populations. (Specific information about sampling procedures has been omitted from this example.)

A possible purpose for reading the study would be to gain information to help in planning an adult literacy program.

[Subjects]

[Target populations]

Two groups of each of 26 adults who were functioning below a grade 9 reading achievement level were selected—one designated as prison inmates and the other as living in mainstream society. Prison inmates were defined as sentenced prisoners in a medium–minimum correctional institution housing approximately 300 prisoners. Adults living in mainstream society were defined as noninstitutionalized adults, that is, not living in prisons, mental, or old age institutions. They were considered "ordinary" people who had freedom of movement, and who could use such city facilities as transportation, recreation, and social interaction. (Fagan, 1988, p. 48)

Because of practical considerations, researchers may not always have equal access to all members of the target population. For example, researchers might wish their target population to be urban, primary grade students in cities of at least 500,000 people having 20 percent or more Spanish-speaking students. An examination of the U.S. Department of Education census shows that there are at least ten such cities, including Los Angeles, Houston, Miami, and New York. The researchers might be able to use the entire target population as their subjects, or they might choose to select some subjects to represent the target population. More realistically, researchers work with **accessible populations**, which are groups that are convenient but are representative of the target population. Practical considerations that lead to the use of an accessible population include time, money, and physical accessibility.

Researchers should fully describe their accessible populations and their specific subjects so that research consumers can determine the generalizability of the findings. It is the research producers' responsibility to provide the necessary descriptive information about target populations and subjects. It is the research consumers' responsibility to make the judgments about the appropriateness of the subjects to their local situation. In evaluating subject sections, research consumers can be critical of the researchers only if they have not provided complete subject information.

The Sampling Process

If researchers' results are to be generalizable to target populations, the subjects must be **representative** of the population. A representative group of subjects, called the **sample**, is a miniature target population. Ideally, the sample would have the same distribution of relevant variables as found in the target population. It is those relevant variables that researchers describe in subject sections. For example, one researcher (Swanson, 1985) felt it important to keep the same ratio of gender and ethnicity in the sample as found in the target population. She investigated whether socioeconomic status, reading ability, and student self-report reading attitude scores were differentiated by teacher judgments or reading enthusiasm.

> The sample consisted of 117 first-grade students from seven classrooms in a school system located in northeastern Georgia. The rural county has a population of approximately 8,000, of which 37.3 percent is non-white. The racial and gender composition of the sample maintained a representative balance. Students repeating first grade, absent during initial testing, and/or not present during reading achievement assessment were deleted from the study. (Swanson, 1985, p. 42)

The most common procedure researchers use to ensure that samples are miniature target populations is **random sampling**. Random sampling works on the principle of randomization, whereby all members of the target population should have an equal chance of being selected for the sample (Borg & Gall, 1983; Gay, 1988; Kerlinger, 1973). And, the subjects finally selected should reflect the distribution of relevant variables as found in the target population. Any discrepancy between the sample and the target population is referred to as **sampling error**.

The following does *not* illustrate a random sample because it is not known whether all classes had an equal chance of being selected and whether the students in selected classes represented all the students in the grade level. The classes may have been heterogeneous, but it was not indicated whether they were equal. Although the principals may have tried to be objective, there may have been an unconscious bias.

> One self-contained, heterogeneous classroom of third-grade students (N = 22) and one self-contained, heterogeneous classroom of fifth-grade students (N = 23) from a rural school district in the midwestern U. S. participated in the study. The third-grade classroom was one of three in a K-4 building, while the fifth-grade classroom was one of two in a 5–8 building. The participating classrooms were selected by the building principals. (Duffelmeyer & Adamson, 1986, p. 194)

The following *is* an example of random sampling because each subject had an equal chance of selection from among the students at each grade level.

> Thirty-two children were tested at each grade level: second, third, fourth, and sixth. An equal number was randomly chosen from each of three different elementary schools in a Midwestern city of 50,000. The city is a predominantly white, middle class community. Subjects were replaced by other randomly selected students if they failed a vocabulary reading test. (Richgels, 1986, p. 205)

Random sampling is conceptually, or theoretically, accomplished by assigning a number to each member of the target population and then picking the subjects by chance. One way researchers used to do this was by placing everyone's name in a hat and drawing out numbers (Popham & Sirotnik, 1967). A simpler way and one which is more commonly used in current research studies is to assign numbers to each possible subject and then use a list of subjects' numbers randomly created by a computer program. The specific way researchers randomize is not important. The important consideration for research consumers is that a randomized sample has a better chance of being representative of the target population than does a nonrandomized one, and therefore, the researchers' results are more likely to be generalizable to the target population.

INTERPRETING EDUCATIONAL RESEARCH

In addition to randomly selecting subjects, it is common in experimental studies for researchers to randomly assign the subjects to treatments. The following subject section, from a study about the occurrence of behaviors that reflect social competence components and informational-processing components of problem solving, illustrates this double randomization procedure.

[Random selection]

[Random assignment]

Subjects for the study were 48 children from a middle-class, midwestern school system who were participants in a larger Logo project. From a pool of all children who returned a parental permission form (more than 80% return rate) 24 first graders (10 girls, 14 boys; mean age 6 years, 6 months), and 24 third graders (13 girls, 11 boys; mean age, 8 years, 8 months) were randomly selected. Children were randomly assigned to either Logo or drill and practice treatment groups, so that 112 in each treatment group were from first grade and 12 were from third grade. (Clements & Nastasi, 1988, p. 93. Copyright 1988 by the American Educational Research Association. Reprinted by permission of the publisher.)

An extension of random sampling involves stratification. In a **stratified random sample**, the subjects are randomly selected by relevant variables in the same proportion as those variables appear in the target population. One example of nonrandomized stratified sampling is shown above in the example with subjects from Georgia. Although the sample was stratified, the researchers did not indicate whether the subjects were randomly selected.

The National Assessment of Educational Progress (NAEP), which is financially supported by the U.S. Department of Education and conducted by the Education Commission of the States, uses a complex form stratified random sampling. To obtain subjects,

NAEP employs a deeply stratified, multistage sampling design. . . . In the first sampling stage, the United States is divided into geographical units, including Standard Metropolitan Statistical Areas and counties or groups of contiguous counties. These are stratified according to region and size of community. In the second stage, schools are randomly sampled within selected first-stage units. Finally, from 10 to 25 age-eligible students are randomly selected within schools, for testing. (Haertel, Walberg, Junker, & Pascarella, 1981, p. 333)

As indicated previously, subjects may be intact groups, for example, classes to which students have been preassigned. When intact groups are selected, the procedure is called **cluster sampling**. Intact groups are selected because of convenience or accessibility. This procedure is especially common in causal–comparative research. If a number of intact groups from a target population exist, researchers should randomly select entire groups as they would individuals.

The following subject description, which illustrates cluster sampling, is from a study that examined the instructional organization of classrooms and tried to explain why students achieved in some classes but not in others. Note that the researchers do not indicate whether their "preselected" classes were chosen through random procedures.

> This study was conducted during the math instruction of eight sixth-grade classes in four elementary schools in a school district in southwest Germany. These classrooms had been preselected out of total population of 113 sixth-grade classes in this school district. . . . Altogether, 195 students and their 8 math teachers participated. (Schneider & Treiber, 1984, p. 200)

Regardless of the nature of researchers' sampling procedures, an important concern in all designs is the use of **volunteer subjects**. Volunteers by nature are different from nonvolunteers because of some inherent motivational factor. Results from the use of volunteer subjects might not be directly generalizable to target populations containing seemingly similar, but nonvolunteer, individuals or groups. For example, researchers using volunteers to study the effect of a particular study-skill instruction on social studies achievement might be able to generalize their results only to students who are motivated to learn and use such a procedure in school. Nonvolunteers might need a different kind of instruction to be successful in that subject. Researchers, then, are faced with a seemingly unanswerable question: Can results from research with volunteers subjects be generalized to nonvolunteer subjects?

The issue has wide implications, especially when human subjects are used in experimental research. It has become uniform practice within the educational research community to require the prior permission of subjects. In cases when the subjects are minors (under the age of 18 years), permissions from parents or guardians are necessary. Granting of permission is a form of volunteering. Permission for including human subjects is not a problem in descriptive or correlational research because (a) confidentiality is maintained through the use of grouped rather than individual data collection procedures and (b) such research does not involve intrusive activities. For example, an ethical and legal concern might be raised by subjects when they are assigned to what becomes a less effective treatment. They may say their educational progress was hindered rather than enhanced by the instructional activity.

Sample Sizes

The size of samples is important to researchers for statistical and practical reasons. There are several practical issues researchers need to consider. In collecting data, researchers must consider factors such as the availability of research personnel, the cost involved in paying personnel and securing instruments and materials, the time available for collecting and analyzing data, and the accessibility of subjects.

More important, researchers who want to generalize from the sample (the smaller group) to the target population (the larger group) should do this with as little statistical error as possible. Statistically, the size of the sample influences the likelihood that the sample's characteristics are truly representative of those of the target population (Borg & Gall, 1983, Gay, 1987; Kerlinger, 1973). That is, the distribution of relevant variables found in the sample should not be significantly different from that of the target population. Any mismatch between the sample and the target population caused by an inadequate sample size will also contribute to sampling error.

ACTIVITIES

Activity 1

Using the focus questions at the beginning of this chapter) as a guide, summarize the chapter's key ideas.

Activity 2

Read each of the following subject sections. The researchers' research purposes have been included for your information. Using the questions and criteria on pp. 109–110, evaluate the studies. For each, list questions and concerns you may have about

a. Characteristics of the subjects
b. The sampling procedures
c. The representativeness of the subjects in relation to the target populations
d. The appropriateness of the subjects for the researchers' purposes

Extract A

The study (a) examined the effectiveness of three methods of teaching social studies concepts to fourth-grade students, (b) tested the effects and interaction of gender and reading ability on the treatments, and (c) tested propositions concerning concept teaching: Is there a need for definitions, examples and nonexamples, and question/practice?

Sample

The sample consisted of 85 subjects drawn from 10 sections of fourth-grade classes at an elementary school located in the suburbs of a small- to medium-sized southern city. Subjects were randomly assigned to one of three treatment groups. Only those subjects who returned parental permission forms were included in the random assignment. Three experienced classroom teachers, all of whom were females, administered the treatment. (McKinney, Larkins, Ford, & Davis, 1983, p. 664)

Extract B

The purposes of the study were (a) to describe children's out-of-school activities, with a special focus on reading, and (b) to examine the relationship of out-of-school activities to reading achievement.

Subjects

The subjects were 155 fifth-grade students, 52 from two classrooms in a village school and 103 from five classrooms in a school in a middle-class area of a small city. Both communities are in east central Illinois. There were 85 boys and 70 girls in the total sample. Although there were some blue collar, low-income, and minority children in the sample, these groups were underrepresented in terms of their proportions in the nation as a whole. On the Metropolitan Achievement test, the sample was above the national average (mean percentile rank = 62.9), but showed a typical spreading in ability (SD = 25.6). Although the sample included a number of poor readers, no child was identified by teachers as a nonreader. (Anderson, Wilson, & Fielding, 1988, p. 287)

FEEDBACK

Activity 1

What are populations and target populations?

The groups of people or objects to whom researchers wish to apply their results constitute populations, which are groups having at least one characteristic that distinguishes them from other groups. A target population is the specific group to which the researchers would like to apply their findings.

What are subjects and samples?

Subjects are the individuals or groups included in the study. A representative group of subjects, called the sample, is a miniature target population. Ideally, the sample would have the same distribution of relevant variables as found in the target population.

What considerations should researchers have about subject selection?

Subjects should be representative of the large population so results can be generalized from the subjects to the target population. Random sampling, or randomization, works on the principle that all members of the target population have an equal chance of being selected for the sample. The subjects finally selected should reflect the distribution of relevant variables as found in the target population.

INTERPRETING EDUCATIONAL RESEARCH

What questions should be used to evaluate subject sections?

From reading the subject sections, research consumers should be able to answer

> What was the intended target population?
>
> Who were the subjects?
>
> How were the subjects selected and did the researchers show bias in their sampling procedures?
>
> Were the subjects truly representative of the target population?
>
> How were subjects assigned to groups or treatments in experimental research?
>
> Will the research results be applicable to my teaching situation and the students I teach (am I part of the target population? are my students part of the target population)?

What considerations should researchers have about sample size?

Research producers and consumers should be sensitive to any mismatch between the sample and the target population caused by an inadequate sample size. The mismatch is a source of error, called sampling error. The probability of making an error relative to sample size is unique to each data analysis procedure.

Activity 2

Extract A

The subjects were volunteer (by parental permission) fourth grade students from one elementary school in a suburban medium-sized southern city. No information was provided about specific demographic characteristics (e.g., age, gender, ethnicity, learning abilities, or percentage of the total student body whose parents volunteered). Since all volunteers in the convenience sample were used, the researchers randomly assigned them so that subject variables were equally distributed across the three treatments. There is no specific way to judge from the given information whether the subjects were representative of the target population or whether the results can be generalized to other fourth grade students. As for the researchers' purposes, the sample seems appropriate.

Questions and concerns might be raised about the characteristics of (a) the subjects in relation to the target population and (b) the volunteered students in relation to the nonvolunteered students. As a consumer, you might ask: Would the results about these instructional programs be appropriate for the students I teach?

Extract B

The subjects were fifth grade students from one rural community and one small city in central Illinois. The demographic characteristics of the subjects in relation to a potential national target population was explained. The actual target population, then, would be middle class fifth graders from the Midwest who scored above average as readers on a standardized achievement test.

Questions and concerns might be raised about (a) whether the sample is representative of villages and small cities in the Midwest (or even Illinois) and (b) the generalizability of these results beyond the target population. As a consumer, you might ask: What applicability would these results have to my teaching situation?

6

Reading and Evaluating Instrumentation Sections

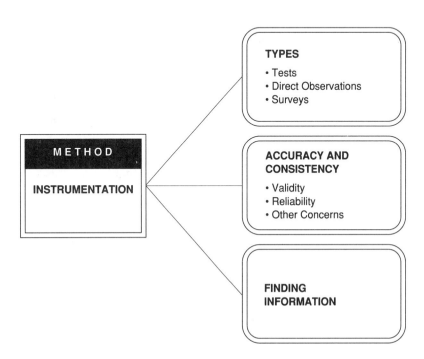

METHOD

INSTRUMENTATION

TYPES
• Tests
• Direct Observations
• Surveys

ACCURACY AND CONSISTENCY
• Validity
• Reliability
• Other Concerns

FINDING INFORMATION

FOCUS QUESTIONS

1. What are the different types of instruments used in research projects?
2. How is information from different instruments reported?
3. What are instrument validity and reliability, and how are they determined?
4. What criteria should be used to determine whether instruments are appropriate for the research?
5. Where can information about instruments be found?
6. How are research report instrument sections read and evaluated?

Researchers use instruments to collect data within all types of research designs. The term **instruments** is used to denote a broad range of specific devices and procedures for collecting, sorting, and categorizing information about subjects and research questions. Research consumers need to understand (a) what instruments are available to educational researchers, how instruments categorize information, and how data from different instruments are reported; (b) what criteria should be used to determine whether instruments accurately present information; and (c) how instrument sections in research reports are read and interpreted.

From an instrument section, research consumers should be able to answer

What type of instruments were used?

Were the instruments valid and reliable for the research project?

Were the instruments appropriate for use with the target population and the research subjects?

Will the research results be applicable to my teaching situation and the students I teach because the instruments are appropriate for use with the students I teach?

Instrument sections should be evaluated using the following questions, which are from Figure 3.1, p. 87.

EVALUATING INSTRUMENT SECTIONS

What instruments are used in the study?

Are they appropriate for the design of the study?

Are the instruments valid for collecting data on the variables in the study?

Are reliability estimates given for each instrument?

Are researcher-made instruments included (or at least samples of the instrument items)?

Is information about the development of these instruments presented?

Are the instruments appropriate for use with the target population and the research subjects?

TYPES OF INSTRUMENTS

Researchers collect data with tests, direct observation, and surveys. These instruments provide data about subjects' characteristics (as reported in subject sections) and about subjects' responses in various situations (as reported in procedure sections) in reports of all three kinds of research. Information about instruments discussed in any section of a research report is usually described in the instruments section.

Tests

Test information includes scores from individual or group standardized norm-referenced tests, standardized criterion-referenced tests, competency tests, and researcher made tests.

A **standardized test** is one for which the tasks and procedures of administering, recording, scoring, and interpreting are specified so other testers can make comparable measurements in different locations (Harris & Hodges, 1981). The test constructors use accepted procedures and research the test's (a) content, (b) procedures for administering, (c) system for recording and scoring answers, and (d) method of turning the results into a usable form. Everything about the test has been made uniform (standardized) so that if all its directions are correctly followed, the results can be interpreted in the same manner, regardless of where the test was administered.

Standardized tests are of two main types: norm-referenced and criterion-referenced. Norm-referenced tests compare individuals' scores to a standardization, or norming, group. A norming group consists of individuals used in researching the standardization of the tests' administration. The section in this chapter called Validity and Reliability of Instruments contains a discussion about how to determine the appropriateness of a relationship between a norm group and a target population.

The scores from norm-referenced tests are reported as standard scores (e.g., SS = 53), grade equivalents (e.g., GE = 4.6), percentiles (e.g., 67th percentile, or percentile rank = 67), stanines (e.g., 5th stanine, or stanine = 5), or normal curve equivalents (e.g., NCE = 72). Each of these scores can be used to describe subjects' characteristics or subjects' relative performance. Additional information about the different types of scores is in Chapter 8, Reading and Interpreting Results Sections.

In the following example, from a subject section, percentile scores are used to describe the subjects.

Purpose of the study: to determine if subject matter text could be rewritten so students' comprehension of unfamiliar topic words could be enhanced.

[Sample]
[Stratified]

Subjects were 55 eighth grade students enrolled in two state history classes at a university laboratory school. They first were stratified by reading ability according to their reading percentile scores on a standardized achievement test (Stanford Achievement Test, 1981), and then grouped by high and average ability levels. The high ability group, with 28 subjects, had scores ranging from 75–99, with a mean score of 89.28 (SD = 7.14). The average ability group, with 27 subjects, had scores ranging from 12–68, with a mean score of 47.80 (SD = 12.59). (From Konopak, 1988, p. 4)

[Percentiles]

Criterion-referenced tests compare students' responses to specified expected learner behaviors or to specified expected levels of performance (Harris & Hodges, 1981). Scores on these tests show students' abilities and performances in relation to sets of goals. They do not show subjects' rankings compared to others, as norm-referenced tests do. A standardized criterion-referenced test is one for which the administration and scoring procedures are uniform but the scoring is in relation to the established goals, not to a norm group.

Direct Observation

When collecting data from **direct observation**, researchers take extensive field notes or use observation forms to record the information. They categorize information on forms in response to questions about subjects' actions or categories of actions. Or, researchers tally subjects' actions within some predetermined categories during a specified time period. Field notes consist of written narratives describing subjects' behavior or performance during an instructional activity. These notes are then analyzed, and the information is categorized for reporting. The analysis can start with predetermined categories, and information from the notes is recorded accordingly. Or, the analysis can be open-ended in that the researchers cluster similar information and then create a label for each cluster.

The following description of an observational assessment and the information in Figure 6.1 are from a naturalistic investigation (Clements & Nastasi, 1988). Notice how the researchers explain their instrument and provide examples of the behaviors to be categorized.

Purpose of the study: To study the occurrence of first- and third-grade students' behaviors that reflect social competence components and information-processing components of problem solving while using computers in school.

Instruments

Observational assessment of social behaviors. The observation scheme was adapted from a more comprehensive instrument (covering six components of social competence) developed by the second author to assess social behaviors (Nastasi & Clements. 1985). Behavioral indicators of social problem solving included cooperative work, conflict, and resolution of conflict. Indicators of effective motivation included self-directed work, persistence, rule determination, and showing pleasure at discovery. Appendix 1 lists the behaviors observed and provides an operational definition of each. Reliability of the instrument was assessed in previous research; interrater agreement, established through simultaneous coding of behaviors by two observers, was 98% (Nastasi & Clements).

Observational assessment of information-processing components. As stated, initial analysis of the data on social behaviors revealed that (a) one of the most striking differences between the experimental (Logo)

Observation Scheme for Social Behaviors

Behavior	Definition
Social problem solving Cooperative work	Child works with another child on an academic task (i.e., jointly engages in computer activity) without conflict. (As opposed to cooperative play—engagement in nonacademic activities or conversation not related to the task at hand.)
Conflict	Child engages in verbal or physical conflict with another child.
Resolution of conflict	Child reaches successful resolution of conflict, without adult intervention.
Effectance motivation Self-directed work	Child initiates or engages in an independent work activity without teacher's coaxing or direction: includes constructive solitary or parallel work.
Persistence	Child persists on a task after encountering difficulty or failure without teacher's coaxing or encouragement.
Rule determination	Child engages in self-determination of rules, for example, making plans or establishing parameters of a problem situation. Includes use of verbal heuristics for solving problems.
Showing pleasure	Child shows signs of pleasure at solving a problem or at discovery of new information (e.g., child cheers after reaching a solution).

Observation Scheme for Information-Processing Components

Component	Definition	Examples
Metacomponents Deciding on nature of the problem	Determining what the task is and what it requires	"What do we make here?" "We gotta go over here, then put lines around it like our drawing."
Selecting performance components	Determining how to solve the problem: choosing lower order components	"Read the list [of directions] again, but change all the LEFTs to RIGHTs for this side." "How are we gonna make this thing go over this way? We did RIGHT 20. What's 90 − 70 . . . 20, right? We need not RIGHT 90, but 70!" "We got to add these three numbers."
Combining performance components	Sequencing the components selected	"First you have to get it over that way a little . . . LEFT 45, then FORWARD 30." "We'll make the turtle go up this way about 10, then RIGHT 90 and 10 down, then FORWARD halfway—5—and we're done."

Figure 6.1 (pp. 123–124) Sample information from an observational assessment. (From Clements, D. H., & Nastasi, B. K. [1988]. Social and cognitive interactions in education computer environments. *American Educational Research Journal, 25*, 87–106. Adapted by permission of the publisher.)

Component	Definition	Examples
Selecting a mental representation	Choosing an effective form or organization for representing relevant information	No verbalizations recorded
Allocating resources	Deciding how much time to spend on various components	"That's enough time talking. We should draw it."
		"We got it" "Let's think and make sure."
Monitoring solution processes	Keeping track of progress and recognizing need to change strategy	"Put 70." "70? We already did 50 . . . type FORWARD 20."
		"You're gonna go off the screen, I'm telling you."
Being sensitive to external feedback	Understanding and acting upon feedback	"I know—if it's wrong it goes 'blub, blub, blub' and sinks down."
Performance components	Executing the task; includes encoding and responding	"5 times 7 is 35." "Type R-I-G-H-T-4-5." "It says, 'What is 305 − 78?' "
Other	Miscellaneous; includes off-task and uninterpretable verbalizations	"They're recording us, you know." "I'm tired of this; can we do another game?"

Figure 6.1 (Continued)

and control (drill and practice) groups was in determining rules and (b) as defined, the construct of rule determination was too general. The rule-determination category involved planning, establishing parameters for problem solving, and use of verbal heuristics. A more detailed framework was needed to differentiate among such metacognitive behaviors. Therefore, a scheme for categorizing information-processing components of problem solving was constructed based on the componential theory of Sternberg (1985). The following metacomponents were delineated in the present study: deciding on the nature of the problem; selecting performance components relevant for the solution of the problem; selecting a strategy for combining performance components; selecting a mental representation; allocating resources for problem solution; monitoring solution processes; and being sensitive to external feedback. Frequencies of behaviors indicative of each metacomponent were recorded. Performance components, used in the actual execution of a task, included such behaviors as encoding, applying, and reporting. These behaviors were relevant to problem solution, but not reflective of metacognitive processing. Because the investigation focused on metacomponential processes, behaviors were not defined more specifically than the "performance" category level. A final category of "other" included off-task behaviors. Appendix 2 presents the definitions and examples of behaviors for each category. Interrater agreement was 87%. (From Clements & Nastasi, 1988, p. 95. Copyright 1988 by the American Educational Research Association. Reprinted by permission of the publisher.)

In the above example, the researchers indicate that the material shown in Figure 6.1 provides an operational definition of each behavior. For example, for the behavior *Social problem solving, cooperative work*, they specify the particular subjects' activities that would be counted as an instance of the behavior. An **operational definition** is a definition of a variable that gives the precise way an occurrence of that variable can be seen. In the Clements and Nastasi study, the operational definitions were verbal. Operational definitions can also be test scores. In the Konopak study, high and average ability students were operationally defined by percentile ranges on the Stanford Achievement Test. (To aid research consumers in understanding technical vocabulary and determining the appropriateness of operational definitions, there are specialized professional dictionaries. Chapter 11, Locating Information About Research Reports, contains information about locating and using these dictionaries.)

Surveys

Surveys include questionnaires, interviews, scales, inventories, and checklists.

Questionnaires require the respondent to either write or orally provide answers to questions about a topic. The answer form may be *structured* in that there are fixed choices, or the form may be *open-ended* in that respondents can use their own words. Fixed-choice questionnaires may be called **inventories**. They may require subjects to simply respond to statements, questions, or category labels with a "yes" or "no," or they may ask subjects to check off appropriate information within a category.

Questionnaires also are used to collect information from files such as subjects' permanent school records. When the respondent answers orally and the researcher records the answers, the instrument is considered an interview. **Interviews** are used to obtain structured or open-ended responses. They differ from questionnaires in that the researcher can modify the data collection situation to fit the respondent's responses. For example, additional information can be solicited, or a question can be rephrased.

The following explanation of a fixed-response questionnaire is from a descriptive study, and sample questions from that questionnaire are presented in Figure 6.2.

Purpose of the study: To determine the nature, extent, and impact of preservice training for special educators working with parents.

Instrument

Survey I questionnaire is displayed as Figure [6.2]. Questions on the survey form included demographic information and series of questions designed to ascertain whether content on working with parents was

1. Approximate number of students in your department:
   undergraduate _____   graduate _____

2. What is your department's emphasis?
   ( ) categorical   ( ) cross-categorical

3. Does your department offer a course on *working with parents of exceptional students*?
   ( ) yes   ( ) no

   a. Is *working with parents of exceptional students* included as a component of another course?
      ( ) yes   ( ) no

   b. Is working with parents of exceptional students offered by another department?
      ( ) yes   ( ) no

   c. Is the course required by your department?
      ( ) yes   ( ) no

      At what level? (mark each that applies)
      ( ) graduate   ( ) undergraduate

   d. Is the course required for certification by your state's Department of Education?
      ( ) yes   ( ) no

Figure 6.2 Sample information from a questionnaire. (From Hughes, C. A., Ruhl, K. L., & Gorman, J. [1987]. Preparation of special educators to work with parents: A survey of teachers and teacher educators. *Teacher Education and Special Education, 10*, 81–87. Reprinted by permission of Special Press and The Teacher Education Division, The Council for Exceptional Children.)

offered [in college courses preparing special education teachers] and, if so, to what extent. Respondents whose departments [of special education] offered a course on this topic were asked to provide a course syllabus, which became permanent product data. (From Hughes, Ruhl, & Gorman, 1987, p. 82)

The following explanation of an inventory is from a study to develop a way to measure student achievement in terms of a school's local curriculum. Sample items from the inventory are presented in Figure 6.3. Notice that although the instrument was labeled an inventory, its items could easily be restructured as questions.

Purpose of the study: To describe a model for a school-wide curriculum-based system of identifying and programming for students with learning disabilities.

The final measure used in the [Curriculum-Based Assessment and Instructional Design] (C-BAID) process is the environmental inventory. Its purpose is to assist teachers in identifying factors that may facilitate or impede instruction in the classroom. It is used to provide information once a particular student is determined to be significantly discrepant from peers either academically, in work habits, or both. The checklist used in C-BAID is an adaptation of ones previously developed [by other researchers]. The inventory is based on the ABC model of instruction

Consequences   Teacher, target learner, and peer responses to learner behavior (c)

C1   Teacher response to correct answer:

meaningful immediate reinforcement _____
meaningful delayed reinforcement   _____
no reinforcement   _____

C2   Target learner response to success:

positive _____   negative _____   no response _____

C3   Peer response to target learner's correct answer:

positive _____   negative _____   no response _____

C4   Teacher response to incorrect answer:

immediate feedback _____   delayed feedback _____
modeled correct responses _____
required learner to imitate correct response _____
no corrective feedback _____
punishment or sarcasm _____

C5   Target learner response to incorrect response or failure:

guessed _____
corrected self _____
gave up and said "I don't know" _____
made another response _____ (please describe) _____
sat and said nothing _____
became negative and refused to work _____
became hostile (i.e., engaged in verbally and/or physically agressive behavior) _____

C6   Peer responses to target learner's incorrect answer:

positive _____   negative _____   no response _____

Figure 6.3 Sample information from an inventory. (From Bursuck, W. D., & Lesson, E. [1987]. A classroom-based model for assessing students with learning disabilities. *Learning Disabilities Focus, 3,* 17–29.)

and thus focuses on the Antecedents, or events taking place prior to or during instruction; the Behavior, or how learners perform; and the Consequences, or events taking place after learners have performed. Many of the variables selected for the inclusion in the environmental inventory have been shown to be positively correlated with academic achievement [by other researchers]. The environmental inventory can be conducted by the school psychologist or principal. Classroom teachers may also complete the inventory after a lesson has ended. A portion of the inventory is shown in Figure [6.3]. (From Bursuck & Lesson, 1987, pp. 23, 26)

Scales commonly measure variables related to attitudes, interests, and personality and social adjustment. Usually, data are quantified in predetermined categories representing subdivisions of the variable. Subjects respond to a series of statements or questions showing the degree or intensity of their responses. Unlike data from tests, which are measured in continuous measurements (e.g., Stanines 1 through 9, or Percentiles 1 through 99), data from scales are discrete measurements. The discrete measurements in scales force respondents to indicate their level of reaction; common forced choices are "Always," "Sometimes," or "Never." This type of data quantification is called a **Likert-type scale**. Each response is assigned a value; a value of *1* represents the least positive response.

The following explanation of a scale is from a study to assess parent attitudes toward employment and services for their mentally retarded adult offspring. Although the report does not include sample items from the survey, the presentation of the results, as shown in Figure 6.4, clearly states that a Likert-type scale was used in the original form.

Purpose of the study: To assess parent/guardian attitudes toward employment opportunities and adult services for their own mentally retarded, adult sons or daughters who are currently receiving services from adult community mental retardation systems.

PARENTAL ATTITUDES TOWARD WORKING CONDITIONS

Perceptions of Current Working Conditions		Preferred Working Conditions	
Condition	Percent	Condition	Percent
Average Current Wages		*Preferred Wages*	
No pay	41%	No pay	5%
Less than $1/hour	23%	Less than now	.4%
$1.01 to $2.50/hour	10%	Same as now	49%
$2.51 to $3.34/hour	3%	More than now	25%
Above $3.35/hour	3%	Much more	12%
Don't know	21%	Not sure	9%
Current Interaction with Nonhandicapped		*Preferred Interactions*	
Never	7%	Less than now	2%
Rarely	13%	Somewhat less	4%
Sometimes	22%	Same as now	54%
Frequently	46%	Somewhat more	30%
Don't know	11%	Much more	10%
Current Responsibility and Advanced Opportunities		*Preferred Responsibility and Advancement Opportunities*	
Never	36%	Less than now	0%
Rarely	13%	Somewhat less	.4%
Sometimes	28%	Same as now	59%
Frequently	25%	Somewhat more	28%
Don't know	17%	Much more	12%

Figure 6.4 Sample information from a Likert-type scale. (From Hill, J. W., Seyfarth, J., Banks, P. D., Wehman, P., & Orelove, F. (1987). Parent attitudes about working conditions of their adult mentally retarded sons and daughters. *Exceptional Children, 54*, 9–23.)

INTERPRETING EDUCATIONAL RESEARCH

Perceptions of Current Working Conditions		Preferred Working Conditions	
Condition	**Percent**	**Condition**	**Percent**
Current Level of Work Without Supervision		*Preferred Level of Work Without Supervision*	
Never	17%	Less than now	0%
Rarely	13%	Somewhat less	2%
Sometimes	28%	Same as now	52%
Frequently	25%	Somewhat more	29%
Don't know	17%	Much more	17%
Requirements to Exhibit "Normal" Behavior During Work		*Preferred Level of Requirements Exhibit "Normal" Behavior During Work*	
Never	14%	Less than now	3%
Rarely	7%	Somewhat less	5%
Sometimes	16%	Same as now	66%
Frequently	25%	Somewhat more	20%
Don't know	38%	Much more	7%
Current Performance of Same Tasks as Nonhandicapped Workers		*Preferred Level of Performance of Same Tasks as Nonhandicapped Workers*	
Never	19%	Less than now	9%
Rarely	14%	Somewhat less	3%
Sometimes	19%	Same as now	61%
Frequently	21%	Somewhat more	28%
Don't know	26%	Much more	7%

Vocational Placement

Current Placement		*Preferred Placement*	
Institution	10.4%	Institution	5.6%
Home (no program)	17.2%	Home	4.0%
Activities center	23.3%	Activities center	25.6%
Sheltered workshop	43.7%	Sheltered workshop	52.0%
Competitive employment	5%	Competitive employment	12.8%

Attitudes Toward Work

Work should be a normal part of life for my son or daughter.

Strongly Disagree	Mildly Disagree	Not Sure	Mildly Agree	Strongly Agree
4%	2%	18%	16%	60%

Figure 6.4 (Continued)

The format of the survey for the attitude section was a Likert-type scale. In this section [of the survey], parents were asked to indicate the degree to which they perceived that their sons or daughters were currently exposed to the six qualitative conditions already listed *and* their opinions regarding the optimal amount of exposure to each practice. Therefore, attitude questions were presented in pairs. The first of the pairs asked for the parents' attitude toward the *current* situation as they perceived it and the second of the pair asked the parents for the *preferred* situation on each issue. The first item of the pairs permitted responding on a four-point Likert scale ranging from "never" (1) to "frequently" (4); a *don't know* response was (5). The responses on the second of the paired items regarding preferences employed a five-point continuum, which ranged from *much less than now* (1) to *much more than now* (5) [see Fig. 6.4]. (From Hill, Seyfarth, Banks, Wehman, & Orelove, 1987, p. 12)

ACCURACY AND CONSISTENCY OF INSTRUMENTS

Researchers are concerned that data they collect with various instruments are accurate and consistent. They wish to be sure they have positive answers to questions such as "Do the data represent real aspects of the variable being measured?" and "Will the data be similar if the instrument is administered a second or third time?" These questions refer to an instrument's validity and reliability. **Validity** refers to the extent that an instrument measures what it is intended to measure. **Reliability** refers to the extent that an instrument measures a variable consistently.

Additional information about the validity and reliability of instruments, including concerning observations, is found in Chapter 7, Reading and Evaluating Procedure Sections.

Validity of Instruments

Instruments have validity when they are appropriate for a specific purpose and a particular population. To use an instrument with confidence, researchers must know the answers to, "Does the instrument measure what it is intended to measure at the time it is being used?" and "Are the results generalizable to the intended target population?" These questions imply that instruments are not universally valid. Instruments are considered valid only for clearly identified situations and populations.

The creators of instruments (tests, observation procedures, and surveys) are responsible for establishing the validity of their instruments. When researchers use others' instruments, they must present evidence that the instrument is valid for the research project. When researchers create new instruments for their projects, they must detail how they established the instrument's validity. Research consumers want to know, "Does the instrument provide a real picture?"

An instrument's validity is investigated using one or more of several generally accepted procedures. Even though each procedure can be used to determine an instrument's validity, research consumers need assurance that the particular way an instrument was validated makes it appropriate for a particular research project.

One validation procedure establishes that an instrument has been developed according to a supportable educational, sociological, or psychological theory. The theory can relate to any human characteristic or to any aspect of society. A theory is based on supportable research and tries to explain the nature of human behavior (such as intelligence

INTERPRETING EDUCATIONAL RESEARCH

or learning) and action (such as teaching). A theory's usefulness depends on how clearly it explains those behaviors and actions. A theory should not be considered as complete; it should be considered adequate only for describing a particular set of conditions, but not all conditions. Any theory must be modified or even discarded as new evidence is encountered, and every theory should (a) explain a complex phenomenon (such as reading ability, the nature of learning disabilities, mathematics aptitude, or the social interaction within a classroom), (b) describe how the phenomenon operates, and (c) provide a basis for predicting changes that will occur in one aspect of the phenomenon when changes are made in other aspects. When an instrument's creator demonstrates the instrument as representing a supportable theory, it is said to have **construct validity**. Research consumers should expect every instrument to have construct validity. It is the researcher producers' responsibility to select an instrument with a construct validity appropriate for the research question, purpose, or hypothesis.

In the example that follows, the developers of a reading comprehension test, the Test of Reading Comprehension (TORC), explain their theoretical frame of reference.

> To many users the *Test of Reading Comprehension: A Method for Assessing the Understanding of Written Language* (the TORC) will represent a significant departure from traditional ways of viewing and measuring reading comprehension. This means that they will need to become thoroughly familiar not only with its administration and interpretation but also with its development and with the philosophies on which it is based.
>
> This chapter is intended to acquaint the practitioner with our frame of reference in regard to the testing of reading comprehension ability. The development of the viewpoints expressed has been guided by (1) our study of the theoretical issues in reading and language behavior, (2) by a review of applied research in reading, language, and test construction, and (3) by noting some of the diagnostic needs expressed by practitioners. The sections that follow provide information about (1) the historical perspectives on reading comprehension, (2) the concepts employed from psycholinguistic theory, and (3) the nature of reading comprehension. (From Brown, Hammill, & Wiederholt, 1978, p. 5)

A second validation procedure establishes that the instrument is measuring a specific body of information. This is an important consideration, especially when the instrument is an achievement or performance test. An instrument that is intended to measure science achievement should contain test items about the specific information the users (subjects or students) had the opportunity to learn in science classes. For example, achievement tests appropriate for use at the elementary level should contain items that test facts, concepts, and generalizations normally found in typical elementary school science curricula. When an instrument's creators demonstrate they represent accurate samplings of specific bodies of knowledge (ie., curricula or courses of study), they are said to have **content validity**. Instruments' creators establish content validity by submitting the instruments' items to groups of authorities in the content areas. It is their expert opinions that determine whether the instruments have content validity. Before research consumers can generalize research results, it must be determined that any instrument's content is appropriate (valid) for their educational situation and student population.

In the following example, from a study to assess the perceptions and opinions of students who completed teacher education programs, the researchers explain the source of their questionnaire's content. (The "Dean's Grant" to which they refer was a federally funded grant competition for the development and implementation of preservice teacher preparation models that would prepare regular and special education teachers for the mainstreaming of special education students.)

Purpose of the study: To assess the perceptions and opinions of students who completed the teacher education program at a large midwestern university.

A questionnaire comprising four parts was used to survey students. In part 1, respondents rated 34 competency statements related to mainstreaming of handicapped students on two scales. On the first scale, the Coverage Scale, respondents rated the extent to which they thought mainstream content had been covered in their teacher education program. On the second scale, the Knowledge Scale, they rated their knowledge of the mainstream curriculum content. The 34 statements were adapted from competency statements developed during the early years of the Dean's Grant that were still being used as guidelines for infusing mainstream curriculum throughout the undergraduate program. (From Aksamit & Alcorn, 1988, p. 54)

An aspect of content validity is **face validity**. Face validity refers only to the extent to which an instrument *appears* to measure a specific body of information. In other words, "Does the instrument look as if it would measure what it intends to measure?" Does a mathematics test look like actual mathematical tasks? Instruments' users, or other subject area experts, usually establish face validity by examining the test without comparing it to a course of study (curriculum).

A third validation procedure establishes the extent an instrument measures something to the same degree as does another instrument. The second instrument must previously have had its validity established by one or more accepted procedures. To establish validity for a new instrument, the instrument's creator administers both instruments to the same group of individuals. The extent to which the results show the individuals correlated, or scored similarly on both instruments, is an indication of **concurrent validity**. This is a common procedure for establishing an instrument's validity, but research producers and consumers must interpret the new instrument's results with some caution. They must be sure of the older instrument's construct and content validity. If the older instrument has questionable construct or content validity, the new instrument may *not* be appropriate even though there is high concurrent validity with that older instrument. Research consumers should expect evidence about the comparison instruments' validity. Research producers should indicate the instrument used to establish concurrent validity and data about the level of correlation.

Information about an instrument's concurrent validity is usually found in studies whose purpose is to develop or assess an instrument. The following example is taken from such a study. It should be noted that the reported negative correlations were a desired result since the two instruments measure students' behavior in inverse ways.

Purpose of the study: To revise and standardize a checklist of adaptive functioning designed for school use at the kindergarten level.

> *Concurrent Validity with Walker Problem Behavior Identification Checklist*
>
> [Twenty] students from grade levels kindergarten, 2, 4, and 6 . . . were also used to examine the concurrent validity of the revised [Classroom Adaptive Behavior Checklist]. The teachers of these selected students were asked to complete both the revised checklist and the Walker Problem Behavior Identification Checklist (Walker, 1976), with a return rate of 70%.
>
> The overall Pearson correlation between the total scores on the revised checklist (where higher scores indicate more adaptive behavior) and on the Walker (where higher scores indicate more problem behavior) was $-.78$ (df = 54, p < .001). The correlation for kindergarten, grades 2, 4, and 6 were, respectively, $-.77$, -84, $-86.$, and $-.95$. (From Hunsucker, Nelson, & Clark, 1986, p. 70)

A fourth validation procedure establishes the extent an instrument can predict a target population's performance after some future situation. This **predictive validity** is determined by comparing a sample's results on the instrument to their results after some other activity. An example of predictive validity is the ability of college admissions officers to predict college students' first-year grade point average from their scores on the Scholastic Aptitude Test (SAT).

Reliability of Instruments

Instruments have **reliability** when they are consistent in producing their results. To use an instrument with confidence, researchers must know the answers to "Does the instrument measure what it is intended to measure in a consistent manner?" and "Are the results going to be similar each time the instrument is used?" The implication of these questions for research producers and consumers has to do with dependability and the degree to which the results can be trusted. Reliability is not an either-or phenomenon; reliability is a statistical estimate of the extent to which the results can be considered dependable.

The creators of instruments (tests, observation procedures, and surveys) are responsible for establishing the reliability of their instruments. When researchers use others' instruments, they must present evidence of the instruments' reliability. When researchers create new instruments for their projects, they must detail how they established the instrument's reliability. Research consumers want to know, "Does the instrument give a dependable picture of data?"

Evidence of an instrument's reliability is demonstrated with one or more of several generally accepted procedures. Even though each procedure is an estimate of an instrument's reliability, research consumers need assurance that the particular way an instrument's reliability was determined deems it appropriate for a particular research project. Whatever procedure is used, the reliability of an instrument is given in a numerical form called the **reliability coefficient**. The coefficient is expressed in decimal form, ranging from .00 to 1.00. The higher the coefficient, the higher the instrument's reliability.

The common procedures for establishing an instrument's reliability are (1) test–retest reliability, (2) equivalent forms reliability, (3) internal consistency reliability, and (4) scorer or rater reliability.

Test–retest reliability is determined by administering the same instrument again to the same subjects after a time period has elapsed. When subjects' results are statistically compared, researchers gain evidence of the instrument's reliability over time, or its stability.

Equivalent forms reliability (sometimes called *parallel forms reliability*) is determined by creating two forms of an instrument. The instruments differ only in the specific nature of the items. The same subjects are given both forms, and their results are statistically compared.

Internal consistency reliability, which is sometimes called *rationale equivalence reliability*, is determined by statistically comparing the subjects' scores on individual items to their scores on each of the other items and to their scores on the instrument as a whole. **Split-half reliability**, a commonly used form of internal consistency, is determined by dividing the instrument in half and statistically comparing the subjects' results on both parts. The most common way to split a test is into odd and even numbered items.

Scorer or **rater reliability**, which is sometimes called *interrater* or *interjudge reliability*, is determined by comparing the results of two or more scorers, raters, or judges. Sometimes scorer reliability is presented as a percentage of agreement and not as a coefficient.

In the following example, which is taken from a previously cited study about the standardization of a behavior checklist (Hunsucker, Nelson, & Clark, 1986), two methods of establishing the instrument's reliability are used. Both methods, test–retest and inter–teacher, involve the use of the Pearson correlation formula, which is explained on p. 192.

Purpose of the study: To revise and standardize a checklist of adaptive functioning designed for school use at the kindergarten level.

Test–Retest Reliability

Subgroups of 20 subjects from grades kindergarten, 2, 4, and 6 were randomly selected from the normative group to examine the test–retest reliability of the revised checklist. The teachers of these students were asked to complete the checklist twice over a 4-week period (X elapsed days = 31.3), with a return rate of 66.2%.

Using the Pearson correlation coefficient on total checklist scores, test–retest reliability was .72 for kindergarten (n = 11), .95 for grade 2 (n = 11), .89 for grade 4 (n = 15), and .67 for grade 6 (n = 26). Using the exact agreement method for specific checklist items (agreements on both occurrence and nonoccurrence divided by total number of items), test–retest reliability was .90 for kindergarten, .92 for grade 2, .90 for grade 4, and .89 for grade 6.

Interteacher Agreement

Subgroups of 15 subjects from grade levels 1, 3, and 5 who were in team-taught classrooms were selected from the normative group to examine interteacher agreement for the revised checklist. Both teachers in the teaching team completed checklists for 68.8% of these selected students.

Using the Pearson correlation coefficient on total checklist scores, interteacher agreement was .92 for grade 1 (n = 11), .86 for grade 3 (n = 10), and .89 for grade 5 (n = 10). Using the exact agreement method for specific checklist items, interteacher agreement was .92 for grade 1, .93 for grade 3, and .86 for grade 5. (From Hunsucker, Nelson, & Clark, 1986, p. 70)

In the following example, from a study involving the use of various phonemic awareness tests, the researcher uses an internal consistency reliability procedure. Note that although the type of reliability procedure is not indicated, the researcher reports a commonly used statistical formula used—the Cronbach alpha. Another commonly used formula for establishing internal consistency reliability is the Kuder–Richardson formula 20.

Purpose of the study: To determine the reliability and validity of tests that have been used to operationalize the concept of phonemic awareness.

The reliability of each test was determined using Cronbach's alpha. Seven of the tests had high internal consistency, with alpha $> .83$. The Roswell–Chall (1959) phoneme blending test showed the greatest reliability (alpha $= .96$) followed closely by the Yopp–Singer phoneme segmentation test (alpha $= .95$). Two tests showed moderate to high reliability: Rosner's (1975) phoneme deletion test (alpha $= .78$) and the Yopp rhyme test (alpha $= .76$). The Yopp modification of Wallach's (1976) word-to-word matching test had the lowest reliability (alpha $= .58$) for this sample. (From Yopp, 1988, p. 168)

Other Concerns About Instruments

A common concern about instruments deals with how and by whom instruments are administered. An instrument may have validity and reliability, but the person using it must be competent and must use it in appropriate settings. For example, certain standardized tests must be administered by fully trained and qualified examiners. Standardized tests requiring special training and certified personnel include the Wechsler Intelligence Scale for Children—Revised and the Stanford–Binet Intelligence Scale, 4th edition. All instruments, whether they are tests, observations, or surveys, should be administered by appropriately trained personnel.

The following three passages illustrate how researchers indicate instrument users' proficiencies.

Purpose of the study: To investigate differences in parent-provided written language experiences of intellectually superior nonreaders and accelerated readers.

Test Administration. All 125 potentially gifted children were administered the *Stanford-Binet Intelligence Test* and Letter-Word Identification subtest from the *Woodcock-Johnson Psycho-Educational Battery* by certified examiners. (From Burns & Collins, 1987, p. 243)

Purpose of the study: To compare students' instructional placements as predicted by a standardized test and an informal reading inventory.

All of the tests were administered over a period of about six weeks (three per grade) by a research assistant trained in the use of both the [*Degrees of Reading Power*] and the [informal reading inventory]. (From Duffelmeyer & Adamson, 1986, p. 195)

Purpose of the study: To determine the effects of education, occupation, and setting on reading practices.

Procedures. A guided interview was constructed based on a review of previous research in measuring reading practice (Guthrie & Seifert,

1984). Two enumerators were recruited who were paid for their services. They had considerable experience in conducting surveys but were not experienced with reading activity inventories. In a 4-hour training session, they were informed about the purpose of the survey, taken step by step through the inventory, and given a demonstration of its administration. The enumerators individually interviewed an adult wage earner in each designated household. (From Guthrie, Siefert, & Kirsch, 1986, p. 152)

A factor that may be important in test administration is the familiarity of the examiner to the subjects. Research evidence seems to show that some subjects' scores increase when they are tested by familiar examiners (Fuchs & Fuchs, 1986, 1989). Since researchers cannot always establish examiner–subject familiarity (because of time constraints or expense), research consumers need to be aware of the possible effect on results of subjects' unfamiliarity with examiners.

A second concern is when, in descriptive research, surveys or questionnaires are mailed to potential respondents. A major concern to researchers is the representativeness of the returned surveys or questionnaires. Usually, a return rate of about 70% is considered adequate to ensure that the obtained responses represent those of the entire target population (Gay, 1987, p. 201). When the percentage of returns is lower, researchers should conduct follow-up activities to get additional questionnaires. Also, when the return rate is the minimum acceptable, research consumers should be concerned whether there is a difference in traits between individuals who respond to the questionnaires and those who do not.

FINDING VALIDITY AND RELIABILITY INFORMATION

Researchers do not always report the available information about instruments' validity and reliability. One reason for omitting validity and reliability information is the extensive reporting of it elsewhere. In such a case, researchers refer readers to the appropriate research report.

In the two examples that follow, the researchers use instruments whose validity information are reported elsewhere. Note that in both examples, the researchers report reliability data established in their research.

Purpose of the study: To improve understanding of the relationships between types of inservice training activities and changes in teaching behavior.

The Stallings Secondary Observation Instrument (SSOI) was used to measure teaching behavior. The validity measures obtained with this instrument in relation to student achievement and attitude has been established in previous studies (e.g., Stallings, Needels, & Stayrook, 1979). High interrater reliability (85% agreement or better) was established for the observers in this study. (From Sparks, 1986, p. 218)

Purpose of the study: To investigate the planning and debugging strategies and group processes that predicted learning of computer programming in small groups with students aged 11 to 14.

Six aptitude and cognitive style measures were administered at the beginning of the workshop. These were a test of mathematical computation and reasoning; a test of verbal inference; a short form of the Raven's Progressive matrices (Raven, 1958) to measure nonverbal reasoning ability; and three tests from the Educational Testing Service (ETS) kit of cognitive factor reference tests (French, Ekstrom, & Price, 1963): Surface Development (spatial ability), Gestalt Completion (holistic vs. analytic processing), and Hidden Figures (field independence). Internal consistency alpha for these tests ranged from .64 to .92 in this sample. (From Webb, Ender, & Lewis, 1986, p. 246)

Another reason for not including validity and reliability information is the instruments' extensive use in educational and psychological projects. It is assumed that their validity and reliability information are known by most of the research reports' readers. This is especially true when researchers use standardized tests such as the Wechsler Intelligence Scale for Children—Revised, the Metropolitan Achievement Tests, or the Woodcock Reading Master Tests.

Research consumers can refer to several readily available sources to locate information about instruments' validity and reliability. When the instrument is a standardized test, research consumers can refer to the administration and technical information manuals provided by an instrument's publisher.

Research consumers may find it helpful to rely on reviews of standardized instruments. These reviews can be found in special yearbooks and handbooks, professional journals, and professional textbooks. Chapter 11, Locating Information About Research Reports, contains information about how to locate and obtain authoritative reviews about instruments' validity, reliability, and appropriateness for target populations.

SUMMARY

What are the different types of instruments used in research projects, and how is information from different instruments reported?

Instruments are used to denote a broad range of specific devices and procedures for collecting, sorting, and categorizing information about subjects and research questions. Three types of instruments are used in research: tests, observations, and surveys. A standardized test is one for which the tasks and procedures of administering, recording, scoring, and interpreting are specified so that other testers can make comparable measurements in different locations. Standardized tests are of two main types: norm-referenced and criterion-referenced. Norm-referenced tests compare individuals' scores to a standardization, or norming, group. Criterion-referenced tests compare students' responses to specified expected learner behaviors or to specified expected levels of performance. Test information includes scores from individual or group standardized norm-referenced tests, standardized criterion-referenced tests, competency tests, and researcher-made tests. When collecting data from direct observation, researchers take extensive field notes or use an observation form to categorize the information. They record information on forms in response to questions about subjects' actions or categories of actions. Surveys include a broad range of devices for data collecting, such as questionnaires, interviews, scales, inventories, and checklists.

What are instrument validity and reliability and how are they determined?

Validity refers to the extent that an instrument measures what it is intended to measure. Reliability refers to the extent that an instrument measures a variable consistently. When an instrument's creator demonstrates the instrument as representing a supportable educational theory, it is said to have construct validity. When an instrument's creator demonstrates the instrument represents an accurate sampling of a specific body of knowledge, it is said to have content validity. An instrument's creator establishes content validity by submitting the instrument's items to a group of authorities in the content area. It is their expert opinions that determine whether the instrument has content validity. When the subjects' results on one instrument correlate, or result in a similar rank order of scores on another instrument, the new instrument is said to have concurrent validity. A fourth validation procedure establishes the extent to which an instrument can predict a target population's performance after some future situation. This is predictive validity.

The common procedures for establishing an instrument's reliability are (1) test–retest reliability, (2) equivalent forms reliability, (3) internal consistency reliability, and (4) scorer or rater reliability. Test–retest reliability is determined by administering the same instrument again to the same subjects after a time period has elapsed. When the subjects' results are compared, researchers gain evidence of the instrument's reliability over time, or its stability. Equivalent forms reliability is determined by creating two forms of an instrument. The instrument should be the same in every aspect except for the specific content of the items. The same subjects are given both forms, and their results are compared. Internal consistency reliability, which is sometimes called rationale equivalence reliability, is determined by comparing the subjects' scores on individual items to their scores on each of the other items and to their scores on the instrument as a whole. Split-half reliability, a common type of internal consistency reliability, is determined by dividing the instrument in half and comparing the subjects' results on both parts. The most common way to split a test is into odd- and even numbered items. Scorer or rater reliability, which is sometimes called interrater or interjudge reliability, is determined by comparing the results of two or more scorers, raters, or judges. Sometimes scorer reliability is presented as a percentage of agreement and not as a coefficient.

What questions should be used to determine whether instruments are appropriate for the research?

Research consumers should answer: What instruments are used in the study? Are they appropriate for the design of the study? Are the instruments valid for collecting data on the variables in the study? Are reliability estimates given for each instrument? Are researcher-made instruments included (or at least samples of the instrument items)? Are the instruments appropriate for use with the target population and the research subjects?

ACTIVITIES

Activity 1

Read each of the following instrument sections. The researchers' purposes have been included for your information. Using the questions and criteria on p. 120, evaluate the researchers' instrumentation. For each, list questions and concerns you may have about

a. The validity of the instruments
b. The reliability of the instruments
c. The appropriateness of the instruments for the target population and research subjects
d. The appropriateness of the instruments for the researchers' purposes

Extract A: The Cognitive Behavior Modification Study

Purpose of the study: To determine the effect of 8 hours of training based on cognitive behavior modification theory in regular grade 1 and 3 classrooms with children who had histories of mild classroom behavior problems.

Pretreatment measures. Classroom teachers completed the teacher rating scale of the Brown–Hammill Behavior Rating Profile Scale (BRP) (1983) for each subject. This tapped teachers' perception of the children's classroom behavior. A list of 30 descriptive words and phrases was rated by the teacher as one of the following: very much like the student, like the student, not much like the student, or not at all like the student. Examples of items are as follows: Is verbally aggressive to teachers or peers, Is disrespectful of others' property rights, and Can't seem to concentrate in class. The numerical range for this measure is a raw score of 0 to 90 and a standard score of 1 to 20.

Baseline observations were made to ascertain whether children were on or off task, with these evaluations made for 10-second intervals over a period of 30 minutes, with the final measure of time on task for a subject expressed as a percentage (number of 10 sec intervals on task/ total number of 10 sec intervals sample [180]). It proved possible for two raters to achieve very high interrater agreement (97%) for these ratings. On-task behavior was defined as eyes toward seatwork material, chalkboard, or other learning display centers; gathering materials immediately followed by other on-task descriptors; writing/drawing in conjunction with eyes on materials; reading assigned materials. Off-task behavior was delineated as being out of classroom; manipulating pencils, rulers, or paper; scribbling or doodling; being out of seat; talking with neighbors; whispering to someone else; motioning; making vocal noises (unrelated to work); making body movements (i.e., head on desk, head cupped in book, arms over head); not having eyes directed toward seatwork; leaning out of desk; manipulating objects on floor; being turned around in desk (Blount, 1985, p. 63). Each rater had participants' names, along with corresponding teachers' names, room numbers, and daily schedules. They used this information to plan the most efficient means of collecting baseline data (i.e., when subjects would be in their classrooms receiving direct instruction or completing independent seatwork while the teacher worked with small groups). (From Manning, 1988, pp. 194–195. Copyright 1988 by the American Educational Research Association. Reprinted by permission of the publisher.)

Extract B: The Voluntary Reading Study

Purpose of the study: To determine the attitudes of teachers, principals, and parents toward the importance of the development of voluntary reading in the school curriculum. The study also sought to determine the factors that contributed to those attitudes and the decisions that ensued from them regarding classroom practice.

MATERIALS

The questionnaire was designed to follow a strategy similar to the "policy capturing approach" described by Shavelson and Stern (1981) in an attempt to capture the judgement and decision-making processes of the individuals in the sample. It opened with a vignette suggesting that the school district with which each individual was affiliated was giving that teacher, principal, or parent authority to design and select materials, methods, and priorities for reading instruction. Four areas of reading instruction were named from which individuals had to make their decisions and define their priorities for the reading program: comprehension, word recognition skills, study skills, and development of voluntary reading.

Other questions sought to discover factors that affected those decisions about program and priority. Participants were asked both to rank and to rate the importance of the four areas of instruction in reading—that is, to assign a different number (1 for "the most important areas" through 4 for "the least important") to each of the four areas, then to rate each of the four on a scale of 1 to 5, 1 representing "most important," and 5 representing "least important." Thus, it was possible for an individual to assign the same rating to two or more areas, but not the same ranking. Similar Likert-type ratings were elicited concerning beliefs about conceptions of voluntary reading, institutional constraints, and personal interests that might determine personal attitudes and decisions. Subjects were told that the purpose of the investigation was to determine their attitudes towards the importance of different skills areas in the reading instructional program.

PROCEDURE

The questionnaires were delivered to teachers and principals by student teachers in the respective schools, then collected one week later. Questionnaires were mailed to parents, with a self-addressed, stamped return envelope enclosed with each questionnaire; follow-up telephone calls helped retrieve late or missing questionnaires.

The same student teachers observed and recorded by checklist the characteristics of classroom library corners, if any, that were maintained and used by teachers who participated in the study. One week after completion of the initial questionnaire, those teachers were asked to complete a checklist of their own indicating what kind of and how often literary activities were included in their own classroom instruction. It was the information from these observations and checklists that was compared with responses to the initial teacher questionnaires to determine relationships, if any, between teachers' attitudes and their classroom practices. (From Morrow, 1985, p. 119)

FEEDBACK

Activity 1

Extract A: The Cognitive Behavior Modification Study
The BRP is a standardized instrument, and the researchers seem to be assuming that readers have access to various sources containing this information. However, the researcher described the instrument and provided sample items. Operational definitions for on- and off-task student behaviors were provided as was reliability information established during the study. The instrument seemed appropriate for the researcher's purpose.

In regard to the instrument's construct validity, however, some

6. What distinguishes simple and complex experimental research designs?
7. What concerns should research consumers have about research procedures that are specific to causal–comparative research designs?
8. What concerns should research consumers have about single-subject, action, and evaluation research designs?
9. What questions should be used to evaluate procedure sections?

Researchers explain the specific way they conducted their research in procedure sections, which are subsections of method sections in research reports. If the researchers detail their procedures completely, other researchers can replicate the study. From a clear explanation of research procedures, research consumers can evaluate whether the study is free from bias and the influence of extraneous variables. Research consumers need to understand (a) how different types of research designs are implemented as studies (see Chapter 2), (b) what information should be included in procedure sections for the different types of research, and (c) what questions are used for determining whether procedure sections are complete.

From reading a procedure section, research consumers should be able to answer

What research design was used in the study?

What special procedures were used to collect data or conduct treatments?

What special materials were used?

Was the research free from researcher bias?

Can the study be replicated from the given information?

Procedure sections should be evaluated using the following questions, which are from Figure 3.1, p. 87.

EVALUATING PROCEDURE SECTIONS

Procedures: Are the research design and data collection procedures clearly described? Is the research design appropriate to the researcher's purpose? Can the study be replicated from the information provided?

Qualitative method: Has the researcher's presence influenced the behavior of the subjects?

Treatment: Are experimental procedures fully explained? Are examples of special materials included?

Research validity: Are the procedures free from the influence of extraneous variables? Does the study contain any threats to its internal and external validity?

UNDERSTANDING PROCEDURE SECTIONS

Besides understanding principles of subject selection (Chapter 5) and instrumentation (Chapter 6), research consumers need to understand steps taken by research producers to collect data, devise special materials, and implement treatments. Although there are unique procedures for some types of research, several procedures are common to all types of educational research.

First, research reports should have clear and complete explanations about every step of the research so that other researchers can replicate the study. In all types of studies, but especially in naturalistic and qualitative research, there should be clear explanations about the settings from which information is collected or in which treatments were given. Research producers should indicate not only what was done but where and when data collection or treatment procedures were carried out. Research consumers can identify vague procedure sections when there is inadequate information for answering the questions in Evaluating Procedure Sections.

Another procedure deals with the use of instructional materials. Researchers often study how subjects react to specific materials such as textbooks, stories, maps, graphs, and charts. These may be commercially produced or specially devised by researchers for the study. Research consumers need to be able to judge the appropriateness of the materials for the research situation and for use with the target population. Therefore, researchers should provide citations of published materials and samples of unpublished, specially devised materials.

A third common procedure deals with trying out the research procedures in a pilot study. A **pilot study** is a limited research project with a few subjects that follows the original research plan. By analyzing the results, research proceducers can identify potential problems. In descriptive, comparative, and experimental studies, researchers can see whether the data collection instruments (questionnaires, interviews, observations) pose any problems to the researchers or subjects. Researchers also have the opportunity to examine the need for modifying specially devised materials. Researchers should indicate that pilot studies were conducted and include information about modifications to instruments, materials, procedures, and treatments that resulted from analyses of the pilot study results.

Procedures in Descriptive Research

Descriptive research designs deal with explaining the status or condition of one or more variables or events. Research consumers should be concerned that information is valid, objective, and reliable and that variables or events are portrayed accurately.

In **observational research**, especially qualitative or naturalistic stud-

INTERPRETING EDUCATIONAL RESEARCH

ies, researchers need to be concerned about factors that might affect the replicability of their studies (LeCompte & Goetz, 1982). They need to be sure the data represent a true picture of what occurred and can be generalized to other situations. This refers to the **validity** of the research. Researchers also need to be sure that they are consistent in identifying aspects of a behavior or event so that others working in the same or similar situations could get similar results. This aspect pertains to the **reliability** of the research.

Several questions can help research consumers determine whether the results from observational studies—whether they be qualitative or quantitative—are valid.

Could the researchers actually have seen what they reported observing?

Are their conclusions applicable to other situations and groups?

Could the observers' presence possibly have influenced the collected data (that is, influenced the way subjects responded or events occurred)?

Could the observers have collected only unique or exotic information (data not representative of usual responses or events)?

Was there a major change in the make-up of the group being observed during the research period?

Several additional questions can help research consumers determine whether results from observational studies—whether they be qualitative or quantitative—are reliable.

What status did the researchers seem to have in the group being studied?

Did the researchers seem to select informed subjects from whom to obtain information?

Did the information seem to be collected in natural social contexts?

Were multiple observers used and was interrater reliability established?

Did it seem that data collection instruments were used unobtrusively?

The following method section is from a qualitative descriptive study. Note that the subjects subsection has also been included. In the procedures section, the researcher has provided information about the classroom instructional activity and about data collection and data analysis procedures.

Purpose of the study: To determine how often, when, and for what reasons a group of second-grade writers used their peers' questions to revise their unfinished pieces.

METHOD

Subjects

The study's site was a heterogeneously grouped second-grade classroom of a cooperative teacher in Delaware who was implementing the process approach to teaching writing as described by Graves (1983). Twenty-four students participated in the study, 16 girls and eight boys.

None of the children had participated in a process-oriented writing program previous to this academic year. All had been participating in such a program for three months when this investigation began.

Procedures

[Class activity]   The writing program was implemented two days per week for approximately one hour each session. Data were collected over 25 writing sessions between January and early June, 1985.

Consistent with Graves' recommendations, each writing session began with a minilesson, which was followed by the writing workshop, which was followed by a sharing session. The questions raised by peers during these group conferences and the revisions made by these young writers in their texts following the sharing sessions were the focus of this investigation.

During each sharing time, the children were divided randomly into three groups. Those children who wished to share an unfinished draft brought it to the group conference. Approximately one to three children shared their drafts during each sharing session in each small group. While children who had not shared recently were encouraged to share their draft, they were never required to receive their peer's questions.

During the sharing sessions, the writers sat in the author's chair, read their pieces, and called upon their peers for questions about the content of the piece. An adult in each group recorded the peers' questions. At the conclusion of each child's reading of his/her piece and receiving the peers' questions, the adult asked the writer what he/she planned to do next and how he/she planned to do it. At the end of the sharing time, the child attached the share questions to the draft and returned both papers to his/her writing folder.

[Data collection]   Prior to the next writing session, both papers were photocopied. This photocopy of the draft provided evidence of the text as it existed prior to the insertion of any of the information identified as missing by the peers' questions.

At the conclusion of the following writing session, the previously shared draft was photocopied a second time. This second photocopy provided evidence of the state of the text after the child had one writing workshop to insert the missing information.

Once every two weeks all folders were examined for evidence of the continuation of writing on a previously shared topic. Discovered drafts were photocopied.

[Data analysis] To determine how frequently the questions raised were used by these young writers, each question was compared against each appropriate text, by the researcher and a second rater, independently, to determine whether or not the child modified the text in the way suggested by his/her peers' questions. The two raters agreed on all but four revisions. These inconsistencies were discussed until agreement was reached.

To determine how the decision to publish a piece (Hubbard, 1985, had suggested that publishing provides children with a sense of audience and a reason for refining their work) affected the frequency of use of the peers' questions, the number of revisions made as a result of peers' questions in eventually published pieces was compared to the number of such revisions in never published pieces.

To determine why these writers chose to use only some of the peers' question, during May each child was questioned at the close of the writing workshop following his/her sharing to determine which peers' questions, if any, were used to revise the piece. If the child had not used all the questions, he/she was asked why he/she had decided not to use some questions. (From Vukelich, 1986, pp. 300–301)

Procedures in Comparative Research

In comparative research, researchers examine the descriptions of two or more variables so they can make decisions about their differences or relationships. Research consumers should use the questions listed above for procedures in descriptive research to determine whether the results from comparative research are valid and reliable.

The following method section, which includes the subject and procedure subsections, is from a quantitative comparative study of the relationship among several variables. The researchers have provided information about materials, instrumentation, scoring, and data analyses.

Purpose of the study: To examine the relationships between children's spelling ability and various aspects of their oral reading performance, specifically, rate, accuracy, and phrasing.

METHOD

Subjects

Seventy-two third-graders were the subjects in this study, 32 from an urban school and 40 from a suburban school, with a balanced number of boys and girls from each school.

Procedures

[Materials] A 500-word reading selection and a 25-word spelling list were used. Reading selections were checked for readability (Dale–Chall), clarity, cohesiveness and general familiarity of topic. The spelling list used was from the inventory standardized by Schlagal (1982). Subjects read the passages orally, knowing that they would be asked about the content afterward. These oral readings were taped and later scored for Rate, Accuracy, and Phrasing. A spelling list was given as a class test and scored for Spelling Accuracy, Phonetic Quality, and State of Spelling Development. Gates–MacGinitie reading tests were also given and scored for each subject.

While scoring procedures for Rate, Accuracy, and Spelling Accuracy were relatively straightforward, those used in generating scores for the other variables need some explanation. Phrasing scores were determined by rater judgment, using a modified version of the six-point scale developed by Allington and Brown (Allington, 1983). Interrater reliability was .96 (Rasinski, 1985). For Phonetic Quality, each spelling was scored either one or zero depending on whether all of the phonemes in the oral pronunciation of the word were represented in the appropriate order in the child's spelling attempt. However, this scoring was purposely extremely "lenient": any reasonable sound–letter pattern was scored one. Patterns typical of Letter Name stage of development (e.g., *chr* for *tr*, nasal omissions) and other later stages were also given credit.

Each child was also assigned to one of the Stages of Spelling Development described by Henderson (1985). These progressive stages of development were discovered and verified in a series of studies based on qualitative analyses of children's spelling attempts (Henderson & Beers, 1980). Procedures used to assign each child to a stage were very similar to ones used in those studies. Two points were allocated to each stage so that children deemed in transition between two stages received odd number scores.

Analyses

The data thus obtained were used to generate multiple correlations and multiple regression equations. A correlation matrix was generated to determine how the different variables were related. Each correlation was tested for statistical significance ($p < .05$). Then, a series of multiple regressions was run in which the spelling variables were used to predict each of the oral reading measures. A canonical correlation relating both sets of variables, reading and spelling, was also generated. Finally, partial correlations were computed using reading achievement test results as the controlling variable. (From Zutell & Rasinski, 1986, pp. 109–110)

Procedures in Experimental Research

In experimental research, researchers set out to answer questions about causation (Borg & Gall, 1983; Gay, 1987; Kerlinger, 1973). They wish to attribute any change in one variable to the effect or influence of one or more other variables. The influencing variable—the one researchers expect to cause change in subjects' responses—is called the **independent variable**. The variable researchers try to change is called the **dependent variable**. Research consumers should be concerned about whether variables other than the independent variables influenced the observed changes in the dependent variable. To have confidence in a study's results, research consumers need to understand (a) how researchers control possible influences of variables other than those under systematic study, and (b) how research producers design studies to ensure the validity of their results.

Controlling Extraneous Variables

Variables that might have an unwanted influence on, or might change, dependent variables are called **extraneous variables**. Researchers can restrict the influence of extraneous variables by controlling subject variables and situational variables. **Subject variables** are variables on which humans are naturally different and which might influence their responses in regard to the dependent variable. **Situational variables** are variables related to the experimental condition (that is, variables outside the subjects) that might cause changes in their responses relating to the dependent variable.

For example, in a study investigating how the learning of syntactic context clues affects students' vocabulary acquisition in science, variables that might influence the results are students' general learning ability (IQ), their reading abilities, and their prior knowledge of the science topic. In this example, researchers can control the possible influence of subject and situational variables by selecting subjects of the same general learning ability and reading ability and by selecting a science topic and materials unfamiliar to all subjects. Another way researchers can account for the influence of these variables is by including them as independent variables. They can do this (a) by selecting students of different general learning and reading abilities and measuring the difference between and among the ability levels, or (b) by testing subjects' knowledge of the topic before the treatment and adjusting the after-treatment results to account for their prior knowledge. Obviously, researchers can only use as independent variables those variables that (a) they are aware of, and (b) they think might influence the dependent variable.

Probably, randomization is the best way to control subject variables because it accounts for all subject variables, even those not known or suspected by the researchers to influence the dependent variable. Chapter 5 contains a detailed explanation and specific examples of randomization.

Other attempts at controlling extraneous subject variables include creating groups that are homogeneous on one or more variables and the matching of subjects on several variables. These procedures, however, do not ensure that other (and possibly influencing) variables have an equally distributed effect on all groups. When subjects cannot be randomly selected or assigned to groups, researchers can equate them statistically. The procedure known as analysis of covariance (ANCOVA) is used to equate subjects on selected variables when known differences exist. The differences, as measured by pretests, must be related to the dependent variables. (ANCOVA is explained further in Chapter 8,

Reading and Evaluating Results Sections.) In the example above, differences in subjects' prior knowledge of a science topic could be used to adjust posttest outcomes statistically.

Experimental Validity

Extraneous variables can invalidate the results of experimental studies in two ways. The first occurs when researchers and consumers cannot attribute their results exclusively to the independent variable(s). The second source of invalidity occurs when the results cannot be used with other subjects and in other educational settings.

When researchers lack assurance that changes to dependent variables can be attributed to independent variables, we say the research lacks **internal validity**. Several factors can affect the internal validity of research. These include:

Current events. Current events include any historical occurrence during the experimental period. For example, a joint USA and USSR spacelab project during a study about changing students' attitudes toward science careers might unduly influence the studies' outcomes. Research consumers may not be aware of the coincidence of such an event during the study, but research producers should be, and they should report them.

Subject growth and development. Subject growth and development includes the physical, emotional, and cognitive maturational changes occurring in subjects and the periodic fluctuations that occur in human responses because of fatigue, boredom, hunger, illness, or excitement. For example, in a study about the influence of daily periods of silent reading on changing subjects' overall reading performance, changes in reading performance might occur because the subjects matured even without the special reading periods.

Subject selection. Subject selection refers to the influence improper or biased subject selection has on results. This phenomenon is discussed above and in Chapter 5.

Attrition. Attrition refers to the loss of subjects during experimental research. The reason for subject loss may be important and may unduly influence the results. For example, in a study about the effects on subjects with differing ethnic backgrounds of using calculators for learning of arithmetic number concepts, a major loss of subjects from any group might influence the results. A loss, say, from an ethnic group with high school dropout rate known to be high may result in a small sample with low achievement scores and an erroneous conclusion that individuals from that group do not benefit from using calculators. When attrition occurs, researchers need to determine why the loss occurred.

Testing. In this context, testing refers to the possible positive and negative influences of pretests on results. For example, subjects' final test scores might be improved because they learned something from taking a pretest. Or, an initial interview might give subjects an inkling about what researchers are studying, thereby influencing their performance on subsequent tasks.

Instrumentation. In this context, instrumentation refers to the influence of unreliable instruments on results. This phenomenon is discussed extensively in Chapter 6.

Statistical regression. Statistical regression refers to the tendency of extreme high and low standardized test scores to regress, or move, toward the group mean. That is, very high and very low subjects' scores on pretests seem to become more like middle scores on posttests—higher scores become lower and lower scores become higher. Research consumers need to understand that this phenomenon may occur "when, in fact, no real change has taken place in the dependent variable" (Kerlinger, 1973, p. 320).

Interaction. Interaction refers to the effect of several factors on each other. For example, attrition might result because of testing (subjects become threatened by the information they are asked on a pretest) or, current events may influence certain subjects because of selection bias (subjects have an advantage because they experienced some event).

When researchers lack assurance that results can be generalized to other persons and other educational settings, we say the research lacks external validity. Several factors can affect the external validity of research. These include

Subject–treatment interaction. Subject–treatment interaction occurs when subjects do not represent a target population and selection procedures produce a sample that is either positively or negatively biased toward a treatment. For example, when researchers use paid subjects, these individuals may undertake the activities solely for the money involved. Volunteer subjects, on the other hand, may have certain personal characteristics (which influence them to be volunteers) that are not present in the target population.

Reactive effects. Reactive effects refer to special situations that make subjects in a treatment group feel special. One reactive effect occurs when they know they are part of an experiment, or they sense that something special is happening to them. This phenomenon is called the **Hawthorne effect**. Another reactive effect occurs when subjects in a comparison or control group know or sense they are in competition with the treatment group, and they produce results above their normal behavior. This phenomenon is called the **John Henry effect**, after the legendary railroad builder.

Multiple treatment interaction. This phenomenon might occur when researchers include more that one treatment in a study. For example, in a study to determine which study skills program might be more effective, subjects are given three content area study strategies: the SQRRR, ReQuest, and Overview methods. If each subject receives instruction about all three, the learning of one might help or hinder the learning of the others. In this case, the order in which subjects learned the strategies might influence the results.

Researcher effects. Researcher or experimenter effects refer to the influences imposed on treatments by researchers themselves. For example, when researchers use an experimental instructional program that they developed, they may exert undue (although not conscious) influence on the subjects to use the program successfully. Also, instructional techniques may be complex, and only those with the researchers' knowledge and dedication could effectively implement them.

Research producers cannot control for the effect of all possible extraneous variables. If they were to do this, much research would be difficult, if not impossible, to undertake. So, researchers do two things. They limit or manipulate pertinent factors affecting their studies' validity, and they identify as possible influences other factors that were not controllable or could not be manipulated. Research consumers need to judge whether researchers have missed or underestimated factors that might affect research validity. To do this, research consumers need to understand the experimental designs researchers use to reduce possible effects of extraneous variables.

Experimental Designs

Experimental designs are the blueprints that researchers use in making decisions about the causative effect of one or more variables on other variables. The plans provide researchers with structures for studying one or more independent variables with one or more groups of subjects. Researchers select designs that best fit their purposes, answer questions about causation, *and* efficiently control extraneous variables.

In studying educational and psychological research, some authorities divide experimental designs into several groups, such as "true experimental," "quasiexperimental," "preexperimental," and "action" research (Borg, 1983, 1987; Campbell & Stanley, 1963; Gay, 1987). The criterion for inclusion, or exclusion, from a group is the strictness with which a design controls for the effect of extraneous variables. The continuum goes from "true experimental," representing the strictest control, to "action," representing the least strict control. Other authorities consider all designs used to answer questions of causation as experimental (Kamil, Langer, & Shanahan, 1985; Wiersma, 1986). These researchers do not identify designs by the above criteria but by other factors. The factors are: (a) the number of independent or treatment variables, and (b) the extent to which results can be generalized from the immediate subjects to a larger target population.

In the discussion here, experimental designs will be presented as a continuum from simple to complex plans. Simple experimental plans deal with a single independent variable, and complex experimental plans deal with multiple independent variables. In reading and evaluating both sets of plans, research consumers are concerned with the question "How generalizable are the results from the research subjects to other individuals and groups?"

Simple experimental designs deal with one independent variable or have subject selection procedures that limit the generalizability of their results. In Chapter 2, single-variable studies were shown to provide limited insight about educational questions. In Chapter 5, subject-selection techniques that produced samples unrepresentative of target populations were discussed. Simple designs are presented here so research consumers can recognize them and understand their limitations.

In some simple experimental designs, two or more groups of subjects are studied with a single independent variable. Subjects are randomly selected and randomly assigned to a group, but each group differs in the experimental condition. An experimental condition refers to how the independent variable is manipulated, varied, or subcategorized. When treatments are involved, one or more groups are randomly designated as treatments or **experimental groups** and the other(s) as **control** or **comparison group**(s). In educational and psychological research, a control group means is one that has received alternative activities, not the one(s) under study. All groups are given the same pretest and posttest (survey, observation, or test). This simple experimental design is called the **pretest–posttest control group**(s) design.

Diagrammatically this simple experimental design is shown in Figure 7.1.

The following method section includes the subject (sample) and procedure subsections. It is taken from a pretest–posttest control group design that has a single independent variable. The independent variable is an activity, a reading strategy, so it is called the *treatment*. Note that there are three dependent variables, but the researchers are trying

Randomized group 1 (experimental group)			
	Pretest	Treatment	Posttest
Randomized group 2 (control or comparison group)			
	Pretest	Alternate treatment(s)	Posttest
Randomized group *n* (other control or comparison groups)			
	Pretest	Alternate treatment(s)	Posttest

Figure 7.1 Pretest–posttest control group design.

to determine whether the change in each is attributable to the single independent variable.

Purpose of the study: To study an experimental instructional program involving the reading of predictable books.

METHOD

Sample

Near the end of the school year, 28 kindergarteners were selected from a public elementary school located in a rural-suburban community in southeastern United States. They were drawn from the pool of the 34 members of the two lowest-progress reading groups in three kindergarten classes. Six of these 34 children were eliminated from the sample because they were able to correctly match their aural memory for a short poem to the printed text on at least one line of print. None of the remaining 28 children were able to correctly match speech to a printed line of text and, thus, became the subjects for the study. The sample was composed of 8 blacks, 20 whites, of which 11 were female, 17 were male. Stratified random sampling on the basis of class membership and reading ability group was used to assign children to the experimental or placebo group.

Procedure

[Instrumentation] Each child referred by the kindergarten teachers for screening was tested individually using a speech/print match task, adapted from Morris (1981). Prior to screening, classroom teachers had been asked to teach the children to recite a four-line poem exactly as written. During testing, each child first demonstrated memory for the poem by reciting it orally. The experimenter then produced a printed copy of the poem, explaining the identity of the text. After demonstrating the reading and finger-pointing of Line 1, the experimenter asked the child to read and point to the words on Line 2. The accuracy of speech/print matching was recorded. This process was repeated for Lines 3 and 4.

[Subject selection] Children selected for the study were unable to correctly match speech to print on any of the test lines. The experimental group was divided in half in order to facilitate instruction, with both groups of seven students receiving 30 minutes of the same experimental treatment daily for 15 school days. A similar division was made for the placebo group.

During the first two days of both treatments, and before the children were introduced to the predictable books, two other tasks were individually administered to each child: a sight vocabulary identification task and an explicit concept-of-word task. In the sight vocabulary identification task, children were asked to identify 10 words, printed in isolation, which had been chosen from the two predictable books used in the study. Five words were selected from each text according to the following criteria: (1) they had been repeated at least three times in the texts; (2) they were not sight vocabulary words at the readiness level, or Levels 1 and 2 of the reading series used in the children's classrooms; and (3) they were not color words which had been learned as sight words.

The explicit concept-of-word task was designed to assess children's conscious ability to identify boundaries of printed words in response to oral requests by the experimenter. In this task the experimenter produced the printed sentence, *Mrs. Rowe likes to work with kindergarteners.*, and read it to the child without pointing to the text. Each child was asked to count the words, and then to isolate with his/her hands one word, one letter, the first and last words, and the longest and shortest words.

After all children were pretested, both groups were instructed using the same two predictable texts, *The Bus Ride* (1971) and *Brown Bear, Brown Bear, What Do You See?* (Martin, 1970). Both books were enlarged to form "big books" (approximately $16'' \times 22''$) so that the pictures and print would be easily visible to all children in the instructional groups. In both treatments the children heard the books read the same number of times.

The major focus of the experimental treatment was providing experimenter-demonstration of correct speech/print matching by pointing to the words of the text during oral reading, and opportunities for children to practice speech/print matching as they read. Lessons also included the use and explanation of such terms as *word* and *letter* in the context of reading the books, identifying individual words using the whole text as support, matching printed words to the text, and marking word boundaries in a line of the text. All of the activities were designed to help children develop a clearer concept of word by using their already well-developed aural memory for the text to support growth of the less-developed ability to get meaning from print. Part of each of the final two lessons was used for posttesting experimental subjects on the speech/print match, sight vocabulary identification, and explicit concept-of-word tasks.

While the two texts were read an identical number of times in the two groups, a major difference in the placebo treatment was that no attention was given to the print. Any questions initiated by the children about the print were answered, but no elaboration or discussion was initiated by the experimenter. Placebo lessons focused on aural memory, visual memory, and oral language skills. Typical of the placebo activities were creative dramatizations using child-created puppets, imagining new story endings, sequencing story events, identifying missing character pictures, and creative art activities related to the story. Placebo children were also posttested during the final two days of the treatment with the speech/print match task, the sight vocabulary identification task, and the explicit concept-of-word task.

Statistical Analyses

[Data analyses]   Scores for the speech/print match, sight vocabulary identification, and explicit concept-of-word posttests were subjected to a multivariate analysis of covariance. The sight vocabulary identification pretest score was used as the covariate, as it was a measure of pretreatment reading ability. (From Rowe & Cunningham, 1983, pp. 227–228)

There are some other less used simple experimental designs. One is the **posttest-only control group(s)** design, in which the experimental and control groups are not pretested. An example of this design is when researchers have two or more randomized groups engaged in alternative activities, but they do not give a pretest. The groups are assumed to be similar because of randomization, but the differences in group results are determined only by the posttest. This procedure's weakness is that there is no assurance that the groups were equal at the start on the dependent measure (such as a reading test). Also, researchers cannot account for the effect of any subject attrition in each group.

A second simple design is the **nonequivalent control group(s)** design. In it, the groups are not randomly selected or assigned and no effort is made to equate them statistically. Obviously, when comparison groups are known to be unequal, the research results can occur from many possible causes. A third simple design is the **matched groups** design. In it, the experimental and control subjects are selected or assigned to groups on the basis of a single subject variable such as reading ability, grade level, ethnicity, or special disabling condition. A major limitation of this design is the possibility that one or more variables, unknown to and unaccounted for by the researchers, might influence the dependent variable.

For all simple experimental designs, extraneous variables affect the internal and external validity of the research. Research consumers should be wary of generalizing the results of simple design research to other educational settings and populations.

More complex experimental designs deal with multiple experimental and subject variables. Some complex designs are built on the pretest–posttest control group design and are expansions of it. In these complex designs, researchers not only study the effect of one variable on one or more other variables, they study the interaction of these variables on the dependent variable. Above, *subject–treatment interaction* and *multiple-treatment interaction* were noted as threats to research validity. Nevertheless, researchers can use complex designs to account for the effect of these interactions.

Not all complex designs use random selection or assignment of subjects. When randomization is not used, statistical procedures are used to account for the possible influence of the differences between and among subjects. Chapter 8 contains a discussion of these statistical procedures.

Two important threats to research validity are *subject growth and development* and *testing*. They can be accounted for in a design called the **Solomon four-group design**. Using random selection and random assignment, four groups are formed. All four groups are posttested. However, only two groups are pretested. One pretested group and one nonpretested group are then given the experimental condition.

Diagrammatically the Solomon four-group experimental design is shown in Figure 7.2.

In addition to the effect of the experimental variable, the possible effects of pretesting can be measured by comparing the posttest results of groups 1 and 3 to groups 2 and 4. If the posttest had an effect, the results of groups 1 and 2 would be higher respectively than those of groups 3 and 4. The possible effect of subjects' growth and development and current events has been controlled because both would have an equal effect on all groups.

The Solomon four-group experimental design is not often used in educational and psychological research, however, because of several limitations. The first limitation is that a large number of subjects is required. In a study employing one independent variable with no factors, approximately 100 subjects (four groups of 25 subjects) would be needed. Each additional independent variable requires another 100 subjects. Therefore, researchers use other experimental designs to control for the effect of pretesting and subjects' growth and development.

Another complex design built on the pretest–posttest control group design is called the **counterbalanced design**. In counterbalanced designs, two or more groups get the same treatments; however, the order of the treatments for each group is different and is usually randomly determined. For this type of design to work, the number of treatments

Randomized group 1 Pretest	Experimental condition	Posttest
Randomized group 2 Pretest	Alternate condition	Posttest
Randomized group 3	Experimental condition	Posttest
Randomized group 4	Alternate condition	Posttest

Figure 7.2 Solomon four-group experimental design.

and groups must match. Although the groups may be randomly selected and assigned, researchers often use this design with already existing groups of subjects, for example, when they use all classes on a grade level. A major problem with this design is the possibility of multiple-treatment interaction. Research consumers need to determine that the individual treatments are unique and that one treatment could not directly increase or decrease the effectiveness of another. Figure 7.3 shows the counterbalanced design for a three-treatment, three-group design.

Educational and psychological researchers are often concerned about questions involving multiple variables. Although the Solomon four-group design accounts for the possible influence of some extraneous variables, its use does not allow researchers to easily study two or more independent variables. In the example shown in Figure 7.2, one independent variable is used with two subcategories: experimental condition and alternate condition. This could represent an experimental science program versus the previously used science program. Many questions are left unanswered in this design. For example, "Does the experimental science program or the existing program produce greater learning with girls? With students with learning disabilities?" or "Does the experimental science program lead to greater learning after shorter periods of instruction?" These are questions of interaction. Questions about the interaction of human variables and instructional and environmental situations are important to educators. Teaching and learning involve the interplay of many variables, and they do not occur in isolation.

Questions of interaction are examined in complex experimental designs called **factorial designs**. The term *factorial* refers to research studies in which there are multiple variables and each is subcategorized into two or more levels, or factors. The simplest factorial design involves two independent variables, each of which has two factors. This is called a 2 × 2 factorial design. Factorial designs can have any

Group 1	Group 2 (randomized or unrandomized) Pretest (all groups)	Group 3
Treatment C	Treatment B Interim Test 1 (all groups)	Treatment A
Treatment B	Treatment A Interim Test 2 (all groups)	Treatment C
Treatment A	Treatment C Posttest (all groups)	Treatment B

Figure 7.3 Counterbalanced experimental design.

INTERPRETING EDUCATIONAL RESEARCH

combination of variables and factors. The practical consideration for research producers is having an adequate number of subjects in each subdivision. Generally, 15 subjects per group is considered the minimum, although group size in factorial designs can be as small as 5 subjects.

Figure 7.4 contains examples of three common factorial designs. Notice how the number of groups increases as independent variables and factors increase. Although multivariable designs can provide educators with valuable insights about teaching and learning, research consumers should be wary of research studies containing what seem to be unnecessary factors. When there are too many possible interactions (because there are many groups), the meaning of the interactions could become confusing. Research consumers need to consider whether the number of variables and factors is appropriate. As a general rule, factorial designs in experimental research larger than $2 \times 2 \times 2$ become unwieldy.

The following method section includes subsections of subjects and design, materials, procedure, and scoring. The study is an example of a $2 \times 2 \times 2$ factorial design. The independent variables and their factors are: reading ability (high and low), treatment (experimental, or induced lookbacks and control, or spontaneous lookbacks), and passage (familiar and unfamiliar).

2 × 2 Factorial Design
   (four groups)

                                    VARIABLE 1

                              F1a | F1b

                                FAa
Variable A
                                FAb

Example variables:
Variable 1 = Student learning ability
   F1a   = Has learning disability
   F1b   = Has no learning disability

Variable A = Science program
   FAa   = Experimental program
   FAb   = Previous program

One example condition: F1a, FAa = Students with learning disabilities using the experimental science program.

Figure 7.4 (pp. 161–162) Common factorial designs.

2 × 3 Factorial Design
        (six groups)

VARIABLE 1

		F1a	F1b	F1c
Variable A	FAa			
	FAb			

Example variables

Variable 1 = Content area study technique
  F1a   = Summary writing
  F1b   = Questions placed in text
  F1c   = Advance organizer

Variable A = Gender
  FAa   = Male
  FAb   = Female

One example condition: F1a, FAa = Males using the summary writing content area study technique.

---

2 × 2 × 2 Factorial Design
          (eight groups)

VARIABLE 1

F1a	F1b

VARIABLE 2

		F2a	F2b	F2a	F2b
Variable A	FAa				
	FAb				

Example variables:

Variable 1 = School grade
  F1a   = Third grade
  F1b   = Sixth grade

Variable 2 = Textbook style
  F2a   = Original textbook
  F2b   = Revised readability textbook

Variable A = Reading ability
  FAa   = Above average
  FAb   = Below average

One example condition: F1a, F2a, FAa = Above average reading ability third grade subjects using the original textbook.

Figure 7.4 (Continued)

Purpose of the study: To investigate the effects of a graphic organizer that was designed to induce students to look back in their texts for information they had missed, misunderstood, or forgotten.

METHOD

Subjects and Design

[Subject selection]

An experimenter-designed questionnaire that assessed students' perceptions of how they would perform on a typical social studies reading assignment was administered to all 10th graders in a small city high school that served a working class neighborhood. Students' self-ratings of their ability to comprehend the assignment were compared with reading scores they achieved on the reading comprehension subtest of the Tests of Achievement and Proficiency (TAP)(Houghton Mifflin, 1978). Students who scored between the 99th and 83rd percentiles on the TAP were designated high-ability comprehenders; those who scored between the 42nd and 18th percentiles were designated low-ability comprehenders. From that pool of 119 subjects, 64 students (32 high and 32 low comprehenders) were selected on the criteria that their self-perceived proficiency ratings matched their actual reading achievement. Next,

[Subject assignment]

blocking on self-perceived high- and low-ability comprehenders, subjects were randomly assigned to one of two treatment groups; the experimental (or induced lookbacks) and the control (or spontaneous lookbacks). Finally, within groups, subjects were randomly assigned to either a familiar or an unfamiliar passage condition. (Passages were defined as familiar or unfamiliar on the basis of earlier pilot tests.) The design was

[Design]

a 2 × 2 × 2 (Reading Ability × Treatment × Passage) factorial.

Materials

Passages were taken from two social studies texts used at the subjects' grade level. Care was taken to ensure that portions selected had not been read earlier. The familiar passage was an historical essay on Louis XIV and contained 998 words; the unfamiliar passage was a historical essay on the diffusion of Western culture and contained 1,007 words. Each passage was distributed over three pages. The full text of the unfamiliar passage appears in the Appendix.

Other materials included a practice passage, "Camp Wildwood," which had been used previously by Garner and Reis (1981), a 10-item open-ended question test over the practice passage, and two 10-item open-ended question tests over material covered in the two experimental passages. For example, some items from the experimental passage on the diffusion of Western culture were: What does diffusion mean? During what historical period was there a cultural diffusion from West to East? What was one benefit of the diffusion of Western culture?

[Instrumentation]

Each of the 10-item open-ended tests contained four lookback questions and six nonlookback questions. Pilot testing of the two experimental passages and their corresponding tests verified which questions were the intended lookback questions. These were the questions that the teacher-experimenter asked after a student had finished page 2 or page

3 of the passage, but the information necessary for answering them was on one of the earlier pages. The nonlookback questions could be answered from the page a student had just finished reading.

Graphic organizers were constructed for the practice passage and each of the two experimental passages. In addition to reflecting the top-level structure of the passage (e.g., comparison/contrast, cause/effect, time/order), a graphic organizer also included specific graphic/pictorial reminders. These graphic/pictorial reminders helped a reader zero in on an area of the text that likely contained information that was missed during the first reading, misunderstood, or forgotten until cued by the teacher-examiner's question. Figure 1 contains the graphic organizer that accompanied the experimental passage of the diffusion of Western culture. The information in that passage was organized according to a time/order sequence explaining the major topics enclosed in the three rectangles. The graphic/pictorial reminders were clues to the information contained under each of the three major topics.

The three parts of the organizer (denoted by broken lines) were revealed, one by one, as a student read the corresponding pages of text. For example, a student who had read only the first page of the text would see only the first segment of the organizer. After reading the second page of the text, a student would be presented with a new organizer that contained the first and second parts of the organizer. After the third page of text, the entire organizer would be revealed.

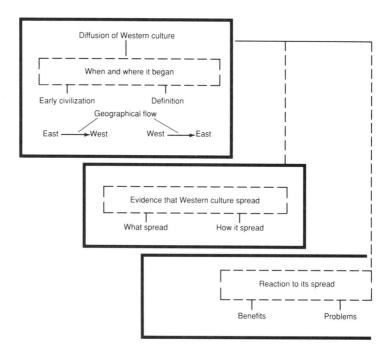

Figure 1 Graphic organizer for the passage on the diffusion of Western culture.

[Procedure]   Subjects were seen individually in conference rooms off the main room of the school library by one of the two social studies teachers who had been trained in the use of the graphic organizer. The experiment took about 55 minutes per subject. The two social studies teachers who were the teacher-experimenters (T-E) followed this procedure when they met with individual students in the experimental group:

[Treatment 1]   First, after putting the student at ease, the T-E read the following set of directions prior to having the student read the practice passage:

> In front of you is a passage that has been divided into three parts. Each part is on a separate page. After you finish reading each part, I'll ask you some questions. You may look back at any part of the passage to answer them. In fact, you *should* look back for answers to questions that you are not sure about. To help you look back, I want you to use this study aid. (T-E shows student the graphic organizer segment that corresponds to the first segment of the practice passage.) Think of the graphic organizer as a "road map" to the passage. It will guide you quickly to the spot in the text where you can find the answer to my question. (T-E demonstrates how the student is to use the organizer.) Do you understand what you are to do? (T-E pauses.) You may begin.

As the student read silently, the T-E took notes on the student's nonverbal behaviors. When the student had finished reading, the T-E asked the first set of questions orally and the student responded orally. The teacher recorded the student's answers on a response form. For the second and third sets of questions, the T-E also recorded whether the student actually looked back to a previous page for an answer to a designated lookback question. (See Garner & Reis, 1981, for a more complete description of this procedure.)

Second, after informing students of their scores on the practice passage, the T-E introduced one of the two experimental passages. The procedure for Step 1 was repeated, including the directions for the use of the graphic organizer.

Third, beginning and ending times for reading and answering questions on both the practice and experimental passages were recorded by the T-E.

[Treatment 2]   The procedure used with students in the control group was the same with the exception that no graphic organizer was provided and the following set of directions was substituted:

> In front of you is a passage that has been divided into three parts. Each part is on a separate page. After you finish reading each part, I'll ask you some questions. You may look back at any part of the passage to answer them. Do you understand what you are to do? (T-E pauses.) You may begin.

Scoring

The open-ended test questions for each of the two experimental passages were scored by two independent raters who achieved an overall agreement rate of .94. In instances where agreement could not be reached through discussion, a third rater was called in. Two scores were obtained for each subject. One score was expressed as a percentage of the total number of questions a subject answered correctly (both lookback and nonlookback questions). The other score was expressed as a percentage of the four designated lookback questions that a subject answered correctly. Students in the experimental group were required to use the graphic organizer to answer the lookback questions. (The T-E's record of a student's nonverbal behavior permitted a check on this last criterion.) (From Alvermann, 1988, pp. 326–328. Reprinted with permission of the Helen Dwight Reid Educational Foundation. Published by Heldref Publications, Washington, D.C. Copyright © 1988.)

Causal–Comparative Experimental Designs

Causal–comparative research is ex post facto, or after-the-fact, research. Researchers use it in trying to establish one or more causal effects between or among existing conditions. The researchers want answers to questions but they cannot manipulate the independent variable(s) for practical or ethical reasons. They realize a condition exists and are unsure about what might have been its cause. Causal–comparative designs are built on the posttest-only control group design.

A major concern for researchers doing causal–comparative research is that the causal effect should be one-way. The distinguishing variables must precede and be the cause of the differences. For example, Chapter 2 presents a representative causal–comparative study about the effect of black students' figurative language on their school language. The existence of out-of-school language experiences preceded their school language experiences; thus, the causal effect can be only one-way.

In using the causal–comparative design, researchers can randomly *select* subjects from target populations that differ in respect to one or more variables. Since there are no manipulated, or treated, independent variables, the subjects cannot be randomly *assigned* to groups. The subjects should be similar except for the variables being studied. For example, selection procedures can assure that subjects are similar in such characteristics as age, socioeconomic status, or intellectual ability, so long as these are not variables that might cause the difference between groups. If it is not possible to select comparable groups, the differences between them can be equated statistically.

For research consumers to generalize the results from causal–comparative studies to other populations and educational situations, they need to be sure that any differences between groups cannot be attributed to one or more important variables that were not accounted for by the researchers. There is always the possibility that these outside variables may be the true causes of the observed differences. Also, they should be sure researchers' description of the subjects is clear and that operational definitions are used to identify and distinguish the comparison groups. Therefore, research consumers should cautiously interpret the results of causal–comparative research, and they should expect researchers to follow up their tentative results with additional experimental research.

The following procedure section contains an example of a causal–comparative design. The researchers sought to determine the effect of a preexisting condition (amount of previous mathematics instruction) on mathematics achievement. It should be remembered that researchers using the causal–comparative design are trying to find *causal relationships* or predictions.

Purpose of the study: To determine the possible effect on students' mathematics achievement of the number of semesters of mathematics courses they took. The researchers took into account the possible influence of several background variables of the subjects.

PROCEDURE

[Statistical procedure] The basic methodology of this study is multiple regression analysis, a statistical procedure for relating variations in a set of predictor variables [Dependent variable] to variation in a criterion variable. Student scores on a mathematics [Independent variables] achievement test served as the criterion or dependent variable. The predictor variables were eight measures of background characteristics plus the number of semesters of mathematics completed by the students. Our approach was to account for as much variance in mathematics scores as possible by entering the nonschool background variables first and then finding the amount of additional variation explained by our measure of school effects, semesters of mathematics completed.

[Instrumentation] The criterion instrument in this study was a booklet of mathematics items administered to a national random sample of 2,216 17-year-old students. The original booklet contained 58 separate items, but a technical analysis of the results suggested the deletion of several items in order to meet appropriate standards for validity and reliability (see Anderson, Welch, & Harris [1980] for details). The resultant achievement measure, NAEP-MATS10, was a 47-item test that sampled the domain of mathematics defined by the National Assessment group. (Specific test characteristics are available from the authors.) The reliability estimate on the present sample was 0.93 using the Cronbach alpha test of internal consistency.

[Independent variables] The background variables were selected to represent the range of home, community, and individual factors that have been found to be related to student learning. These variables typically account for substantial variation in achievement, but are those over which the school has little control. The eight background variables used in this study included Welfare (percent in community on welfare), Professional Status (percent of professionals living in the community), Minority (percent racial minority in school), Title 1 (percent Title 1 qualifiers in school), Parent Education (mean level of schooling), Printed Material (extent of reading material in the home), Ethnicity (percentage of minority students), and Grade Level of 17-year-old at time of testing.

[Setting] The semesters of mathematics studied included those found in the traditional sequence in secondary schools: algebra, advanced algebra, geometry, trigonometry, and calculus. It did not include business, general mathematics, or prealgebra because these courses tend to enroll large numbers of remedial students. However, the results reported in this study are similar whether all mathematics courses are included or only those in the traditional sequence.

[Replication]   The complete study was replicated using two different mathematics tests, each involving an additional 2,200 17-year-old students who were randomly selected within the United States. Test booklets NAEP-MATS1 and NAEP-MATS3 are mathematics achievement tests similar in scope to MATS10 described earlier. All were used in the 1978 National Assessment surveys. The former contains 45 items, and the alpha reliability index is 0.92. The MATS3 contains 53 items with a reliability

[Replication]   coefficient of 0.93. (From Welch, Anderson, & Harris, 1982, pp. 147–148. Copyright 1982 by the American Educational Research Association. Reprinted by permission of the publisher.)

OTHER RESEARCH PROCEDURES

Single-subject research, action research, and evaluation research are other ways researchers describe, compare, and draw causative conclusions about educational problems and questions.

Single-Subject Research

Many insights gained from single-subject and case study research have greatly influenced educational and psychological practice. Classic examples of single-subject and case study research that have produced significant hypotheses are those of Jean Piaget and Sigmund Freud. Single-subject experimental designs are variations of pretest–posttest counterbalanced designs. Figure 7.5 shows three forms of single-subject experimental designs. In single-subject research, the pretest is called a **baseline measure** and can sometimes take the form of several measurements. Also, each posttest can consist of several measurements because they become the baseline for subsequent treatments. Baselines are the results to which posttest results are compared to determine the effect of each treatment.

Because of the unique relationship that can develop between researcher and subject and because of the possible effect of multiple testing and treatment, single-subject research can have its external and internal validity threatened in several ways. Single-subject research and case-study research should have clear, precise descriptions of the subject. This is most important. The results of research with a single subject are not directly generalizable to a target population without replications with other individuals or without follow-up descriptive, comparative, or experimental research with larger samples. The threats to the internal validity of single-subject research include testing, instrumentation, subject–treatment interaction, reactive effects, and researcher effects. Research consumers should anticipate that research

```
                    Pretest–Posttest Two-Treatment

            A-B Design
              Pretest
                Treatment A
                  Posttest 1
                    Treatment B
                      Posttest 2


            Pretest—Posttest Counterbalanced Two-Treatment

         A-B-A Design
           Pretest
             Treatment A
               Posttest 1
                 Treatment B
                   Posttest 2
                     Treatment A
                       Posttest 3


       A-B-A-B Design
         Pretest
           Treatment A
             Posttest 1
               Treatment B
                 Posttest 2
                   Treatment A
                     Posttest 3
                       Treatment B
                         Posttest 4
```

Figure 7.5 Single-subject experimental designs.

producers will follow the same guidelines as would be used for conducting descriptive and experimental research.

The following method section is from research done with a single subject in a pretest–posttest two-treatment design (referred to as an A-B design in Figure 7.5). The subsections have clarifying headings.

Purpose of the study: To determine the effects of a peer-tutoring procedure on the spelling behavior of a mainstreamed elementary school student with a learning disability.

METHOD

Subjects and Setting

The subject (tutee) was an 11-year-old learning disabled male student in a regular grade six classroom in a large urban school. Scores on the *Wide Range Achievement Test* (Jastak, Bijou, & Jastak, 1965) ranged from 2.2 to 2.4 grade equivalents for spelling and reading. The subject (S-A) demonstrated a four-year deficiency in at least two academic areas. Subject A had spent five years in and out of special education classes before he was mainstreamed at the request of his mother. Teacher reports indicated that the subject should be academically able to perform well in a lower level spelling group.

The tutor (S-B) was a male student from the same classroom as the above-mentioned subject. He was 11 years old and excelled in all academic areas. Results on the *Wide Range Achievement Test* and *Wechsler Intelligence Scale for Children-Revised* (Wechsler, 1974) indicated superior achievement and intelligence. However, the tutor did not participate in any extracurricular activities and tended to interact with few students.

The classroom was self-contained, equipped with the usual facilities, with 27 students and one certified teacher. The spelling class was divided into two groups according to achievement. Tutoring sessions occurred at a worktable in a corner of the classroom.

Response Definition

The following two dependent variables were employed in the study.

Percent correct. Data were collected from biweekly spelling tests. The words for the spelling test were obtained from *Basic Goals in Spelling* (Kottmeyer & Claus, 1976). A response was defined as correct if it matched the spelling in the word list. The percent correct was calculated by dividing the number of correct responses by the total number of possible words for each test.

Clinical significance. During the experimental condition the two subjects were requested to write self-reports. They were asked to indicate whether they liked the program, worked harder in it, and/or performed better than in the regular classroom lesson. In addition, the subjects rated how well they felt they were learning by marking two pluses (+ +) for very good, one plus (+) for satisfactory (same as in the regular class), and one minus (−) for unsatisfactory. Subjects entered their opinions in small notebooks at the end of each week.

Design Elements and Experimental Conditions

An AB design was employed to examine the effects of peer tutoring (Hersen & Barlow, 1976). A description of the experimental condition follows.

Baseline. During the baseline condition, students were given spelling tests at the middle and end of the week. The tests were corrected upon completion and feedback was communicated in the form of percent correct. This procedure was in effect for two weeks for Subject A. The same procedure was applied to Subject B in order for the experimenter to monitor whether the experimental treatment had any effect on his spelling behavior.

Peer tutoring. In this condition, the tutee met with the peer tutor for 15 minutes each day during the regular spelling time. The peer tutor was instructed for two days using a modeling method. The experimenter presented the teaching procedure and the peer tutor was encouraged to emulate it. On the third day, the peer tutor conducted the entire session under the guidance of the experimenter. The tutor represented a good example of academic behavior, and it was anticipated that the tutee would model his behavior. The tutor presented a list of 10 words taken from *Basic Goals in Spelling* (Level 5), which coincided with the lessons of the lower spelling group. The first two word lists were taken from the lesson currently under study in the class. The third word list consisted of difficult words from the previous spelling lesson. The tutor read the words aloud, then asked the tutee to read the word list after which he orally spelled the words. Flashcards and games were used to enhance the teaching process. If the tutee experienced difficulties with a word or words, he was requested to write them out 10 times. The tutor was encouraged to offer assistance, helpful hints, and praise. On Wednesday and Friday the tutor dictated 20 words from the word lists. He checked the completed tests against his word list and tabulated the results before handing back the papers to the tutees. Difficulties and mistakes were discussed at this time. The condition was in effect for five weeks for Subject A.

Reliability

Reliability of measurement as to the percent correct on the spelling tests was assessed biweekly by having the experimenter check the tests prior to having either the peer tutor or the classroom teacher mark them. A third individual who was unaware of the experimental outcomes checked all test papers. An agreement was defined as all graders scoring a word as spelled either correctly or incorrectly. A disagreement was defined as any grader failing to score a word in the same manner as the other two. Intergrader reliability for percent correct was 96.4 percent.

Reliability of measurement as to the use of the peer-tutoring procedure was checked twice during the intervention by the principal and another classroom teacher. Reliability of measurement as to the implementation of the treatment was 100 percent. (From Mandoli, Mandoli, & McLaughlin, 1982, pp. 186–187)

Action Research

Action research is descriptive, comparative, or experimental research in which results are not generalized beyond the study's specific subjects and educational setting. Action researchers seek answers or solutions to specific questions or problems. Their goal is to create immediate change. Action researchers can use both quantitative and qualitative research methods.

For quantitative method studies, they use the same general plans and procedures as used in more controlled research. However, there are differences in how they select and assign subjects. Also, they do not apply strict procedures to control for the possible influence of extraneous variables. They do identify a problem area and seek out what others have done, create operational definitions, select appropriate instruments, identify possible influencing variables and factors, select appropriate designs for collecting data, and analyze data either qualitatively or quantitatively. Most often, action researchers use convenience samples. Since students are usually assigned to classes before the research begins, random selection and assignment are not possible. Experimental action research is usually done with a simple design such as a pretest–posttest control group(s) design with one or two independent and dependent variables. If the groups are known to differ on important variables, the groups can be equated statistically.

Qualitative educational action research is the collecting of information in order to understand what is happening in particular educational settings. It is an attempt to go beneath surfaces to reveal the possible reasons for the situations. As with quantitative action research, qualitative action research begins with a sense that something needs attention and possible change.

Even though action research has only local generalizability, this form of research can be relevant to research consumers. If there are similarities in subject variables, educational setting, or treatment(s), research consumers may wish to replicate the study in searching for answers to their own educational questions. Therefore, research consumers should expect published action research reports to have the same specificity in detail as other research reports.

Action research, especially qualitative action research as described below, is often used in researcher/classroom teacher collaborative projects. When classroom teachers act as teacher researchers, they usually undertake action research.

The following section reports the procedures from a qualitative action research project. Note that in keeping with the purposes of action research, the researchers focus on the solving of local instructional problems.

Purpose of the study: To report action research showing how a teacher/ university researcher collaboration resulted in changing the teacher's instructional practice.

Description of the Action Research Model

During the school year 1987–88, the Department of Physical Education and the Greensboro Public Schools have been engaged in a collaborative project involving the development, delivery, and assessment of a middle school physical education program. The partnership is the first of its kind in Greensboro and represents a unique model whereby university and public school combine resources to provide effective physical education instruction for children.

One goal of this project is to assist as many of the middle school teachers ($n = 12$) as possible in solving various instructional problems. Prior to the beginning of the school year, the first of two workshops was held. Attention was given to familiarizing the teachers with the middle school curriculum and to discussing the goals of the project for the upcoming school year.

A second workshop was then held midway into the fall semester and was followed by a series of planning sessions at the school site of each teacher. The purposes of the workshop and sessions were to help teachers identify instructional concerns and to plan research strategies to help address these concerns in their own setting. The content of the workshop and the follow-up sessions was determined from the guidelines suggested by Tikunoff, Ward, and Griffin (1979). These guidelines provide the essential stages that users need to go through if action research is to be successful.

The first stage focuses on identifying a solvable problem that the teacher is grappling with. The responsibility for identifying the problem belongs to the teacher, with help from university, peer, and administrative personnel. In the second stage the action research team assists the teacher in developing a plan of action for working on (researching) the problem. During this stage, university and administrative personnel assist by providing appropriate materials, research, and evaluation tools for the teacher to use in researching the problem. Stage 3 is the implementation of the action research project. The research team consult and assist the teacher when needed.

During Stage 4 the teacher and the rest of the team discuss and analyze the results of the action research project. Specific successes and failures are discussed at this point. Then follows the last stage, during which an overall evaluation and recommendations are discussed and a new cycle of action research is implemented.

STAGE 1—IDENTIFICATION OF INSTRUCTIONAL PROBLEMS

During the second workshop the participants were grouped into research teams. Each team was composed of two to three teachers, a university facilitator, and an assistant principal. It was the university facilitator's job to help the teams develop those areas of concern into solvable action research questions. Among the areas identified during this workshop were teacher communication (i.e., teacher feedback, questioning techniques, direction giving) and classroom management problems.

Following the workshop, the first of the series of planning sessions was held so each team could further discuss their ideas for the action research project. At this session the concerns identified in the workshop were revisited. For example, two teachers of one team decided that improving instructional feedback and increasing student time on task would be the focal points of their respective research projects.

As previously stated in this chapter, only one teacher's project will be presented. The research project of this target teacher was designed to look at the effects of selected teaching strategies on time on task. The following sections will describe the remaining stages of this project.

STAGE 2—DEVELOPMENT OF THE
RESEARCH STRATEGY

A second planning session was scheduled to help the target teacher decide on a plan of action for addressing the instructional problem. At this time a research design was also formulated by the teacher and the team members to evaluate the effects of the teacher's planned strategy. During this session the university facilitator presented the teacher with some possible instructional strategies to use as well as observational tools for assessing their impact.

After reviewing the materials, the teacher decided to design an action research strategy that would work on increasing the time on task of three of his most disruptive students in a specific class. For evaluation of student time on task, the teacher selected a tool for coding the following student behaviors: (a) On-task-Active, (b) On-task-Inactive, and (c) Off-task. An event recording format was used to record the student behaviors.

The teacher's plan of action included utilizing two instructional strategies. The first was to implement a reciprocal teaching approach (Mosston, 1983) whereby each target student would be given some of the instructional responsibility during classes. The second strategy was to have each student assume the role of squad captain, which involved organizing team membership, monitoring the behavior of other classmates, and helping to keep score of small group games.

The research design included collecting baseline data by the university researcher during actual class time, analyzing the data, implementing the strategies for change, and collecting and analyzing postintervention data. It should be noted that the classes were also videotaped so the teacher could gain additional information about the use of his strategies and perhaps identify other problems that could be addressed in the future.

STAGE 3—IMPLEMENTATION OF THE
ACTION RESEARCH PROJECT

Two baseline (preintervention) and two postintervention observations were made during the implementation stage of the project. All coding was done live by the university researcher. During the coding periods only the three target students were observed. They were engaged in lead-up basketball game playing for each of the observational periods.

During baseline instruction the target students participated without the implementation of the planned instructional strategies (reciprocal teaching and squad captain assignments). The implementation phase lasted eight instructional periods. During that time the teacher appointed the target students as squad captains and also used them to help with various aspects of the class. It was felt that the responsibilities associated with their assigned roles would make them take a more active interest in the class and thereby increase their time on task. (From Martineck & Butt, 1988, pp. 215–217. Copyright 1988 by Human Kinetics Publishers. Reprinted by permission.)

Educational **evaluation research** has developed to a great extent because of federal and state mandates to assess the impact (influence) of funded compensatory programs for students who are educationally disadvantaged, have limited English proficiency, and have special educational needs. It is the systematic study of existing educational programs (treatments). Evaluation researchers wish to know whether a particular instructional program or technique results in improved student performance or achievement. They can use both quantitative and qualitative research methods.

Qualitative research methods differ from quantitative methods. Qualitative analysis is inductive. Researchers use observed data to draw a conclusion. It emphasizes an examination and explanation of the processes by which the educational programs do or do not work. Qualitative analyses focus on how instruction (teaching and learning) happens from the point of view of the students, teachers, and administrators. Quantitative research methods are deductive. They begin with predefined goals—most often the goals of the programs themselves—and focus on whether particular outcomes have been reached (Bogdan & Biklen, 1982).

Evaluation research differs from action research in several ways. These are (a) the complexity of the research designs, (b) the degree to which the possible effects of extraneous variables are controlled, and (c) the extent to which the results can be generalized to other educational settings.

Research consumers can use the following questions to help them judge the appropriateness of the evaluation researchers' statement of the problem, identification of subjects, selection of instruments, collection of data, and analysis of data. These questions are based on standards established by a consortium of educational associations and by educational researchers (Bogdan & Biklen, 1982; Joint Committee, 1981).

In evaluation research using quantitative methods, could the research be useful to the school or agency conducting the study in that its results answer a clearly defined question or problem?

In evaluation research using qualitative methods, could the research be useful to the school or agency conducting the study in that its results provide meanings for and understandings about the processes occurring during teaching and learning?

In both quantitative and qualitative designs, was the evaluation research appropriate to the educational setting in that it was minimally disruptive to the subjects (administrators, teachers, students, and other school personnel)?

Were the rights and well-being of the participating administrators, teachers, and students protected and was information about individuals obtained and stored in such a way that confidentiality was maintained?

Was the evaluation research report clearly written so that the reliability and validity of the collected data and the internal and external validity of the study could be determined?

ACTIVITIES

Activity 1

Using the Focus Questions at the beginning of the chapter as a guide, summarize the chapter's key ideas.

Activity 2

Read the following sections containing research procedures for two studies. The researchers' purposes have been included for your information. Using the questions and criteria discussed in this chapter (on p. 145), evaluate the studies. For each, list questions and concerns you may have about
   a. The appropriateness of the research designs to the researchers' purposes
   b. The research designs and data collection procedures
   c. The replicability of the study
   d. The studies' internal and external validity

Extract A: Teachers' Work Behavior Study

Purpose of the study: To examine the work behavior of five teachers of second through fourth grades in diverse elementary schools.

PROCEDURES

The structured observation technique is simple. The observer stays with the observee through the entire workday, recording each activity in field notes. Included are a description of the activity, its location and origin, the subjects involved, the beginning and ending times of the activity (with its duration to the nearest minute), and its purpose.

The field notes are used to construct four records. The chronological record shows the activities and time allotted, the correspondence record describes the action taken on each piece of written or printed material, the contact record provides details on verbal and personal interactions, and the analysis of purpose groups activities in terms of intended ends.

Structured observation is flexible because the various records can be adapted to the type of position being observed by creating categories appropriate to that position and eliminating those used in past research. This has been done in previous studies (Martin & Willower, 1981) and in this study, although an effort was made to maintain sufficient consistency with the companion study so that comparisons could be made.

Also, techniques in addition to structured observation can be used when feasible. For example, in the present study, an anecdotal record was kept. This record provided information on context and meaning. In addition, the teachers kept logs of their work after school hours. After the field work was completed, telephone interviews averaging 1 hour were conducted with the observed teachers for their reactions on the results of the research. The observations were made in April and May of 1984, and the interviews were conducted in November and December of the same year.

During a pilot study, an observer, who had extensive experience in elementary schools as a teacher and principal, felt sufficiently practiced in structured observation recording procedures following 8 to 9 hours of observations.

Sample

Five elementary school teachers were observed for 5 consecutive work-days each, for a total of 25 days of observations, as was the case in the companion and complementary studies. The sample schools, from five different school districts, were chosen with heterogeneity in mind. They were located in the following settings: one urban center city, two rural, one suburban, and one middle-sized city. The study was explained to the school principals, who agreed to furnish lists of teachers in first through fourth grades with over three years of experience and limited or no use of an aide, conditions thought to emulate typical teaching situations. The principals also were asked to eliminate teachers in odd or special circumstances. Names were drawn from the lists using a table of random numbers. However, in one school the principal furnished the name of a single volunteer, stating this was standard practice in his school. Meetings were then held with the five first choices to explain the research and seek their participation. All 5 teachers became part of the study. These teachers, identified by single fictitious names, and their situations, are briefly described below.

Primera has taught for 20 years. She is 42 years old and has two school-aged children and a husband who teaches high school in a neighboring district. Primera teaches fourth grade and has a normal class schedule, but was designated head teacher in her 280-pupil building even though there was a full-time secretary and the district's elementary principal worked at the school on a daily basis. The modern school was located about a mile from a small village. The community was rural and included several dairy farms.

Materna, 56, is married to a retired teacher. She has 17 years of teaching experience, and began her career after her two sons reached their teens. She teaches second grade in a recently renovated 650-student school located in the relatively well-off suburbs of a small industrial city.

Novitia is 28 and recently married, with 6 years of teaching experience, the least of the 5 teachers. She teaches third grade in a school of 525 pupils. The setting is rural, although there is a small community nearby.

Productivia is 34 and married, with two sons. She is a fourth-grade teacher with 14 years' experience. Her school is an old, two-story building located in a middle-sized city. There are about 200 students in the school.

Luxor, 41, is married and has two children. He has taught in several schools and previously served 3 years as an assistant principal. He teaches fourth grade in an old but well-maintained central city school. The school enrolls fewer than 300 students, the majority of whom are bused to what the district labels an academic prep school. Both the faculty and student body are racially diverse.

Class sizes varied from 20 to 31, but they also varied for each teacher because the numbers changed depending on what subject was being taught and what kind of grouping was used. The observer attempted to strike a balance between unobtrusiveness and objective friendliness during the study. She was excluded from confidential meetings only once, during a parent conference over a suspended child. The time lost was 26 minutes. (From McDaniel-Hine & Willower, 1988, pp. 274–275. Reprinted with permission of the Helen Dwight Reid Educational Foundation. Published by Heldref Publications, Washington, D.C. Copyright © 1988.)

Extract B: Learner Achievement in Science Study

Purpose of the study: To examine (a) the effects of learner control and program control of seeing the information context on students' performance and attitudes during computer-assisted instruction (CAI); and, (b) the effects on achievement of reading ability and gender.

METHOD

Subjects

Subjects were 98 eighth-grade science students in a suburban junior high school. The mean standardized reading ability score, based on tests administered the previous year and expressed as grade equivalent, was 8.1.

Materials

The unit that served as the base for this study covered an introduction to solar energy. The content was developed from *Energy Choices and Challenges* (1984), part of The Energy Source Program, a nationally distributed energy education series. The material was first scaled down to a seventh-grade reading level, and practice and test questions were generated. Two classroom tryouts were conducted in pencil-and-paper format and one in computer-based format, each with accompanying revisions. The unit was designed as a series of informational screens containing text and graphics. Fifteen multiple-choice practice questions, with four response options each, were interspersed with the text and graphics screens.

Treatments

We used two instructional treatments: learner control and program control of content in CAI on solar energy. The instruction was the same for both the treatment groups. Subjects in both groups proceeded through the unit at their own pace, answered practice questions, and received feedback. After correct answers, all subjects received feedback such as "That's right. Today, most solar systems are used to heat water and inside air," or "That's right. A big problem with solar cells is that they cost a lot of money."

In the learner-control condition, subjects were told that their answer was incorrect immediately after a wrong answer and were asked, "Do you want to review before trying to answer the question again?" When a subject responded "Yes," he or she was returned to the program segment covering the pertinent content. At the end of that review segment, the subject was presented with the practice question once again. A "No" response resulted in a second presentation of the practice question.

In the program control condition, subjects were also told that their answer was not correct immediately after a wrong response. Next they were told, "Let's review before you try to answer the question again." Then the subjects reviewed the relevant material. After the review, a second chance was given to answer the practice question.

Both learner control and program control groups received three tries at each question, with attendant options for reviews after the first two incorrect answers. On the third incorrect answer, all subjects were given the correct answer and then continued on with the instruction.

The CAI that served as a base for this research was designed so that sound instructional procedures were incorporated regardless of whether learners chose high or low amounts of additional instruction through review. All learners progressed through the same base instruction on solar energy, and all had opportunities for appropriate practice and feedback.

Instruments

The instruction was followed by a posttest of 25 multiple-choice items with four response options each. Of these posttest items, 15 paralleled content covered by the practice questions and are referred to as "principal items." Interitem consistency for principal items across all subjects was calculated with the Kuder-Richardson Formula 20 to be .71.

An additional 10 items ("incidental items") were included in the posttest to measure incidental learning. All of the content for the incidental items was included in the initial presentation and in the available review screens, but not in practice questions.

After the posttest, students completed a seven-item questionnaire on attitudes and computer use. Students were asked about ease of understanding for the CAI, how well they liked it, how interesting they found it, whether they would like to learn more about solar energy, how much they felt they had learned, and how important they felt solar energy was for the future. Students were also asked how often they used a computer.

Procedures

To establish the experimental groups, we first separated participating students according to sex. Next we conducted a median split on standardized reading ability test scores. The median grade equivalent score was 8.0 for girls and 8.4 for boys. Students from the resulting four cells were then randomly assigned to either the learner control or program control treatments.

The study was conducted in the school's computer laboratory over four consecutive days. Apple II+ and IIe computers were used. Administration of the instructional treatment and dependent measures was completed within a single class period for each subject.

At the laboratory, students went directly to the computer that displayed their name on the screen and contained their preassigned instructional program. The experimenters explained that the instruction would be followed by a test to see how much they learned and a questionnaire to find out how they felt about the instruction. The students were told that although test scores would not count toward their class grade, their instructors would be looking over their tests, and so they should try hard to do well. The number of repeated practice questions, the number of reviews selected/assigned for each question, and the time to completion were recorded for each student.

Unequal group sizes resulted for two reasons: First, there were more boys than girls in the participating classes; second, some of the students who had been assigned were absent. Because equal numbers of subjects were desired for the analyses, subjects from each group were randomly dropped from consideration. As a result, data from 84 students were included in the analysis; each Sex × Treatment group contained 21 students.

Data from all dependent measures were analyzed with multiple regression techniques. Posttest performance, proportion of reviews selected/assigned, and time to completion were analyzed singly. Attitudinal and computer use data from the questionnaire were analyzed in multivariate multiple regression analyses.

The multiple regression analyses were performed on all dependent variables in accordance with techniques outlined by Pedhazur (1982). Standardized reading ability scores were entered first and were followed by effects for sex and treatment (girls = 1, boys = −1; learner control = 1, program control = −1). The four interaction products were entered in the first analysis and then excluded from the remaining analyses when no significant interactions were found. (From Kinzie, Sullivan, & Berdel, 1988, pp. 300–301. Copyright 1988 by the American Psychological Association. Reprinted by permission.)

FEEDBACK

Activity 1

What concerns should research consumers have about research procedures that are common to descriptive, comparative, and experimental research designs?

All research reports should have clear and complete explanations about every step of the research. All instruments should be valid and reliable and be administered by trained examiners. Research procedures should be tested in pilot studies.

What concerns should research consumers have about research procedures that are specific to descriptive research designs?

In observational research, especially qualitative or ethnographic studies, researchers need to be concerned about factors that might affect the replicability of their studies. They need to be sure the data represent a true picture of what occurred and can be generalized to other situations. This refers to the validity of the research results. Researchers also need to be sure that they are consistent in identifying aspects of a behavior or event and that others working in the same or similar situations would get similar results. This refers to the reliability of the research results.

What concerns should research consumers have about research procedures that are specific to comparative research designs?

Research consumers should use the questions for procedures in descriptive research to determine whether the results from comparative research are valid and reliable.

What concerns should research consumers have about research procedures that are specific to experimental research designs?

Research consumers should be concerned about whether variables other than the independent variables caused the observed changes in the dependent variable. Variables that might have an unwanted influence on, or might change, dependent variables are called extraneous variables. One of the best ways to control subject variables is through randomization. When subjects cannot be randomly selected or assigned to groups, researchers can equate them statistically.

How are extraneous variables controlled in experimental research?

Variables that need to be controlled to maintain the internal validity of experimental research are current events, subject growth and development, subject selection, attrition, testing, instrumentation, statistical regression, and interaction. Variables that need to be controlled to maintain the external validity of experimental research are subject–treatment interaction, reactive effects, multiple-treatment interaction, and research effects.

What distinguishes simple and complex experimental research designs?

Simple and complex experimental research designs are distinguished by (1) the number of independent or treatment variables, and (2) the extent to which results can be generalized from the immediate subjects to a larger target population. Experimental designs are a continuum from simple to complex plans. Simple experimental plans deal with single independent variables, and complex experimental plans deal with multiple independent variables. Simple experimental designs deal with one independent variable or have subject selection procedures that limit the generalizability of their results. More complex experimental designs deal with two or more experimental and subject variables.

What concerns should research consumers have about research procedures that are specific to causal–comparative research designs?

A major concern for researchers doing causal–comparative research is that the causal effect should be one-way. Since there are no manipulated, or treated, independent variables, the subjects cannot be randomly assigned to groups. For research consumers to generalize the results from causal–comparative studies to other populations and educational situations, they need to be sure that any differences between groups cannot be attributed to one or more important variables that were not accounted for by the researchers. There is always the possibility that these outside variables may be the true causes of the observed differences. Also, they should be sure researchers' description of the subjects is clear and that operational definitions are used to identify and distinguish the comparison groups.

What concerns should research consumers have about single-subject, action, and evaluation research designs?

Single-subject research is any research in which there is only one subject or one group that is treated as a single entity. Single-subject research may be descriptive or experimental. Action research is directed to studying existing educational practice and to producing practical, immediately applicable findings. The questions or problems studied are local in nature. Evaluation research is applying the rigors of experimental research to the judging of the worth or value of educational programs, projects, and instruction. Threats to the internal validity of single-subject research include testing, instrumentation, subject–treatment interaction, reactive effects, and researcher effects. Research consumers should expect research producers to adhere to the same guidelines as used for conducting descriptive and experimental research. Research consumers should expect published action research reports to have the same specificity in detail as other research reports. Research consumers can use several questions to help them judge the appropriateness of the evaluation researchers' statement of the problem, identification of subjects, selection of instruments, collecting data, and analyzing data.

What questions should be used to evaluate procedure sections?

To evaluate research design and procedure research consumers should use these questions: Are the research design and data collection procedures clearly described? Is the research design appropriate to the researcher's purpose? Can the study be replicated from the information provided? To evaluate qualitative experimental research, the question is: Has the researcher's presence influenced the behavior of the subjects? In studies with treatments: Are experimental procedures fully explained? Are examples of special materials included? To determine research validity: Are the procedures free from the influence of extraneous variables? Does the study contain any threats to its internal and external validity?

Activity 2

Extract A: Teachers' Work Behavior Study
This was a qualitative comparative study in which the researchers made observations during the school day. Since the purpose was to examine the work behavior of teachers, the design was appropriate to their purpose. The structured observation technique was identified and the research consumer was referred to a previous study. No mention, however, was made about the validity and reliability of the observation procedure for collecting data (field notes) nor of the telephone interviewing procedure. The researchers did mention that all techniques were tested in a pilot study, but no mention was made of any changes made in procedures nor what "sufficiently practiced in structured observation" means. The sample consisted of nominated volunteers. Descriptions of the five teachers were provided, but no mention was made of the criteria for including or eliminating teachers as candidates. The results might not be representative of typical elementary school teachers. Although the study might provide insight about five teachers' work behavior, research consumers need to be wary about extending generalizations to other teaching situations because reporting was insufficient to demonstrate that there were no threats to the research's validity and the reliability of the data.

Extract B: Learner Achievement in Science Study
Overall, the designs were appropriate to the researchers' purposes. The design used in the first part of this experimental research was a 2×2 factorial in a posttest-only control group design. The experimental variable was type of instruction (learner control and program control), and the second independent variable was gender. For the second part of the study, a multiple regression analysis was done to determine the influence on achievement of attitude about using CAI, prior computer experience, and reading ability. The descriptions of the subjects were sketchy; other variables with that possibly could influence achievement are intelligence, prior science knowledge and achievement, and learning style. Since a multiple regression analysis was done, the possible influence of these other variables could have been measured and analyzed. The materials were explained, but no sample passages and questions were provided, and there was no in-

dication as to the type of revisions made after the pilot study, so research consumers have no evidence of their validity. The researchers provided data about their reliability. Because of limited subject descriptions and lack of specific materials, replication of this study from the given information would be difficult. Research consumers should consider this study's results as tentative.

8

Reading and Interpreting Results Sections

DATA ANALYSIS IN QUANTITATIVE RESEARCH
- Normal Distribution
- Statistical Significance
- Interval Scale Data
- Nominal and Ordinal Scale Data

RESULTS

DATA ANALYSIS IN QUALITATIVE RESEARCH

READING RESULT SECTIONS
- Qualitative Description Quantitave Comparison
- Experimental
- Single-Subject
- Action

FOCUS QUESTIONS

1. What are the different ways quantitative data are recorded?
2. What is a normal distribution curve?
3. What statistical procedures are used in educational and other behavioral science research?
4. What is statistical significance?

5. What are the ways data are analyzed in qualitative research?
6. What criteria should be used to read and evaluate results sections?

After collecting data, researchers use several methods to describe, synthesize, analyze, and interpret the information. In all types of quantitative research, statistical procedures facilitate understanding of a vast amount of numerical data. These procedures are the techniques by which researchers summarize and explain quantitative data and determine the existence of relationships and causal effects. In qualitative research, the outcomes of research are the generation of hypotheses and research questions, not the verification of predicted relationships or outcomes. Therefore, qualitative researchers use verbal rather than statistical procedures to analyze data. These inductive analytic procedures involve organizing data, identifying patterns, and synthesizing key ideas as research questions and hypotheses.

Research consumers need to understand (a) the way researchers match data analysis procedures to research designs, (b) the different statistical analyses available to educational and other behavioral and social science researchers, (c) the assumptions researchers make about those analyses to use them effectively, (d) the concept of statistical significance and the criteria generally used to set the point at which results can be considered as reliable, (e) the assumptions researchers make about qualitative data analyses, and (f) the way to read and interpret results sections in quantitative and qualitative research reports.

From reading results sections, research consumers should be able to answer

What types of data analysis were used?

What statistical analyses did the researchers use?

Were the statistical analyses appropriate for the researchers' questions, purposes, or hypotheses and for the research design?

Were the qualitative analyses appropriate and logical?

What were the research results?

Were the results of quantitative research statistically significant?

Were the results of practical use and importance?

Will the results be applicable to the other educational settings, especially the one in which I teach?

Results sections should be evaluated using the following questions, which are from Figure 3.1, p. 87.

INTERPRETING EDUCATIONAL RESEARCH

Are the statistical procedures for data analysis clearly described and are they appropriate for the type of quantitative research design?

Are statistical significance levels indicated?

Does the research have practical significance?

In qualitative research, are the processes for organizing data, identifying patterns, and synthesizing key ideas as hypothesis and research questions clearly described.

DATA ANALYSES IN QUANTITATIVE RESEARCH

Data analyses in quantitative research involve the use of statistics. **Statistics** are numerical ways to describe, analyze, summarize, and interpret data in a manner that conserves time and space. Researchers select statistical procedures after they have determined what research designs and types of data will be appropriate for answering their research questions. For example, in answering descriptive research questions, statistics let researchers show the data's central tendencies and variability. In answering comparative and experimental research questions, other statistics allow researchers to draw inferences and make generalizations about target populations. In all three types of research, the specific statistical procedures are determined by the research design and by the type of data that are collected. And, in comparative and experimental research, statistics are tools that let researchers gain two other insights: They allow researchers to determine (a) an estimate of the sampling error—the error (or difference) between the research sample and the target population, and (b) the confidence with which research producers and consumers can accept the results.

The way quantitative data are recorded depends on the instruments (measuring devices) used. Data are recorded as: (a) intervals, (b) rankings, (c) categories, and (d) ratios. Each means of recording data requires the use of different statistics. **Interval scales** present data according to preset, equal spans. They are the most common form of data reporting in education and the social sciences, and they are identified by continuous measurement scales: raw scores and derived scores such as IQ scores, standard scores, normal curve equivalents. They are the way data from most tests are recorded. Rankings, or **ordinal scales**, show the order, from highest to lowest, for a variable. There are no indications about the value or size of differences between or among items in a list; the indications refer only to the relative order of the scores. For instance, subjects can be ranked according to their performance on a set of athletic tasks, and what will be reported is the order in which they scored (e.g., first, second, third), not their actual accumulation of points. Olympic medal winners are reported as ordinal scales. Data from surveys and observations are often recorded in this manner. Categories separate data into two or more discrete aspects, such as male–female, red–white–blue, or always–frequently–infrequently–never. The data can be reported as number of items or as percentages of a total. Data recorded this way are considered **nominal scales**. Data from surveys and observations are often recorded in this way. **Ratio scales**, less frequently used in educational and other behavioral and social science research than the other three, show relative relationships among scores, such as half-as-large or three-times-as-tall. In dealing with educational variables, researchers usually do not have much use for these presentations.

Normal Distribution

Chapter 2 contains an explanation of central tendency and variability. The most common form of each of these statistics for interval scale data are the mean and standard deviation. To reiterate, the **mean** is the arithmetic average score, and the **standard deviation** (SD) shows how far from the mean are most of the other scores. The SD is based on the concept that given a large enough set of scores, they will produce a graph in the shape of a bell. This graph is called the **normal distribution curve**. This graph, which is shown in Figure 8.1, represents a theoretical statistical picture of how most human and nonhuman variables are distributed. Using a human variable such as ability to draw human figures as measured by a test as an example, the curve would show that few people have scores indicating little of the trait (the extreme left end of the graph), that is, an inability to draw human figures, and few people have scores showing a great deal of the trait (the extreme right end of the graph), that is, a great ability to draw human figures. The center of the graph shows that most people have scores indicating some ability to draw human figures. This description is commonly called the **norm**.

There is a direct relationship between the SD and the normal distribution curve. Starting at the center, or mean, of the distributed variable, each SD represents a fixed, specific proportion of the population. For example, in Figure 8.1, the range between the mean and either extreme end of the graph (left or right) equals 50% of the population represented by the graph. And, each of the ranges between the mean and +1 SD (the area M → A) and the mean and −1 SD (the area a ← M) equals a little more than one-third (34%) of the distributed population. Each of the ranges +1 SD to +2 SDs (A → B) and −1 SD to −2 SDs (b ← a) equals about 14% of the population. Therefore, the range of scores included between ± 1 SD (a ↔ A) equals about 68% of the population, and between ± 2 SDs (b ↔ B) equals slightly over 95%. Most statistical procedures are based on the assumption that data approximate the normal distribution curve. In reality, the graphs produced from the data of many research studies are not as symmetrical as the normal distribution curve.

INTERPRETING EDUCATIONAL RESEARCH

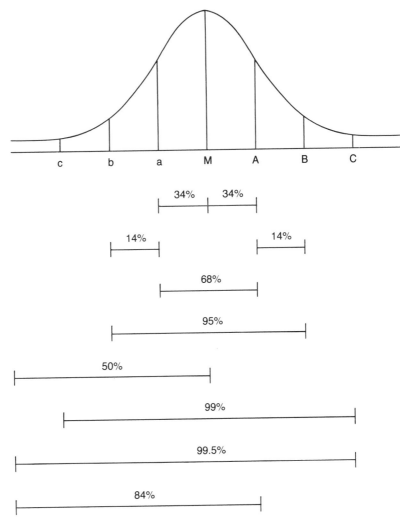

Figure 8.1 The normal distribution curve.

Statistical Significance

The normal distribution curve is also called the *normal probability curve* because it is used to estimate the likelihood of an interval score or set of interval scores happening by chance. In comparative and experimental research, researchers want to be sure that the observed differences between the means of two or more groups of subjects or two or more variables are truly different. That is, they want to know if the difference is a reliable one. If these means differ, researchers need to know the extent to which the difference could have happened by chance. When the observed difference between these means is large enough to be beyond a predetermined chance level, the difference is considered as significant. **Statistical significance** occurs when results exceed a predetermined chance level. Therefore, researchers can know how confident they can be about the conclusions they can make from their findings.

Three interrelated factors are usually considered in a statistical analysis: (1) the difference between group means, (2) the variability of the groups, and (3) the number of subjects in each group. All other things being equal, there is an increased likelihood that difference(s) between the means of two or more sets of scores are statistically significant when (a) the differences between the means become larger, (b) the variability of each set of scores becomes smaller, or (c) the size of the sample increases. These three relationships can be seen in Figure 8.2.

When researchers statistically conclude if a difference or relationship exists, there is the possibility of error. Two kinds of error can occur: (1) Researchers can accept the results as true when they are not and (2) researchers do not accept the results as true when they actually are.

For example, in the first error, researchers find what appears to be a statistically significant difference in student performance over previous performance when using a new instructional program. However, because of imperfections in sampling procedures (subject selection error) and the measuring instruments (reliability estimates), there may not be a true difference in student performance after using the new program. In such a case, the researchers will have concluded that the new instructional program is better than the old one when in fact that is not true. In the second error, researchers do not find a significant difference in student learning when actually there is a difference. In this case, there is a change resulting from teachers' use of an instructional technique, but the researchers do not observe it. The second error may also result from imperfections in the sample and instrumentation.

In educational and other behavioral and social science research, researchers try to avoid making the first type of error, but to do this they increase the possibility of making the second. Relative to the

The possibility of statistical significance increases as		
Differences between Means	Variability	Sample Size
or		or
gets larger	gets smaller	gets larger

Figure 8.2 Factors affecting statistical significance.

discussion of the normal probability curve, researchers have agreed to use certain probability levels. These conventional levels correspond to the extreme ends of the curve and designate a very small chance of the first type of error. It is important to realize that research producers and consumers *never* know whether either of these two error types is being made.

Researchers report the probability that the first type of error has occurred as a decimal. The probability level is shown in research reports as $p = .05$. This means that the chances of concluding that differences or relationships exist when they truly do not exist are no more than 5 chances out of 100. These are odds similar to those for reporting one's likelihood of winning a state lottery. Sometimes researchers report the probability level as $p < .05$, which is read as "the probability is less than 5 chances out of 100," or as $p \le .05$, which is read as "the probability is equal to or less than 5 chances out of 100." Of course, when researchers realize the probability is even less than $p = .05$, they sometimes may report it as $p = .01$ or even as $p = .001$.

Research consumers need to be wary of accepting any results (even if they are statistically significant) without considering whether the results are practical or meaningful in educational settings. What is of prime importance to research consumers is the usefulness of the results in terms of improving teacher effectiveness, student learning, and efficient uses of instructional resources. To determine whether research results have **practical significance**, research consumers need to answer: How effectively can the results be used in my teaching situation?

Statistics with Interval Scale Data

Statistical procedures used with interval scales are based on certain assumptions, all of which are related to the concept of a normal distribution curve. These statistics procedures are called **parametric statistics**. In using parametric statistics, researchers are trying to draw some conclusion from the differences between the means of sample groups or sets of scores.

The assumptions for using parametric statistics are:

The variables are measured in interval scales.

The score of any subject is not influenced by those of any other subjects; that is, each is an independent phenomenon.

The subjects are selected from and represent a normally distributed population.

When the research involves two or more groups of subjects, each of which represents different populations, the variables that distinguish each population are similarly distributed among each population.

A common parametric statistic is the *t*-**test**. It is used when there are two sets of scores and is reported as numbers such as $t = 1.6$ or $t = 3.1$. After determining the value of t, researchers consult a statistical table to determine whether the value is a significant one. A *t*-test can be used, for example, to examine the mean scores in reading and mathematics for one group of subjects, or it can be used to examine mean scores in reading for two different groups of subjects. The *t*-test is used frequently in single-variable comparative and experimental research, and its use is limited by the same factors that limit single-variable research.

Another parametric statistic used with interval data in comparative research is the **product-moment correlation**, which refers to the quantified relationship between two sets of scores for the same group of subjects. The results of the arithmetical computation is a **coefficient of correlation**, which is expressed as r, a decimal between -1.0 and $+1.0$. The most common interval scale correlation coefficient is the Pearson product-moment r. Correlations show whether two or more variables have a systematic relationship of occurrence—that is, whether high scores for one variable occur with high scores of another (a positive relationship) or whether they occur with low scores of that other variable (a negative relationship). The occurrence of low scores for one variable with low scores of another is also an example of a positive relationship. A correlational coefficient of zero (0) indicates that the variables have no relationship with each other, that is, are independent of each other.

Correlations can also be used to establish predictions. When a strong relationship has been established between two variables, a correlation can be used to predict the possible occurrence of either variable. The predictive use of correlation is important for such educational endeavors as early intervention programs for students with special needs. For example, certain tests, including tests of basic concepts and cognitive abilities, are appropriate for young children and are highly predictive of students' later school performance.

Table 2.3 (Chapter 2, p. 34) shows how correlation coefficients are reported in table format from a study about the relationships between topic-specific background knowledge and measures of overall writing quality. When coefficients of correlation are statistically significant, they indicate that the variables are probably systematically related. In other words, the two variables *go together*; significant correlations do not indicate that there are any causal effects of one variable on the other. In Table 2.4, the relationship between the holistic scoring method and teachers' marks is positive and significant—high coherence scores were given to the same students' work that received high teacher marks. On the other hand, the relationship between coherence and the number of words and clauses, which is negative, was not significant, and therefore the two scoring methods can be said to be unrelated. Again, no causality is implied, nor should it be assumed.

When research designs call for examining differences among the means of two or more groups of subjects or two or more variables, they frequently use the **analysis of variance** (ANOVA), which is reported in F ratios. The advantage in using an ANOVA is that several independent variables as well as several factors can be examined. In its simplest form, ANOVA can be thought of as a multiple t-test. The ANOVA is appropriate for use with some comparative research designs and with experimental research designs such as the pretest–posttest with multiple control groups, the Solomon four-group design, counterbalanced designs, common factorial designs, and causal–comparative designs. The ANOVA procedure can be used when more than one independent variable is involved. Table 2.4 (Chapter 2, p. 39) shows the ANOVA results for a three-way factorial design from a study using three independent variables: The effect of three different sentence organizations (format of text) during cloze tests (students' comprehension) on fourth and fifth grade readers (grade level). Notice that the researchers indicated three significance levels: $p < .05$, $.01$, and $.001$. The results show that there were differences in results based on the type of sentence organization (format of text), the students' grade level, and the comprehension ability of the students (students' comprehension). The results also indicated that particular types of text format were most effective at certain grade levels with specific ability students (format $\times$ grade $\times$ comprehension).

An important feature of ANOVA is that it can show the **interaction effects** between and among variables. In Chapter 7, the negative consequence of treatment interaction was discussed, as well as the possibility of measuring the interaction in factorial designs. Interactions are also expressed as F-ratios within a ANOVA table, and often the interaction is illustrated in a graph. For research consumers, treatment interactions permit instructional modifications for particular groups of learners. For example, referring again to Table 2.4, there is a significant three-way interaction (format $\times$ grade $\times$ comprehension). The researchers report that this significant finding can be interpreted to mean that a specific group (fifth grade good comprehenders) produce the highest comprehension scores when reading meaning-preorganized material. For other groups of students, reading specific types of materials does not similarly increase comprehension scores.

In previous chapters, reference was made to situations in which two or more groups of subjects differ on one or more variables, thereby limiting the generalizability of the studies' findings. The differences might have occurred because preexisting groups of subjects were used instead of randomly selected and assigned groups of subjects. When research producers think these variables might influence the dependent variables under study (and the variables are not features that are used to distinguish between groups, e.g., distinguishing between male and female, or high and low mathematical performance), they use a statistical procedure to equate the groups on these independent variable factors.

One frequently used procedure is known as **analysis of covariance** (ANCOVA). Its use allows researchers to examine differences among the means of groups of subjects as if the means were equal from the start. They do this by adjusting the differences in the means to make them hypothetically equal. The procedure is similar to the use of a "handicap" in bowling or golf leagues to balance out differences among players and teams. In all other ways, ANCOVAs are interpreted as ANOVAs.

When researchers wish to examine the relationships among more than two variables, they can use a **multiple correlation** technique (also called *multiple regression* technique). The procedure is interpreted similarly to a single correlation coefficient. Multiple correlations can also be used to make predictions. Prediction scores are reported as a multiple correlation coefficient, or R, and have the same range as single correlations. Multiple regression coefficients are used frequently in causal–comparative experimental research because they combine ANOVA and correlational techniques. Research consumers need to keep in mind that the causality in causal–comparative research is *assumed* because of a strong, highly predictive relationship. This assumed causality needs to be reconfirmed by further experimental studies.

Statistics with Nominal and Ordinal Scale Data

When researchers collect data that are measured in nominal and ordinal scales, they must use different types of statistics. These statistics, called **nonparametric statistics**, work on different assumptions. Nonparametric statistics are used when:

The populations do *not* have the characteristics of the normal distribution curve.

Symbols or numbers are used as labels on categories (nominal scales).

An expected or rank order is apparent but the order is not necessarily equally spaced as is the case with interval data.

For each parametric statistical procedure there are corresponding nonparametric procedures. In general, nonparametric statistics are less frequently used in educational and other behavioral and social science research than are parametric. Table 8.1 shows corresponding parametric and nonparametric statistics.

One popular nonparametric statistical procedure is the **Chi square test** (X^2). It is used to test the significance of group differences when data are reported as frequencies or percentages of a total or as nominal scales. Table 2.2 (Chapter 2, p. 33) shows an example of Chi square reporting from a study that examined how teachers responded when students made miscues (deviant oral reading responses). In their anal-

Table 8.1   Corresponding Parametric and Nonparametric Statistics

Parametric	Nonparametric
t-Test	Mann-Whitney *U* Test
ANOVA	Friedman two-way analysis of variance Kruskal–Wallis one-way analysis of variance
Pearson product-moment correlation	Spearman rank–order correlation

ysis, the researchers found that teachers who dealt with unattempted miscues significantly supplied words more often than they did when faced with all other types of student responses.

Indications of statistical significance are interpreted the same for nonparametric statistics as they are for parametric statistics.

DATA ANALYSIS IN QUALITATIVE RESEARCH

In qualitative studies, researchers' verbally analyze data. This involves examining and organizing notes from interviews and observations and reducing the information into smaller segments from which they can see patterns and trends. In addition, researchers interpret the meanings of these patterns and trends and create research hypotheses and questions for verification in further research. Qualitative researchers begin their analyses while still in the research setting and finish it after all data have been collected. An important point about qualitative research is that qualitative researchers often do measure and count; in other words, they quantify some data. However, they do not use statistical analyses to verify or support their results and conclusions, nor do they consider statistical probabilities.

Research consumers should expect qualitative researchers to fully explain their analysis methods so that the logic of their decisions can be followed and evaluated. In Chapter 2 there is a discussion of the features of qualitative research methods, and in Chapter 7 are questions that can be used to determine the validity and reliability of observational research. Research consumers may wish to review those sections before continuing the discussion here, which is a synthesis of the ideas of several scholars who use qualitative research methods (Bogdan & Biklen, 1982; Firestone, 1987; Howe, 1988; Jacob, 1987; Lincoln & Guba, 1985; Van Maanen, Dabbs, & Faulkner, 1982; Wiersma, 1986; and, Wilson, 1977).

In the research setting, commonly called the field, qualitative researchers continually make decisions that narrow their study. They may start out with broad questions and begin looking at an entire educational setting, but as their study proceeds they concentrate on smaller issues and create more specific analytical questions. Data collection is an additive process. New information is looked for and collected on the basis of previous data, because the qualitative researchers are interpreting as they assemble additional information. This does not mean they discard or selectively omit information. On the contrary, they maintain extensive on-site field notes. It is the influence of the events in the field and their on-going interpretation of those events that guide researchers in their search for additional information. For example, while observing middle school science lessons to study teachers' use of graphic organizers, a qualitative researcher may take note in one class of students' collaborative activities in examining and recording the mealworm's life cycle. What the researcher notes is a combination of formalized small group behaviors and seemingly unstructured, random student interaction. Noting this, the researcher was later able to seek out information leading to a hypothesis about a possible interrelationship among teachers' teaching style, their development of student collaborations, and students' use of graphic organizers.

One procedure used by qualitative researchers to support their interpretations is **triangulation**, a procedure for cross-validating information. Triangulation is collecting information from several sources about the same event or behavior. For example, in studying parents' attitudes about their involvement in their children's homework activities, data would be collected from interviews with parents, students, siblings, and teachers and from observations of parent–student behaviors during homework activities.

After collecting data in the field, qualitative researchers organize their data by sifting through the information and clustering seemingly similar ideas. These categories of information are labeled for ease of use and cross referencing. Qualitative researchers start with broad categories:

Settings (where teaching and learning occur)

Situations (when an activity or behavior occurs)

Activities (what teachers and students do)

Behaviors (how teachers and students act and respond)

Techniques or methods (how and why teachers and students respond to an event)

Socializations (with whom teachers and students regularly interact)

Depending on the nature of their data, these categories may be expanded, subdivided, eliminated, or renamed. Some notes may be cross referenced because they contain information relevant to more than one category.

Research consumers need to know the coding categories qualitative researchers use and how the classification systems were developed and revised. Since qualitative analyses are subjective, producers of qualitative research should be explicit about their theoretical formulations and their conceptual positions regarding the topic being investigated. When these are not explicitly stated in research reports, research consumers need to be aware that these formulations and positions usually are reflected in researchers' purpose questions and classification systems.

READING RESULTS SECTIONS

The results sections of research reports are usually the most difficult for research consumers to read and interpret. Often research consumers are intimidated by the statistical procedures and the presentation of numerical data in charts and tables. However, these sections can be read systematically if the reading plan outlined in Chapter 3 is followed. By the time research consumers read the results sections, they should already know the researchers' purposes, questions, and research designs; major results and conclusions; target populations and subject selection techniques; instrumentations; and, research methods. What is left to understand are the specific results relative to the research questions.

Results sections are read during the third phase of the reading plan, when the research consumer is confirming predictions and knowledge (see Chapter 3, p. 43). The goal of this phase for research consumers is to verify that their (not the research producers') purposes have been met and to decide what information supports the researchers' purpose and adds to their (the consumers') knowledge base.

In reports of quantitative research, the results of statistical procedures such as the *t*-test, correlation, and ANOVA are not always put into table format; the numerical information may be part of the general discourse of the report because of space limitations. Research consumers should expect, however, that the reports' authors give an explanation of the numerical information whether it is within the text or in tables.

You should review the questions in the Evaluating Results Sections at the beginning of this chapter before reading the following portions of this chapter, in which the results sections for each of the methods sections discussed in Chapter 7 are presented. In the quantitative studies, the researchers' explanations of the statistical information are highlighted.

Reading a Qualitative Descriptive Research Report

The following results section is from a qualitative descriptive study (see Chapter 7, pp. 148–149 to review the method section). Note two things about the results section. The researcher has answered specific questions that relate to her data analysis procedures. And, although some quantification was done (percentages of responses), the data were verbally analyzed, not statistically analyzed.

Purpose of the study: To determine how frequently, when, and for what reasons a group of second grade writers used their peers' questions to revise their unfinished pieces.

RESULTS

How frequently did the children insert the requested information into their texts?

To answer this question the percentage of changes made by each child in his/her texts as a result of the questions raised during the sharing sessions was calculated.

Six of the 24 children (25%) made no changes in their texts as a result of their peers' questions. Three of these six children chose to share only once between January and June.

Eighteen of the 24 children (75%) inserted into their texts, typically at the end, at least some of the information identified as missing by their peers' questions. Six of these 18 children incorporated responses into their texts to more than 50% of the questions they received from their peers. The range of these children's percentage of questions used was from 60 to 100%. Two of these children were nondiscriminating; every question asked was answered by inserting the missing information at the end of their pieces. For one of these two children, the change over the data collection period was from inserting the requested information in phrases, for example, in response to "Why did you have to go to the hospital?," Mathy inserted "Because my eye puffed up." at the end of her text to inserting the requested information in sentences, for example, in response to "How sunburned did you get?," Mathy inserted "I got a little bit of sunburn." The other 12 of these 18 children used their peers' questions sometimes, but not often, to modify their text. The range of these 12 children's percentage of changes made as a result of their peers' questions was from 14 to 40%.

Did publishing affect how frequently these writers used their peers' questions for text revisions?

To answer this question the percentage of revisions made in eventually published and in never published drafts by those fourteen children who had shared both kinds of drafts was calculated and compared.

For slightly more than half (57%) of these children, more revisions were made in eventually published than in never published drafts. For five of these children, the decision to publish had a significant effect on their decision to use their peers' questions; they made no revisions based on their peers' questions in never published pieces. Those three children who made some revisions based on their peers' questions in both eventually published and never published drafts made from 15 to 86% more revisions in drafts which were eventually published.

Four of the 14 children (28%) used their peers' questions more frequently to revise never published pieces.

Two children (14%) revised, based on their peers' questions, equally as often in published and never published drafts. One of these children made no changes based on his peers' questions in either eventually published or never published drafts; the other child inserted information based on every question asked by her peers in eventually published and never published drafts.

What reasons did the children provide for their decisions not to use their peers' questions?

During one month (May) the children were asked to provide reasons for their decisions not to use their peers' questions. The most frequently provided reason (30%) was that the child did not know the answer to the question raised by his/her peer. Typically, these rejected questions were requests for specific information, for details, for example, "Why did Baby Anna put her hand in the garbage?," which the writer did not possess. (Roni answered, "I can't answer that! I can't read her mind!")

While the second and third most frequently provided reasons seem similar, the focus of the child's response was different. The focus of the "I didn't want to use the question." response (20%) was the quality of the piece as it existed; the writer liked it as it was. The focus of the "The question wasn't good." (15%) was the value of the question of the piece. In the writer's opinion, the question "What day did that happen?" was unimportant.

Five other reasons were provided by the children. Fifteen percent of their responses were of the "I'm not going to publish this piece" type. This response implied that since the child did not intend to publish the piece no revising to make the meaning clear for others was necessary. "I already answered that question in my piece." was suggested 8% of the time as the reason for rejecting a question. The writer contended that the question-asker had not listened carefully to the reading of the pieces. Six percent of the responses focused on the relationship between the writer and the question-asker. "I didn't like (a child's name)." was typical of the responses in this category. Since the question-asker was not liked, his/her question was not used to guide the piece's revision. Four percent of the responses were of the "I already answered that question during sharing time." type. These responses suggested that the answer to the question had been given orally during the sharing session. Finally, "My parents wouldn't want me to answer that question." was suggested once as the reason for rejecting a question. This response indicated that the answers to some questions were unacceptable.

Every child questioned provided a reason for his/her discision not to insert the requested information into the text. (From Vukelich, 1986, pp. 302–303)

Reading a Quantitative Comparative Research Report

In comparative research, researchers examine the descriptions of two or more variables and make decisions about their differences or relationships. They can also make predictions about one variable based on information about another. Research consumers should be concerned that only appropriate generalizations are made from comparative and predictive data. The following results section is from a comparative study of the relationship among several variables (see pp. 149–150).

Purpose of the study: To examine the relationships between children's spelling ability and different aspects of their oral reading performance, specifically, rate, accuracy, and phrasing.

RESULTS

All correlations were positive, high, and statistically significant. Individual correlations between the spelling and oral reading variables ranged from .56 (Phonetic Quality and Rate) to .73 (Phonetic Quality and Accuracy). Surprisingly, Accuracy was more highly correlated with Phonetic Quality (.73) than with either of the other reading variables, Rate (.68) or Phrasing (.69). Spelling variables predicted 46% of the variance in Rate, 59% of the variance in Accuracy and 43% of the variance in Phrasing. Spelling Accuracy accounted for almost all of the explained variance in Rate and Phrasing while Phonetic Quality was the best predictor of Accuracy. The canonical correlation revealed that 62% of the variance was shared between the two sets of variables. (See Tables 1 and 2.)

Table 1   Spelling, Reading Correlations

	Sp. Score	Phon. Qual.	Sp. Stage	Rate	Accuracy	Phrasing
Sp. Score						
Phon. Qual.	.78					
Sp. Stage	.88	.78				
Rate	.68	.56	.60			
Accuracy	.70	.73	.62	.68		
Phrasing	.65	.57	.56	.86	.69	

Table 2   Partial Correlations—Reading Achievement Controlled

	Rate	Accuracy	Phrasing
Sp. Score	.39	.46	.34
Phon. Qual.	.19*	.57	.25
Sp. Stage	.38	.43	.31

*Only nonsignificant correlation ($p < .05$).

Table 3   Regression Analyses—Spelling Variables on Each Reading Measure

	Variable	Multiple *R*	*R* Square	*RSQ* Change
Rate	Sp. Score	.6812	.4640	.4640
	Phon. Qual.	.6823	.4656	.0016
	Sp. Stage	.6826	.4659	.0003
Accuracy	Phon. Qual.	.7345	.5394	.5394
	Sp. Score	.7613	.5796	.0401
	Sp. Stage	.7671	.5885	.0089
Phrasing	Sp. Score	.6477	.4196	.4196
	Phon. Qual.	.6563	.4307	.0111
	Sp. Stage	.6591	.4344	.0038

As expected, all the reading and spelling variables were highly correlated with standardized test scores of reading achievement, and correlations were reduced when achievement scores were used as a control. However, the pattern of correlations remained essentially the same, and all but one of the correlations remained statistically significant. The correlation between Accuracy and Phonetic Quality remained particularly high (.57). (See Table 3.) (From Zutell & Rasinski, 1986, pp. 110–111)

In addition to computing common correlation coefficients (Table 1) the researchers computed two other correlations, both of which were indicated in the method section. One, a canonical correlation, involves the use of multiple variables in combination to predict a combination of other variables. In the study about spelling ability and reading performance, the reading variables shown in Table 1 (rate, accuracy, phrasing) were used in combination with each other to predict spelling variables (score, quality, and stage).

The second, a partial correlation, also involves the use of several variables, but it is used when researchers wish to determine whether one or more variables may have an underlying influence on the others. This is done because the subjects are known to differ on these possibly influencing variables. In the spelling ability and reading performance study, reading achievement is different and is "partialed out"; that is, the researchers wished to know whether the correlations between the spelling variables and the reading variables of rate and accuracy were still statistically significant after reading achievement was held constant.

Research consumers should carefully consider whether the variable(s) controlled in partial correlations can have an influence. All assumptions about the possibility of causality based on correlations should be fully explained by researchers so that research consumers can determine the logic of their argument. In the above study, the researchers computed a partial correlation because they found that all of the variables correlated highly with reading achievement. Therefore, whatever reading achievement is, the researchers wished to know if it might have influenced all the other statistically significant correlations.

Reading an Experimental Research Report

Researchers use experimental designs when conducting research about the causative effect of one or more variables on other variables. The plans provide researchers with structures for studying one or more independent variables with one or more groups of subjects. Researchers select designs that best fit their purposes, answer questions about causation, and efficiently control extraneous variables.

The common experimental designs are discussed in Chapter 7 and illustrated in Figures 7.1 (p. 156), 7.2 (p. 159), 7.3 (p. 160), 7.4 (pp. 161–162), and 7.5 (p. 169).

The following results section is taken from a pretest–posttest control group design that has a single independent variable and three dependent variables. In this section, the results of an analysis of covariance (ANCOVA) are presented, but they are not presented in table form. Since the subjects differed at the start on sight-vocabulary identification scores, this was statistically corrected for in the ANCOVA. The table shows only the groups' means and standard deviations. (See pp. 156–158.)

Purpose of the study: To study an experimental instructional program involving the reading of predictable books and instruction and practice in matching speech to print.

RESULTS

The multivariate analysis of covariance for the three tasks was significant, $F (3, 23)$, $p < .04$. The univariate F tests were then conducted to explain the significant multivariate effect. Results of these tests indicated that the experimental group's posttreatment ability to match speech to print was significantly greater, $F (1, 25) = 4.37$, $p < .05$, than that of the placebo group. There was also a significant difference, $F (1, 25) = 8.74$, $p .01$, in favor of the experimental group, in posttreatment ability to identify sight vocabulary words. There was no significant difference, $F (1, 25) = 0.12$, $p .73$, between the experimental and placebo groups on the explicit concept-of-word variable. (For cell means and standard deviations, see Table 1). (From Rowe & Cunningham, 1983, p. 228)

Table 1 Means and Standard Deviations of Speech/Print Match, Sight Words and Explicit Posttest Scores Adjusted by Sight Word Pretest Scores

Group	Speech/Print Match		Sight Words		Explicit	
	M	SD	M	SD	M	SD
Experimental	6.12	1.82	1.92	1.87	4.94	1.54
Placebo	4.88	1.64	.87	.61	5.14	1.46

The next results section is from a $2 \times 2 \times 2$ factorial design. The independent variables and their factors are reading ability (high and low), treatment (experimental, or induced lookbacks, and control, or spontaneous lookbacks), and passage (familiar and unfamiliar). (See Chapter 7, pp. 163–166 for the method sections of this study.) Notice that the ANCOVA results are not presented in table form, but the interaction effects are graphed. If the lines in an interaction graph intersect, there is an interaction; if the lines do not cross, there is no interaction.

Purpose of the study: To investigate the effects of a graphic organizer that was designed to induce students to look back in their texts for information they had missed, misunderstood, or forgotten.

RESULTS

Preliminary data analyses were run to determine if there were any effects for passage or for time spent reading and answering the questions. The results of these analyses indicated that there were no differences ($F = 0.16$, $p > .60$) for passage (Louis XIV vs. diffusion of Western culture) on either of the two dependent measures. Consequently, the data were collapsed across passages for the final analyses. However, the preliminary analyses did reveal differences on both dependent measures for time spent reading and answering the questions. As a result of these analyses, time was entered as the covariate in each of the separate two-way analyses of covariance (ANCOVAs).

Table 1 [on p. 204] contains the means and standard deviations for the total number of questions answered correctly and for the lookback-only questions answered correctly by treatment group and self-perceived reading ability. The mean scores for both treatment groups were adjusted for differences due to time spent reading and answering the questions.

The results of the analysis of covariance run on the total number of questions answered correctly showed a main effect for reading ability— $F (1, 59) = 47.57$, $p < .001$, but not for treatment, $F (1, 59) = 3.13$, $p < .09$. However, there was an interaction effect for Treatment $\times$ Reading Ability—$F (1, 59) = 6.13$, $p < .02$. A similar pattern resulted from the analysis of covariance with lookback-only questions as the dependent variable. A main effect was found for reading ability—$F (1, 59) = 41.36$, $p < .001$, but not for treatment, $F < 1$. However, there was an interaction effect for Treatment $\times$ Reading Ability—$F (1, 59) = 4.12$, $p < .05$. As shown in Figure 2 [on p. 204], tests of simple main effects ($p < .05$) for total number of questions answered correctly indicated that the self-perceived low-ability comprehenders who were exposed to the graphic organizer treatment performed significantly better than the self-perceived low-ability comprehenders who were in the control group. There were no significant differences between the self-perceived high-ability comprehenders. Likewise, as shown in Figure 3 [on p. 205], tests of simple main effects ($p < .05$) for the number of lookback-only questions answered correctly indicated that the self-perceived low-ability comprehenders who were exposed to the graphic organizer treatment per-

Table 1   Means and Standard Deviations for Total Questions Correct and Lookback-Only Correct by Treatment Group and Self-Perceived Reading Ability

Reading Ability	Graphic Organizer (Induced)		No Graphic Organizer (Spontaneous)	
	Total	Lookback-Only	Total	Lookback-Only
Self-perceived high-ability comprehenders				
M	76.92[a]	61.13[b]	79.30	71.26
(SD)	(3.79)	(6.48)	(3.71)	(6.34)
Self-perceived low-ability comprehenders				
M	60.20	31.71	44.82	16.66
(SD)	(3.64)	(6.21)	(3.90)	(6.66)

[a]Percentage correct out of a possible 10.
[b]Percentage correct out of a possible 4.

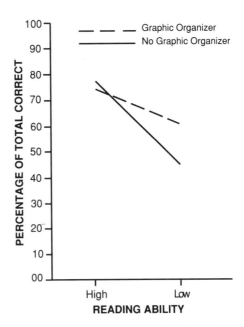

Figure 2 Interaction between treatment and reading ability for total correct.

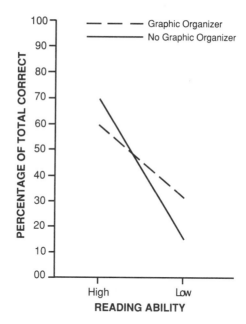

Figure 3 Interaction between treatment and reading ability for lookback-only correct.

formed significantly better than the self-perceived low-ability compre-henders who were in the control group. There were no significant dif-ferences between the self-perceived high-ability comprehenders. (From Alvermann, 1988, pp. 328–329. Reprinted with permission of the Helen Dwight Reid Educational Foundation. Published by Heldref Publica-tions, Washington, D.C. Copyright © 1988.)

Causal–comparative research is *ex post facto*, or after-the-fact, re-search because researchers are trying to establish a causal effect be-tween existing conditions. Researchers want answers to questions but cannot manipulate the independent variable(s) for practical or ethical reasons. They realize a condition exists and are unsure about what might have been its cause. Causal–comparative designs are built on the posttest-only control group design.

The following results section contains an example of a causal–com-parative design (see Chapter 7, pp. 167–168). The researchers sought to determine the effect of a preexisting condition (amount of previous mathematics instruction) on mathematics achievement. It should be remembered that researchers using the causal–comparative design are trying to find *causal relationships* or *predictions*.

Purpose of the study: To determine the possible effect on students' mathematics achievement of the number of semesters of mathematics courses they took. The researchers took into account the possible in-fluence of several background variables of the subjects.

RESULTS

The means, standard deviations and correlations of the predictor and criterion variables are shown in Table 1. The achievement test was the 47-item MATS10. With the exception of the percent of Title I qualifiers in the school, all background variables correlated with the criterion variable with values greater than 0.20. The rather large skewness of this variable, positive 3.2, may explain the low correlation with the criterion variable. Nearly half of the sample reported no Title I qualifiers at all. Especially noteworthy is the 0.73 correlation between quantity of mathematics and the measure of mathematics achievement.

The multiple regression analysis was performed by entering the nonschool variables first and then testing the contribution of mathematics courses. The findings are reported in Table 2.

The eight background variables accounted for 24 percent of the variation in achievement scores, suggesting a substantial community and home environmental influence. However, the variation in the amount of mathematics studied accounted for an additional 34 percent of the total variance, far more than reported in previous studies.

The regression analysis was repeated on two other random samples of 17-year-olds using different criterion instruments. These samples included 2,294 and 2,273 students, respectively, each group using a different mathematics test.

In the first replication, (NAEP-MATS1), the background variables accounted for 28.5 percent of the total variance, while semesters of mathematics explained an additional 28 percent. In the second replication (NAEP-MATS3), the background variables explained 30.1 percent of the variance, while semesters of mathematics accounted for an additional 30.6 percent. A summary of these findings is shown below.

Test	Variance Due to Background (Percent)	Additional Variance Due to Semesters Math (Percent)
MATS10	24.5	34.5
MATS1	28.5	28.0
MATS3	30.1	30.6

In each replication, the nonschool variables were a significant determinant of learning, accounting for an average of 28 percent of the variance in achievement. However, there were also substantial effects due to mathematics studied. When precise and accumulative measures of schooling effects were used, an average 31 percent of additional variance was explained.

Strong relationships were found in this study between nonschool background variables and mathematics achievement. Even stronger relationships were found for the amount of mathematics studied in schools. The results are further confirmed by a triple replication of a large nationally drawn sample using different measures of mathematics achievement.

INTERPRETING EDUCATIONAL RESEARCH

Table 1 Means, Standard Deviations, and Correlation of Predictor and Criterion Variables

Variable	1	2	3	4	5	6	7	8	9	10	Mean	S.D.
Welfare	1.00	—	—	—	—	—	—	—	—	—	8.47[a]	10.06
Professional Status	-.42	1.00	—	—	—	—	—	—	—	—	24.07[a]	20.50
Minority Ratio	.66	-.20	1.00	—	—	—	—	—	—	—	17.76[a]	21.50
Title I	.31	-.27	.31	1.00	—	—	—	—	—	—	5.81[a]	13.01
Parent Education	-.14	.31	-.12	-.11	1.00	—	—	—	—	—	4.37[b]	1.19
Printed Material	-.15	.09	-.14	.03	.13	1.00	—	—	—	—	4.09[b]	1.48
Ethnicity	-.32	.13	.48	-.14	.18	.04	1.00	—	—	—	82.94[b]	37.63
Grade Level	-.06	.04	-.08	.02	.06	.11	.09	1.00	—	—	10.98	.50
Semesters Math	-.20	.25	-.14	-.06	.29	.23	.14	.26	1.00	—	3.48	2.67
Math Achievement	-.28	.25	-.26	-.08	.31	.26	.27	.20	.73	1.00	61.21[a]	22.16

[a]Values expressed in percent.
[b]Scale range is 1–6.

Table 2 Multiple Regression Analysis Summary Predicting Math Achievement

Variables Entered	Multiple R	R^2	Percent Added Variance	F	P
Background	.494	.245	24.5	44.48	.001
Semesters of math	.768	.590	34.5	923.59	.001

In previous studies, schooling effects have been rather modest when qualitative or noncumulative quantitative measures were used. They have seldom accounted for more than one-third of the variance explained by home and background variables. In most studies, less than 25 percent of the total variance can be explained by a combination of home and school effects. In this study, it was possible to implement many of the recommendations made by previous researchers (Bridge et al., 1979; Karweit, 1976). The results are dramatic; nearly 60 percent of the variance has been explained, with home and school effects each accounting for about one-half of the total.

Our results support a hypothesis proposed by some (Coleman, 1975; Wolf, 1979) that the more likely a subject is to be learned only in school (e.g., a foreign language), the stronger the school effects. Wolf found that school effects explained only 2 percent of the reading variation, but jumped to 8 and 20 percent for science and French listening, respectively. While direct comparisons with the Wolf data are not possible because of differences in total explained variation, it does appear from our study that much of the mathematics children learn occurs in school. (From Welch, Anderson, & Harris, 1982, pp. 149–151. Copyright 1982 by the American Educational Research Association. Reprinted by permission of the publisher.)

Reading a Single-Subject Research Report

Single-subject research, action research, and evaluation research are other ways researchers describe, compare, and draw causative conclusions about educational problems and questions.

The following results section is from research done with a single subject in an A-B design. Note that although data were collected and presented in graph form, no tests of statistical significance were performed. Therefore, the research consumer does not know whether the subject's increased spelling scores after tutoring differed significantly from those before tutoring or whether the difference might be attributed to chance or error variations. (See pp. 169–171.)

Purpose of the study: To determine the effects of a peer-tutoring procedure on the spelling behavior of a mainstreamed elementary school learning disabled student.

RESULTS

Percent Correct

The overall results indicated that the tutee obtained a greater percent of accuracy on the spelling tests during the peer-tutoring condition than during the baseline condition. As shown in Figure 1, the student increased his mean percent correct from 61.25 percent in baseline to 77.5 percent in the peer-tutoring condition, that is, an improvement of 16.25 percent. The spelling performance of the peer tutor (S-B) did not decrease during either of the experimental conditions; it was 100 percent.

Clinical Significance: Student Self-Reports and Ratings

Both the tutee and the tutor rated the peer-tutoring procedure favorably (see Table 1). The program was rated as very good five times, satisfactory on four occasions, and unsatisfactory once. Subject A rated the program as unsatisfactory on the day when he scored 45% on his spelling test. (From Mandoli, Mandoli, & McLaughlin, 1982, pp. 187–188)

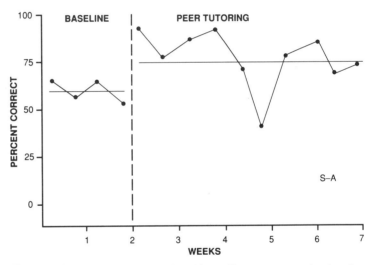

Figure 1 The percent correct on biweekly spelling tests across the duration of the study. Solid horizontal lines indicate condition means.

Table 1 Weekly Subject Ratings of the Experimental Treatment

Subjects	Rating		
	Very Good	Satisfactory	Unsatisfactory
A	2	2	1
B	3	2	

Action research is descriptive, comparative, or experimental research in which results are not generalized beyond the study's specific subjects and educational setting. Action researchers seek answers to immediate questions or problems.

The following method section reports the procedure from a single-subject action research project (see Chapter 7, pp. 172–174). Note that in this action research study no tests of statistical significance were done on the tabulated data. The researchers' purpose was the process of collaboration and its impact on solving a problem of concern to the participating teachers. Action research is useful to research consumers if there are similarities in subject variables, educational setting, or treatment(s). In such cases, research consumers may wish to replicate the study in searching for answers to their own educational questions.

Purpose of the study: To report action research showing how a teacher/ university researcher collaboration resulted in changing the teacher's instructional practice.

Figure 1 shows three graphic profiles of the overall percentage of each teacher for pre- and postintervention phases. The figure shows a 7% increase in on-task behaviors (from 73 to 80%) and a 12% decrease of off-task behaviors (from 27 to 19%). Pre- and postintervention coding data for each of the three students are provided in Figure 2.

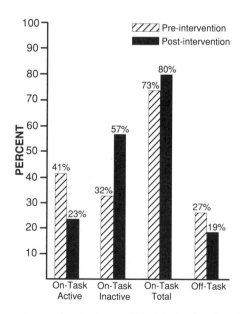

Figure 1 Percentages of on-task and off-task behaviors for all three target students combined.

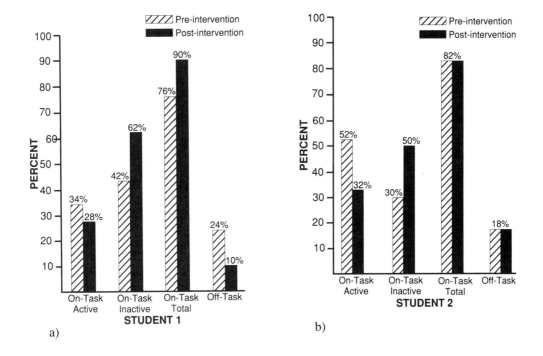

a)

b)

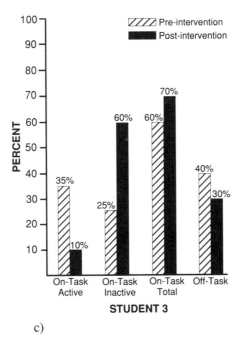

c)

Figure 2 Percentages of on-task and off-task behaviors for each of the three target students.

The data showed that Student 1 had a 14% increase in on-task behavior (from 76 to 90%) and a 14% decrease in off-task (from 24 to 10%). No changes in on-task and off-task behavior for Student 2 were indicated. It should be noted, however, that a high level of on-task behavior (82%) and a relatively low level of off-task behavior (18%) was maintained throughout the project for Student 2. Substantial changes were found for Student 3, with a 10% increase in on-task behavior (60 to 70%) and a 10% decrease in off-task behavior (from 40 to 30%). The data reveal that most of the increase in on-task behavior was attributed to more inactive behaviors (i.e., attentiveness during teacher lecture or direction-giving).

STAGES 4 and 5—DISCUSSION OF RESULTS AND FUTURE RECOMMENDATIONS

After the data were tabulated and summarized, they were shared with the teacher and team members; the discussion centered on two major areas. First, it was determined that the results indicated the research project goals had been reached. In this case the teacher felt that the overall goal of reducing off-task behavior was met. Although still evident, there was a substantial decrease in off-task behavior after the instructional strategies were employed for two of the students observed.

A second area of discussion was to make an overall evaluation of the project. From this, recommendations were made and a new cycle of action research was implemented. For example, one team member suggested that increasing active on-task behavior would be a future goal for the teacher. A possible way to accomplish this would be to change the structure of the game in which the students participate. Most of the games observed (e.g., sideline basketball) were structured so that students had to wait to receive the ball or wait for their turn to participate. A useful strategy therefore would be to restructure the games so that smaller groups would participate in games focusing on only one or two game skills. This would ensure greater opportunity for the students to become more physically active during game play. Given these suggestions, the teacher is placed in a position to begin a new cycle of research with this goal as a focus. Another suggestion was to work more on Student 2, the student who showed no change after the intervention. If the teacher was interested in affecting change in this student, perhaps this could be the focus of a new cycle of action research. (From Martineck & Butt, 1988, pp. 217–220. Copyright 1988 by Human Kinetics Publishers. Reprinted by permission.)

SUMMARY

What are the different ways quantitative data are recorded?

Statistics are numerical ways to describe, analyze, summarize, and interpret data in a manner that conserves time and space. Researchers select statistical procedures after they have determined what research designs and types of data will be appropriate for answering their research questions.

In answering descriptive research questions, statistics let researchers show the data's central tendencies and variability. In answering comparative and experimental research questions, other statistics allow researchers to draw inferences from samples and make generalizations about target populations. In all three types of research, the specific statistical procedures are determined by the research design and the type of data that are collected. And, in comparative and experimental research, statistics are tools that let researchers gain two other insights: They allow researchers to determine (a) an estimate of the error (or difference) between the research sample and the target population, and (b) the confidence with which research producers and consumers can accept the results.

Data are recorded as: (a) categories, (b) rankings, (c) intervals, and (d) ratios. Each requires the use of different statistics. Interval scales present data according to preset, equal spans. They are the most common form of data reporting in education and social science, and they are identified by continuous-measurement scales: raw scores and derived scores such as IQ scores, standard scores, and normal curve equivalents. Interval scores are the form in which data from most tests are recorded. Rankings, or ordinal scales, show the order, from highest to lowest, for a variable. There are no indications as to the value or size of differences between or among items in a list; the indications refer only to the relative order of the scores. Subjects can be ranked according to their performance on a set of athletic tasks, and what will be reported is the order in which they scored (e.g., first, second, third), not their actual accumulation of points. Data from surveys and observations are often recorded in this manner. Categories separate data into two or more discrete aspects, such as male–female, red–white–blue, or always–frequently–infrequently–never. The data can be reported as number of items or as percentages of a total. Data recorded in this way are considered nominal scales. Data from surveys and observations are often recorded in this way. Ratio scales, less frequently used in educational and other behavioral and social science research than the other three, show relative relationships among scores, such as half-as-large or three-times-as-tall.

What is a normal distribution curve?

Parametric statistics are based on the concept that if a set of scores is large enough, the scores will be distributed systematically and predictably. They will produce a graph in the shape of a bell, which is called the normal distribution curve. There is a direct relationship between the SD and the normal distribution curve. Starting at the center, or mean, of the distributed variable, each SD represents a fixed, specific proportion of the population.

What statistical procedures are used in educational and other behavioral science research?

A common parametric statistic is the *t*-test. It is used when the difference between two sets of scores is being tested. It is reported as numbers such as $t = 1.6$ or $t = 3.1$. Another parametric statistic used with interval data in comparative research is the product-moment correlation, which refers to the quantified relationship between two sets of scores for the same group of subjects. The result of the arithmetical computation is a coefficient of correlation which is expressed as *r*, a decimal between -1.0 and $+1.0$. When research designs call for examining differences among the means of two or more groups of subjects or two or more variables, they frequently use the analysis of variance (ANOVA), which is reported in *F*-ratios. The advantage in using an ANOVA is that two or more variables as well as two or more factors can be examined. In its simplest form, ANOVA can be thought of as a multiple *t*-test. The ANOVA is appropriate for use with some comparative research designs and with experimental research designs such as the pretest–posttest with multiple control groups, the Solomon four-group design, counterbalanced designs, common factorial designs, and causal–comparative designs. Analysis of covariance (ANCOVA) allows researchers to examine differences among the means of groups of subjects as if the means were equal from the start. They do this by adjusting the differences in the means to make them hypothetically equal. In all other ways, ANCOVA are interpreted as ANOVA. When researchers wish to examine the relationships among more than two variables, they can use multiple or partial correlation techniques. These procedures are interpreted similarly to a single correlation coefficient.

For each parametric statistical procedure there are corresponding nonparametric procedures. In general, nonparametric statistics are less frequently used in educational and other behavioral and social science research than are parametric.

What is statistical significance?

In comparative and experimental research, researchers want to be sure that the differences between the means of two or more groups of subjects or two or more variables are truly different. If the means differ, researchers need to know whether the difference happened by chance. When the difference between the means is large enough that it cannot be attributed to chance, the difference is considered as significant and, therefore, reliable. Statistical significance occurs when results exceed a particular *p*, or chance, level, and researchers are confident about the conclusions they make from their findings. When researchers determine whether a difference or relationship exists, there is the possibility of error. Two kinds of error can occur: (a) researchers accept the results as true when they are not, and (b) researchers do not accept the results as true when they actually are.

What are the ways data are analyzed in qualitative research?

In qualitative studies, researchers analyze data by examining and organizing notes from interviews and observations and reducing the information into smaller segments from which they can see patterns and trends. In addition, they interpret the meanings of these patterns and trends and create research hypotheses and questions for verification in further research. Qualitative researchers begin their analyses while still in the field and finish it after all data have been collected. An important point about qualitative research is that qualitative researchers often do measure and count; in other words, they quantify some data. However, they do not use statistical analyses to verify or support their results and conclusions, nor do they consider statistical probabilities. In the field, qualitative researchers continually make decisions that narrow their study. They may start out with broad questions and begin looking at an entire educational setting, but as their study proceeds they concentrate on smaller issues and create more specific analytical questions. Data collection is an additive process: New information is sought and collected on the basis of previous data, because the qualitative researchers are interpreting as they assemble additional information. One procedure used by qualitative researchers to support their interpretations is triangulation, a procedure for cross-validating information. Triangulation is collecting information from several different sources about the same event or behavior.

What questions should be used to read and evaluate results sections?

Research consumers need to be able to answer these questions about research reports: What types of data analyses were used? What statistical analyses researchers used? Were the statistical analyses appropriate for the researchers' questions, purposes, or hypotheses and for the research design? What were the research findings? Were the results of quantitative research statistically significant? Were the qualitative analyses appropriate and logical? Were the results of practical use and importance? Will the results be applicable to the other educational settings, especially the one in which I teach?

ACTIVITIES

Activity 1

Read the results sections in A and B. They are from the same studies as the method sections presented in the Activities portion of Chapter 7, pp. 176–180. Using the questions and criteria discussed in this chapter, evaluate the studies. For each, list questions and concerns you may have about

a. The appropriateness of the statistical procedures to the researchers' purposes and designs
b. The indicated statistical significance levels
c. The practical significance of the research
d. If it is a qualitative study, the processes for organizing data, identifying patterns, and synthesizing key ideas as hypotheses and research questions.

Extract A: Teachers' Work Behavior Study

Purpose of the study: To examine the work behavior of five teachers of second through fourth grades in diverse elementary schools.

FINDINGS

The teachers averaged a 37.5 hour in-school week; an additional 6.6 hours of after-school work was primarily devoted to checking papers or preparing lessons. The average secondary teacher in the companion study (Cypher & Willower, 1984: 18–19) had a longer in-school week by over 1 hour and worked almost 4 hours more after-school time. Chissom's (1987) sixth-grade teachers had heavier loads in both categories, but were only slightly higher than the secondary teachers.

The Chronological Record

The chronological record for the elementary teachers' in-school time is given in Table 1. As in the companion study, a division was made between instructional and noninstructional activities. However, in order to be true to the realities of the elementary school, our categories *within* these broad divisions differ somewhat from those in Cypher and Willower and in Chissom, who did not devise new categories.

Instructional acitivies included the time a teacher and students actually devoted to a subject area and should not be confused with a scheduled period for a subject. The broad category included seven specific areas. Group instruction involved lecturing or the presentation of a new skill. Elementary teachers rarely lecture. This activity accounted for 3.8% of the teachers' time. More time was devoted to question and answer activities (14%) and to individual help (16.8%) given to students. Providing directions and giving tests were somewhat less salient, accounting, respectively, for 2.7% and 1.4% of the teachers' total time. Reading to class covers the time three of the teachers read stories or student papers to their classes. It took 0.9% of the observational time. Organizing was devoted to such duties as distributing and collecting papers, assigning students to groups, and focusing a projector. This activity consumed 5.5% of the teachers' time. Overall, instructional activities took 45.1% of the teachers' time. This compares with 38.6% in the secondary school study. The figure for the sixth-grade teachers was 48.5%.

The other broad category, noninstructional activities, included events both within and outside the classroom; some involved students and some

Table 1   The Chronological Record

Activity	Number of Activities	Total Time in Minutes	Percentage of Total Time	Range
Instructional activities				
Group instruction	62	423	3.8	2.2–5.0
Question-answer	161	1,579	14.0	10.6–17.7
Individual help	257	1,888	16.8	12.8–24.6
Giving directions	329	310	2.7	1.6– 3.9
Giving tests	12	159	1.4	0.0– 2.5
Reading to class	14	99	0.9	0.0– 2.5
Organizing	222	625	5.5	2.3–10.9
Subtotals	1,057	5,083	45.1	
Noninstructional activities				
Transition-supervision	190	763	6.8	5.6– 8.2
Recess-supervision	114	846	7.5	3.5–11.6
Clerical-mechanical	80	156	1.4	0.3– 2.6
Desk work	177	1,381	12.3	7.6–14.7
Travel	170	354	3.1	1.4– 4.7
General conversations (staff)	86	911	8.1	1.2–12.5
Planning with staff	133	453	4.0	1.0– 7.4
Conversations (student)	179	680	6.0	3.0–10.6
Planning with students	51	82	0.7	0.0– 1.2
Private	39	212	1.9	0.9– 3.0
Miscellaneous	109	329	2.9	1.6– 4.4
Subtotals	1,328	6,167	54.7	

did not; some included time with and without students. Transition and supervision was the in-classroom time between lessons and the time spent preparing for lunch or dismissal. Often periods of higher noise level, these activities used 6.8% of the teachers' time. Recess and supervisory duties differed from the preceding category in location. These duties involved supervision of the playground, cafeteria, and hallways. This kind of supervision took 7.5% of the teachers' time. Clerical-mechanical tasks refer to routines like taking the attendance and lunch count and performing the standard opening exercises. These tasks consumed 1.4% of the total time. Desk work refers to time spent completing reports, checking assignments, lesson plans, and so forth. It accounted for 12.3% of the teachers' time. Travel was the time spent moving from the classroom to another location, inside or outside of the building. About half of the travel time occurred while accompanying students to recess, lunch, or a special class. Travel took 3.1% of the teachers' time.

General conversations with staff describes talk that was not oriented to work. These conversations consumed 8.1% of the time. Planning with staff, on the other hand, consumed 4% of the teachers' time and included discussing work-related matters, usually in informal settings. Conversations with students occurred during such times as transition periods, travel, and recess. These talks were informal and sometimes personal, and they used 6% of the time. Planning with students was a label for explicit efforts to plan something with a class, as distinct from instructing it. This took 0.7% of the teachers' time. Private activities were those few moments when the observer did not stay with the teacher, such as during lavatory use. This category accounted for 1.9% of the time. Miscellaneous was a final category, totaling 2.9% of the time, for activities that did not fit elsewhere. They included a parent conference and Primera's administrative duties.

Next are considered three categories that did not figure in the time totals. They are scheduled meetings, unscheduled meetings, and exchanges. The time expended in the first two of these activities is given but the time for all three of the categories was counted as part of other activities in figuring total time and percentages. For instance, an exchange between a teacher and student dealing with instructional subject matter was included as part of the time under the appropriate instructional category. This presents a clear picture of time use and avoids a problem that occurred in past studies where exchanges were defined as 1 minute in length when they were in fact shorter. Data are presented in Table 2.

Scheduled meetings were not common in our sample. Only four were held during the whole 5 weeks of observation. They averaged less than one per teacher per week and took 1.1% of the teachers' total time. Unscheduled meetings distinguished from exchanges because their duration is longer than 1 minute, used 13.6% of the teachers' time. They averaged almost 8 minutes in length. Over half occurred in the teachers' classrooms, and nearly half involved giving information to others. Over 60% were with other teachers, while almost 30% were with students. About 40% of the unscheduled meetings were initiated by the teachers, 45% by others, and almost 15% mutually by the meeting participants. Exchanges were divided into those occurring outside of classroom teaching and those occurring during teaching. The 5 teachers had 6,344 out-of-class exchanges, an average of 254 per teacher per day. Almost 95% of them occurred with students, more than 66% were teacher initiated, and 88% occurred in the classroom but not during class time. These elementary teachers had less than four times as many out-of-class exchanges as the teachers in the companion secondary school study. Exchanges during teaching also were recorded. There was a total of 9,266 for the elementary teachers, an average of 371 per teacher per day. Over 75% of these exchanges were initiated by the teachers, and nearly 80% were with individual students. Our elementary teachers had more than

Table 2 Meetings and Exchanges

Activity	Number of Activities	Total Time in Minutes	*M* per Teacher per Day
Scheduled meetings	4	125	0.16
Unscheduled meetings	198	1,535	7.9
Exchanges			
Out-of-class	6,344		254
In-class	9,266		371
Total exchanges	15,610		625

twice as many in-class exchanges as their counterparts in the secondary school study. Chissom did not separate in- and out-of-class exchanges, but the totals for his sixth-grade teachers were lower than those of the teachers in each of the other studies.

Activities. Our elementary teachers engaged in 2,385 in-school activities that were timed in the chronological record. However, they also had 6,344 out-of-class exchanges, totaling 8,729 activities. These figures were substantially higher than those for the secondary school study, which were compiled in the same manner. The secondary teachers engaged in a total of 3,201 activities, including 1,688 out-of-class exchanges. A record of in-class exchanges was kept but not counted in either the time or activity totals. Their total of more than 9,000 in the present research compared with 3,977 for the teachers in the companion study. Clearly, the elementary teachers engaged in more discrete activities than their secondary school counterparts. They engaged in slightly under twice as many activities as Chissom's sixth-grade teachers, not counting exchanges, which would increase the differences even more.

Interruptions. A total of 2,042 of the observed activities of the elementary teachers were interrupted. This compares with 1,450 interruptions in the companion study. Chissom (1987) did not record interruptions, but stated that "almost all" activities were interrupted (p. 253). About 70% of the interruptions in the current study occurred during teaching. About one fourth of the interruptions were in the form of teacher reprimands in response to student misbehavior. These reprimands were almost evenly distributed between in-class and out-of-class time. When reprimands were counted as pupil-induced interruptions, students were responsible for 67.6% of all interruptions. Interruptions to an activity initiated by the teachers themselves accounted for 28.7%. Fellow teachers were sources of 2.3% of the interruptions, and others such as custodians, office personnel, or administrators were responsible for 1.4%. The majority of the interruptions by fellow teachers occurred in class, while more than half of those by others took place out of class.

Individual differences. That there were individual differences among the 5 teachers can be seen in the ranges given in Table 1. They are based on percentages of total in-school time for individual teachers. For example, the range of 2.2 to 5.0 under group instruction indicates that 1 teacher (Luxor) spent 2.2% of his in-school time on this activity, while another (Productivia) spent 5% of hers on the same activity.

The range was sometimes inflated by a single outlier who reflected special circumstances. The observations and notes on context helped to account for these individual differences. For instance, Productivia taught in a district and school that were emphasizing task-oriented teaching. She had the highest percentage of time in the instructional categories overall and in testing, organizing, and group instruction. She also had the largest number of in-class exchanges. In addition, she did less desk work than the other teachers and spent only minutes on clerical-maintenance tasks. Luxor made substantial efforts to individualize instruction, which influenced his work behavior. He did less group instruction than the rest of the teachers, was lowest in giving directions, and was highest in the individual help category. Luxor was highest in desk work because of his efforts to correct individual student papers. He was lowest in general conversations with staff and highest in general conversations with students, had the largest number of interruptions in and outside of class, and reprimanded students more times than any of the other teachers. Some other examples of outliers include Materna's high travel time, due largely to the size and plan of her building and the distance between her classroom and the faculty room where she spent each planning period. Also, Novitia's extensive transition and supervision duties were associated with the movement of students in the most departmentalized arrangement observed.

The Correspondence Record

Student papers constituted the largest source of written material received and sent by the teachers. If these papers were not counted, mail was a minor part of the work lives of the teachers. Excluding the student papers, the teachers received 77 items and sent 60. Notes and excuses were the largest categories of incoming correspondence, with parents and the office the leading sources. Attendance slips and notes were the largest outgoing categories, with the office as the leading target. The correspondence of the elementary teachers differed from that of the companion secondary teachers in that there were more items received from parents and fewer from the office and fellow teachers, and more were sent to parents and fewer were sent to other teachers. Chissom (1987: 250) stated that correspondence was not important to his teachers, so he did not record it.

The Contact Record

The teachers' contacts with others can be easily summed up as overwhelmingly brief, verbal, and student dominated. The contact record is derived from the data for scheduled and unscheduled meetings, exchanges, and telephone calls. The first and last of these contributed little; there were only four of each. Unscheduled meetings and exchanges have already been discussed. It can be added that over 95% of the teachers' contacts included students. Excluding in-class exchanges, the teachers had a total of 6,546 contacts. The comparable figure for the secondary teachers was 1,818. If in-class exchanges are added, the figures are 15,812 and 5,795, respectively. Of the elementary teachers' nearly 16,000 contacts, only 1.3% lasted more than 1 minute. They averaged a new contact about every 43 seconds.

The teachers spent over 75% of their time with students. Over half of the time they spent without students was devoted to instruction and student-related work such as grading papers and preparing materials. During their time without students, the teachers maintained the fast pace and fragmented activity that characterized their time with students. They engaged in a new activity every 8 or 9 minutes when without students, an inflated figure, because it includes the teachers' lunch periods, which averaged just under 30 minutes.

The Analysis of Purpose

The analysis of purpose led to the development of four main categories. Instructional activities accounted for 39.6% of the total observation time. This category consisted of all the instructional activities in the chronological record except organizing. Instructional support took 23.8% of the time. It included organizing, desk work, planning with staff and students, and out-of-class activities dealing with instructional materials or schedules. The third category, organizational routine with students, included transition and supervision, recess, clerical-mechanical activities, travel with students, and interruptions and out-of-class exchanges that were noninstructional in nature. This category amounted to 24.6% of the total time. The final category, private and personal, covered 11.7% of the observational time. It consisted of general conversations with staff, including lunch periods, travel without students, private time, and appropriate miscellaneous activities. Chissom (1987: 252) saw the lack of private time as the "most striking dissimilarity" between his sample and Cypher and Willower's. Our elementary teachers' private time was a meager 1.9% of their total time compared with only 3.5% for the secondary teachers. Since Chissom reported 3.7% for his sixth-grade teachers, he probably compared his private time category with Cypher and Willower's combined private-personal analysis of purpose category, which included interactions with others on nonschool matters and totaled 11.6%.

The elementary teachers spent 63.4% of their time either giving or supporting instruction. The secondary teachers' study reported a comparable 62.2%, with a somewhat higher proportion of support activities. The category in the companion study closest to organizational routines with students was called pupil control. It took 19.3% of the secondary teachers' time, less than was expended by the elementary teachers. The secondary teachers' percentage of private and personal time was nearly the same as the elementary teachers' at 11.6%, although it did not include travel. Chissom did not do an analysis of purpose for the sixth-grade teachers. This probably caused him to underestimate work done to support instruction. Activities classed in the chronological record as, for instance, desk work or scheduled meetings, often turned out in the analysis of purpose to be concerned with instruction.

Extract B: Learner Achievement in Science Study

Purpose of the study: To examine (a) the effects of learner control and program control of seeing the information context on students' performance and attitudes during computer assisted instruction (CAI) and (b) the effects on achievement of reading ability and gender.

RESULTS

Mean scores for the groups on reading ability, principal and incidental posttest items, and computer use are shown in Table 1 [on p. 222]. Results for these measures are reported as follows. Preliminary exami-

Table 1 Means Scores on Dependent Measures by Sex and Treatment

Variable	Sex		Treatment	
	Male (*n* = 42)	Female (*n* = 42)	Learner Control (*n* = 42)	Program Control (*n* = 42)
Reading ability[a]				
M	83.8	80.2	83.1	90.9
SD	15.8	14.4	15.5	14.8
Posttest principal items[b]				
M	10.12	8.95	10.21	8.86
SD	2.53	2.76	2.56	2.68
Posttest incidental items[c]				
M	1.17	1.38	1.24	1.31
SD	0.93	0.91	0.85	1.00
Prior computer use[d]				
M	3.67	2.69	3.02	2.93
SD	1.46	1.49	1.60	1.66

[a]Scores are expressed as mean grade equivalents.
[b]Scores are mean number correct (out of 15 possible).
[c]Scores are mean number correct (out of 10 possible).
[d]Responses were rated on a scale from 1 (*low*) to 5 (*high*).

nation of correlation coefficients indicated minimal intercorrelations between the independent variables: The coefficient of correlation was—.12 between reading ability and sex and .08 between reading ability and treatment.

Principal Items

Principal items on the posttest were those items parallel to the practice items included in the CAI. Multiple regression analysis resulted in significant effects for reading ability, $F(1, 80) = 40.18$, $MS_E = 4.67$, $p < .0001$, and treatment, $F(1, 80) = 5.87$, $MS_E = 4.67$, $p < .02$. The main effect for sex approached significance, $F(1, 80) = 2.98$, $MS_E = 4.67$, $p < .09$.

As might be expected, higher reading ability was associated with higher scores on these items (range of possible scores was 0 to 15). Scores for subjects in the learner control treatment ($M = 10.24$) were significantly higher than scores for subjects under program control ($M = 9.02$).

Incidental Items

Performance on the content for which there was no direct practice was reflected by scores on the incidental items. When examined across the Sex × Treatment groups, these scores ranged from a high mean of 1.38 correct (out of 10 possible) to a low mean of 1.17 correct. Because the scores were so low (overall $M = 13\%$ correct, and between-group range = 12–14%), they were not analyzed statistically.

Attitudes and Computer Use

Students' attitudes toward instruction were generally positive, as indicated by an overall mean of 2.93 (1 = *low*, 4 = *high*) on the attitude items. The multivariate multiple regression analysis yielded significant main effects for reading ability, $F(7, 74) = 2.42$, $p < .03$, and sex $F(7, 74) = 3.16$, $p < .006$. There were no significant treatment effects.

Univariate multiple regression analyses were undertaken for each of the attitude and computer use items to determine how much of the variance in student responses was accounted for first by reading ability and then by the addition of sex. Significant univariate effects were found only for amount of prior computer use (range = 1 to 5). Higher ability students reported more frequent computer use, $F(1, 80) = 16.96$, $MS_E = 1.91$, $p < .0001$. Boys ($M = 3.67$) reported a higher frequency of computer use than did girls ($M = 2.29$), $F(1, 80) = 16.90$, $MS_E = 1.91$, $p < .0001$.

Proportion Reviews Selected/Assigned

During the instructional treatment, subjects in the learner-control condition had the choice of reviewing or not reviewing the relevant content for each practice item that they missed. Data on performance during instruction revealed that the learner-control subjects chose to review content for 35% of the practice items that they missed and not to review it for the remaining 65% of missed items.

The multiple regression analysis revealed that reading level was significant in the proportion of reviews selected by learner-control subjects, $F(1, 36) = 4.50$, $MS_E = 1484.36$, $p < .05$; higher ability subjects selected a higher proportion of possible reviews. No significant sex differences were noted.

Time to Completion

The overall mean time to completion for the instruction, posttest, and questionnaire was 30.8 min. Time to completion was similar across treatment groups and sexes: 30.5 min for learner-control subjects, 31.1 min for program-control subjects, 29.9 min for boys, and 31.7 min for girls. Reading ability was the only significant predictor of time to completion, $F(1, 80) = 6.17$, $MS_E = 22.13$, $p < .02$; higher ability readers took less time.

Proportion of Variance Accounted For

As indicated earlier, reading ability accounted for the largest proportion of variance on the principal posttest items ($R^2 = .31$). Treatment accounted for a smaller but significant portion of additional variance ($R^2 = .045$). Reading ability accounted for significant proportions of the variance in reported amount of computer use ($R^2 = .15$) and time to completion ($R^2 = .07$). Reading ability also explained a significant amount of variance in proportion of reviews selected by learner control subjects ($R^2 = .11$). The factor of sex added a significant amount to the variance accounted for by reading ability in reported computer use ($R^2 = .15$). (From Kinzie, Sullivan, & Berdel, 1988, pp. 301–302. Copyright 1988 by the American Psychological Association. Reprinted by permission.)

Extract A: Teachers' Work Behavior Study

In qualitative observational studies, researchers should identify the categories for organizing their data. This the researchers do; however, they do not provide a rationale for these "chronological record" (Table 1) and "analysis of purpose" categories (as logical as they may seem), for the assumptions made for placing events into a category, or for how their categories differ from those of the companion study. This is especially important when assigning a particular occurrence to a specific purpose. Since some information was presented in table format, it might be easier for readers if all information were so tabulated. Research consumers might want to know whether purpose was determined by the researcher or by the teacher. This question might have been answered if the researchers indicated whether triangulation was used in the data collection. Research consumers, therefore, need to interpret this study and its results as representing the impressions of the observer about teachers' work behavior.

Extract B: Learner Achievement in Science Study

The researchers used a multiple regression procedure to examine the influence and interaction of several variables. Multiple regression analysis is a generalized form of ANOVA which incorporates correlational techniques. In this case it is used as part of an ANCOVA; however, the researchers did not specify why they were conducting an ANCOVA instead of ANOVA. They present the results of their analyses (reported as F-ratios. The one table presents only mean scores. Presenting all scores in table format facilitates readers' identification of significant treatment effects and interactions. After presenting each series of F-ratios, the researchers do provide an explanation of each score. In the subsections "Proportion Reviews Selected/Assigned" and "Proportion of Variance Accounted For," the researchers provide the multiple correlation R^2 scores, which show the extent to which different scores varied as a result of particular variables. Although the researchers do not indicate the significance level ($p = .05$), it is assumed they are referring to the .05 level when they say the results are significant. Overall, the finding section is difficult to interpret because information was not presented in table form.

9

Reading and Evaluating Discussion Sections

DISCUSSION

UNDERSTANDING AND EVALUATING

FOCUS QUESTIONS

1. What information should research consumers get from discussion sections of research reports?
2. What criteria should be used to evaluate discussion sections?
3. What is the plan for reading discussion sections?

In Chapter 3, a plan for reading research reports is set out. The plan calls for the reading of the discussion section as part of the second stage of the plan. The demonstrations for that plan show that discussion sections usually contain several types of information: (a) a restatement of the researchers' purposes (or research questions or hypotheses), (b) a summary of the results, (c) a discussion or interpretation of those results, (d) and recommendations based on those results. By reading the discussion section together with the abstract, research consumers have an overview of the research project.

From reading discussion sections, research consumers should be able to answer

What were the researchers' purposes for the study?

What were the researchers' major results?

How did the researchers interpret their results?

What recommendations did the researchers make for applying the results to instructional situations or for future research projects?

Are the researchers' issues and concerns relevant to me as a professional or to my teaching situation?

Discussion sections should be evaluated using the following questions, which are from Figure 3.1, p. 87.

EVALUATING DISCUSSION SECTIONS

Are the conclusions related to answering the research question(s)?
Are they appropriate to the results?
Is the report free from inappropriate generalizations and implications?

UNDERSTANDING AND EVALUATING DISCUSSION SECTIONS

Some researchers label the discussion sections as conclusions, summary, or implications, and they may subdivide the section to highlight specific information. As a research consumer, you will have determined the specific format of research producers' discussion sections during the first, or preview, phase of the reading plan.

A common procedure for research producers is to begin discussion sections with a statement of the research purpose and then to follow that with a statement of their results and, in the case of quantitative studies, whether the results were statistically significant. In the remainder of the section, they usually explain (a) whether the results answered their research questions, (b) how their results relate to related literature presented in the introduction, and (c) what implications the results have for practitioners and other researchers.

The following section, called Conclusions by the researchers, has all the elements of a discussion section.

Purpose of the study: To investigate a broad-based program to foster children's social development that includes supportive teacher–student relationships, and opportunities for students to interact and collaborate in cooperative groups.

CONCLUSIONS

[Purpose]   The goal of the present project was to devise, implement, and assess the effectiveness of a comprehensive school-based program designed to enhance children's prosocial orientations. In this paper we have demonstrated, through quasi-experimental analyses, that the program was

[General results]

implemented by classroom teachers and that it had substantial positive effects on children's interpersonal behavior in the classroom (without impeding their achievement).

[Specific results]   Children in the first-cohort classrooms participating in the program over 5 years of program implementation were observed to be more supportive, friendly, and helpful, and to display more spontaneous prosocial behavior toward one another than children in a group of comparison classrooms. A replication with a second cohort, in kindergarten and grade 1, produced similar results. Outcomes such as these have not often been investigated in classroom observational studies, despite a growing concern with problems relating to students' interpersonal behavior in classrooms and recent calls for schools to renew their emphasis on preparing students for responsible roles in our democratic society (e.g., Bastian, 1985; Honig, 1985). If social development is a legitimate goal of elementary education, then research identifying factors that can serve to promote it is essential. The project described in this paper is one such effort.

When the program developed in this project is being fully implemented, students exercise considerable autonomy and self control: they help make decisions about their classrooms, participate in rule-development and revision, discuss and help solve classroom problems, and in general develop a shared sense of membership in, and responsibility for, their community. It is our expectation, as Dewey (1916) suggested long ago and others have more recently (e.g., Wood, 1986), that engaged participation in activities such as these should help to prepare students for adult democratic responsibilities.

[Relation to other research] The approach to classroom organization and activity embodied in this program, particularly its attempt to minimize the use of extrinsic incentives, represents a fairly radical departure from some of the classroom management systems currently in vogue (e.g., Canter's, 1976, "assertive discipline"). It is, however, quite consistent with the ideas and findings of much recent research concerning the conditions that enhance intrinsic motivation. Several researchers (see Lepper, 1983) have investigated the deleterious effect on intrinsic motivation of the use of external incentives (rewards in particular), often from an attributional perspective. Ryan, Connell, and Deci (1985), in a discussion of classroom factors that influence the development of students' self-regulation and intrinsic motivation for learning, emphasize teachers' provision of autonomy and decision-making opportunities, and the minimization of external control "in a context of adequate structure and guidance" (p. 44). The present findings suggest that these factors may also play a role in enhancing students' social orientations and behavior.

[Significance] The two general aspects of classroom life that have been found to be related to children's social development in prior research—establishment of supportive teacher-student relationships and provision of opportunities for collaborative interstudent interaction—are incorporated in our Positive Discipline and Cooperative Activities program components, respectively. These aspects have previously been investigated separately. Our approach has been to combine these, along with other consistent elements (providing experiences in helping and understanding others; exposure to and discussion of examples of prosocial behavior, motives and attitudes) into a general, pervasive, and coherent whole. We believe that the data reported in this paper indicate that the total program has had clear and strong effects on children's classroom behavior. We do not know whether these results could have been obtained with less than the total program (for example, with Developmental Discipline alone, or Developmental Discipline combined with Cooperative

Activities). Because these elements are designed to be mutually supportive and interrelated (and are in fact intercorrelated), it is somewhat arbitrary and perhaps somewhat misleading to describe them as separate "components." We do intend, however, to conduct a series of natural variation analyses to try to assess the relative influence on student social behavior of various combinations of teacher behavior and classroom activity measures.

[Implications]   It is our hope and expectation that through participating in an environment in which certain central values of the society are both discussed and exemplified (e.g., mutual concern and respect, responsibility, helpfulness), such values and behaviors consistent with them will become more deeply ingrained in the children. While the present data, indicating substantial effects on students' behavior in the classroom, reflect only some surface aspects of the kinds of change we hope to engender, including a long-range commitment to democratic values, they do suggest that such changes may result from participating in this program.[5] In other papers, we will be describing effects outside the classroom and on other areas of children's functioning. (From Solomon, Watson, Delucchi, et al., 1988, pp. 545–546. Copyright 1988 by the American Educational Research Association. Reprinted by permission of the publisher.)

Research consumers need to evaluate research producers' interpretation of results carefully for unwarranted or overgeneralized conclusions. They need to examine four aspects of research producers' conclusions: (a) predicted results, (b) unpredicted results, (c) statistical and practical significance, and (4) further research or replications of the studies.

Researchers should explain whether results logically answer their research purposes or questions. Also, they need to indicate whether results are consistent with results of other researchers. As stated in Chapter 4, background sections provide three major kinds of information: problem areas and their educational importance, related literature, and research purposes. Research consumers need to compare research producers' conclusions about predicted results with the information provided in background sections. Also, research consumers need to determine whether research producers have drawn appropriate conclusions from the research designs and statistical procedures they used. For example, research producers should not conclude causality from descriptive or comparative research, and they should not generalize beyond the target population in any category of research.

Since comparative studies provide information about the existence of relationships (similarities and differences), it is not appropriate for research producers and consumers to infer a causal effect among variables. Most research producers avoid making this error, as did the researchers of the spelling program noted in Chapters 7 and 8 (pp. 149–150 and 200–201), who found the existence of strong relationships. They appropriately indicated as a result of their study that "the results support the idea of a common conceptual base for varying aspects of word knowledge" (Zutell & Rasinski, 1986, p. 111). This is not a statement of causation but of coexistence.

Nevertheless, the error of inferring causality from relational studies is common. In the following passage, taken from a newspaper article about issues related to improving high schools, note the italicized portion. That statement implies causation, an inappropriate conclusion based on correlation data.

The sociologist found several strong correlations between self-discipline on the part of students and the overall performance of the schools they attended, beginning with the amount of homework they did. "Homework is an important measure of self-discipline because students must do it on a regular basis and without close supervision," he said.

The data showed that students in "high performance" schools in both sectors did considerably more homework than students in average schools. For example, 5.4 percent of public high schools require students to do more than 10 hours of homework a week, but 12.7 percent of "high performing" public schools require that amount. In the private sector the number requiring 10 hours of homework ranges from 13.3. percent in Roman Catholic schools to 19.8 percent in others, but among "high performing" private schools the figure rises to nearly half, or 47.9 percent. . . .

Asked about his own agenda for improving schools, [the sociologist] said he would put more rigorous homework at the top of his list. "Homework is the golden opportunity to develop self-discipline because you take it, you go to the library or a quiet corner of the house and you bring it back," he said. (Fiske, 1983, p. C1)

The sociologist's statement seems inappropriate because factors other than the type of school students attend might be responsible for the amount of homework they do. In the next example, taken from a newspaper article about the relationship between television viewing and school achievement, a more appropriate statement is made. (It has been italicized for emphasis.)

A team of social scientists in California is not prepared to say that watching "B. J. and the Bear" made students do poorly in school, but the researchers do maintain that children who watched the show regularly were the students most likely to have low scores on standard achievement tests. The next most likely shows to have been viewed by low-achieving students were "The Incredible Hulk" and "Dance Fever."

New results such as these are providing fresh insight into the possible links between television viewing and classroom achievement. Several such studies from around the country were discussed publicly for the first time last week at the annual meeting of the American Educational Research Association in New York City.

It is widely believed that children who spend more time watching the popular programs on commercial television tend to be lower achievers in school, but researchers have yet to show that television causes that poor performance. (Maeroff, 1982, p. C9)

Researchers sometimes need to explain results that they did not expect. For example, one researcher found that one of his treatments did not produce an anticipated outcome. The following discussion section is an example of how that researcher explains possible reasons for the unexpected finding.

Purpose of the study: To investigate the effects of one approach to cooperative learning on the acquisition of one set of problem-solving skills, and to provide additional data on sex differences in small-group learning.

DISCUSSION

[Results]

The two treatments in which there was an overt attempt to teach problem-solving skills directly outperformed the control condition, in which intellectual skill development was expected to occur as a by-product of knowledge acquisition. This finding confirms the results of previous studies (Maynes & Ross, 1984; Ross, 1981, 1986; Ross & Maynes, 1983; Ross & Robinson, 1987).

[Relation to other research]

[Unexpected results]

Less expected is the finding that the cooperative method was less effective than the whole-class treatment in promoting learning of problem-solving skills. Because previous investigations have reported that cooperative approaches consistently outperform whole-class approaches when basic computational skills and the recall of simple facts are addressed, there would seem to be an interaction between type of objective and the effects of cooperative grouping. It is clear that cooperative learning, operationalized in these studies as Student Teams Achievement Divisions (STAD), made little contribution to the acquisition of a particular set of problem-solving skills in a grade 4 social studies program. The question is why.

[Possible explanations]

First, the amount of independent practice may have been insufficient to achieve mastery. When STAD is used for teaching computational skills, students are typically given 20 to 30 short items to work through in each group session. In contrast, the practice exercises in these studies typically involved one or two long problem-solving items in each session (see, for example, Figure 2). Although it is possible to have shorter and fewer items, the task to be practiced inevitably takes more time, particularly when an attempt is made to integrate problem-solving development with acquisition of subject-specific knowledge. Burns & Lash (1986) discovered a similar tendency: They found that when math teachers shifted from computational skills to problem solving, the number of items given for practice declined dramatically. In these studies, students in the cooperative treatment were assigned the same amount of practice as students in the whole-class treatment. Time was kept constant. But cooperative students may have taken longer to complete each practice activity (because they were also interacting with each other), with the

INTERPRETING EDUCATIONAL RESEARCH

result that the amount of practice actually completed might have been lower.

Second, the distribution of cognitive demands across the task may have had unintended effects. In Studies 1 and 2, cognitive activity was concentrated in the initial phase of the practice task. In Figure 2, for example, the most difficult mental action is undertaken at the outset, with the construction of a framework containing alternatives as one dimension and advantages and disadvantages as the other. This massing of demands may have been counterproductive, for previous researchers (e.g., O'Donnell et al., 1985) have found that spreading cognitive activity evenly across the exercise is more effective. The concentration of demands at the beginning may also have increased the consequences of social loafing. Latane, Williams, & Harkins (1979) found that in group situations some students will allow others to do most of the work. If students prone to loafing were slower to get going on the exercise—a reasonable hypothesis—the most difficult part of the task would be completed by others, with the result that the loafers would receive practice only on the less demanding problem-solving operations.

Third, student learning in groups may have been impeded by the lack of competent/confident students able to given direction to others. When computational skills are the object of instruction, it is reasonable to anticipate that in each heterogeneous group there will be at least one person who knows how to do the task on entry. Furthermore, many arithmetic skills can be mastered easily by bright students in short periods of time. In cooperative settings, these masters become available to help others. One might speculate that the presence of at least one master in the group is an essential condition. For example, Webb (1980) found that math groups that lacked a master experienced motivational problems and tended to be unproductive. In Studies 1 and 2, most students performed very poorly on all the skills pretests, and the tasks to be learned were substantially more challenging than the acquisition of computational skills. It is likely that the most competent person in each group was at best an incomplete master, reluctant and unable to provide effective tutoring to others.

Fourth, helping behaviors may not have occurred in the cooperative groups to the degree required to achieve mastery. Research into unstructured cooperative settings has found that certain types of student-student interactions are critical. For example, providing explanations to others contributes to achievement because it involves rehearsal and elaboration of the material to be learned (Peterson, Janicki, & Swing, 1981; Peterson & Swing, 1984; Webb, 1982; Webb & Cullian, 1983). Receiving explanations in response to a request also improves performance (Webb, 1982; Webb & Kenderski, 1984), as does providing procedural information on group progress and other metacognitive acts (Peterson, Wilkinson, Spinelli, & Swing, 1984). These effective behaviors are relatively infrequent in groups composed of young children: Peterson & Swing (1984) found that only a few mature and bright students were able to provide good explanations, even on tasks related to lower order objectives.

The absence of sex differences in the cooperative treatment in Studies

1 and 2 also warrants comment. Previous researchers have found that males tend to derive greater benefit from peer interaction within small groups. The cooperative learning groups treatment in the present investigation can be distinguished from treatments in previous studies by a number of factors that reduce sex effects. The most important of these factors concerns degree of structure. Previous studies of cooperation in which male superiority has been reported have involved low-structure activities—either naturally occurring cooperation or small groups established with little direction other than that students should help each other. In contrast, the present investigation involved activities that were more highly structured. There is some evidence that girls prefer high structure to low structure (Huston & Carpenter, 1985) and that this preference can lead to superior performance of girls in cooperative games (Peterson & Fennema, 1985).

A second feature distinguishing this investigation from previous ones is domain of learning. Previous studies have tended to focus on mathematics. Societal expectations in this domain encourage children to anticipate that boys will be more competent than girls. This anticipation is typically reinforced within the group: Boys consistently outperform girls on quantitative tasks (Halpern, 1986). In contrast, the present investigation involved social studies learning for which there is greater equality in expectations and the activities undertaken by students involved a combination of verbal tasks (favoring girls) and spatial tasks (favoring boys). In addition, the content of the activities included topics of particular interest to girls to balance topics of particular interest to boys.

Finally, previous research has found that the disadvantage of girls in group situations is greatest when girls are underrepresented or overrepresented in the group (Webb, 1985). In the present investigation, there were equal numbers of girls and boys in most groups.

Implications for Teachers

The main implication for teachers is that attempts to teach problem-solving skills directly are likely to be more successful than strategies in which complex intellectual skill development is expected to occur as a by-product of knowledge acquisition.

The second implication concerns the findings related to cooperative learning. If cooperative learning is no more effective than a whole-class method in promoting the acquisition of higher order objectives under the conditions that existed in these two studies, what conditions might be more fruitful?

Modest improvements of the impact of cooperative learning might be achieved by adjusting the tasks undertaken in the group sessions. The number of independent practice activities might be increased by reducing the knowledge demands of the task or by providing practice of component operations rather than the whole procedure. In addition to providing more practice, this would have the added effect of distributing task demands more evenly across the session. The obvious trade-off in this strategy is that it would reduce the validity of the practice.

Changing the instructional context might increase the effectiveness of cooperative learning. Older children are more likely than younger ones to be able to provide effective tutoring within the cooperative group. Similarly, children who have had prior training in the problem-solving tasks to be reinforced might function more effectively as tutors: Limiting cooperative learning to distributed practice tasks might thereby increase its impact. Training students how to help others might also be beneficial; the tutoring literature provides some evidence that training tutors contributes to student learning (Devin-Sheehan, Feldman, & Allen, 1976).

Finally, the impact of cooperative learning on higher order cognitive objectives might be enhanced if an alternate method to STAD were adopted. All the successes of cooperative learning with more complex intellectual objectives have been with group investigative techniques such as the Johnsons' Cooperative Learning Method or Sharan's Small-Group Teaching Method (Rolheiser-Bennett, 1986). (From Ross, 1988, pp. 586–589. Copyright 1988 by the American Educational Research Association. Reprinted by permission of the publisher.)

For some reason, quantitative research reports published in journals all seem to have statistically significant results. Less often published are studies with nonsignificant results. Reports of this kind sometimes occur when one set of researchers attempt to show that particular treatments do not produce results that other researchers have previously produced. It is important that professionals examine each others' work and that researchers be able to replicate their work. In fact, many journals will ask for "responses" from researchers when publishing studies that seem to refute their position. Research consumers need to examine both sets of reports for biases, and they need to determine the practical significance of all research. Consumers need to be concerned with the applicability of the results to their educational situation: Are the results generalizable to my local educational setting and can the treatment, when there is one, be implemented with practical considerations given to time, effort, money, and personnel?

Researchers often cite questions that their research has left unanswered. These questions can, and often do, become the research purposes in future studies by the researchers themselves or by other researchers. The questions might be about research design, research procedures, subject selection, instrumentation, data analysis, or research results. Research consumers need to examine the logic of these recommendations.

ACTIVITIES

Activity 1: Teachers' Work Behavior Study

Read the following discussion section, which is from the study presented in part of the activities section in Chapters 7 and 8. (You may wish to refer to those portions of the reports and to the Feedback sections.) Using the questions and criteria discussed in this chapter, evaluate the discussion section. List questions and concerns you may have about the applicability of the results to your teaching situation and about the researcher's (a) purposes for the study, (b) major results, and (c) recommendations for applying the results to instructional situations and future research projects.

DISCUSSION

[1] Our most salient finding is the extent to which elementary teachers' work is varied, choppy, and fast paced. Previous structured observation studies showed this hectic pattern of work behavior to be typical of administrators, and Cypher and Willower reported an even more pronounced pattern for secondary school teachers. Chissom's (1987: 252) data indicated that sixth-grade teachers were close to the secondary teachers in terms of busyness. Our second- through fourth-grade elementary teachers were at the pinnacle; their work was the most frenetic and fragmented of all. The teachers in the present study undertook a new activity every 77 seconds. If their in-class exchanges were counted, a new activity was performed every 37 seconds.

[2] The hours of the elementary teachers in our sample were shorter than those of the teachers in both the companion and complementary studies. It is not the total time but the variety and number of activities that are crammed into the elementary teachers' workdays that result in their overwhelming busyness. For instance, when our elementary teachers engaged in group instruction, an average period of such instruction lasted less than 7 minutes, compared with more than 27 minutes for the secondary teachers and about 16 minutes for the sixth-grade teachers. Most activities had short durations. Planning with staff averaged 3.4 minutes per session, planning with students only 1.6 minutes. Even traveling was done quickly with a mean time of about 2 minutes per occurrence.

[3] Our elementary teachers' work was literally child centered. They were with students or performing student-related work during most of their time at school. Over 95% of their contacts were with students. Generally, the students successfully sought their teachers' attention. To illustrate, a phenomenon we called flocking was often observed when the teachers sat at their desks. Sitting was apparently a sign that the teachers were open for business, and students flocked to the desk for help, which they received. Younger students might feel freer than older ones about approaching teachers for a variety of help. Also, teachers of younger students likely respond to a wide array of needs, accounting for the differences in the activity levels between our elementary teachers and the sixth-grade and secondary teachers.

[4] Another indication of the teachers' responsiveness to students was given in the post-research interviews. After looking at the chronological record, some of the teachers commented that they intended to reduce the time spent on activities like desk work to give more time to activities such as helping individual students.

[5] Although Luxor defined himself and acted as a "loner" with regard to his colleagues and principal, and the newly married Novitia made every effort to avoid bringing work home, all five of the teachers said they enjoy teaching and like their jobs and the students. The teachers spent considerable time maintaining good pupil control, but the student misbehavior that occurred seemed more a result of exuberance and close quarters than of deliberate opposition. Relations with students were generally amicable, and the teachers sometimes were the objects of obvious student affection.

[6] The intensity of the work life of the teachers seems to stem largely from the classroom organization—1 teacher with many students in one room—and the many tasks that are to be accomplished at school. In other words, the physical and task structures of schools have a major effect on the work behavior of teachers. The idea that administrative interruption prevents teaching was not supported in our data. Teachers were not interrupted by administrators, but by students, themselves, and fellow teachers. We also failed to find a heavy burden of office-generated paperwork. Most of the teachers' paperwork involved correcting student assignments and preparing lessons.

[7] One element of possible administrator influence did surface. The fact that Productivia's district and school were stressing a task-oriented program as a matter of policy, coupled with that teacher's task-oriented work behavior, suggests that policy can affect what happens in the classroom. However, we have no data on what occurred in this case.

[8] The teachers, all with extensive experience, adapted well to the demands of their jobs. They were sometimes polychronic, doing two things at once, for instance, gesturing approval or disapproval to one student while talking with another. More important, they were able to accomplish their work while emphasizing those aspects that appealed to them. Luxor, for example, felt that to teach effectively, he had to know his students. He was highest by far in the category of conversations with students. Novitia enjoyed reading to her class and did so more than twice as much as the next highest teacher. The teachers also used humor and empathy to make their jobs easier. They joked with colleagues, were sympathetic listeners, and referred to their work with comments about "getting through another day (or week)" that were at once clichés and expressions of shared ordeal. Moreover, they were able to give a normative dimension to their efforts undertaken on behalf of "the kids," an expression mentioned several times during the interviews.

[9] Next this study emphasizes the limitations inherent in structured observation research. This kind of investigation probes the allocation of time and attention. It can miss important features of context and might overemphasize common but unimportant activities while deemphasizing rare but important ones. It suffers from all of the limitations of small sample size research and the possibility of observer-influenced changes in work behavior. In the present case, the teachers assured us in the post-research interviews that their observed work weeks were typical and that they did nothing different because of the observer's presence. Perhaps so, but caution must be taken about generalizing from such research. Peculiarities of the teachers observed, the nature of their current student groups, and even of the time of the school year are just

three of many possible examples of particular circumstances that could make these teachers unrepresentative. Nevertheless, this kind of inquiry can lead to useful interpretation and speculation that, taken together with other studies, adds to our understanding of educational organizations and their participants. Ultimately, studies of how time and attention are allocated raise the issue of how they should be allocated.

[10] This brings us to the question of implications for policies directed toward the improvement of teaching. Obviously, small-sample research has severe limitations in this regard. Still, when placed in the larger mosaic of past research and current theorizing, some comments can be made.

[11] The overwhelming busyness, fragmentation, and intensity of the work of teaching found in the structured observation studies has been noted by others. For instance, Jackson (1968: 11) asserted that the elementary teacher "engages in as many as 1,000 interpersonal interchanges each day." (Teachers continue to be busy even when not interacting with others.) Because Hilsum and his colleagues found British teachers busy with so many details, they suggested that many of the teachers' activities were chores that should be carried out by teacher helpers (Hilsum & Cane, 1971). This echoed a recommendation made after an observational study done in Bay City, Michigan, in the 1950s. There, the idea was to use teacher aides to relieve teachers of time-consuming duties that did not require professional training (Park, 1956).

[12] These recommendations suggest restructuring the work of teachers by adding assistants. A contemporary version would see the teacher as manager of a classroom team of aides and volunteers having planning connections to the administration, staff specialists, and other teacher-led teams.

[13] A technological option would provide large-group instruction via television or individualized instruction using computers to free teachers to plan and assess their work in less hectic circumstances. The extended time option in which teachers work a longer school year but with the extra time as planning time without students in attendance is another option. Another choice is the reduction of class size.

[14] These are some possibilities for dealing with the overload that characterizes the work of teachers. Oddly, even though pronouncements on how to improve teaching have become a growth industry, few of them have examined the work of teaching.

[15] Work overload can lead to job dissatisfaction and exhaustion. It can also lead to coping strategies and a shared rhetoric of survival of the kind exhibited by the teachers in our sample. Overload is endemic to school organizations where many people and activities are found in a small space. School principals exhibit the same pattern of intense and fragmented work (Kmetz & Willower, 1982; Martin & Willower, 1981) that teachers exhibit, although as we have noted, elementary teachers are the extreme case. Obviously, greater attention to the problem of work in educational organizations is needed at the levels of both inquiry and policymaking.

[16] This study illustrated policy options stemming from findings about the work of teachers. However, a variety of empirical questions remain. Some examples are, "What are the thresholds of work overload

in teaching, and do they differ for particular individuals and settings?" and "What are the consequences of exceeding such thresholds for teachers and for their students?" Studies of work in educational organizations should move beyond their present focus on the allocation of time and attention to questions of this kind. (From McDaniel-Hine & Willower, 1988, pp. 279–280. Reprinted with permission of the Helen Dwight Reid Educational Foundation. Published by Heldref Publications.)

Activity 2: Vocabulary Acquisition Study

Read the following abstract and general discussion sections from a research report about vocabulary acquisition in young children. The abstract has been included to provide a general sense of the researcher's procedures and results.

Using the questions and criteria discussed in this chapter, evaluate the discussion section. Using the limited information available to you, list questions and concerns you may have about the applicability of the results to your teaching situation and about the researcher's (a) purposes for the study, (b) major results, and (c) recommendations for applying the results to instructional situations and future research projects.

Vocabulary Acquisition from Listening to Stories

[1] In two experiments, classroom teachers in New Zealand read stories aloud to elementary school children, and administered pretests and posttests to measure the extent of the new vocabulary the children acquired from the reading. Results showed that oral story reading constitutes a significant source of vocabulary acquisition, whether or not the reading is accompanied by teacher explanation of word meanings. In the first study, seven classes of 7-year-olds showed vocabulary gains of 15 percent from one story, without any teacher explanation. In the second study, after hearing one story, three classes of 8-year-olds who received no teacher explanation showed gains of 15 percent, and three classes that did receive explanation showed gains of 40 percent. By contrast, the same groups produced gains of less than half these figures on a second story with different characteristics. Follow-up tests showed that this incidental vocabulary learning was relatively permanent, and that low-scoring children gained as much as high-scoring children. In addition, the features that best predicted whether a particular word would be learned were frequency of the word in the text, depiction of the word in illustrations, and the amount of redundancy in the surrounding context. The author recommends future studies to investigate further the benefits from stories read aloud, and to clarify the factors that yield differences in children's interest in stories.

GENERAL DISCUSSION

[2] The findings from both experiments support the assumption that young children can learn new vocabulary incidentally from having illustrated storybooks read to them. As in previous studies, teachers' additional explanations of unknown words as they are encountered can

more than double such vocabulary gains. Furthermore, the evidence from these studies indicates that students who start out with less vocabulary knowledge gain at least as much from the readings as the other students, and that the learning is relatively permanent. Both studies also suggest several identifiable features in the stories that appear to account for a large portion of variance in the likelihood that children will learn a certain word: the frequency of occurrence of the word in the story, the helpfulness of the context, and the frequency of occurrence of the word in pictorial representation.

[3] However, several questions remain unanswered. The contrasting results obtained for the two stories in Experiment 2 raise the specter of story specificity, a problem that has also confused interpretation of the findings from research on vocabulary learning during silent reading (Nagy, Herman, & Anderson, 1985). Other than the order in which they were presented, the two stories in Experiment 2 were read under identical conditions. Apparently, some features of stories are critical in determining whether they produce effective language learning. Which are the critical story features?

[4] Clearly, for new learning to occur, the text must contain some vocabulary beyond the pupils' present understanding. Moreover, the unfamiliar words should be supported by a helpful verbal or pictorial context, and there should normally be more than one exposure to each word. As each story in the current investigation was read three times, over 1 week, it is not possible to generalize about other levels of frequency. However, the number of occurrences of a word within the story correlated well with the gain score in each experiment (.43 and .60), suggesting that frequency of exposure is a key variable (see also Stahl & Fairbanks, 1986; Sternberg, 1984). Thus, one possible reason children learned less vocabulary from *The White Crane* may have been that only 2 of the target words occurred more than once in the story. However, in the other story in Experiment 2, only 4 words occurred more than once, so the contrast is not very great. Thus, explanations must be sought elsewhere.

[5] One distinguishing feature of *The White Crane* mentioned by several participating teachers was the "lack of involvement" of their children with this story. The setting of the story was a severe winter in a distant place, Japan; the lifestyle was foreign; the main characters were probably not easy for children to identify with; and there was little action and no humor. Certainly there were elements of suspense and surprise, but the plot might have been too incredible for many pupils to follow, and these elements may also have lost their force in repeated readings.

[6] A general hypothesis that would explain the differences between the results for these stories requires a motivational theory more sophisticated than those currently in existence. Of the constructs cited in the literature, the arousal theory of Berlyne (1960) may well prove most useful. For children to derive new word meanings from context surely requires persistent attention to the meaning of the stories. It is conceivable, as Berlyne maintains, that attention levels are greatest when they are aroused by such "collative variables" as novelty, humor, conflict, suspense, incongruity, vividness, and the like. Stories like *Gumdrop at Sea* and *Rapscallion Jones* were well endowed with such features, and

these stories certainly kept the children's attention. For instance, in the first story, the engine of Gumdrop (a car) exploded, a yacht capsized, everyone fell in the water, Gumdrop was caught in the rising tide, and the story ended happily as a new engine was fortuitously discovered for Gumdrop. *Rapscallion Jones* was similarly entertaining. Rapscallion, a fox, was portrayed as a figure of fun, too proud to work for his living. He told far-fetched stories, pretended to be a doctor, and had a sick crocodile jumping on his bed while he (Rapscallion) rifled the refrigerator. However, he had his come-uppance when he nearly died of a fever, and he then confessed his sins to the minister. Again, there was a pleasing resolution to the story. Thus, both stories had many features to attract and hold children's attention.

[7] What we need is a model that could relate such sources of attention in stories to the child's depth of processing, extent of elaboration, and incidental learning, and to contextual variables. Such a model might help clarify the conditions under which students will benefit from particular storybook experiences. One suspects, for instance, that the pictures in these stories may have provoked children to generate more elaborated networks of meaning, which would enhance learning and retention of the content of the story (Anderson & Reder, 1979). Some support for such a model might be found in the tradition of research that has postulated intensity of affect as a key influence in verbal retention (Dutta & Kanungo, 1975; Weiner, 1966) and from studies of the newly defined concept of text-based interest, or interestingness, in discourse processing (Hidi & Baird, 1986).

Implications

[8] The two experiments outlined above provide evidence that reading stories aloud to children is a significant source of vocabulary acquisition, that teachers' additional explanation of words as they are read can more than double such gains, that the new learning is relatively permanent, and that students who score low on vocabulary at the outset can gain at least as much as students who score higher. Each of these findings has significant implications. School systems, teachers, and parents vary considerably in the emphasis they place on story reading to children. New Zealand elementary school teachers spend approximately 30 minutes each day reading aloud (Elley, 1985). But a recent survey of Singapore schools (Ng, 1983) showed that virtually no teachers in the first three grades ever did so, and pupils in the South Pacific islands rarely heard stories read aloud until recently (Elley & Mangubhai, 1983). The pattern in U.S. schools and kindergartens is variable (Mason & Allen, 1986). If an appealing 8- to 10-minute story, read three times, with only brief explanation of word meanings, can produce 40% gains in vocabulary for typical children, there are clearly good linguistic grounds for increasing this activity, over and above the recreational and cultural reasons for doing so.

[9] These two studies have also highlighted a fruitful field for further research. There is potential for numerous related studies on language acquisition from story reading, at varying age levels, with different kinds of stories, with and without pictures, and with varied numbers and forms

of presentation. Follow-up interviews would be helpful in probing children's misconceptions and their level of understanding, and measures of comprehension and syntax should be used as dependent variables to assess the degree of transfer of the new knowledge gained in this way.

[10] Many teachers and parents have known intuitively of the numerous benefits of story reading. It is reassuring to discover empirical evidence of one of the advantages of story reading, the expansion of children's vocabulary. To maximize such benefits, more research is needed to help determine which characteristics of stories are critical in contributing to children's learning. (From Elley, 1989. Reprinted with permission of W.B. Elley and the International Reading Association.)

FEEDBACK

Activity 1: Teachers' Work Behavior Study

The discussion section does not have a restatement of the researchers' purposes. The researchers have summarized their results in paragraphs 1 and 2, and they have interpreted the results in paragraphs 3 through 7. Implications of their results are presented in paragraph 8. In paragraph 9 they have acknowledged certain limitations to their study. In paragraphs 10 and 11 they link their results to other studies; these are followed by recommendations which have not been too broadly generalized. Paragraph 16 contains questions for further research.

In the Feedback to Chapter 7 Activities, some reservations about the design of the study were raised (see last sentences of Feedback on pp. 183–184). The researchers have made appropriate generalizations by recognizing the limitations of their study. In the Feedback to Chapter 8 Activities (see p. 224), research consumers were warned that these results might just be impressions because triangulation was not reported. On the other hand, the researchers have tried to substantiate their results by comparing theirs with those of other researchers.

Activity 2: Vocabulary Acquisition Study

In paragraph 1, the researcher summarized his results without providing a restatement of the studies' purposes. These results were presented in relation to other, unspecified studies. In paragraph 2, questions left unanswered by the research are identified. Paragraphs 3 to 5 contain discussions about why the unexplained results might have occurred. Paragraph 6 contains a recommendation as to how the unanswered question and unexplained results might be rectified. In paragraphs 7 to 9, implications of the two studies are discussed and generalizations are made by comparing the results to those obtained with subjects from other cultures. Further research is recommended and generalizations are not inappropriately broad.

Both studies represent conservative interpretations of results by the researchers.

10 Reading and Interpreting Reviews of Research

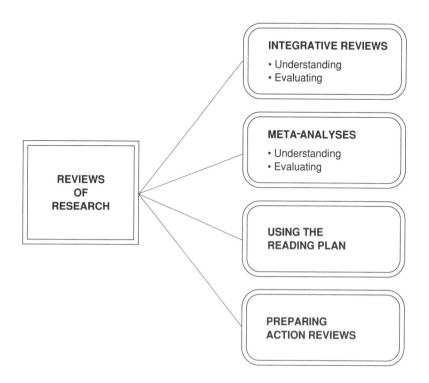

REVIEWS OF RESEARCH

INTEGRATIVE REVIEWS
- Understanding
- Evaluating

META-ANALYSES
- Understanding
- Evaluating

USING THE READING PLAN

PREPARING ACTION REVIEWS

FOCUS QUESTIONS

1. What are integrative reviews of research?
2. What criteria are used to evaluate integrative reviews of research?
3. What are meta-analyses?
4. What criteria are used to evaluate meta-analyses?
5. How are integrative reviews of research prepared?

In Chapter 4, part of the discussion about introductory sections dealt with researchers' brief summaries of other researchers' results that were related to a research problem area. In these limited reviews, called **literature reviews**, researchers indicate strengths from research under review that they used in their own research and weaknesses or limitations in the reviewed research that were changed. A set of questions was given in Chapter 4 so that research consumers could evaluate how critically researchers analyzed related research. These limited literature searches, however, are not intended to be comprehensive, or in-depth, reports of research related to a problem area. When researchers report comprehensive reviews of research related to problem areas, they do so in integrative reviews of research or in meta-analyses of research.

Comprehensive reviews of research are important to educators—both research producers and research consumers. First, preparers of research reviews provide overviews of the research related to a particular problem area. They explain why the problem area is important as a research concern and also report the extent to which the problem area has been researched. Second, research reviewers provide information about the types of research designs used to study the problem, and they may show methodological changes over time in how research producers approached the problem. Third, they identify and define key terms related to the problem area, and they may discover differences in the operational definitions researchers used. Fourth, research reviewers can provide insights about the appropriateness of research producers' methodology. This is important for research consumers when they wish to determine the generalizability of results from various research situations to other teaching and learning situations. Fifth, and possibly the most important reason for these reviews, reviewers join together and interpret the results from a group of research studies dealing with the research problems. Through their interpretation of the collective results and their general commentary, research reviewers in education indicate trends in the development of concepts about learning and instruction. These ideas help research producers understand possible areas for future research and help research consumers gain insight about school-related issues.

Research consumers need to understand (a) researchers' reason(s) for preparing reviews of research, (b) the way research reviewers prepare integrative reviews of research, (c) the rationale underlying meta-analyses of research and the procedures for doing meta-analyses, and (d) the way to read and interpret integrative reviews and meta-analyses of research.

From reading integrative reviews and meta-analyses of research, research consumers should be able to answer

How did research reviewers define their problem areas?

What questions did research reviewers seek to answer and why did they think the answers would be important for educators to know?

How did research reviewers locate relevant research reports?

How did research reviewers determine what studies to include in their reviews?

What procedures did research reviewers use to analyze and interpret the results of the research?

What conclusions did research reviewers make from the research?

Research consumers should keep in mind that research related to any educational problem can be summarized, interpreted, and reported for different purposes and for different consumers (Ladas, 1980). For example, research can be reviewed to point out weaknesses or limitations in instruction and make recommendations for improvement in teaching practices. Or, it can be reviewed to establish the improvement of research practices. Or, it can be reviewed to influence broad educational policy and provide conclusions for applied use. The reviews can be directed at audiences such as researchers, those in power or influential positions, practitioners, or the public at large. Research consumers, then, need to identify the intended audience(s) of integrative and meta-analytic reviews of educational research.

INTEGRATIVE REVIEWS OF RESEARCH

Integrative reviews are undertaken as research projects in which the sources of data are the primary research reports of other researchers. These reviews are more than summaries of research; **integrative reviews of research** are critical examinations of research producers' methods and conclusions and of the generalizability of their combined results.

Understanding Integrative Reviews of Research

Integrative reviews consist of five stages (Cooper, 1982; Jackson, 1980): (1) problem formation, (2) data collection, (3) evaluation of data quality, (4) data analysis and interpretation, and (5) presentation of results.

The stages of integrative reviews are summarized in Table 10.1. The table includes the characteristics of each stage of the review process and the issues research reviewers need to address. For each stage, these include (a) a research question that needs to be asked, (b) the activities that need to be done, (c) the sources of differences among reviewers that can cause variations in their conclusions, and (d) the possible sources of threats to the validity of the review. The discussion that follows is based on ideas expressed in several sources (Abrami, Cohen, & d'Apollonia, 1988; Cooper, 1982; Jackson, 1980).

Problem Formulation

The first stage begins with a search of *existing* integrative reviews for ideas about questions or hypotheses. Ideas are sought for questions

Table 10.1 The Integrative Review Conceptualized as a Research Report

Stage Characteristics	Stage of Research				
	Problem Formulation	Data Collection	Data Evaluation	Analysis and Interpretation	Public Presentation
Research Question Asked	What evidence should be included in the review?	What procdures should be used to find relevant evidence?	What retrieved evidence should be included in the review?	What procdures should be used to make inferences about the literature as a whole?	What information should be included in the review report?
Primary Function in Review	Constructing definitions that distinguish relevant from irrelevant studies.	Determining which sources of potentially relevant studies to examine.	Applying criteria to separate "valid" from "invalid" studies.	Synthesizing valid retrieved studies.	Applying editorial criteria to separate important from unimportant information.
Procedural Differences That Create Variation in Review Conclusions	1. Differences in included operational definitions. 2. Differences in operational detail.	Differences in the research contained in sources of information.	1. Differences in quality criteria. 2. Differences in the influence of nonquality criteria.	Differences in rules of inference.	Differences in guidelines for editorial judgment.
Sources of Potential Invalidity in Review Conclusions	1. Narrow concepts might make review conclusions less definitive and robust. 2. Superficial operational detail might obscure interacting variables.	1. Accessed studies might be qualitatively different from the target population of studies. 2. People shared in accessible studies might be different from target population of people.	1. Nonquality factors might cause improper weighting of study information. 2. Omissions in study reports might make conclusions unreliable.	1. Rules for distinguishing patterns from noise might be inappropriate. 2. Review-based evidence might be used to infer causality.	1. Omission of review procedures might make conclusions irreproducible. 2. Omission of review findings and study procedure might make conclusions obsolete.

Source: From Cooper, 1982. Copyright 1982 by the American Educational Research Association. Adapted by permission of the publisher.

about the phenomenon being researched and variations in methods that might account for variations in results. In addition, questions might be formulated from available theory and the reviewers' own insights. Research reviewers then set out operational definitions for key concepts within the problem area. These definitions may reflect those used by primary researchers or may be created for the research review. Research reviewers use the operational definitions to identify relevant primary research studies for inclusion in the integrative review. For example, the following is how one research reviewer operationally defined a key concept, classroom evaluation. Note that for the purposes of this review the definition limits the concept to formal testing.

Purpose of the review: To examine the relationships between classroom evaluation practices and student learning outcomes.

Classroom evaluation is defined as evaluation based on activities that students undertake as an integral part of the educational programs in which they are enrolled. These activities may involve time spent both inside and outside the classroom. This definition includes tasks such as formal teacher-made tests, curriculum-embedded tests (including adjunct questions and other exercises intended to be an integral part of learning materials), oral questions asked of students, and a wide variety of other performance activities (cognitive and psychomotor). It also includes assessment of motivational and attitudinal variables and of learning skills. (Crooks, 1988, p. 439)

Data Collection

In collecting, organizing, and summarizing data, research reviewers try to use as many information sources as possible. An important responsibility of research reviewers is to identify the target population, the accessible population, and the sample of primary research reports. The target population of primary research reports is the total body of research reports about which generalizations can be made. Therefore, accessible populations of research reports may be determined by the availability to researchers of library holdings and electronic data bases. The sample population of research reports is the specific research reports the reviewers select for review. Practical considerations for reviewers about selection relate to the resources for locating primary research reports (see Chapter 11, Locating Information About Research Reports) and the time period(s) to be covered (e.g., examining only research published between 1980 and 1990). Also, research reviewers cluster research reports by research designs, since each type of research must be judged by separate criteria.

Data Evaluation

In evaluating data quality, research reviewers set up evaluation criteria before they search the literature. As a rule, research reviewers use critical questions about research that are similar to those included in this text about primary research reports (see Figure 3.1, p. 87, and Chapters 4 to 9).

Analysis and Interpretation

In analyzing and interpreting data, the research reviewers should explicitly state how they made inferences, and they should distinguish between inferences they made on the basis of individual studies and those they made as a result of their review of a group of studies.

Public Presentation

In presenting their results, reviewers try to avoid omitting details and evidence. In other words, in making an integrative review of research comprehensible, they attend to the same factors that make a primary research report understandable.

The article on pp. 247–253 is taken from an integrative research review about the role of elementary school principals in program development. It includes a portion of the review in which the research reviewers state the problem area, their method for obtaining the sample of studies to review, their method of analysis, and the results and discussion of their analysis of the research methodologies. Also, included is a portion of their conclusion about the generalizability of the summarized results. What has not been included in this example are the results and discussion of the dimensions of principals' behavior that were revealed by the literature and the researchers' conclusions about those substantive (or problem area–related) results.

Evaluating Integrative Reviews of Research

Research consumers need to determine whether research reviewers have critically analyzed and interpreted the data they presented. The information in Table 10.1 under the dashed line (the lower portion of the table) and the following discussion indicate characteristics in research reviews that may lead them to be invalid. Research consumers need to identify whether research reviewers controlled variables that could threaten the internal and external validity of their reviews.

Procedural Differences That Create Variation in Review Conclusions and Sources of Potential Invalidity in Review Conclusions

In the problem formulation stage, research reviewers should identify differences that exist among their operational definitions, those of other reviewers, and those found in the sampled research. Reviewers should

(Text continued on p. 253)

Leithwood, K. A., & Montgomery, D. J. (1982). The role of the elementary school principal in program improvement. *Review of Educational Research*, 52, 309–339. Copyright 1982 by the American Educational Research Association. Reprinted by permission of the publisher.

The Role of the Elementary School Principal in Program Improvement

K. A. Leithwood and D. J. Montgomery
The Ontario Institute for Studies in Education

In the search for factors that influence school effectiveness, the role of the elementary school principal has emerged as critical. Yet the bulk of past research focused on that role has provided limited insights to explain how principals go about improving the effectiveness of their schools; surprisingly few studies have asked that question directly. Using a framework for planned change, this study assessed the status of knowledge about effective and ineffective principal behaviours. Obstacles that principals face in their attempts at school improvement were also reviewed. Results point to areas of existing knowledge in which confidence can be placed and to useful approaches to subsequent research.

The problem for this study emerges from the now well-documented failure of a large proportion of past program improvement efforts (Fullan & Pomfret, 1977; Goodland & Klein, 1970; Gross, Giacquinta, & Bernstein, 1971; Smith & Keith, 1971) and a growing body of research identifying factors associated with success. Reviews of research (Austin, 1979; Averch, 1971; Fullan, 1981; Reinhardt et al., 1979; Sikorski, 1976), large-scale evaluations of federally funded change projects (Berman & McLaughlin, 1978; Emrick, 1977) and clinically oriented investigations of educational change (Goodlad, 1975; Gross, Giacquinta, & Bernstein, 1971; Sarason, 1971) coalesce in support of the elementary school principal as a potentially critical determinant in the success of efforts to improve. However, only a small proportion of those in the role seem to realize this potential. Available data suggest that about 50 percent of elementary principals actually attempt to assist the teacher in improving instructional programs (Berman & Pauly, 1975; Blumberg & Greenfield, 1980; Leithwood, Ross, Montgomery, & Maynes, 1978); those who would provide such assistance confront pervasive norms of teacher autonomy (Deal & Celloti, 1980; Dreeben, 1973; Jackson & Belford, 1965; Lortie, 1975;

Packard, 1976; Warren, 1975) and minimal direct control over those aspects of classroom life that teachers find most rewarding. Some principals are successful in spite of these obstacles. Why? What are they doing? How does this compare with typical principal behaviour? What is presently known about effective principal behaviour that would be of value to practicing principals and those responsible for their training?

General questions addressed by this review were further specified in the context of a framework for planned educational change (Leithwood & Robinson, 1979; Leithwood & Montgomery, 1982). This framework draws together and shows the relationships among concepts central to most research on educational change including the process of growth, the role of the agents involved in the change, and forms of intervention. Change, or program "improvement," is defined as the realization of valued outcomes by students. The change process is conceptualized as a complex form of individual and organizational learning, resocialization, or growth. The amount and nature of growth required of the teacher is determined largely by the experiences necessary for student growth toward the attainment of valued outcomes; the teacher is a central agent in the creation of those experiences. Similarly, principal behaviours are increasingly "effective" to the extent that they facilitate necessary teacher growth and thereby indirectly influence student learning or impinge on other factors known to effect such learning. This logic is extended to the role of other educational agents as well. However, growth in the complex behaviours of educational agents implied by curriculum guidelines and other curriculum innovations, for example, does not occur naturally. Obstacles (lack of knowledge and skill, disincentives, inappropriate organizational arrangements, lack of material resources, etc.) prevent such growth. Intervention is usually necessary if such obstacles are to be overcome (Leithwood, 1981b). Five types of information about the behaviour of each agent involved in planned change are required within this briefly described framework: categories or dimensions of behaviour most directly associated with program improvement; desired status within these dimensions; behaviours of the typical or modestly effective principal; patterns of growth within each dimension from current to preferred status; and obstacles. Research could be located relevant to three of these questions or categories of needed information; virtually no attention has been given to growth in principal behaviour, and attention to critical dimensions of principal behaviour is not yet sufficiently self-conscious to make a useful review possible. Therefore, questions about typical principal behaviours, effective principal behaviours, and obstacles to growth in principal effectiveness constitute the focus for this review.

As the framework indicates, "principal effectiveness" has been defined in terms of effects on student learning either directly or through mediating variables. This orientation toward effectiveness is in line with much current thinking in educational administration (Erickson, 1979; Silver, 1980–1981) and certainly in curriculum development. Boyan (1981), nevertheless, urges recognition of the framework-dependent na-

ture of such a definition. Approached from the orientation of school governance, for example, the dependent variables for research on effectiveness might be "enfranchisement of the previously disenfranchised, professional vs. lay control of policy decisions and procedures, resolution of ideological conflicts" (p. 10), and so forth.

METHOD

Sample

Three categories of studies were reviewed. Those concerned with the role of the principal in general comprised one category. These studies frequently focused on leadership, management, and administration concepts. The second category included research on school change and the implementation of educational innovations. This body of research was concerned specifically with the effect of the principal's behaviour on innovative thrusts initiated within as well as outside the school.

School effectiveness research comprised the third category. These studies, only four in number, located schools with unusual patterns of student achievement and then searched for explanations of such achievement; principal behaviours were identified as one set of variables potentially accounting for observed student achievement patterns. Erickson (1979) suggested that this line of research is presently the most promising and relevant for scholars of educational administration because

(a) it draws fertile insights from research in classrooms; (b) it seems far more seminal, catalyzing inquiry that constantly breaks out in new directions; (c) it departs from the "black-box" tradition that has moved us [scholars of educational administration] substantially nowhere; (d) it features provocative practical implications and explanatory appeal; and (e) its conceptualizations, rather than being so abstract as to defy empirical challenge, are well grounded in the observable world. (page 10)

The results of our review support Erickson's assertion. Nevertheless, the particular questions guiding the review were not addressed, even by implication, by many school effectiveness studies, hence the limited size of the sample included here.

Initial sources of information used to locate research included the Eric system, Dissertation Abstracts, library indexes, the library card catalogue, and the visible file of journal titles. The *Canadian Index of Journals in Education and Resources in Education* from 1974–80 was searched using as descriptors (a) academic achievement, (b) program effectiveness, (c) principals, (d) leadership responsibility, (e) teacher effectiveness, (f) school role, (g) school supervision, (h) school administration, (i) teacher-administrator relationship, and (j) outcomes of education. Descriptors used in searching the Ontario Institute for Studies in Education's library card catalogue included (a) teacher-principal relationships, (b) high school principals, (c) junior high school principals, (d) elementary school principals, and (e) school superintendents and principals. The initial journals searched included the *National Elementary Principal* and the *National Association of Secondary School Principals' Bulletin*. Sources of information following this initial search consisted primarily of the references used in papers/books as they were read.

Several limitations of the search procedure should be noted. First, no systematic search was made for studies outside North America. The studies finally reviewed included one from the United Kingdom (McGeown, 1979–80); three of the North American studies were carried out in Canada (Dow & Whitehead, 1980; Leithwood et al., 1978; Wilson, 1981); and the remainder in the United States. Second, most studies reviewed were from published sources. Gage (1978) recently reviewed evidence related to the argument that published studies are biased toward significant results; there

does not appear to be convincing support for this claim. Finally, studies of the secondary school principal's role exclusively-were eventually dropped from our analysis on the grounds that the elementary and secondary school contexts are sufficiently different to warrant independent attention to the two principal roles. Several studies included in the review examine both roles without an attempt to identify differences.

Yin, Bingham, and Heald (1976) examined the difference in research results between high- and low-quality studies. Because it is based on case study research, their analysis is especially relevant to research reviewed in this paper, as is evident in Table 1. Results from methodologically low- and high-quality studies did not differ significantly, although fewer positive treatment effects were demonstrated by lower quality studies. This conclusion was supported by Ladas's (1980) subsequent analysis. For this reason, a very coarse screen was used in sifting those studies to be reviewed out of the studies identified by the above search procedure. A study had to meet two criteria; (a) it had to provide direct empirical data about one or more of the three questions of concern to the review, and (b) the methodology had to be interpretable from the written report of the research. The quality of studies selected using these criteria is discussed in the body of the review.

Analysis

Literature reviews present two data analysis problems: How best to summarize the data presented in many individual studies, and how to organize or classify the data for purposes of summary. The first of these problems has been systematically addressed largely in the context of quantitative correlational or experimental data (Glass, 1976; Ladas, 1980) to this point. However, studies included in this review frequently consisted of extended qualitative descriptions of behaviours or obstacles that principals encounter. Given such data and the questions

Table 1 Dimensions of Principal Behavior

Dimensions	Subdimensions
1. Goals	
2. Factors	1. Factors affecting student classroom experiences
	1.1 The teacher
	1.2 Program objectives and emphasis
	1.3 Instructional behaviors of the teacher
	1.4 Materials and resources
	1.5 Assessment, recording, and reporting procedures
	1.6 Time/classroom management
	1.7 Content
	1.8 Physical environment
	1.9 Interpersonal relationships in the classroom
	1.10 Integration
	2. Factors affecting student school-wide experiences
	2.1 Human resources
	2.2 Material and physical resources
	2.3 Relationships with community
	2.4 Extracurricular and intramural activities
	2.5 Relationships among staff
	2.6 Relationships with out-of-school staff
	2.7 Student behavior while at school
3. Strategies	Categories of Strategies Used by Principals
	1. Building/maintaining interpersonal relationships and motivating staff
	1.1 Involving staff
	1.2 Doing things with staff
	1.3 Being positive, cheerful, and encouraging
	1.4 Being with/available or accessible to staff
	1.5 Being honest, direct, and sincere
	1.6 Getting staff to express/set their own goals
	2. Providing staff with knowledge and skill
	3. Collecting information
	4. Using vested authority
	5. Providing direct service to students
	6. Assisting with and supporting teachers' regular tasks
	7. Facilitating within-school communication
	8. Providing information to staff
	9. Focusing attention on the special needs of students
	10. Facilitating communication between the school and the community
	11. Using goal and priority-setting and planning
	12. Finding nonteaching time for staff
	13. Establishing procedures to handle routine matters

Note: Detailed definitions of categories are avaiable from the authors.

guiding the review, content analysis methods were used to summarize the data.

The lens a reviewer uses to examine phenomena of interest determines the framework or organization of data. In this case, the results of the review were intended to be of maximum use to principals as well as academics. Therefore, an attempt was made to organize and describe the data in a form meaningful to principals. The categories selected to organize the data had to reflect a pattern that made sense to principals; the data itself had to capture an interpretation of school events that would be understood by principals. These requirements raised several basic questions inadequately addressed by extant research: (a) What cognitive frameworks do principals use in thinking about their roles? (b) What language do principals use to describe their own professional activities and problems? (c) How can principals' behaviours be classified so that subsequent descriptions will be meaningful to principals as well as focused on critical aspects of their behaviour? To answer these questions an original study was conducted prior to the detailed review of the literature.

The original study involved deriving a set of "grounded" dimensions (Glaser & Strauss, 1967) or categories of principal behaviour from intensive interviews with a sample of principals drawn from four school systems. Preliminary data used to develop an adequate interview schedule were collected in an open-ended interview of approximately 3 hours' duration with one principal known by the researchers to be an active curriculum leader in his school. After further field testing of the instrument with 2 more principals from a different school system, it was administered to volunteer principals in a third school system. Preliminary analysis of these data indicated that the instrument was suitable and another 10 randomly selected principals from a fourth school system were interviewed; all interviews were audiotaped. The sample of 23 interviews ranged from 1½ to 3 hours and were conducted by the researchers. Audiotapes initially were transcribed by recording discrete behaviours or actions identified by interviewers on separate file cards. All cards were then sorted into "natural clusters" of similar actions resulting in some 21 grounded dimensions or categories.

Although additional investigation suggested that these discrete actions could be reliably assigned to the 21 dimensions, eventually it was concluded that the dimensions did not provide the meaningful pattern of behaviour that was needed; interview tapes were reanalyzed more holistically and three major dimensions with subdimensions (see Table 1) were identified. This set of

dimensions better recognized the interrelatedness of a principal's actions (e.g., the value of a particular action depends significantly on its intended purpose). Subsequent consultation with two groups of principals confirmed the value of these three sets of dimensions for principals; they readily thought about their work in such terms. We found these dimensions to be compatible, usually implicitly, with behaviour classes described in much of the literature eventually included in the review. The dimensions were used as categories for organizing the data in the studies reviewed and for reporting the results.

RESULTS AND DISCUSSION
Methodological Characteristics of the Research Reviewed

Methodological characteristics of individual studies is an important issue in selecting studies for review, as already discussed. Such characteristics of the whole sample of studies are critical also, because they substantially determine how much confidence can be placed in accumulated knowledge resulting from the review. It is not necessarily the case that the integration of many weak studies permits little confidence to be placed in the outcome. As Glass (1976) argued, many imperfect studies can converge on a true conclusion. This is the case when such studies are flawed in dissimilar ways and possess different methodological strengths; such studies together are likely to control for most serious threats to internal and external validity. The major exception to this occurs when congruent findings emerge from a cluster of studies each flawed in similar ways. All findings under these circumstances are likely to share the same bias (Jackson, 1968). Investigating the possible existence of such bias was a central reason for analyzing the methodological characteristics of the 39 studies providing the primary source of data for this review. . . .

With respect to design, 17 studies were surveys, 15 were case or field studies, and

2 combined survey and case study designs. Of the remaining five studies, two were ethnographies, two "preexperiments," and one a conference. (Houts [1975] reports and discusses opinions presented by principals and academics at a conference on the role of the principal. Houts was in the role of participant observer. The data may be considered "expert judgment.") In most instances, the label used to classify a study's design was the original investigator's. Studies classified as ethnographic (Wolcott, 1978; Morris, Van Cleve, Crowson, & Porter-Gehrie 1981) were comparable to many classified as case studies or field studies, the primary difference being the intensity and duration of direct observation, which was greater in the case of the two ethnographies. We applied the term "preexperiment" to Wiggins (1972) and Chesler, Schmuck, and Lippitt (1975); it indicates a design characterized by two sets of data collection separated by a period during which some treatment occurred but with serious threats to internal and external validity left uncontrolled (Campbell & Stanley, 1963).

Subjects from whom data were collected included principals alone in 8 studies, teachers alone in 2 studies, principals as well as teachers in 11 studies, and principals and some role other than teachers (e.g., district administrator, student, trustee) in 3 studies. Fifteen studies incorporated data from principals, teachers, and several other roles as well.

Of the 21 studies using the individual as the sampling unit, subjects ranged in number from 1 to 1,448 with a mean of 333. Twelve studies used the school as the sampling unit; in these cases the number of schools included ranged from 1 to 103 with a mean of 20. Projects designed to introduce some type of innovation into a classroom, school, or cluster of schools (e.g., teacher cooperation) were used as the sampling unit in 3 studies; 4 projects in the case of Rosenblum and Jastrzab (n.d.) and 293 and 100 projects in the case of first and second parts of the *Rand Change Agent Study* (1974–75;

1976–78). In the three studies using districts as the sampling unit, one, four, and five districts were included. Sampling procedures included random (11 studies), selected (20), total population within a preselected unit (4), and a combination of random and selected procedures (2). Procedures used could not be determined from reports by Krajewski (1979) and Williams et al. (1974).

Data were collected through questionnaires only (9 studies), interviews only (7), and observations only (2). In more than half the studies (21), multiple measures were used, which frequently involved some form of document analysis.

Do the methodological features described above permit confidence to be placed in the knowledge resulting from an integrative review? The answer depends on which of the three research questions is examined. In combination, detailed ethnographies employing direct observation, less intense, interview-based case studies, and surveys involving the collection of massive amounts of questionnaire data seem capable of presenting an unbiased description of the range of typical principal behaviours and obstacles principals faces in their work setting. Knowledge resulting from the review about "effective" behaviours is more tenuous, however. The question of effectiveness is causal in nature. While there is variation in design among studies addressing this question, it is within a restricted range that does not include experimental or quasi-experimental alternatives; such alternatives provide well-recognized controls for addressing causal questions that are difficult to duplicate in other ways. Further, substantial variation in the operational definition of the dependent variable "improved student outcomes," "effectiveness," or "program improvement" also should be noted in interpreting the studies reviewed. We considered student achievement the most defensible definition; only the four studies of school effectiveness operationally defined the dependent variable in this way, however. Most studies focused on leadership, management, and administration, or permitted the dependent variable to be defined intuitively and subjectively by the research subjects. This seems likely to introduce a systematic bias linked to conventional images of effective teacher practice and those behaviours that facilitate such practice. Several studies in this category identified a mediating variable (usually "school climate") as the dependent variable. The value of resulting data depends on additional evidence linking the mediating variable to improved student achievement; such evidence is not yet overwhelming. Studies of school change typically considered degree of use of a new program or practice in the classroom as the definition of the dependent variable. These studies did not attempt to link such use to improved student outcomes in typical school settings. If there is a systematic bias in practices advocated by the developers of innovations it is toward a liberal, open view of classroom practices. Recent evidence casts serious doubts on the effects of such practices on student achievement (Peterson &

Walberg, 1979; Crocker, 1981). It will be important to compare the findings of the school effectiveness studies with other results as the review proceeds.

Finally, this review of effective principal behaviours was conducted using a relatively large number of behavioural "dimensions" (Table 1), described in more detail below. The effect of this refinement was to increase the number of specific questions asked of the research and reduce the number of studies available to address most of the questions. As a result, it is important to consider the confidence that can be placed in the outcomes of the review for each research question. This was done by describing the nature of the sample of studies available to address each question, as well as the nature of the total sample of studies (already described). . . . These results, although painted in very broad strokes, receive support from a body of data of uneven quality but few conflicts. Conservative use of the results as guides to practical action seems warranted.

indicate how the specific details of the reviewed studies differ. Research consumers should be able to distinguish precisely between aspects of primary researchers' methods that research reviewers believe are relevant to their critique and those that are not.

In the data collection stage, research reviewers should identify differences that exist between the target population of available studies, their sample of studies, and studies used in other reviews. The target population of research studies consists of all published research reports related to the problem area. The studies selected for analysis constitute the review sample. Research consumers need an understanding of the target population of studies and the representativeness of the reviewers' sample of studies. Also, research reviewers determine their own criteria for including or excluding primary research reports from their reviews, so it is possible for research reviewers to select different samples of studies for analysis. (This limitation is similar to the one discussed in Chapter 5 about the need for research consumers to be sensitive to primary researchers' identification of their target populations and subject selection techniques.) Research reviewers should explain the time span covered by the research and the type of research designs used. And, research consumers need assurance that there was no selection bias. Differences in conclusions by different research reviewers can result from differences in their samples.

Also, research consumers need to understand subject sampling procedures used by primary researchers. It is possible for several primary researchers to use similar labels for their subjects while actually dealing with different target populations. Research consumers should expect research reviewers to delineate the operational definitions used in primary researchers' subject selection.

In the data evaluation stage, research reviewers should indicate what differences exist between the criteria they used for evaluating the research and those used by other reviewers. Research reviewers should indicate whether their critical evaluations were limited by the absence of information in the primary studies. Also, more than one evaluator should be used in reviewing the primary studies, and interevaluator agreements should be reported.

In the analysis and interpretation stage, research reviewers should indicate how their method of interpretation and their conclusions differ from those of other research reviewers. They need to indicate how they distinguished between relevant information (patterns of results) and extraneous information (noise). Research consumers need to identify whether reviewers effectively synthesized results and noted trends, or whether they made inaccurate inferences such as basing causality on relationship results or drawing conclusions not directly related to their purpose questions or extending beyond the data.

In the public presentation stage, research reviewers might not be responsible for differences in editorial guidelines; however, research consumers should be critical of research review reports that are not complete. Omissions restrict the replicability of an integrative review, thereby limiting the effective use of the reviewers' results and conclusions.

Research consumers can use these questions when evaluating integrative reviews of research:

Are there differences in operational definitions among the integrative reviewers, other reviewers, and the primary researchers. Are those differences explained?

Has the target population of research been identified? Are there differences between the samples of research in the review and other reviews? What is the nature of those differences?

Are there explicit evaluation criteria? Do they differ from those of other reviewers? Have the integrative reviewers cited studies with methodological limitations? Have those limitations been explained?

Have the reviewers drawn conclusions that are different from those of other reviewers? Are those differences discussed?

Does the review report present information in a standard research format? Is the report complete?

META-ANALYSES OF RESEARCH

Meta-Analyses of research are ways of critically examining primary research studies that use quantitative data analyses. Research reviewers use meta-analyses as "analyses of analyses" (Glass, 1976, p. 3), that is, statistical data analyses of already completed statistical data analyses. In them, they convert the statistical results of the individual studies into a common measurement so that they can obtain an overall, combined result. Research reviewers convert primary researchers' statistical results into standard numerical forms, and then they analyze those measures by traditional statistical procedures. The following discussions about understanding and evaluating meta-analyses are synthesized from several sources (Abrami, Cohen, & d'Apollonia, 1988; Carlberg et al 1984; Glass 1976; Joyce 1987; Slavin 1984a, 1984b, 1986, 1987b; Stock et al 1982).

Understanding Meta-Analyses of Research

The meta-analysis approach was devised as an attempt to eliminate reviewer biases in synthesizing results from primary quantitative research reports. Some researchers wished to reduce the possible influence of reviewers' biases in the selection and interpretation of research reports. To do this, they designed several quantitative procedures for tabulating and comparing research results from a large number of primary research reports, especially experimental research. A simple quantitative tabulation for estimating the effectiveness of a treatment is called vote counting. *Vote counting* consists of tabulating the number of positive significant results ($+$), the number of negative significant results—those in which the control results exceed the treatment ($-$), and the number of studies without significant results (0). Vote counting, however, can provide misleading ideas about the effectiveness of a treatment or the relationship among variables because vote counting does not take into account the magnitude of the effect or relationship. *Magnitude* can be thought of as the size of the difference between two or more variables.

A quantitative procedure that research reviewers use to account for the magnitude of an effect or relationship is **meta-analysis**. The meta-analysis procedure has become increasingly popular with research reviewers because it is systematic and easily replicable. Given the same set of research reports and by using the same statistical procedures, all research reviewers should get the same results. Also, its users say meta-analyses can be used with the results of research projects with varying methodological quality and with similar but not exactly the same statistical procedures. And, it allows research reviewers to concurrently examine the degree of influence or relationship among the methods, subjects, treatments, duration of treatments, and results of primary research (regardless of whether they are significant or not).

Meta-analyses have stages similar to those of integrative research reviews. In meta-analyses, (1) problems are formed, (2) research studies are collected, (3) pertinent data are identified, (4) analyses and interpretations are made of the data, and (5) results are presented to the public. Meta-analyses begin with reviewers doing an exhaustive, or complete, search to locate previous integrative research reviews and meta-analyses and *all* primary research studies relating to the education questions or problems under review.

In the following example, two subsections are included: literature search and classification of studies. Note that the research reviewers indicate the procedures used to obtain studies, to identify those for inclusion in the review, and to select the variables for analysis. These procedures are similar to those used in integrative reviews.

Purpose of the study: To conduct a meta-analysis of research about the effect of three types of feedback on students' learning.

LITERATURE SEARCH

[Identifying target populations]

The search for studies is an integral part of the process: indeed, it is at this point that the most serious form of bias is likely to occur (Glass et al., 1981). The relevant body of literature was defined as all research studies of the effects of any type or combination of reward and punishment feedback on children's discrimination learning reported in English between 1956 (the starting point for both previous integrative studies) and 1981. The bibliographies of both previous reviews were used as starting points, as well as computer searches of *Psychological Abstracts* and ERIC. The following descriptors were used: discrimination learning, concept learning, feedback, knowledge of results, reinforcement, punishment, with children. In addition, a number of journals were hand searched; 36 journals (including *Dissertation Abstracts*) were included.

[Search procedures]

[Criteria for exclusion]

These searches produced almost 300 documents that initially appeared to be appropriate. However, the number actually used in this analysis was 89. Among the studies not analyzed were comparisons that could not be defensibly included. Included, for instance, were topics such as the relative effectiveness of two types of symbolic reward, immediate versus delayed feedback, "filled" versus "empty" delayed feedback, high incentive and reward versus "unknown incentive reward." Data from such studies were not included because (a) there were too few of them to use as the basis for drawing any meaningful conclusions, and (b) it was almost impossible to determine exactly what effects were estimated. Other studies eliminated included those with populations of college age or special education students and studies in which the statistics could not be transformed to a common metric.

CLASSIFICATION OF STUDIES

Characteristics used to describe Coding Categories of the studies included the following: date of publication, form of publication, author's theoretical commitment (incentive or information), author's institutional affiliation (e.g., university, government), total sample size, mean age of subjects, socioeconomic status, grade level of the subjects, task complexity, instruction, feedback training, feedback delivery, incentive value, measure of dependent variable (i.e., either number of correct responses, number of errors, number of trials to criterion, or percentage of problems solved), and control for sequence effects. (From Getsie, Langer, and Glass, 1985)

In the second step, the reviewers describe and code the selected studies' characteristics and results. To ensure accurate coding, meta-analysis researchers use multiple raters and report interrater reliability. Summaries of the coding are usually reported in table form. In the following example, taken from a meta-analysis of vocabulary instruction research, two tables are partially reproduced. Table 1 [on p. 258] of their review lists studies reflecting treatments in which control groups did not get any chance to see target words before the pretests; Table 2 [on p. 259] lists studies reflecting treatments in which control groups did not get any instruction in how to study.

Purpose of the study: A meta-analysis of studies concerned the effects of vocabulary instruction on the learning of word meanings and on comprehension.

After coding, meta-analysis reviewers use statistical procedures to examine the combined research results. They group the research according to their research designs. Most often, meta-analyses are done with research using experimental designs. Meta-analysts create an effect size for each experimental study. **Effect sizes** are standard scores created from a ratio derived from the mean scores of the experimental and control groups and the standard deviations of the control groups. Effect size scores show the size of the differences between the experimental and control groups in relation to the standard deviation. For example, an effect size of $+.50$ would mean the experimental group scored about one-half a standard deviation above the control group, and an effect size of $-.50$ would mean the experimental group scored about one-half a standard deviation below the control group.

These effect sizes can be averaged, and significant differences (e.g., t- or F- ratios) can be determined between treatment and control groups or among several other independent variables.

The following portion from a results section illustrates how research reviewers report their results from meta-analyses. In a separate section

Table 1 List of Studies Used in Analysis with Classifications (No-Exposure Control Group)

Study/treatment	Grade	Emphasis[a]	DOP[b]	Exposures[c]	Group/Ind.	Time per Word	Effect Size	Comments
Contextual vocabulary measures								
Ahlfors (1979)								
Context	6	4	G	ME	group	[d]	1.710	Sentence anomaly (delayed)
							1.579	Sentence anomaly (immediate)
Definitions	6	1	A	MR	ind.	[d]	1.512	Sentence anomaly (delayed)
						1.128		Sentence anomaly (immediate)
Experience	6	3	G	ME	group	[d]	1.116	Sentence anomaly (delayed)
							.661	Sentence anomaly (immediate)
R. C. Anderson & Kulhavy (1972)								
Context	college	3	G	SE	ind.	.10	1.980	
Repetition	college	1	A	MR	ind.	.10	1.230	
Jenkins, Pany, & Schreck (1978)								
Meaning given	[d]	2	A	SE	ind.	.25	.160	
Meaning practiced	[d]	2	A	MR	ind.	1.67	2.204	
Johnson & Stratton (1966)								
Classification	college	1	A	SE	ind.	1.50	.795	
Definitions	college	2	C	ME	ind.	1.50	.651	
Mixed	college	3	G	ME	ind.	1.50	1.181	
Sentences	college	5	C	ME	ind.	1.50	.916	
Synonyms	college	1	A	MR	ind.	1.50	.807	
Pany & Jenkins (1977)								
Meaning given	[d]	2	A	SE	ind.	.25	.852	
Meaning practiced	[d]	2	A	MR	ind.	1.67	3.782	
Stahl (1983)								
Definitional	5	2	G	ME	group	10.00	1.421	Sentence cloze

Source: From Stahl & Fairbanks, 1986, p. 87. Copyright 1986 by the American Educational Research Association. Adapted by permission of the publisher.

Table 2 List of Studies Used in Analysis with Classifications (No-Instruction Control Group)

Study/treatment	Grade	Method Factors			General Setting Factors			
		Emphasis[a]	DOP[b]	Exposures[c]	Group/Ind.	Time per Word	Effect Size	Comments
Contextual vocabulary measures								
Anderson & Kulhavy (1972)	college	4	G	SE	ind.	.10	3.000 1.710	First trial Second trial
Aurentz (1983)	12	K	K	K	ind.		.704 .368	Immediate Delayed
Crist & Petrone (1977)	college	4	C	ME	ind.	d	.784	
Gipe (1979) Context	3 5	3 3	G G	ME ME	ind. ind.	3.75 3.75	.897[c] 1.200[e]	
Jenkins et al. (1978)	d	2	A	MR	ind.	1.67	.866 1.691 1.785 2.439	Ave. sent. cloze Ave. paraphrase LD sent. cloze LD paraphrase
Johnson & Stratton (1966)								
Classification	college	1	A	SE	ind.	1.50	−.015	
Definition	college	2	C	ME	ind.	1.50	−.191	
Mixed	college	3	G	ME	ind.	1.50	.456	
Levin, Dretzke, Pressley, & McGivern								

Note: Identifications in the "comments" column are given only for studies with multiple measures where some confusion might occur. See original reference for full information about each measure.

[a] I = defintions only; 2 = definitional emphasis; 3 = balanced; 4 = contextual emphasis; 5 = context only; k = keyword.

[b] A = associative; C = comprehension; G = generation; K = keyword.

[c] SE = one or two exposures; MR = multiple repetitions (sure information); ME = multiple exposures (different information); K = keyword.

[d] Not enough information given in study.

[e] Since three treatments met our criteria for comparison group, effect size was calculated using the combined means of association, classification, and definition groups.

Source: From Stahl & Fairbanks, 1986, p. 88. Copyright 1986 by the American Educational Research Association. Adapted by permission of the publisher.

and table, the researchers had reported the effect sizes for the individual primary studies. In this portion they report the results of a statistical analysis to determine whether any variables had significant effects.

Purpose of the study: A meta-analysis of selected studies on the efficacy of bilingual education.

Major Variables Influencing Effect Sizes

Table 2 presents the analysis of variance that includes the most parsimonious combination of variables for explaining variation in the effect sizes. The variables in this model were extracted from a group of 12 variables identified during the first stage of analysis that were essential conceptually or that had R^2 values of sufficient magnitude to warrant their further study. Among the variables in the first stage of analysis that did *not* demonstrate sufficient systematic variation to be retained for further study were the grade level of the samples and sample size. Bivariate regressions of effect size with grade level and with sample size yielded R^2 values of only .01 and .03, respectively, and p values of .38 and .12. Consequently, effect sizes were aggregated across grade levels and sample sizes for the remaining analyses.

In the model presented in Table 2, six variables were found to account conjointly for about 50% of the total variance of effect sizes. These include the types of programs compared, academic domain of the criterion instrument, language of the criterion instrument, assignment of students to programs (random vs. matched groups and unknown types of assignment), and two variables that demonstrated sufficient systematic variation to necessitate their inclusion for statistical control—the formulas used to calculate effect sizes and the types of scores reported in the studies (e.g., raw scores, percentiles, grade equivalents, or others). Each of the six variables accounted for a significant portion of the variance in effect sizes even with the variance of the remaining variables held constant.

In examining more detailed information concerning the variables in Table 2, it was noted that 466 of the 495 effect sizes came from com-

Table 2 Analysis of Variance of Effect Sizes with Multiple Independent Variables[a]

Variable	df	Sum of Squares[b]	F value	PR F
Types of program compared	4	2.20	5.29	.0004
Academic domain of criterion	8	2.53	3.04	.0024
Language of criterion	1	6.72	64.70	.0001
Assignment to programs	2	2.54	12.20	.0001
Effect size formula	6	7.97	12.78	.0001
Type of score	5	3.33	6.40	.0001

Note: SS model = 48.85; SS error = 48.63; df = 26/468; F = 18.08; p = .0001; multiple R^2 = .50.
[a]Effective sizes weighted by independent sample within domain of test.
[b]SS value takes into account the presence of all variables in the model.

INTERPRETING EDUCATIONAL RESEARCH

parisons of bilingual programs to submersion programs. The thin spread of data over the remaining types of comparisons precluded the examination in this model of the interaction of domain of test by language of test, a variable that would add too many categories to the analysis. (From Willig, 1985, pp. 287–288. Copyright 1985 by the American Educational Research Association. Reprinted by permission of the publisher.)

EVALUATING META-ANALYSES OF RESEARCH

Research consumers need to determine whether research reviewers using meta-analysis techniques have critically analyzed and interpreted the data they presented. Research consumers need to know how research reviewers using meta-analyses controlled variables that could threaten the internal and external validity of their review.

Although meta-analyses are systematic and their results may be replicable, several major limitations affect the usability and generalizability of their results. Some of these limitations are common to both integrative and meta-analytic research reviews. Research consumers need to understand what these limitations are and how to critically evaluate meta-analytic reviews of research.

In evaluating meta-analyses, research consumers need to have the same understandings about the stages of problem formulation, data collection, data evaluation, analysis and interpretation, and public presentation as they have about these stages in integrative reviews.

A limitation specific to evaluating meta-analyses in the data evaluation stage is the possible lack of appropriate data in the primary studies. Meta-analytic reviewers must have the means, standard deviations, and sample sizes for all subject groups. When data are insufficient, primary studies are excluded; therefore, meta-analyses are only effective in examining the results of well-reported research.

And, meta-analyses involve the specific coding of primary research reports on several factors. The coding procedures involve rational or subjective, not statistical or objective, judgments. Therefore, meta-analysis reviewers should use more than one coder, and they need to report the consistency, or reliability factors, among coders.

Another limitation of meta-analyses is that they can examine only primary research with direct quantitiative evidence. Direct evidence comes from the examination of explicit variables and specific defined subjects. However, one benefit of integrative reviews of research is that reviewers can provide indications of indirect evidence that might give research producers and consumers insight about possible effects or relationships. And, integrative reviewers can analyze and synthesize results from qualitative research.

Also, meta-analyses include all primary research studies with complete data in the analyses. Primary research studies that have major methodological weaknesses or problems are not excluded. Consequently, poorly designed and implemented research studies are given equal status with well designed and implemented studies.

These problems have been highlighted by some researchers who reviewed meta-analyses of research. One reviewer team did an integrative critique and comparison of six meta-analyses of research concerning the validity of college students' rating of instruction (Abrami, Cohen, and d'Apollonia, 1988). These reviewers found that all six meta-analyses resulted in different conclusions about students' rating of instruction. They concluded that they, the integrative reviewers,

> found differences at each of five steps in the quantitative synthesizes which contributed to the discrepant conclusions reached by the [six meta-analytic] reviewers. The [six] reviewers had dissimilar inclusion criteria; thus the operational definitions of the problems were not the same, making the questions addressed somewhat incomparable. . . . Only one reviewer coded study features. This suggests an undue emphasis on single summary judgments of the literature without attempts to analyze thoroughly factors contributing to variability in the main relationship[s]. Agreement among the reviewers in reported effect magnitudes were low. . . . [so] extracting data from reports and then calculating individual study outcomes appears more difficult than was initially envisioned. Finally, methods of analysis differed, most noticeably with regard to variability in effect magnitudes where opposite conclusions about the importance of outcome variability were reached.
>
> Overall, the differences uncovered [by the reviewers of the meta-analyses] were in both conception and execution, not limited to technical details of quantification. Clearly, computing effect magnitudes or sizes provided no assurance of an objective review. Thus the enterprise of quantitative synthesis must be conceived broadly by reviewers to include both statistical and substantive [or problem-related] issues. Attention must be paid to the procedures used and decisions reached at each step in a quantitative synthesis. (pp. 162–163)

Research consumers can use these questions when evaluating meta-analysis reviews of research:

> Are there differences in operational definitions among the meta-analysis reviewers, other reviewers (integrative and meta-analytic), and the primary researchers? Are those differences explained?
>
> Have the target populations of studies been identified? Are there differences between the samples of studies in the meta-analysis and other reviews?
>
> Are there explicit coding and evaluation criteria? Do they differ from those of other meta-analysis reviewers? Have the meta-analysis reviewers produced separate results for methodologically strong and weak studies? Has more than one coder been used and are interrater reliability coefficients provided?

Have the meta-analysis reviewers drawn conclusions that differ from those of other reviewers? Are those differences discussed?

Do the meta-analysis reports present information in a standard research format? Are the reports complete?

READING INTEGRATIVE RESEARCH REVIEWS AND META-ANALYSES

Research consumers can read reviews of research using a plan similar to that for reading primary research reviews. The idea is to understand the purposes and conclusions of the research reviewers before reading their data collection and data analyses. As you read, keep in mind the evaluative questions.

Read the title and abstract, if one is provided.

Read the problem formation section. Often, research reviewers will not use this label, and they will subdivide the discussion of the research problem into two or more subsections. But, the section or sections usually provide background information about the topic, definition of terms, and a review of previous research reviews. Research reviewers will often state their purposes near the beginning of these sections.

Read the analysis and interpretation section and the conclusion section, if there is one.

Read the data collection and data evaluation sections. You should examine any tables and figures included in these sections, because they often summarize pertinent information. In meta-analyses, check the tables for indications of significant results.

When you have completed reading the integrative review or meta-analysis, you should understand (a) the reviewers' purposes, (b) their major results and conclusions, and (c) the appropriateness of their review.

PREPARING ACTION REVIEWS OF RESEARCH

Research consumers may need to synthesize, or bring together, the results of research concerning a school-related organizational, learning, or instructional issue. For example, teachers and supervisors in a middle school may wish to examine the research relating to alternative ways to integrate special education students into general education classes. Or, the members of a high school English department may wish to examine research related to the holistic scoring of students' writing. Or, the staff of an early childhood center may wish to gain additional insights about the development children's self-concept during structured and spontaneous play.

Reviews of research are prepared by going through stages similar to those shown in Table 10.1. However, research reviews produced for local use can be considered **action research reviews** rather than full integrative reviews. Action research reviews are to integrative reviews what action research is to comparative and experimental research (see Chapters 7 and 8).

To prepare action research reviews, research consumers can use the concept of **best evidence** (Slavin, 1986, 1987b). Best evidence is an idea about selecting and reviewing studies that (a) have purposes specifically related to an immediate issue or concern, (b) are methodologically adequate, and (c) are generalizable to the local situation. In selecting studies specifically related to an immediate issue, research consumers would include only studies that have explicit descriptions of independent and dependent variables. The early childhood staff, for example, would only select studies that clearly define "self-concept," "structured play," and "spontaneous play." Since no research project is without some methodological limitation, research consumers need to determine what aspects in the primary research they would expect to have been rigidly controlled and for what aspects they could tolerate less rigorous controls. That is, studies without complete information about instrument reliability or subject selection procedures might be included, but studies without full documentation of structured play as a treatment would not be. And, primary studies in which the subjects are not representative of local students and those containing apparent researcher biases or influences should be excluded.

The first steps in conducting action research reviews are to locate, summarize, and interpret the most recent integrative and meta-analytic reviews of research. (Chapter 11 contains discussions about locating primary research reports and research reviews.) Then, using the principle of best evidence, you should locate, summarize, and interpret the most recent primary research, working back to studies published in the previous five to eight years. As an aid to organizing information from these two steps, you can use forms such as those in Figures 10.1, 10.2, and 10.3. Figure 10.1 contains a form for summarizing information from integrative reviews of research and meta-analyses. Figure 10.2 contains a form for summarizing information from primary research. Figure 10.3 contains a form for synthesizing the major results from the reviews and primary research reports.

To complete Figure 10.1

Enter the appropriate information in the heading; on the *location* line, indicate the place (i.e., the specific library) where the original research review is located—in case it has to be reexamined.

Summarize the pertinent information about the type of review

Authors: _____
Date: _____
Title: _____
Journal: _____
Volume: _____
Pages: _____
Location: _____

Type of review: _____ Integrative _____ Meta-analysis

Purpose:

_____
_____

Operational definitions:

_____
_____
_____

Conclusions:

_____
_____
_____

Generalizability of conclusions to local issue:

_____
_____
_____

Evaluation:

    Appropriateness of reviewers' evaluation criteria:

_____
_____

    Appropriateness of reviewers' explanation of differences in definitions or selection criteria/coding with other reviewers:

_____
_____
_____

    Appropriateness of reviewers' explanation of differences in conclusions with other reviewers:

_____
_____
_____

Figure 10.1 Summarizing information from integrative research reviews and meta-analyses.

Authors: _____

Date: _____

Title: _____

Journal: _____

Volume: _____

Pages: _____

Location: _____

Type of research: _____ Descriptive _____ Comparative _____ Experimental

_____ Quantitative _____ Qualitative

Purpose:

_____

_____

Instruments:

_____

_____

Operational definitions:

Subjects: _____

Treatments: _____

Special Materials: _____

Results and conclusions:

_____

_____

_____

Generalizability of results and conclusions to local issues:

_____

_____

_____

Evaluation:

Validity and reliability and appropriateness of instruments:

_____

_____

Possible influence of extraneous variables:

_____

_____

Possible threats to internal and external validity:

_____

_____

Figure 10.2 Summarizing information from primary research.

				Synthesis
Purpose				
Design				
Subjects				
Instruments				
Procedures Treatment Materials				
Results				
Generalizability				
Weaknesses				

Figure 10.3 Synthesizing information about primary research.

and the stated purposes, definitions, and conclusions of the reviewers.

Enter your decisions about the generalizability of the reviewers' conclusions to your local situation.

Enter your evaluative comments about the appropriateness of the reviewers' evaluation criteria, definitions, coding procedures, and conclusions.

To complete Figure 10.2

Enter the appropriate information in the heading; on the *location* line, indicate the place (i.e., the specific library) where the primary research report is located.

Summarize pertinent information about the primary research.

Indicate the generalizability of the primary researchers' results and conclusions to your local situation.

Enter your evaluative comments about the appropriateness of the primary researchers' methodology.

Figure 10.3 is a prototype of a form for synthesizing information from several primary research reports. It is shown foreshortened and should be redrawn to accommodate the number of primary research studies obtained. The last column, *Synthesis*, should remain the same.
To complete Figure 10.3

List the citations for the selected research reviews in the spaces along the top of the form; use the authors' last names and the date of publication. For example, the integrative review of research about the role of the principal in the elementary school would be listed as Leithwood & Montgomery (1982); and, the primary research study about peer tutoring (discussed in Chapters 7 and 8) would be listed as Mandoli, Mandoli, & McLaughlin (1982).

Place pertinent information about each integrative review, meta-analysis, and primary study in the appropriate box for each of the evaluative topics; your comments should be taken from the information you entered on the summary forms shown in Figures 10.1 and 10.2.

Synthesize the results, generalizability to your local situation, and weaknesses of the reviews and primary research; appropriate synthesizing comments reflect a conclusion you have drawn about the research result *as a whole*, and not just a repeat of individual results. These sentences would become key or main ideas when preparing action reports; each could be used as a main idea for paragraphs or subsections.

SUMMARY

What are integrative reviews of research?

Integrative reviews are undertaken as research projects in which the sources of data are the primary research reports of other researchers. These are critical examinations of research producers' methods and conclusions and of the generalizability of their combined results. They consist of five stages: (1) problem formation, (2) data collection, (3) evaluation of data quality, (4) data analysis and interpretation, and (5) presentation of results.

What questions are used to evaluate integrative reviews of research?

These questions can be used to evaluate integrative reviews:

Are there differences in operational definitions among the integrative reviewers, other reviewers, and the primary researchers?

Are those differences explained?

Has the target population been identified?

Are there differences between the samples of studies in the review and other reviews?

Are there explicit evaluation criteria?

Do they differ from those of other reviewers?

Have the integrative reviewers cited studies with methodological limitations? Have those limitations been explained?

Have the reviewers drawn conclusions that are different from those of other reviewers?

Are those differences discussed?

Does the review report present information in a standard research format?

Is the report complete?

What are meta-analyses?

Meta-analyses of research are ways to critically examine primary research studies that used quantitative data analyses. Research reviewers use meta-analyses as analyses of analyses (data analyses of already done data analyses). In them, they convert the statistical results of the individual studies into a common measurement so they can obtain an overall, combined result. Meta-analyses have stages similar to those of integrative research reviews. In meta-analyses, (1) problems are formed and research studies are collected, (2) pertinent data are identified, (3) analyses and interpretations are made of the data, and (4) results are presented to the public. Meta-analyses begin with reviewers doing an exhaustive, or complete, search to locate previous integrative research reviews and meta-analyses and all primary research studies relating to the education questions or problems under review.

What questions are used to evaluate meta-analyses?

In addition to the questions for evaluating integrative research reviews, these questions can be used:

Are there differences in operational definitions among the meta-analysis reviewers, other reviewers (integrative and meta-analytic), and the primary researchers?

Are those differences explained?

Have the target populations of studies been identified?

Are the differences between the samples of studies in the meta-analysis and other reviews?

Are there explicit coding and evaluation criteria?

Do they differ from those of other meta-analysis reviewers?

Have the meta-analysis reviewers produced separate results for methodologically strong and weak studies?

Has more than one coder been used and are interrater reliability coefficients provided?

Have the meta-analysis reviewers drawn conclusions that differ from those of other reviewers?

Are those differences discussed?

Do the meta-analysis reports present information in a standard research format?

Are the reports complete?

How are integrative reviews of research prepared?

Reviews of research are prepared by going through stages similar to those for preparing integrative reviews. Research reviews produced for local consumption can be considered action research reviews rather than full integrative reviews. To prepare action research reviews, research consumers can use the concept of best evidence. Best evidence is an idea about selecting and reviewing studies that (a) have purposes specifically related to an immediate issue or concern, (b) are methodologically adequate, and (c) are generalizable to the local situation.

ACTIVITY

Peer Status Review of Research

Read the integrative review of research on pp. 272–296. Use the following reading plan, which is based on the one discussed in Chapter 3 for reading research reports.

Read the title and abstract

Determine a purpose for reading the review

Survey the subheadings

Read the conclusion section

Read the entire review

As you survey and read the review, check for the stages of (1) problem formulation, (2) data collection, (3) evaluation of data quality, and (4) data analysis and interpretation. Then judge the completeness of the report using the questions on pp. 254–255 to evaluate the integrative review of research.

Wiener, J. (1987). Peer status of learning disabled children and adolescents: A review of the literature. *Learning Disabilities Research, 2,* 62–79.

Peer Status of Learning Disabled Children and Adolescents: A Review of the Literature

Judith Wiener
Ontario Institute for Studies in Education

Peer status of learning disabled children has been a focus in the literature since Tanis Bryan investigated the issue in 1974. This article reviews 25 studies investigating peer status of learning disabled children. The studies either compare the peer status of learning disabled and nondisabled children or identify correlates of peer status in learning disabled children. The review reveals that the underlying assumption of most of the studies is a unidirectional relationship between peer status and social skills. The results are reinterpreted in terms of a bidirectional model based on Bell and Harper's (1977) reciprocity theory. Peer status is seen to be the outcome of reciprocal interactions between the learning disabled child and family, teachers, and peers.

A major indicator of social competence and social adjustment is the degree to which a child is accepted by peers (Ladd, 1985). Support for this assumption has come from three types of findings. First, longitudinal studies have shown that children receiving negative nominations or ratings are more likely than others to have a variety of psychological adjustment problems (French & Waas, 1985; Weintraub, Prinz, & Neale, 1978) and to be at risk for adjustment problems as adolescents and young adults (Cowen, Pederson, Bibigian, Izzo, & Trost, 1973; Hartup, 1983; Roff, Sells, & Golden, 1972). Second, several studies have shown that accepted children tend to behave in ways that are valued by society. For example, they are proficient at cooperative play and social conversation, maintain lengthy interactions with peers, and are considered to be leaders (Asher, Oden, & Gottman, 1977; Dodge, 1983; Putallaz, 1983; Rubin, Daniels-Beirness, & Hayvren, 1982). Unpopular children, on the other hand, have been found to be aggressive, poor leaders, unwilling to share, and inept in social interaction (Dodge, 1983; Dodge, Coie, & Brakke, 1982; Putallaz, 1983; Putallaz & Gottman, 1981). Finally, friends are

an important source of emotional support for children (Asher & Renshaw, 1981; Freud & Dann, 1951). They teach children how to engage in more complex play (Gottman & Parkhurst, 1980) and manage aggression and sexual relationships (Fine, 1981). As suggested by Asher (1983), there may be a bidirectional relationship between peer status and social behavior. Children who behave inappropriately may alienate their peers. In so doing, they do not get enough practice at interacting with other children to develop their social skills adequately.

The study of peer relationships of learning disabled (LD) children may illustrate the dynamics of the bidirectional relationship to which Asher (1983) referred. By definition, LD children have academic/cognitive problems (Hammill, Leigh, McNutt, & Larsen, 1981). The importance of studying LD children's peer relationships lies in the clarification it brings to several issues in the relationship between cognitive and social development. In 1974, Tanis Bryan published a report of a study in which she used sociometric procedures to compare the peer status of LD and non-learning disabled (NLD) children. She found that LD children tended to be rejected by their peers. The publication of Bryan's study sparked considerable interest among researchers in the area of peer status and social skills of LD children and adolescents. The underlying assumption of this research, however, is a unidirectional relationship between peer status and social skills.

The purpose of this article is to review the research on peer status of LD children and adolescents. The adequacy of the theoretical models on which this research is based is discussed. The research is then reinterpreted in terms of a reciprocity model of peer status that is based on Asher's (1983) bidirectional proposition and Bell and Harper's (1977) reciprocity theory. The major tenet of this model is that the psychological processing deficits of LD children affect the strategies they use for social interaction. Inappropriate strategies may set up negative interaction patterns with family, teachers, or peers; i.e., LD children are treated differently from NLD children by significant others. Because this differential treatment may include isolation or rejection, LD children's opportunities to practice social skills may be reduced, leading to poor skill development and increasingly negative peer status.

The literature review begins with a brief discussion of the problems involved in measuring peer status and social skills. This is followed by a review of 25 studies. These studies were identified through computer search of the *Psychological Abstracts, Dissertation Abstracts*, and ERIC data bases. Each of the studies, in some way, addressed one or both of the following questions: (1) Are LD children less accepted/more rejected by their peers than NLD children? (2) What are the correlates of peer status in LD children? The article concludes with a discussion of the reciprocity model of peer status.

MEASUREMENT OF PEER STATUS AND SOCIAL INTERACTION

Gresham (1983) divided measures of social skills into three categories or "types." Type

I measures involve ratings of the child by significant others (e.g., peers, teachers, parents) or objective outcome measures such as school attendance, suspension records, recidivism rates, and probation violations. According to Gresham, these measures are socially valid because they assess "social outcomes valued by society." Type I measures tend to be valid in that they correlate highly with one another and correlate moderately with Type II measures that involve direct observation of behavior in naturalistic settings. While Type I measures identify children who are at risk, Type II measures describe the specific behaviors that contribute to the Type I outcomes. Type III measures are processing measures in the areas of social perception and social cognition. They include role-play measures (e.g., Reardon, Hersen, Bellack, & Foley, 1979), social problem-solving measures (e.g., Spivack, Platt, & Shure, 1976; Weissberg et al., 1981), and social cognitive measures such as role-taking based on a Piagetian perspective (e.g., Chandler, 1973; Flavell, Botkin, Fry, Wright, & Jarvis, 1968; Selman, 1981). Reviews of these Type III measures indicated low correlations with Type I measures; i.e., poor concurrent validity (Enright & Lapsley, 1980; Hasselt, Hersen, & Bellack, 1981; Urbain & Kendall, 1980). Unlike naturalistic observation measures, processing measures were not found to be related to important social outcomes. Analysis of Type III measures reveals that many demand considerable verbal skill; thus, they may measure language and cognitive development more than social interaction skills.

Because most of the studies reviewed below compare LD and NLD children on a Type I measure, a sociogram measuring peer status, it is important to examine the psychometric properties of sociometric procedures. Two kinds of sociometric procedures are commonly used to assess peer status. Nomination procedures involve asking children to name members of their group (class, playgroup) who have certain characteristics (e.g., are helpful, shy, fight a lot) or meet certain criteria (e.g., like most, like least, like to play with). All are based on the procedure developed by Moreno (1934). Rating-scale procedures require children to rate every member of their group on a continuum with negative and positive ratings at each pole. Both nomination and rating-scale procedures have good psychometric properties (Asher & Hymel, 1981; Oden & Asher, 1977).

There are two basic kinds of nomination sociograms. Positive nomination sociograms require children to name those whom they like; they measure peer acceptance. Negative nominations ask children to name those whom they do not like; they measure peer rejection. Acceptance and rejection, however, are not poles on the same continuum. Many children who receive few positive nominations also receive few negative nominations (Asher & Renshaw, 1981); these children are considered to be isolates or neglected. Several investigators have recommended using composite positive and negative nomination sociograms in order to differentiate between neglected and rejected children (Coie, Dodge, & Coppotelli, 1982; French, Waas, & Tarver-Behring, 1985).

Rating-scale measures normally involve 3- or 5-point scales. Because sex bias is often evident in children's ratings, many investigators choose to calculate scores based on same-sex ratings only. A rating scale measure that has been used frequently with LD and other handicapped children is the *Peer Acceptance Scale* (Bruininks, Rynders, & Gross, 1974). This scale gives 3 points for the rating of "friend," 2 points for "all right," and 1 point for "wouldn't like." The labels are accompanied by line drawings of the three choices.

There have been questions raised in the literature as to whether nomination and rating-scale sociometric procedures measure the same aspects of peer status. Using positive nomination sociograms, Gresham (1982) found that acceptance based on rating-scale procedures predicted children's

behavior in receiving social interaction from peers, whereas acceptance based on nomination procedures predicted children's behavior in initiating interactions. French and colleagues (1985), however, found considerable convergence between the two types of measures. Their studies differed from Gresham's in that composite positive and negative nomination sociometric procedures were used. Children rated as rejected on both measures were rated lower by teachers than children rated as rejected on one measure.

To conclude, sociometric measures are reliable and have good concurrent and predictive validity. There is also support for operationally defining peer status and social competence in terms of sociometric ratings.

COMPARISON OF PEER STATUS BETWEEN LD AND NLD CHILDREN

Nineteen studies were identified that provide information pertaining to differences in peer status between LD and NLD children. In 15 of the studies, LD children were rated by their peers as being lower in peer status than NLD children. Eight of these 15 studies used nomination sociometric procedures (Bryan, 1974; Bryan, 1976; Garrett & Crump, 1980; Horowitz, 1981; Scranton & Ryckman, 1979; Siperstein, Bopp, & Bak, 1978; Siperstein & Goding, 1983), and three used the *Peer Acceptance Scale*, a 3-point rating scale (Bruininks, 1978a, 1978b; Sheare, 1978). Four studies measured peer status using other rating-scale procedures (Bender, Wyne, Stuck, & Bailey, 1984; Gresham & Reschly, 1986; Hutton & Polo, 1976; Perlmutter, Crocker, Cordray, & Garstecki, 1983). Subjects in 14 of the studies were elementary school children. Grade 10 students were the subjects of the Perlmutter et al. (1983) study. Although urban, suburban, rural, middle class, working class, black, and white children participated in the various studies, the majority of the samples were composed of white middle class suburban children.

Four studies were identified in which LD and NLD children did not differ significantly in peer status (Bursuck, 1983; Prillaman, 1981; Sabornie & Kauffman, 1986; Sainato, Zigmond, & Strain, 1983). These studies had methodological shortcomings such as small sample size, unorthodox sociometric procedures, and comparison of LD children with an undefined sample of low achievers. These shortcomings may have contributed to failure to find the results that were consistent in the other 15 studies.

Thus, the data reported in the literature overwhelmingly indicated that LD children obtain lower peer status scores than NLD peers in elementary school and grade 10. Four secondary questions have emerged from these findings and have been addressed in the literature:

1. Do LD boys and girls differ in peer status?
2. Is the low peer status of LD children a result of having few very popular children, many isolated children, or many rejected children?
3. Are peer and teacher ratings of LD children's social status correlated?
4. To what extent are the differences in peer status between LD and NLD children predicted by differences in IQ?

Gender Differences

Three studies reported gender differences in peer status of LD children (Bryan, 1974; Hutton & Polo, 1976; Scranton & Ryckman, 1979). In all three studies, the lower peer status of LD children was more pronounced for girls. Significant gender differences were not reported in the other 11 studies.

A practical difficulty in studying the question of gender differences is the relatively small number of LD girls compared to LD boys. The small sample size for LD girls generally mitigated against any meaningful comparisons. Furthermore, in sociometric studies, it has been found that children tend to make same-sex nominations for friendship and rate their own sex more

reliably (Gronlund, 1959). Consequently, it has been considered good practice to ask children to rate/nominate their own gender only. Due to the small number of LD girls, most of the studies were unable to use same-sex nomination/ratings only.

The issue of gender differences in peer status among LD children has not been resolved. Although there is some indication that LD girls may have more serious problems in this area, the data are inconclusive.

Acceptance Versus Rejection

Validity studies of sociometric measures have indicated that acceptance and rejection are not necessarily two poles on a continuum, but are independent factors (Asher & Renshaw, 1981; Gresham, 1982). Thus, positive nomination sociograms indicate the degree to which children are accepted and negative nominations the degree to which they are rejected.

Several studies have indicated that it is important to distinguish between neglected and rejected children. As suggested by Asher and Dodge (1986), the two groups are quite different when assessed on behavioral measures. Rejected children are more likely than neglected children to be aggressive and disruptive and to remain unaccepted when they move into a new group (Coie & Kupersmidt, 1983; Dodge, 1983). Rejected children more often report that they experience loneliness and social dissatisfaction than neglected children (Asher, Hymel, & Renshaw, 1984). It seems that rejected children may be more at risk than those who are neglected. Studies that used composite positive and negative nomination sociograms provide investigators with the opportunity to distinguish between popular, rejected, and neglected children (Coie et al., 1982). Popular children receive many positive nominations and few negative nominations, rejected children receive many negative nominations and few positive ones, and neglected children receive very few nominations.

Five studies used composite positive and

negative nomination sociometric procedures when comparing the peer status of LD and NLD children. Two of these studies, however, combined the positive and negative nominations to obtain a single score (Garrett & Crump, 1980; Horowitz, 1981). Bryan (1974, 1976) and Scranton and Ryckman (1979) analyzed positive and negative nomination data separately. The findings were consistent: LD children received significantly more negative nominations and fewer positive nominations than NLD children. Unfortunately, none of these investigators reported the number of neglected children. Clearly, reports on these data are needed.

Three studies investigated the question of the proportion of LD children who are popular or rejected informally through post hoc analyses. Perlmutter et al. (1983), in their study of sociometric status of LD adolescents, found that 22 of 28 LD children had a sociometric rating below the median rating for NLD adolescents and 9 of 28 were in a range the investigators rated as disliked. Six of the 28 LD students were highly rated and labeled well-liked. Similar data were not provided for the NLD adolescents, and contingency table analyses were not done.

As assessed by unlimited choice positive nomination sociograms, children were labeled "stars" if they were nominated by 60% (Siperstein et al., 1978) or 70% (Siperstein & Goding, 1983) of their classmates and isolated/rejected if they received one or zero nominations (Siperstein et al., 1978) or one or zero unreciprocated nominations (Siperstein & Goding, 1983). Siperstein and colleagues (1978) found no stars among their 22 LD subjects and the LD children were not overrepresented among the isolated/rejected children. Studying a larger sample of LD children ($n = 38$), Siperstein and Goding (1983) found that 26% of LD children were isolated/rejected compared to 9% of NLD children (a significant difference) and that 5% of LD children were stars compared to 11% of NLD youngsters (a difference that was not statistically significant).

To conclude, the evidence suggests that fewer LD children were positively rated by their peers and more LD children were negatively rated by their peers than NLD children. The research published to date, however, has not indicated clearly whether negative ratings represent isolated or rejected status.

Peer Ratings Versus Teacher Ratings

Three studies were identified in which teachers rated the social performances of LD and NLD children. Perlmutter et al. (1983) asked the regular and special teachers of the LD subjects to rate the social and academic ability of each of their grade 10 students. Although regular classroom teachers viewed LD children as having academic problems, special education teachers were more concerned about the LD students' social behavior. Correlations between peer and teacher ratings were not reported. Regular classroom teachers, however, rated well-liked LD students as less anxious than disliked LD students.

Both Siperstein and Goding (1983) and Garrett and Crump (1980) used Q-sort procedures to obtain teacher ratings. Siperstein and Goding asked teachers to divide their students into three categories (high, middle, and low) on the basis of academic and social behavior. Garrett and Crump asked teachers to place their students into nine categories from "most preferred" to "least preferred." Siperstein and Goding found that teachers consistently placed LD students in the lowest third of the class for academic and social behavior. Low but significant correlations were found between peer status and teacher ratings on both dimensions. (The exact correlation coefficients were not reported.) Garrett and Crump found that LD children were less preferred by teachers than NLD children and that in 78% of the classrooms there was a low but significant correlation between peer status and teachers' preference. To conclude, it appears that teachers' and pupils' ratings of LD pupils' social status were related.

It is important to note that these studies examined correlations between teachers' views or ratings of LD children and peer ratings. No studies were identified in which teachers were asked to predict peer ratings and teacher predictions correlated with sociometric status. As discussed below, sociometric studies with handicapped children have many practical difficulties. If teachers' predictions are highly correlated with actual peer status, it may be legitimate to substitute teacher prediction ratings for sociometrics.

The Effect of IQ

Of the 19 studies comparing LD and NLD children with regard to peer status, three provided information about intellectual functioning (Horowitz, 1981; Sabornie & Kauffman, 1986; Sainato et al., 1983), and only one made an attempt to control for IQ (Horowitz, 1981).

Horowitz (1981) administered the *Otis-Lennon Test of Mental Abilities* (Elementary I: Form J), a forced-choice positive and negative nomination sociogram, and a 6-point rating scale to assess perceived peer status. Mean IQ of the 29 LD children was 95.3; of the 29 NLD children, 108.5. Because peer status and IQ were highly correlated for both groups, analysis of covariance was used to adjust for IQ. Although LD children had significantly lower peer status scores than NLD children when the unadjusted means were compared, the differences were not significant when IQ was used as a covariate.

The results of the Horowitz (1981) study raise questions about the necessity of controlling for IQ in sociometric studies with LD children. Because IQ and achievement tests measure some of the same processes, LD children generally obtain lower IQ scores than their NLD counterparts (Siegel & Heaven, 1985). Horowitz's study sug-

gested that controlling for IQ does not provide information about the child behavior and group dynamics that contributed to peer status.

Summary

Although the results of 15 of the 19 studies comparing peer status of LD and NLD children supported the conclusion that LD children and adolescents were less accepted by their peers than NLD children, several issues merit further study. First, all of the studies employed samples of LD children identified by the school district. This is problematic because school districts vary in their criteria for identification as learning disabled (Ysseldyke, 1983). A more complete discription of the learning abilities of the subjects would allow for comparison of studies. Second, larger samples of LD subjects are needed to ensure more adequate representation of girls. It may then be possible to ascertain whether LD girls have more problems acquiring positive peer relationships than LD boys.

Third, the data are clear that LD children receive fewer positive and more negative ratings/nominations than NLD children. The studies have not, however, differentiated between rejected and neglected status. Because there is evidence that rejected and neglected children behave differently (Asher & Dodge, in press; Coie & Kupersmidt, 1983; Dodge, 1983) and possibly require different forms of intervention, distinguishing between these groups is important.

Fourth, it seems valid to conclude that there is a positive correlation between teacher and peer ratings of social status. Finally, investigators should consider the relationship between IQ and peer status when doing sociometric studies.

Establishing that a group of children, in this case LD children, are less accepted and more rejected by peers merely indicates that they are at risk; the factors contributing to their lower acceptance were not evident. An examination of the correlates of peer status, however, may elucidate the dynamics of the bidirectional relationship between peer status and social skills.

CORRELATES OF PEER STATUS IN LD CHILDREN

The LD literature is replete with studies comparing LD and NLD children on a variety of social skills including social perception, social cognition and pragmatic competence. (See Bryan, 1981; Dudley-Marling, 1985; Maheady & Sainato, 1986, for reviews.) Other studies have examined the differential treatment of LD and NLD children in the family (Bryan, Pearl, Zimmerman, & Matthews, 1982) and school (Bryan & Wheeler, 1976; Bryan, Wheeler, Felcan, & Henek, 1976) environments. Many of these investigators have found differences between LD and NLD children in these areas, and have speculated that the lower peer status of LD children may be a result of their poor social skills. Very few studies, however, have investigated the relationship between social skills and peer status directly. It is these studies that are reviewed here.

Four hypotheses have been advanced to explain the low peer status of LD children:

1. *The discrepancy hypothesis.* The LD children are less accepted by their peers because they lack abilities that are valued by the peers. Specifically, LD children are low achievers. If achievement is valued by the peer group, LD children may be rejected due to the discrepancy between their achievement and the expectations of the group. This hypothesis predicts that LD children and other low achievers would not differ in peer status, that LD children attending schools in which academic achievement is not valued by the peer culture would not differ in peer status from NLD children, and that LD children with other attributes

valued by the peer group (e.g., physical attractiveness, intelligence, athletic ability) would be more accepted than other LD children.

2. *The psychological processing deficit hypothesis.* Perceptual, cognitive, and linguistic deficit theories have been the basis of considerable research on the academic problems of LD children (Wong, 1979). Closely related to these theories is the hypothesis that LD children are not accepted by their peers because of deficits in social perception, social cognition, or pragmatic competence. This hypothesis predicts that different subtypes of LD children, who presumably process information differently, would have different levels of peer acceptance. Further, LD children's performance on measures of social perception, social cognition, and pragmatic competence would correlate positively with measures of peer acceptance.

3. *The strategic deficit hypothesis.* The proposition that LD children are inactive learners who achieve poorly because they do not use appropriate strategies to learn (Torgesen, 1982) has also been applied to explain their low peer status. This hypothesis predicts that LD children's peer status would be correlated with specific strategies they use in social situations (e.g., approach behavior, accepting and giving positive and negative feedback) and that LD children who are not accepted by peers would have different patterns of attributions for success and failure in the social domain.

4. *The differential treatment hypothesis.* Some investigators have postulated that LD children's low peer status is related to differential treatment by family, teachers, and peers. Consequently, LD children may not have the opportunities NLD children have to learn social skills.

The Discrepancy Hypothesis

The discrepancy hypothesis was first advanced by Bryan (1974) to explain the finding that white LD girls were less accepted and more rejected by peers than white LD boys or black LD children. Bryan suggested that elementary-school-age girls may value achievement more than boys do and that white children may value achievement more than black children do. Seven studies have been identified that provide evidence regarding the predictions of the discrepancy hypothesis.

As stated, the discrepancy hypothesis predicts that peer status and academic achievement are positively correlated and LD children and other low achievers do not differ in peer status. There is evidence in the developmental literature to suggest that there is a significant positive correlation between peer status and academic achievement (Hartup, 1970). With respect to LD children, Wiener (1980) compared the peer status of LD children defined as mildly disabled (a discrepancy of less than two grades between age and achievement) and severely disabled (a discrepancy of more than two grades between age and academic achievement), using a limited choice positive and negative nomination sociogram. The children, who were 8 to 12 years of age, were attending a residential summer camp program for LD children. A significant difference in peer status was found between the mildly and severely disabled children, with those defined as mildly disabled receiving more positive and fewer negative nominations from their LD peers.

Bursuck's (1983) study supported the prediction that LD children and other low achievers do not differ significantly with regard to peer status, but that both groups were less accepted by peers than high achievers. Bursuck compared 12 LD boys with 12 "low achieving" boys who were matched with the LD boys on race, classroom behavior, and reading achievement. None of the children had repeated a grade. All of the LD children received special education assistance from the resource teacher, but none were withdrawn for more than half the day. No significant differences were found between the groups on a "play with" rating-scale questionnaire and a limited choice positive nomination sociogram. Significant differences in peer status were found between the LD, low achiever, and middle achiever groups and a group of high-achieving youngsters on the positive nomination sociogram, but not the rating scale. The Bursuck study suggested that high achievement is related to popularity but did not provide evidence that low achievement is related to rejection.

The degree to which LD children are accepted by peers who do not value academic achievement compared to those who do has not been investigated. According to Bruininks and colleagues (1974), however, mildly retarded children from *urban* schools received significantly higher same-sex peer ratings than nonretarded children; mildly retarded *suburban* children received significantly lower ratings than nonretarded children. Although the investigators claimed that a possible reason for the urban/suburban differences is that "peer group value structure in suburban schools may reflect a greater emphasis on school attainment than is true of values held by peer groups in urban settings" (p. 382), the support for this statement was not provided. The mean IQ of the urban mildly retarded children was significantly higher than that of the suburban children. Because the IQs of the nonretarded children were not reported, it cannot be determined whether the discrepancy in IQ between nonretarded and retarded was greater in suburban than urban schools. Furthermore, the degree to which the nonretarded children in either setting value intelligence and achievement was not measured.

The discrepancy hypothesis predicts that LD children who, in spite of low academic achievement, have characteristics valued by the peer group would obtain higher peer status scores. There is considerable support for this prediction. Two studies examined the relationship between peer acceptance of LD children and intellectual ability. As discussed above, Horowitz (1981) found a significant positive correlation between IQ and peer status. Anderson (1983) used open and forced choice nomination sociograms to assess the peer status of 49 integrated LD children in grades 3 through 6. Their WISC-R IQ scores were found to be a significant predictor of peer status; i.e., LD children with higher IQ scores were more accepted. Both the Horowitz and Anderson studies supported the conclusion that IQ is an important predictor of peer status in LD children. Thus, the hypothesis that low-achieving LD children may be more positively accepted if they are more intelligent has some support.

Siperstein et al. (1978) and Siperstein and Goding (1983) investigated the relationship between peer status of LD children and nominations by NLD children as "best athlete," "smartest," and "best looking." Because similar findings were evident in both studies, but the methodology of the Siperstein and Goding study was more refined and the sample size larger, only the results of the latter study will be reported. Siperstein and Goding found that nominations for "best athlete," "best looking," and "smartest" correlated significantly with peer status ($p < .001$) in LD children. Furthermore, LD children who received nominations (approximately half of the sample) had a higher peer status score than the other LD children, and those LD children who nominated themselves ($n = 4$) had a peer status rating that was slightly higher than the mean score for NLD children. To conclude, these studies supported the conclusion that LD children, who are low achievers by definition, may receive positive peer status ratings if they are judged to have redeeming features such as physical attractiveness or intellectual or athletic ability.

None of the available evidence contradicted the predictions of the discrepancy hypothesis, and the data supporting the prediction that popular LD children have characteristics valued by their peer group was well supported. Nevertheless, the discrepancy hypothesis may not be an adequate

explanation of the low peer status of LD children. With the exception of the Siperstein (Siperstein et al., 1978; Siperstein & Goding, 1983) studies, characteristics children value in their peers were not ascertained. Rather, investigators inferred that intelligence and academic achievement were valued by children. Further, achievement and IQ may be correlated with other abilities that are more likely to produce acceptance or rejection from peers. For example, IQ was positively correlated with social perception abilities (Horowitz, 1981) and achievement was correlated with interpersonal problem-solving skills (Wiener, 1978). Thus, the discrepancy hypothesis has some predictive value, but the support was not sufficiently strong to conclude that it provides an adequate explanation for a significant portion of the data.

The Psychological Processing Deficit Hypothesis

The basic tenet of psychological processing deficit theories is that the academic and social problems of LD children result from deficits in perception, cognition, or language. Consequently, the paradigm of most of the social skills research has been to compare LD and NLD children on various measures of social perception, social cognition, and pragmatic competence. For example, studies have shown that LD children are less proficient than NLD children at interpreting facial expressions and nonverbal cues (Bruno, 1981; Bryan, 1977; Wiig & Harris, 1974) and at role taking (Bruck & Hebert, 1982; Dickstein & Warren, 1980; Wong & Wong, 1980). Reviews by Bryan (1981) and Dudley-Marling (1985) have indicated that LD children have problems with various subtle pragmatic skills. Of interest here are those studies that examined the relationship between psychological processing deficits and peer status. One study (Martin, 1985) focused on social perception, six on social cognition (Bruck & Hebert, 1982; Bruininks, 1978a, 1978b; Garrett & Crump, 1980;

Horowitz, 1981; Perlmutter et al., 1983), and two on pragmatic competence (Anderson, 1983; Simon, 1982).

Martin (1985) examined the relationship between sociometric status and social perception in 35 LD children (31 male and 4 female) and 22 NLD children (16 male and 6 female) in grades 5 through 8. Although LD children were found to be less well-liked than NLD children on a combined rating-scale and positive nomination sociometric measure, the two groups did not differ on two social perception measures (the *Test of Social Inference* and a soap opera videotape). The correlations between the sociometric and social perception measures were not significant. Thus, the hypothesis that social perceptual abilities are predictors of peer status was not supported. It cannot be inferred, however, that social perception and peer status are not related. As suggested by Martin and by Maheady, Harper, and Sainato (1985), the predictive validity of most social perception measures, including the ones used in the study, is questionable. Also, the correlation coefficient may not be a sensitive statistic in this case because of the restricted range of the scales.

The studies investigating the relationship between peer status and social cognition included investigations of role taking, social insight, and social attributions. Bruck and Hebert (1982) studied the peer status and role-taking skills of 20 LD children (7 girls and 13 boys) from an LD clinic and 20 control children matched on age, gender, and socioeconomic status from a public elementary school classroom. Cognitive and affective role-taking tasks were administered to the children and a peer-interaction checklist was filled out by the teachers and parents of each subject. The checklist consisted of 36 items (e.g., quarrelsome with peers, plays mostly with younger children) on which the parents and teachers were asked to rate the children using a 4-point scale. The LD and NLD groups differed significantly on the role-taking tasks, with NLD children obtaining higher scores than LD children, but no significant differences were found between the groups on parent and teacher ratings of peer interaction. Furthermore, the correlations between role-taking scores and parent/teacher ratings were not significant. Bruck and Hebert (1982), however, found that scores on the *Conners Rating Scale*, a measure of hyperactivity, were good predictors of the peer interaction ratings. They speculated that samples of LD children in previous studies might have included more hyperactive children than their own study, resulting in significant differences between groups in peer acceptance.

The lack of significant positive correlations between role taking and peer status in the Bruck and Hebert (1982) study is consistent with findings in the developmental literature. Enright and Lapsley (1980), in their review of role-taking measures, came to the conclusion that the validity of these measures needs to be examined more carefully. Bruck and Hebert's conclusion that peer status differences between LD and NLD children may be a function of the number of hyperactive children in the sample is of interest and demands further study using peer sociometric measures.

Bruck and Hebert's (1982) findings were supported by Horowitz's (1981) study of role taking in 29 LD (20 boys and 9 girls) and 29 NLD children matched on gender and classroom. The children were attending grades 3 and 4. Horowitz also found significant differences between the LD and NLD children on a role-taking task, with NLD children performing better than LD children. These differences, however, were eliminated when IQ was controlled through analysis of covariance. Similarly, as discussed above, the peer status differences between the LD and NLD children were not significant when IQ was covaried. As in the Bruck and Hebert (1982) study, the correlations between role taking and peer status were not significant.

Horowitz (1981) also administered a measure of "social insight" that was defined as the ability to predict one's own peer status.

Nomination sociometric techniques were used to measure peer status and rating-scale techniques to assess social insight. When IQ was controlled, there were no significant differences between LD and NLD children in predicting their peers. Horowitz did not report whether there were significant differences when IQ was not controlled.

Four other studies examined the issue of social insight. Garrett and Crump (1980) and Perlmutter et al. (1983) found that when overall means of difference scores between actual and perceived status for LD and NLD children were compared, no significant differences were evident. Garrett and Crump (1980) measured actual status using a composite positive and negative forced choice nomination sociometric procedure; they measured perceived status using the *Peer Acceptance Scale*. Because rating-scale and nomination procedures may measure different aspects of social acceptance (Gresham, 1982), it is not surprising that the NLD children generally underestimated their perceived status. The results of this study were questionable, however, due to the comparison of two different types of measures of peer status. The same criticism may be applied to the Horowitz (1981) study.

Perlmutter et al. (1983) compared actual and perceived status of LD and NLD adolescents using the same rating-scale procedure. No significant differences were found in the two groups' ability to predict their status. Well-liked LD adolescents, however, were found to be significantly more accurate than other LD subjects at predicting their peer status.

Bruininks (1978a, 1978b), on the other hand, found that LD pupils were less proficient at predicting their peer status on the *Peer Acceptance Scale* than NLD pupils. In the first of the two studies (Bruininks, 1978a), actual and perceived status for each group (LD and NLD) were compared separately using one-tailed t tests. Garrett and Crump (1980) criticized this procedure as being inappropriate because the differences between means for entire groups were being compared instead of the differences between actual and perceived status for each subject. Bruininks (1978b), however, used a two-way ANOVA with repeated measures to analyze these data in the second study. A significant interaction between groups (LD and NLD) and type of status (perceived and actual) was found. The LD children were significantly lower in peer status than NLD children and rated themselves significantly higher than their actual peer status in the classroom.

The results of the five studies investigating LD children's social insight suggested that they may be deficient in this ability. When the same methods were used to measure and predict peer status, differences in LD and NLD children's ability to predict were apparent in two of the three studies. According to Horowitz (1981), the social insight task is, in effect, a role-taking task because the individual must assume the perspective of another person. Unlike most other role-taking tasks, the social insight task was not verbally loaded. Furthermore, it may be more ecologically valid because children are making predictions about people they know instead of contrived situations. Consequently, further study of social insight is warranted. Specifically, it would be important to determine whether social insight correlates positively with peer status.

The question of the pragmatic competence of LD children has received considerable attention in the literature during the past 8 years. Dudley-Marling (1985), for example, reviewed 19 studies completed since 1976. Only two studies were identified, however, that investigated the relationship between pragmatic competence and peer status.

Anderson (1983) investigated the relationship between several language comprehension measures, WISC-R IQ, and peer status in 49 LD children in grades 3 to 6. Many of the language tasks—indirect request, idiomatic expression, riddle, analogy, context clue, and semantic restriction—may also be considered to be measures of pragmatic competence. Peer status was assessed through open and forced choice nomination sociometric procedures. Using multiple regression analyses, Anderson found that WISC-R, idiomatic expression, and context clue scores were significant predictors of peer status for boys on the forced choice sociogram.

Simon (1982) compared the use of persuasive strategies and politeness forms in 12 highly popular NLD children, 12 less popular NLD children, and 12 LD children. The children were 10 to 12 years of age. They were videotaped in two situations in which they had to request a favor from a peer. The three groups did not differ significantly in the total number of persuasive stategies and politeness forms. The highly popular children, however, used a significantly higher number of persuasive strategies than the other two groups. Unfortunately, the methodology used in the Simon study did not allow for examination of the correlation between use of persuasive strategies and politeness forms and peer status in LD children.

To conclude, the evidence suggested that the psychological deficit hypothesis should not be rejected. Although there was little support for the position that social perception problems contribute to the low peer status of LD children, there was evidence to suggest that social, cognitive, and pragmatic problems may be contributors. Scores on contrived cognitive role-taking tasks were not significantly correlated with peer status, but there were data to indicate that LD children are poor at predicting their peer status. Furthermore, well-liked LD adolescents obtained scores on a social insight task that were at least as high as NLD adolescents. Finally, the Anderson (1983) study showed a positive relationship between various aspects of pragmatic competence (idiomatic expression and context clues) and peer status. Anderson used valid sociometric procedures and had a relatively large sample of LD children ($n = 49$). Replication of this study and further research

exploring the relationship between other areas of pragmatic competence and peer status would be appropriate. Nevertheless, the value of the psychological processing deficit hypothesis in explaining the peer status of LD children was limited. Only a small part of the variance is accounted for by role-taking or pragmatic competence scores.

The Strategic Deficit Hypothesis

The strategic deficit hypothesis is based on Torgesen's (1982) proposition that LD children are inactive learners; their deficits are in the area of metacognition. Consequently, LD children who are not well accepted by their peers may not have learned specific strategies that are necessary for social interaction. Furthermore, LD children may be more apt to attribute success or failure in social situations to factors they cannot control (e.g., luck).

Studies by Bryan et al. (1976) and Schumaker, Hazel, Sherman, and Sheldon (1982) have indicated that LD children and adolescents perform differently from their peers in social situations. Bryan et al. found that LD children in a summer school program made significantly more competitive statements than NLD children, and LD males were more frequently ignored by peers and were less likely to respond to peer initiations. Schumaker et al. used role-play techniques to assess social interaction strategies of 60 NLD adolescents who were in grades 10, 11, and 12, 119 LD students from the same grades, and 57 court-adjudicated youths (JD) of approximately the same age. The LD and JD adolescents differed significantly from the NLD adolescents on eight strategies, including accepting negative feedback, conversation, giving negative feedback, giving positive feedback, negotiation, problem solving, and resisting peer pressure. No differences between the three groups were observed for following instructions. The LD and JD groups differed significantly on one strategy, resisting peer pressure, with the JD youths being less capable.

Three studies investigated the relationship between social interaction strategies and peer status. Perlmutter et al. (1983) compared well-liked LD adolescents with not-as-well-liked LD adolescents using teacher and peer ratings. Peers found popular LD students to be more independent than disliked LD students and more withdrawn than other LD students. Teachers found the popular LD students to be less anxious than other LD students.

Bursuck (1983) compared LD children with low achievers and found no significant differences in peer status. In addition, Bursuck devised two teacher rating scales and a hypothetical situations measure to assess social performance stategies. The situation-specific teacher rating scale consisted of 12 items, 6 representing conflict situations (e.g., disagreeing over the rules of a game) and 6 representing initiation (e.g., joining an ongoing game) and maintenance (e.g., responding to a friend showing a new baseball glove) situations. Each item contained a short vignette describing the situation and three possible responses: a friendly/prosocial response, a nasty/abusive response, and withdrawn/avoidance response. Teachers were asked to rate the children on a scale of 1 to 5 from "not very likely" to "very likely." The second scale was a general scale in which teachers rated children in terms of the frequency of their engaging in certain behaviors (e.g., "is helpful," "resolves disagreements easily"). The hypothetical situations measure assessed children's knowledge of the correct response in the situations listed on the situation-specific teacher rating scale. Bursuck found no significant differences between LD and low-achieving children on any of these measures.

Gresham and Reschly (1986) administered a parent rating scale, a teacher rating scale, a "play with/work with" peer rating scale, and the *Structured Peer Assessment Scale* (which is similar to the "Guess Who"

technique) to 100 LD children and their NLD peers. All children were 7½ to 11½ years old. The LD children were compared to a randomly selected group of 100 NLD children from the same schools. Parents and teachers gave the LD children low ratings on task-related behavior (attending behavior, completing tasks, on-task behavior, following directions, and independent work). Parents, teachers, and peers indicated that LD children demonstrated significant deficits in interpersonal and self-related behavior (accepting authority, helping others, expressing feelings, and having a positive attitude). Although Gresham and Reschly found that LD and NLD children differed significantly on the task-related and interpersonal dimensions as rated by teachers, parents, and peers, they did not report whether scores on the three behavior rating scales predicted peer status.

The issue of the relationship between peer status and social interaction strategies of LD children has not been resolved. This issue was not the main question investigated in the Perlmutter et al. (1983) research. Consequently, the post hoc analyses involved small n's in each cell. Bursuck (1983) compared LD children with low achievers instead of a more broadly defined sample of NLD children. Bursuck and Gresham and Reschly (1986) did not report correlations between the strategies/behavioral measures and peer status measures. Research involving behavioral observation of LD children in the classroom or in play situations should include measures of peer status. Similar developmental research (e.g., Dodge, 1983; Putallaz, 1983; Putallaz & Gottman, 1981) has revealed that nondisabled children who were rejected are more likely to be aggressive and disruptive and to initiate interaction inappropriately than accepted children; they are less likely to be cooperative and good leaders. Is the low peer status of LD children a result of their problems with social interaction strategies, or are they rejected because of low academic achievement, as the discrepancy hypothesis would predict? These questions have not been addressed in the research published to date.

The prediction that LD children possessing low peer status have different attribution patterns for social situations than high status children has been examined in one study. Sobol, Earn, Bennett, and Humphries (1983) investigated the social attributions of 7- to 12-year-old LD children. They compared 24 LD children (14 males and 10 females) who attended a hospital clinic with (a) 24 NLD children who were matched with the LD children on age, gender, and social acceptance ratings and labeled Low Acceptance (LA) and (b) 24 NLD children matched on age and gender but who obtained higher social acceptance ratings (HA). Social acceptance was assessed through teacher ratings on the *Pupil Rating Scale* (Myklebust, 1971). An open-ended interview format (Elig & Frieze, 1975) was used to examine social attributions. It consisted of 12 social situations with different outcomes (successful or unsuccessful for the protagonist) and different initiators (the child or peer). Children were asked to explain the reason for the outcome. In addition, the children completed a questionnaire to assess expectancy of social success and a modification of the *Coopersmith Self Esteem Inventory* (Coopersmith, 1967) to examine peer-related self-esteem.

The attributions provided by the LD children differed significantly from the LA and HA groups for self-initiated and other-initiated success situations, and other-initiated failure situations. For self-initiated success situations and other-initiated failure situations, the LD children were more likely to attribute the outcome to luck than the NLD children and less likely to attribute outcome to "personality interaction" (e.g., "We are friends," "We don't get along"). For other-initiated success situations, all three groups attributed outcome to personality interaction most frequently. The LD children, however, attributed outcome to others' mo-

tives more frequently (e.g., "He wanted to be nice") and were the only group to use the personality interaction by personality category (e.g., "He thinks I'm a nice person"). The LD children also had the lowest expectation of social success and, along with the LA group, had lower social self-esteem than the HA group.

The Sobol et al. (1983) study showed important differences between LD and NLD children matched on social acceptance level as rated by teachers. A major problem in this study, however, was that the validity of the *Pupil Rating Scale* as a social acceptance measure has not been established. The investigators also did not determine whether social attribution was a predictor of peer acceptance in LD children. In spite of these limitations the study did provide some support for the strategic deficit hypothesis. The LD children were not only inactive learners in academic situations; they also believed more than NLD children that variables not under their control (e.g., luck, others' motives) were the reasons for their social success or failure. As a result of these attributions, they may not see the need to observe carefully how others interact and to learn strategies for social interaction.

The Differential Treatment Hypothesis

Some investigators have postulated that LD children's low peer status is related to differential treatment by family (Elardo & Freund, 1981; Freund & Elardo, 1978), teachers (Bryan & Wheeler, 1976), and peers (Bryan et al., 1976). With regard to differential treatment by family, for example, Elardo and Freund (1981) concluded that mothers of LD children who value children, who are considerate of other people's feelings, who are socially responsible, and who point out the consequences of their misbehavior to other people, produce children with good role-taking and interpersonal problem-solving skills. The issue of family contributions to the social development of

LD children is very complex and beyond the scope of this review. It is important to note, however, that no empirical studies were identified that investigated the relationship between family factors and peer status.

Only two studies investigated the relationship between differential treatment and peer status, and only with regard to differential treatment by teachers. In a classroom observation study, Siperstein and Goding (1983) found that grade 7 teachers interacted significantly more often with LD children receiving few positive ratings from their peers than with high status NLD children. This involved initiating more frequently, following up initiations for longer periods, correcting the LD children more often, and displaying both more verbal nonsupportive behavior and negative nonverbal affective behavior. Differences in behavior between LD and NLD children, however, were not observed in seven of the eight classrooms. The differential treatment was attributed to the LD label. Following a training program focused on making teachers aware of their differential behavior, teachers maintained their high level of interaction with LD children, but reduced the frequency of verbal nonsupportive and negative nonverbal affective behavior. Siperstein and Goding did not determine whether the changes in teacher behavior were maintained over time and resulted in improved peer status for the LD children. Siperstein and Goding (1985) replicated the study with children in grades 5 and 6 and obtained essentially the same results.

The differential treatment hypothesis suggested that LD children were not accepted by their peers because a pathological family situation produces behavior disorders that alienate peers or because teachers treat them negatively, possibly due to their poor academic achievement. This analysis, however, omits an important factor. Does the child behave in ways that provoke this differential treatment?

AN ALTERNATIVE CONCEPTUALIZATION OF CHILDREN'S PEER STATUS

The data show clearly that LD children in regular classrooms are less likely to be accepted and more likely to be rejected by NLD peers than are NLD children. Furthermore, some LD children are well liked, and some NLD children are disliked. Because peer status is a significant predictor of psychological adjustment and rejection is a risk factor, these findings are important. Their importance, however, rests on an understanding of the factors producing this relationship and the ability to devise interventions based on this understanding.

The literature review revealed four hypotheses that have been the basis of research on peer status of LD children. Although the discrepancy, psychological processing deficit, strategic deficit, and differential treatment hypotheses all received some support from research findings, none provided a sufficient explanation of the problem. The discrepancy and differential treatment hypotheses do not account for the positive correlations between pragmatic competence and social attributions with peer status. The psychological processing and strategic deficit hypotheses do not account for the fact that LD children are treated differently by family, teachers, and peers and that LD children who are considered by peers to be intelligent, attractive, and athletic tend to be well accepted. Consequently a new theoretical formulation is needed.

The reciprocity model and control theory advanced by Bell and Harper (1977) may have explanatory value in interpreting the low peer status of LD children. As articulated by Bell and Harper, "parent-child interaction occurs in a reciprocal social system in which much of the progress toward cultural norms involves mutual adjustment and accommodation" (p. 65). For the present analysis, the words "parent–child" should be replaced by "peer." According to control theory, "when the upper limit for one participant is reached, the reaction of the other is to redirect or reduce the excessive inappropriate behavior (upper-limit control reaction)" (Bell & Harper, 1977, p. 65). There exists considerable evidence that LD children's behavior is excessive or inappropriate (e.g., Bryan, 1974; Bryan et al., 1976; Speece, McKinney, & Appelbaum, 1985) and that LD children who engage in these excessive or inappropriate behaviors are more likely to be disliked or rejected by peers and teachers (Bruck & Hebert, 1982; Perlmutter et al., 1983). Thus, methods of upper limit control that are easily used by peers are to associate with the offending child as little as possible or to act aversively toward that child, thus discouraging the child from approaching. As suggested by Asher (1983), the effect of this rejection for the LD child may be a lack of practice at interacting with peers with a resultant reduced rate of learning the skills needed for appropriate interaction.

An assumption underlying a reciprocity model of peer interaction is that peer status is an outcome measure that reflects the quality and quantity of the reciprocal interactions between peers (Coie & Kupersmidt, 1983; Dodge, 1983; Ladd, 1985; Putallaz, 1983). This relationshiip was illustrated in Dodge's (1983) study in which boys in grade 2 were placed in small play groups with seven children they did not know. A composite positive and negative nomination sociogram was administered, and behavioral observations were made. Dodge found that popular children engaged in high rates of cooperative play and social conversation and avoided verbal and physical aggression. They approached peers at a similar rate to average children, but maintained longer interactions. They were considered by their peers to be good leaders and people who shared things. Neglected boys were viewed by peers as shy and socially inept. Rejected boys, on the other hand, were seen as aggressive, poor leaders, and unwilling to

share. They engaged in antisocial behavior (e.g., insults, threats, contentious statements, exclusion of peers from play and physical aggression). Both neglected and rejected boys approached others with high frequency in the earlier sessions, but reduced the frequency of approach behavior in later sessions, possibly as a result of being rebuffed. The final group, controversial boys, displayed the prosocial behaviors of the popular children and the aggressive behavior of the rejected children. Dodge's study showed that there is a reciprocal relationship between the strategies children use in social situations and the ways their peers view them. The peer evaluations are translated into actions that then affect the children in question.

As shown in Figure 1, the reciprocity model integrates the predictions that can be derived from the discrepancy, psychological processing deficit, strategic deficit, and differential treatment hypotheses. Social perceptual, social cognitive, pragmatic, and metacognitive deficits may affect the strategies LD children use for social interaction. If these strategies are inappropriate (child effect), the quality of the peer interaction may change and become negative—the LD child receives differential treatment (peer, parent, teacher effect). Should the LD child, however, be viewed as intelligent, physically attractive, or athletic and should these qualities be viewed by the peer group as valuable, this differential treatment may be mitigated. Rejection or isolation may reduce the LD child's opportunities to practice social interaction strategies, reducing his or her skill effectiveness even further. Families may also teach LD children inappropriate ways of interacting by modeling or reinforcing excessive or bizarre behaviors. Effective strategies used by parents, however, may not be carried on outside the home. Parents, for example, may use upper limit control strategies (e.g., structure, redirection) effectively with their attention-deficit-disordered child. Because the child continues to

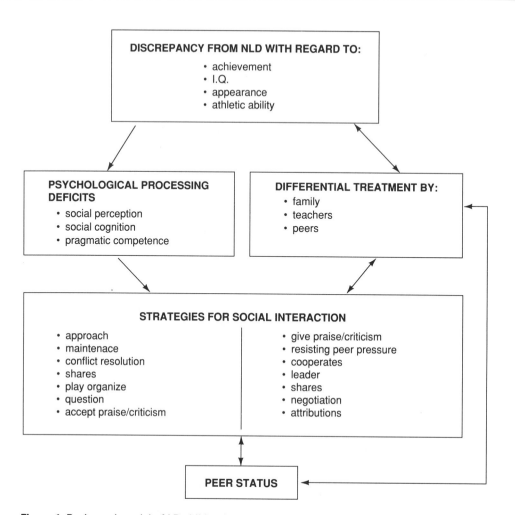

DISCREPANCY FROM NLD WITH REGARD TO:
- achievement
- I.Q.
- appearance
- athletic ability

PSYCHOLOGICAL PROCESSING DEFICITS
- social perception
- social cognition
- pragmatic competence

DIFFERENTIAL TREATMENT BY:
- family
- teachers
- peers

STRATEGIES FOR SOCIAL INTERACTION
- approach
- maintenace
- conflict resolution
- shares
- play organize
- question
- accept praise/criticism
- give praise/criticism
- resisting peer pressure
- cooperates
- leader
- shares
- negotiation
- attributions

PEER STATUS

Figure 1 Reciprocal model of LD children's peer relationships.

need control strategies at school, the teacher may provide controls in the form of verbal nonsupportive and nonverbal affective behavior (i.e., yelling, frowning, and sarcasm) (Siperstein & Goding, 1983). The other pupils then imitate the teacher. They reject the child. In this hostile environment, the LD child does not learn appropriate strategies for social interaction and is rejected further. All of these factors may play a part in establishing LD children's peer status.

Conceivably, the reciprocity model can be used to generate hypotheses for research on the peer status and social skills of LD children. In this article, however, the focus is on four.

1. *Low but positive correlations would be found between peer status and measures of social perception, social cognition, and pragmatic competence, assuming that these measures are reliable and valid. These measures would account for only a small portion of the variance in peer status of LD children. As reported above, some support for this prediction was pro-*

vided by Anderson (1983). Instead of merely differentiating LD and NLD children on these psychological processes, investigators need to determine the extent to which these processes are predictors of peer tatus.

2. *Popular, neglected, and rejected LD children would be differentiated on the basis of the strategies they use in social interaction.* As found by Dodge (1983), in play groups with unfamiliar children, normally popular children tend to use prosocial strategies, rejected children use antisocial strategies, and neglected children are socially inept. Measures of peer status that distinguish between neglected and rejected children need to be used in further research with LD children. In addition, studies need to be done comparing the social interaction strategies of LD children with different levels of peer status.

3. *Parents, teachers, and peers would use different control strategies with LD children who have different kinds of behavior patterns.* Using the *Classroom Behavior Inventory*, Speece et al. (1985) identified a relatively large cluster of LD children who were not task oriented or sensitive to others' needs and who tended to be distractible and hostile. All of these children were boys. Children with this type of behavioral profile are often identified as having Attention Deficit Disorder (ADD). Bruck and Hebert (1982) found that ADD children obtained low teacher ratings of peer status. Reciprocity theory predicts that parents, teachers, and peers would use upper limit controls with this group. Speece et al., (1985) also identified a sizable cluster of LD children, with an overrepresentation of girls, who were dependent and introverted. Reciprocity theory predicts that lower limit controls would be employed with this behavioral subgroup by parents and teachers and by peers in dyadic interaction. In large groups, peers may be more likely to ignore them. Ob-

servational studies of the interaction patterns of LD children with their parents, siblings, teachers, and peers are clearly required.

4. *LD children who display excessive or inappropriate social behavior would be more likely to be rejected by NLD peers the more time they spend in regular class settings. LD children whose social interaction strategies are within normal limits would be more likely to receive positive nominations the more time they spend in regular class settings.* With two exceptions, all of the studies on peer status of LD children have been done in regular classrooms. The LD subjects have generally received special education services from a resource teacher for less than one hour per day. (The two exceptions both involved clinical populations.) Research needs to be done with LD subjects who are integrated for different time periods to test this prediction.

Reciprocity theory explains the data accumulated to date regarding the correlates of peer status in LD children and generates hypotheses for further research. An implication of this theory is that the success of interventions in the social domain with LD children should be evaluated in terms of improvements in peer status (Ladd, 1985). According to reciprocity theory, changes are not likely to occur using an intervention aimed at only one of the participants in a reciprocal relationship (e.g., social skills training). An analysis of the interactions of the LD child with family, teachers, and peers may need to be done prior to developing a treatment plan. Depending on the situation, family therapy, consultation with the teacher regarding differential treatment of the LD child, and peer-mediated social skill training (Strain, Odom, & McConnell, 1984) may be required.

CONCLUSION

This article reviewed twenty-five studies that compared the peer status of LD and

NLD children and adolescents or provided information about the correlates of peer status in LD children. The data indicate overwhelmingly that LD children and adolescents who were integrated into regular classes are lower in peer status than NLD peers. There was some suggestion, though the data were not conclusive, that lower peer status of LD children is true mainly for girls and may be a function of LD samples having lower mean IQ scores than NLD samples. Furthermore, LD children were awarded fewer positive nominations and more negative nominations than NLD children; i.e., few LD children were rated as popular, and more than would be expected were rejected. There was a significant positive correlation between teacher and peer ratings of peer status. The studies to date have not differentiated between rejected and neglected children.

Four hypotheses were identified that were the bases for the research on the correlates of peer status in LD children. The discrepancy hypothesis received support because peer status was found to be related to both IQ and academic achievement. The LD children who were rated by peers as intelligent, attractive, or athletic were also more accepted, in spite of low academic achievement. The results of studies investigating the psychological processing deficit hypothesis have been equivocal. There was some evidence that peer status of LD children is related to aspects of pragmatic competence and that LD children are deficient in social insight—the ability to predict their own peer status. Methodological problems in the studies, however, have mitigated against drawing conclusions about the relationship between social perception, role taking, and peer status. Although LD children have been found to have difficulty using appropriate strategies for social interaction, the relationship between these difficulties and peer status was unclear due to the paucity of studies investigating the issue. The one published study compared LD children with low achievers and did not examine

the relationship between social interaction scores and peer status even though peer status measures were available. Differential treatment of low peer status LD children by teachers was the subject of one study. There was some evidence that LD children with low peer status were treated differently from high status NLD children by their regular grade 7 class teachers. Interactions with low status LD children were more frequent and negative.

Four methodological problems, common to most of the studies, have made it necessary to qualify the conclusions. First, all but three of the studies used samples of LD children identified by the school district and adopted school district definitions. Characteristics of the samples were poorly described. Furthermore, in all but the same three studies, the children were placed in regular classrooms and received remedial assistance from resource teachers. It is possible that the peer status of severely disabled children, who tend to be placed in self-contained special classes, has not been studied. (The three studies for which this does not apply examined clinical populations; two of them used teacher ratings of social status.)

Second, the IQ scores of LD and NLD children in most of the samples were not reported and only two studies took steps to control for IQ differences between LD and NLD groups. Because IQ has been found to be a major predictor of peer status in LD and NLD children, properly controlling for IQ may be important.

Third, the sample sizes in most of the studies were too small to explore gender or developmental differences. Furthermore, acceptance of the null hypothesis with these small sample sizes may constitute a Type II error. There were practical difficulties in dealing with this problem. Sociometric research demands that the classmates of the target children must participate in the study as raters. Normally, there are between one and three identified LD children in regular class. Consequently, in order to acquire, for example, a sample of 50 LD children, at least 500 children, whose parents have provided consent, must become raters.

The fourth methodological problem is remedied more easily. Although many of the studies used positive and negative nomination sociograms, none of them provided information about the proportion of LD children who were neglected; i.e., received very few nominations. As suggested by Asher and Dodge (in press), the two groups are quite different when assessed on behavioral measures. Rejected children were more likely than neglected children to be aggressive and disruptive and to remain unaccepted when they move into a new group (Coie & Kupersmidt, 1983; Dodge, 1983). Rejected children more often report that they experienced loneliness and social dissatisfaction than neglected children (Asher et al., 1984). Different kinds of intervention may be needed for neglected and rejected children. Clearly, neglected and rejected LD children should be differentiated through the use of positive and negative nomination sociograms in future research.

The literature review demonstrated the conceptual and empirical weaknesses of the four hypotheses that have been the bases of the research on correlates of peer status of LD children. All four hypotheses assume a unidirectional relationship between peer status and social skills. Investigators either took the position that LD children are the architects of their low peer status because of psychological processing or strategic deficits, or assumed that the LD label led to differential treatment or rejection. Analysis of the results from all studies reviewed suggested a different interpretation based on a reciprocity model and control theory (Bell & Harper, 1977). According to this model, peer status should be viewed as an outcome measure that reflects the quality *and* quantity of the reciprocal interactions between peers. From a developmental point of view, LD children, who may behave differently during infancy, possibly due to psychological processing deficits, may set up an interaction pattern with parents that does not facilitate social development. Consequently, when they come to school their behavior is viewed as immature or inappropriate by teachers and peers. Differential treatment by teachers to accommodate to LD children's behavior patterns and rejection from peers then follows. In addition to secondary affective results such as anxiety and negative self-concept, LD children do not acquire the social interaction strategies that are learned from interacting with peers, leading to increased rejection. To conclude, the reciprocity model integrates the predictions that can be derived from the discrepancy, psychological processing deficit, strategic deficit, and differential treatment hypotheses.

REFERENCES

Anderson, J.P. (1983). *The relationship between comprehension of verbal communication and social status in elementary school learning disabled students.* Unpublished doctoral dissertation, Fordham University.

Asher, S.R. (1983). Social competence and peer status: Recent advances and future directions. *Child Development, 54,* 1427–1434.

Asher, S.R., & Dodge, K.A. (1986). Identifying children who are rejected by their peers. *Developmental Psychology, 22,* 444–449.

Asher, S.R., & Hymel, S. (1981). Children's social competence in peer relations: Sociometric and behavioral assessment. In J.D. Wine & M.D. Smye (Eds.), *Social competence* (pp. 125–156). New York: Guilford.

Asher, S.R., Hymel, S., & Renshaw, P.D. (1984). Loneliness in children. *Child Development, 55,* 1456–1464.

Asher, S.R., Oden, S.L., & Gottman, J.M. (1977). Children's friendships in school settings. In L.G. Katz (Ed.), *Current topics in early childhood education* (Vol. 1) (pp. 37–53). Norwood, NJ: Ablex.

Asher, S.R., & Renshaw, P.D. (1981). Children without friends: Social knowledge and social-skill training. In S.R. Asher & J.M. Gottman (Eds.), *The development of children's friendships* (pp. 273–296.) Cambridge: Cambridge University Press.

Bell, R.Q., & Harper, L. (1977). *Child effects on adults.* New York: Wiley.

Bender, W.N., Wyne, M.D., Stuck, G.B., & Bailey, D.B., Jr. (1984). Relative peer status of learning disabled, educable mentally handicapped, low achieving and normally achieving children. *Child Study Journal, 13,* 209–216.

Bruck, M., & Hebert, M. (1982). Correlates of learning disabled students' peer-interaction patterns. *Learning Disability Quarterly, 5,* 353–362.

Bruininks, R.H., Rynders, J.B., & Gross, J.C. (1974). Social acceptance of mildly retarded pupils in resource rooms and regular classes. *American Journal of Mental Deficiency, 78,* 377–383.

Bruininks, V.L. (1978a). Actual and perceived peer status of learning disabled students in mainstream programs. *Journal of Special Education, 12,* 51–58.

Bruininks V.L. (1978b). Peer status and personality characteristics of learning disabled and nondisabled students. *Journal of Learning Disabilities, 11,* 484–489.

Bruno, R.M. (1981). Interpretation of pictorially presented social situations by learning disabled and normal children. *Journal of Learning Disabilities, 14,* 350–352.

Bryan, T. (1974). Peer popularity of learning disabled children. *Journal of Learning Disability, 7,* 621–625.

Bryan, T. (1976). Peer popularity of learning disabled children: A replication. *Journal of Learning Disabilities, 9,* 307–311.

Bryan, T. (1977). Learning disabled children's comprehension of nonverbal communication. *Journal of Learning Disabilities, 10,* 36–41.

Bryan, T. (1981). Studies of learning disabled children's pragmatic competence.

Topics in Learning and Learning Disabilities, July, 29–39.

Bryan, T., Pearl, R., Zimmerman, D., & Matthews, F. (1982). Mothers' evaluations of their learning disabled children. *Journal of Special Education, 16,* 149–159.

Bryan, T., & Wheeler, R. (1976). Teachers' behaviors in classes for severely retarded, multiply trainable, mentally retarded, learning disabled and normal children. *Mental Retardation, 14*(4), 41–45.

Bryan, T., Wheeler, R., Felcan, J., & Henek, T. (1976). Come on dummy: An observational study of children's communications. *Journal of Learning Disabilities, 9,* 661–669.

Bursuck, W.D. (1983). Sociometric status, behavior ratings, and social knowledge of learning disabled and low achieving students. *Learning Disability Quarterly, 6,* 329–338.

Chandler, M. (1973). Egocentrism and antisocial behavior: The assessment and training of social perspective taking skills. *Developmental Psychology, 9,* 326–332.

Coie, J.D., Dodge, K., & Coppotelli, H. (1982). Dimensions for types of social status: A cross-age perspective. *Developmental Psychology, 18,* 557–570.

Coie, J.D., & Kupersmidt, J.B. (1983). A behavioral analysis of emerging social status in boys' groups. *Child Development, 54,* 1400–1416.

Coopersmith, S. (1967). *The antecedents of self esteem.* San Francisco: Freeman.

Cowen, E.L., Pederson, A., Bibigian, H., Izzo, L.D., & Trost, M.A. (1973). Long-term follow-up of early detected vulnerable children. *Journal of Consulting and Clinical Psychology, 41,* 438–446.

Dickstein, E.B., & Warren D.R. (1980). Role-taking deficits in learning disabled children. *Journal of Learning Disabilities, 13,* 33–37.

Dodge, D.A., Coie, J.D., & Brakke, N.P. (1982). Behavior patterns of socially rejected and neglected pre-adolescents: The roles of social approach and aggression. *Journal of Abnormal Child Psychology, 10,* 389–410.

Dodge, K.A., (1983). Behavioral antecedents of peer social status. *Child Development, 54,* 1386–1399.

Dudley-Marling, C. (1985). The pragmatic skills of learning disabled children: A review. *Journal of Learning Disabilities, 18,* 193–199.

Elardo, R., & Freund, J.H. (1981). Maternal child-rearing styles and the social skills of learning disabled boys: A preliminary investigation. *Contemporary Educational Psychology, 6,* 86–94.

Elig, T.W., & Frieze, I.H. (1975). A multidimensional scheme for coding and interpreting perceived causality for success and failure events. *JSAS Catalogue of Selected Documents in Psychology, 5,* 313.

Enright, R.D., & Lapsley, D.K. (1980). Social role-taking: A review of the constructs, measures and measurement properties. *Review of Educational Research, 50,* 647–674.

Fine, G.A. (1981). Friends, impression management, and preadolescent behavior. In S.R. Asher & J.M. Gottman (Eds.), *The development of children's friendships* (pp. 29–52.) Cambridge: Cambridge University Press.

Flavell, J., Botkin, P., Fry, C., Wright, J., & Jarvis, P. (1968). *The development of role-taking and communication skills in children.* New York: Wiley.

French, D.C., & Waas, G.E. (1985). Behavior problems of peer rejected and neglected elementary age children: Teacher and parent perspectives. *Child Development, 56,* 246–252.

French, D.C., Waas, G.A., & Tarver-Behring, S.A. (1985). *Nomination and rating scale sociometrics: Convergent validity and clinical utility.* Biennial meeting of the Society for Research in Child Development, Toronto.

Freud, A., & Dann, S. (1951). An experiment in group upbringing. *Psychoanalytic Study of the Child, 6,* 127–168.

Freund, J.H., & Elardo, R. (1978). Maternal behavior and family constellation as predictors of social competence in learning disabled children. *Learning Disability Quarterly, 1,* 80–86.

Garrett, M.R., & Crump, W.D. (1980). Peer acceptance, teacher preference, and self-appraisal of social status among learning disabled children. *Learning Disability Quarterly, 3*(3), 42–48.

Gottman, J.M., & Parkhurst, J.T. (1980). A developmental theory of friendship and acquaintanceship processes. In W.A. Collins (Ed.), *Minnesota symposia on child psychology* (Vol. 13) (pp. 197–253). Hillsdale, NJ: Lawrence Erlbaum.

Gresham, F.M. (1982). Social interactions as predictors of children's likeability and friendship patterns: A multiple regression analysis. *Journal of Behavioral Assessment, 4,* 39–54.

Gresham, F.M. (1983). Social validity in the assessment of children's social skills: Establishing standards for social competency. *Journal of Psychoeducational Assessment,* 209–307.

Gresham, F.M., & Reschly, D.J. (1986). Social skill deficits and low peer acceptance of mainstreamed learning disabled children. *Learning Disability Quarterly, 9,* 23–32.

Gronlund, W.E. (1959). *Sociometry in the classroom.* New York: Harper.

Hammill, D.D., Leigh, J., McNutt, G.E., & Larsen, S.E. (1981). A new definition of learning disabilities. *Learning Disability Quarterly, 4,* 336–342.

Hartup, W.W. (1970). Peer interaction and social organization. In P.H. Mussen (Ed.), *Carmichael's manual of child psychology,* (Vol. 2) (pp. 361–456). New York: Wiley.

Hartup, W.W. (1983). Peer relations. In E.M. Heatherington (Ed.), *Handbook of child psychology* (Vol. 4): *Socialization, personality and social development* (pp. 103–196). New York: Wiley.

Hasselt, V.B., Hersen, M., & Bellack, A.S. (1981). The validity of role play tests for assessing social skills in children. *Behavior Therapy, 12*, 202–216.

Horowitz, E.C. (1981). Popularity, decentering ability, and role-taking skills in learning disabled and normal children. *Learning Disability Quarterly, 4*, 23–30.

Hutton, J., & Polo, L. (1976). A sociometric study of learning disability children and types of teaching strategy. *Group Psychotherapy and Psychodrama, 29*, 113–120.

Ladd, G.W. (1985). Documenting the effects of social skill training with children: Process and outcome assessment. In B. Schneider, K. Rubin, & J. Ledingham (Eds.), *Children's peer relations: Issues in assessment and intervention* (pp. 243–269). New York: Springer-Verlag.

Maheady, L., Harper, G.L., & Sainato, D.M. (1985). Social perception deficits: Have we misinterpreted data? (Unpublished manuscript).

Maheady, L. & Sainato, D.M. (1986). Learning disabled students' perceptions of social events. In S. Ceci (Ed.), *Handbook of cognitive, social and neuropsychological aspects of learning disabilities* (Vol. 1) (pp. 381–402). New York: Academic Press.

Martin, J.S. (1985). *Relationship between sociometric status and social perception in learning disabled children.* Unpublished doctoral dissertation, University of Georgia.

Moreno, J.L. (1934). *Who shall survive? A new approach to the problem of human interrelations.* Washington, DC: Nervous and Mental Disease Publishing.

Myklebust, H. (1971). *The pupil rating scale: Screening for learning disabilities.* New York: Grune & Stratton.

Oden, S., & Asher, S.R. (1977). Coaching children in social skills for friendship making. *Child Development, 48*, 495–506.

Perlmutter, B.F., Crocker, J., Cordray, D., & Garstecki, D. (1983). Sociometric status and related personality characteristics of mainstreamed learning disabled adolescents. *Learning Disability Quarterly, 6*, 20–30.

Prillaman, D. (1981). Acceptance of learning disabled students in a mainstream environment: A failure to replicate. *Journal of Learning Disabilities, 14*, 344–352.

Putallaz, M. (1983). Predicting children's sociometric status from their behavior. *Child Development, 54*, 1417–1426.

Putallaz, M., & Gottman, J.M. (1981). Social skills and group acceptance. In S.R. Asher & J.M. Gottman (Eds.), *The development of children's friendships* (pp. 116–149). Cambridge: Cambridge University Press.

Reardon, R.C., Hersen, M.O., Bellack, A.S., & Foley, J.M. (1979). Measuring social skill in grade school boys. *Journal of Behavioral Assessment, 1*, 87–105.

Roff, M., Sells, S.B., & Golden, M.M. (1972). *Social adjustment and personality development in children.* Minneapolis: University of Minneapolis Press.

Rubin, K.H., Daniels-Beirness, T., & Hayvren, M. (1982). Social and social-cognitive correlates of sociometric status in preschool and kindergarten children. *Canadian Journal of Behavioral Science, 14*, 338–349.

Sabornie, E.J., & Kauffman, J.M. (1986). Social acceptance of learning disabled adolescents. *Learning Disability Quarterly, 9*, 55–60.

Sainato, D.M., Zigmond, N., & Strain, P.S. (1983). Social status and initiations of interaction by learning disabled students in a regular education setting. *Analysis and Intervention in Developmental Disabilities, 3*(1), 71–87.

Schumaker, J.B., Hazel, J.S., Sherman, J.A., & Sheldon, J. (1982). Social skill performances of learning disabled, non-learning disabled and delinquent adolescents. *Learning Disability Quarterly, 5*, 388–397.

Scranton, T.R., & Ryckman, D.B. (1979). Sociometric status of learning disabled children in an integrative program. *Journal of Learning Disabilities, 6*, 402–407.

Selman, R.L. (1981). The child as a friendship philosopher. In S.R. Asher & J.M. Gottman (Eds.), *The development of children's friendships* (pp. 242–272). Cambridge: Cambridge University Press.

Sheare, J.B. (1978). The impact of resource programs upon the self concept of peer acceptance of learning disabled children. *Psychology in the Schools, 15*, 406–411.

Siegel, L.S., & Heaven, R.K. (1986). Defining and categorizing learning disabilities. In S. Ceci (Ed.), *Handbook of cognitive, social and neuropsychological aspects of learning disabilities* (Vol. 1) (pp. 95–122). New York: Academic Press.

Simon, J.E. (1982). *The use of persuasive strategies and politeness forms in peer interactions by learning disabled, highly popular nondisabled, and less popular nondisabled children.* Unpublished doctoral dissertation, University of Cincinnati.

Siperstein, G., Bopp, M.J., & Bak, J.J. (1978). Social status of learning disabled children. *Journal of Learning Disabilities, 11*, 98–102.

Siperstein, G., & Goding, M.J. (1983). Social integration of learning disabled children in regular classrooms. *Advances in Learning and Behavioral Disabilities, 2*, 227–263.

Siperstein, G., & Goding, M. (1985). Teachers' behavior toward LD and NLD children: A strategy for change. *Journal of Learning Disabilities, 18*, 139–144.

Sobol, M.P., Earn, B.M., Bennett, D., & Humphries, T. (1983). A categorical analysis of the social attributions of learning disabled children. *Journal of Abnormal Child Psychology, 11*, 217–228.

Speece, D.L., McKinney, J.D., & Appelbaum, M.I. (1985). Classification and validation of behavioral subtypes of learning-disabled children. *Journal of Educational Psychology, 77*(1), 67–77.

Spivack, G.E., Platt, J.J. & Shure, M.D. (1976). *The problem solving approach to adjustment.* San Francisco: Jossey-Bass.

Strain, P.S., Odom, S.L., & McConnell, S. (1984). Promoting social reciprocity of exceptional children: Identification, target behavior selection, and intervention. *Remedial and Special Education, 5*(1), 21–28.

Torgesen, J. (1982). The learning disabled child as an inactive learner: Educational implications. *Topics in Learning and Learning Disabilities, 2*(1), 45–52.

Urbain, E.S., & Kendall, P.C. (1980). Review of social-cognitive problem solving interventions with children. *Psychological Bulletin, 88*(1), 109–143.

Weintraub, S., Prinz, A.J., & Neale, J.M. (1978). Peer evaluations of the competence of children vulnerable to psychopathology. *Journal of Abnormal Child Psychology, 6*, 461–473.

Weissberg, R.P., Gesten, E.L., Rapkin, B.D., Cowen, E.L., Davidson, E., Flores De Apodaca, R., & McKim, B.J. (1981). Evaluation of a social problem-solving training program for suburban and inner-city third-grade children. *Journal of Consulting and Clinical Psychology, 8*, 251–261.

Wiener, J. (1978). *A theoretical model of the affective and social development of learning disabled children.* Unpublished doctoral dissertation, University of Michigan.

Wiener, J. (1980). A theoretical model of the acquisition of peer relationships of learning disabled children. *Journal of Learning Disabilities, 13*, 506–511.

Wiig, E.H., & Harris, S.P. (1974). Perception and interpretation of nonverbally expressed emotions by adolescents with learning disabilities. *Perceptual and Motor Skills, 38*, 239–245.

Wong, B.Y.L. (1979). The role of theory in

learning-disabilities research. *Journal of Learning Disabilities, 12,* 585–595.

Wong, B.Y.L., & Wong, R. (1980). Role-taking skills in normal achieving and learning disabled children. *Learning Disability Quarterly, 3,* 3–11.

Ysseldyke, J.E. (1983). Current practices in making psychoeducational decisions about learning disabled students. *Journal of Learning Disabilities, 16,* 226–232.

FEEDBACK

Peer Status Review of Research

In the introductory section, the research reviewer sets out the problem area and ends with an explanation of the data collection procedure. In the section "Measurement of Peer Status . . . ," the reviewer provides operational definitions. In the section "Comparison of Peer Status . . . ," the researcher examines and critiques research related to four questions. In the section "Correlates of Peer Status . . . ," the reviewer critiques research related to four hypotheses. The discussion of the previous researchers' limitations are embedded within each subsection. For example, the discussions of gender and "isolate" subjects are within the discussion of "comparisons." Her conclusion is that the previous research in both areas is limited and that the questions and hypotheses remain unanswered. Beginning with the heading "An Alternate Conceptualization . . . ," the reviewer provides an alternative theory with reference to research studies, supporting that theory and explaining its plausibility.

However, a major limitation of this integrative review of research is that the research supporting the alternative theory is not critically analyzed by the same standards applied to the previous research or by evaluative questions and criteria such as those set out in this text.

11

Locating Information About Research Reports

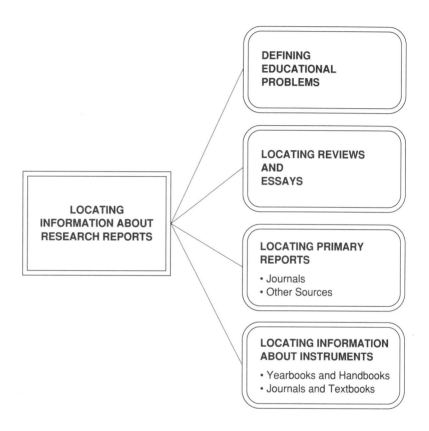

FOCUS QUESTIONS

1. How is an educational problem defined before primary research reports are located?
2. How are integrative reviews and essays about research located?
3. How are primary research reports located?
4. Where can information about instruments be located?

To reiterate from Chapter 1: Educators, whether they are college or university instructors, school practitioners, administrators, or researchers, are continually making decisions about curriculum, teaching, classroom management, and learning. These decisions are based on their experiences, others' experiences, and their understanding of accumulated knowledge about education. Much of this accumulated knowledge is in the form of research reports and interpretations of research. The sign of a productive profession such as education is that its members systematically examine the knowledge base upon which it functions. The chapters in this text are aimed at helping educators examine and interpret research from education, psychology, and related areas in the social sciences.

This chapter provides research consumers with some guidance for locating primary research reports and integrative research reviews and meta-analyses, as well as evaluations of instruments used in research. Most of the resources for locating these reports, and the reports themselves can be found in college and university libraries. Some of these resources can be found in public libraries. Research consumers need to know (a) what resources exist for locating reports and reviews of instruments and (b) how to locate reviews of research, primary research reports, and reviews of instruments.

Initially, a research consumer needs to identify an educational question or problem. Then, the consumer must decide what kind of information is required to answer the question. For purposes of illustration, a representative educational question is used here. In the following sections, the question's subject area (or topic) is used with the different kinds of resources available to research consumers.

DEFINING THE EDUCATIONAL PROBLEM

The general subject area to be used for demonstration is cooperative learning. The educational questions are "How is cooperative learning used in middle schools, grades 5 to 8?" and How does cooperative learning affect students' school performance and learning?"

The first step in answering these questions is to be clear about the definitions of key terms. Precise definitions allow research consumers to pose answerable questions and locate relevant studies. Since the target population is defined—fifth and sixth grade students—a key term remains to be defined: *cooperative learning*.

Possible sources of definitions, in addition to definitions that may appear within primary research articles, are textbooks on the subject, dictionaries of educational terms, and educational encyclopedias. Textbooks can be found through the libraries' card catalog under the appropriate subject heading (e.g., cooperative learning). Although textbooks may not be a source of research, their authors often include references to and syntheses of primary studies. For example, a search of one university's card catalog did not uncover the subject heading *cooperative learning*, but it did show two books with the term in their titles:

Slavin, R. E. (1987). *Cooperative learning: Student teams.* Washington, D.C.: National Education Association.

Slavin, R. E. (1983). *Cooperative learning.* New York: Longman.

In the first book, *cooperative learning* is defined as

a term that refers to instructional methods in which students of all performance levels work together in small groups toward a group goal. (Slavin, 1987, p. 8)

And, in the second book, *cooperative learning methods* is defined as

techniques that use cooperative *task structures*, in which students spend much of their class time working in 4–6 member heterogeneous groups. They also use cooperative *incentive structures*, in which students earn recognition, rewards, or (occasionally) grades based on the academic performance of their groups. (Slavin, 1983, p. 3)

The card catalog showed as subject headings for these books: *Group work in education* and *Team learning approach in education*. These subject headings were noted as possible sources of other materials related to the educational question.

Educational and psychological dictionaries, usually found in libraries' reference sections, contain definitions of technical and professional terms used in these fields. Dictionaries that are important to educators are:

A Comprehensive Dictionary of Psychological and Psychoanalytic Terms: A Guide to Usage

A Dictionary of Reading and Related Terms

Dictionary of Education, 3rd edition

Dictionary of Philosophy and Psychology

Encyclopedic Dictionary of Psychology

International Dictionary of Education

Longman Dictionary of Psychology and Psychiatry

The Concise Dictionary of Education

In the *Dictionary of Education*, 3rd edition, the following appears:

cooperative learning
   see learning, cooperative
learning, cooperative: changes in behavior resulting wholly or in part from shared experiences of two or more persons. (Good, 1973)

Obtaining these definitions and the insight that information about cooperative learning might be found under headings such as *group work* and *team learning* is preparatory to seeking summaries and interpretations of the research related to cooperative learning.

LOCATING INTERPRETIVE REVIEWS AND ESSAYS

Several sources provide interpretive reviews and essays about educational, psychological, and other related social science topics. These sources include

American Educators' Encyclopedia

Encyclopedia of Special Education

The Encyclopedia of Educational Research, 5th edition

The Encyclopedia of Education

Handbook of Research on Teaching, 3rd edition

The International Encyclopedia of Education

The International Encyclopedia of Education: Research and Studies

The International Encyclopedia of Teaching and Teacher Education

Review of Research in Education

Among other subject headings, a sampling of the indexes of these handbooks and encyclopedias contain references to the following (the numbers after the entries refer to pages in the particular encyclopedia):

International Encyclopedia of Teaching and Teacher Education

Cooperation
    in the classroom 345–49
    grouping (instructional purposes) 229

Encyclopedia of Education Research, 5th edition

Cooperation
    in classrooms 750–51, 761–62
Cooperative learning 269

The International Encyclopedia of Education: Research and Studies

Cooperation
    in the classroom 2:1003–6
    grouping (instructional purposes) 4:2103, 2104

Upon referring to the pages noted in the indexes, several interpretive essays are found. As noted in one essay,

> Recent years have seen a surge in popularity of methods of teaching that promote student–student interaction (*International Encyclopedia of Education: Research and Studies*, **2**:1003).

Each of the interpretive essays contains a bibliography of all references discussed within the essay. These are excellent sources of additional interpretive essays and reviews. For example, this reference to an integrative research review appears in more than one encyclopedia essay:

> Slavin, R. E. (1980). Cooperative learning. *Review of Educational Research*, *50*, 315–42.

The journal in which the Slavin review appears, *Review of Educational Research (RER)*, is published quarterly by the American Educational Research Association. It is an excellent source of integrative research reviews and meta-analyses. Research consumers can locate reviews in *RER* through the sources discussed in the next section.

LOCATING PRIMARY RESEARCH REPORTS

Educational, psychological, and other social science journals containing primary research reports are usually located in the periodicals sections of libraries. To locate specific research reports—and, for the discussion here, reports about cooperative learning—research consumers need to use two sources that index all journal articles (research and nonresearch). These are the *Education Index (EI)* and the *Current Index to Journals in Education (CIJE)*. To locate primary research reports that are not published in journals two other sources need to be examined. These are *Resources in Education (RIE)* and Exceptional Child Educational Resources *(ECER)*.

Locating Research Reports in Journals

The *Education Index (EI)* and the *Current Index to Journals (CIJE)* contain up-to-date information about research and general (nonresearch) articles published in almost 800 educational journals. Other information contained in these indexes includes information found in several different kinds of educational documents: yearbooks, bulletins, and reports. Although there is a great deal of overlap in the information they provide, both indexes should be consulted because it is possible that information about a research report may appear in one and not the other.

Both *EI* and *CIJE* are published monthly with semiannual and annual compilations (*EI* provides quarterly consolidations). Both present information alphabetically by subject headings, but they use different systems of subject listings and present bibliographic information differently. *CIJE* provides short annotations for each listing, something *EI* does not do.

Examining the December 1988 quarterly compilation of *EI* for *cooperative learning* reveals this entry:

Cooperative learning *See* Learning, Psychology of—Team learning (p. 87).

Following that lead, the entries for "Learning, Psychology of—Team learning" are located. These are shown in Figure 11.1. (To this example and the ones that follow, explanatory labels have been added to assist you in understanding the entries.)

To conserve space, entries in *EI* contain abbreviations for journal titles and dates. A listing in the front of each issue explains the abbreviations. When the article is a primary research report, the listing is preceded by the subheading *Research*. Since that heading does not appear, research consumers can assume that each of the listings for "Learning, Psychology of—Team learning" is a general or interpretive article.

CIJE is a publication of the Educational Resources Information Center (ERIC), a national network supported by the Office of Education Research and Improvement of the U.S. Department of Education. The purpose of **ERIC** is to provide access to current research results and related information in the field of education. It is a decentralized system composed of about sixteen clearinghouses, each specializing on a major education area. For example, some of the clearinghouses within the ERIC network are Elementary and Early Childhood Education; Hand-

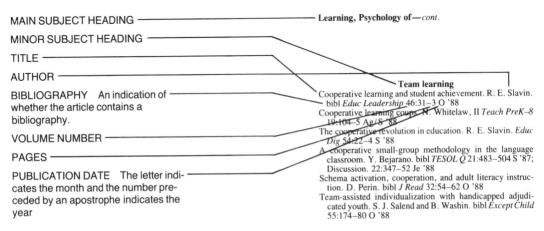

Figure 11.1 *Education Index* subject entry. (From *Education Index*, 1988, Dec., p. 201)

icapped and Gifted Children; Reading and Communication Skills; Science, Mathematics, and Environmental Education, Social Studies/Social Science Education; and Teacher Education. The clearinghouses collect, index, abstract, and disseminate information that is available through a central computerized facility. This information appears monthly in *CIJE*.

To use *CIJE*, the *Current Index to Journals in Education*, research consumers refer first to a guide for determining appropriate subject headings. To maintain uniformity of subject listings, the ERIC system publishes a *Thesaurus of ERIC Descriptors*, which is updated periodically. **Descriptors** are key words used in indexing documents. The thesaurus indicates the terms that are used to index a topic. For example, checking the 11th edition of the thesaurus, published in 1987, there is no listing for *cooperative* learning. What one finds is the entry for "cooperation" shown in Figure 11.2.

The scope note (SN) for *cooperation* shows a definition consistent with those found in other sources for cooperative learning. One of the related terms (RT) is *group activities*, which is consistent with other information obtained in card catalogs and educational encyclopedias. The entry for *cooperative activities* also suggests using the heading *group activities*.

When a specific subject listing is not used in the ERIC thesaurus, research consumers can use a researcher's name to locate references in *CIJE*. Since the name "R. E. Slavin" consistently appears in the card catalog, encyclopedic essays, and *EI*, that name is located in the

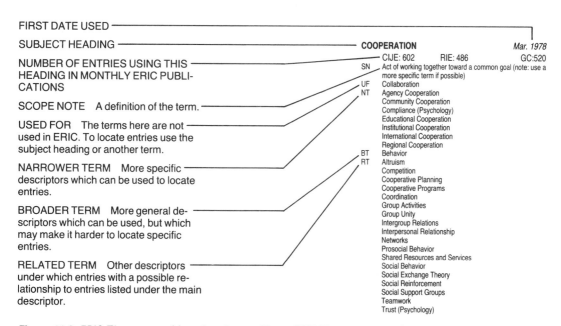

Figure 11.2 *ERIC Thesaurus* subject descriptors. (From *ERIC Thesaurus,* p. 50)

author index of the January–June 1988 semiannual compilation of *CIJE*. The entries for "Slavin, R. E." are shown in Figure 11.3.

Using the EJ-prefixed accession number appearing after the first title, the entry as found in the main entry section is shown in Figure 11.4.

This journal article by Slavin, "Cooperative Learning: Where Behavior and Humanistic Approaches to Classroom Motivation Meet," is listed within *CIJE* under all subject headings listed as descriptors and marked with an asterisk. That is, it is found in the subject index under the headings *Student motivation*; "*Elementary school students; Group dynamics*"; and so on. It is also listed under the headings listed as identifiers, which are headings that reflect terms currently used by researchers and other authors that have not been officially recognized as ERIC descriptors. By going to the subject heading, *Cooperative learning* in the subject index, one finds the entries as shown in Figure 11.5.

Each of the entries under *Cooperative learning* in the *CIJE* subject index is located in the main entry section. After reading the annotations, the researcher selects a journal article. The full text of the selected article can be found in the periodicals section of the library or on microfilm in the library's microform section.

Locating Research Reports in Other Sources

As indicated previously, ERIC is a national network of educational clearinghouses that collect, index, abstract, and disseminate a wide variety of educational information. *CIJE* is the publication indexing articles in professional educational journals. The main ERIC publication for indexing educational documents is *Resources in Education (RIE)*. Like *CIJE*, *RIE* is published monthly with semiannual and annual consolidations. It is the means for finding research reports, literature reviews, general descriptive articles, papers presented at conferences, descriptions of educational products, curriculum guides,

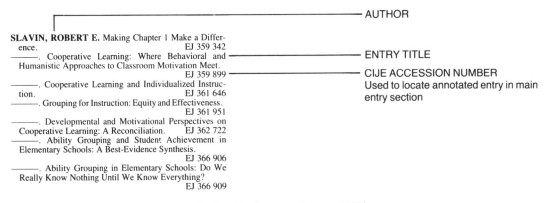

Figure 11.3 *CIJE* author entry. (From *CIJE*, 1988, January–June, p. 1009)

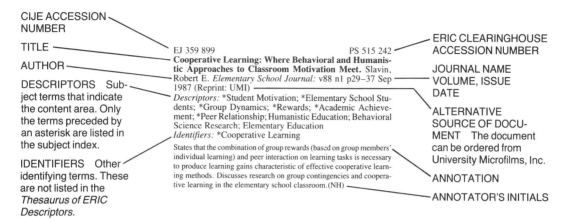

CIJE ACCESSION NUMBER

TITLE

AUTHOR

DESCRIPTORS Subject terms that indicate the content area. Only the terms preceded by an asterisk are listed in the subject index.

IDENTIFIERS Other identifying terms. These are not listed in the *Thesaurus of ERIC Descriptors*.

EJ 359 899   PS 515 242
Cooperative Learning: Where Behavioral and Humanistic Approaches to Classroom Motivation Meet. Slavin, Robert E. *Elementary School Journal:* v88 n1 p29–37 Sep 1987 (Reprint: UMI)

Descriptors: *Student Motivation; *Elementary School Students; *Group Dynamics; *Rewards; *Academic Achievement; *Peer Relationship; Humanistic Education; Behavioral Science Research; Elementary Education
Identifiers: *Cooperative Learning

States that the combination of group rewards (based on group members' individual learning) and peer interaction on learning tasks is necessary to produce learning gains characteristic of effective cooperative learning methods. Discusses research on group contingencies and cooperative learning in the elementary school classroom.(NH)

ERIC CLEARINGHOUSE ACCESSION NUMBER

JOURNAL NAME VOLUME, ISSUE DATE

ALTERNATIVE SOURCE OF DOCUMENT The document can be ordered from University Microfilms, Inc.

ANNOTATION

ANNOTATOR'S INITIALS

Figure 11.4 *CIJE* document resume. (From *CIJE*, 1988, January–June, p.65)

and government reports. Most of these documents are unpublished and noncopyrighted materials that would otherwise be hard to find.

Locating an entry in *RIE* is similar to finding one in *CIJE*. That is, both use the same system of descriptors and identifiers, list entries under subject headings and author indexes, and use a similar accession number system. However, ERIC accession numbers are prefixed with ED instead of EJ.

After an item listed in *RIE* has been determined to fit the problem area being searched, the full text of the document can usually be found on small sheets of microfilm called **microfiche** (pronounced *MY-krow-feesh*), which can be read only on special microfiche readers. ERIC microfiche collections and microfiche readers can be found in college and university libraries and some public libraries. *RIE* contains information for ordering a document on microfiche or in printed-copy form. In some cases, documents are not available from the ERIC document reproduction service.

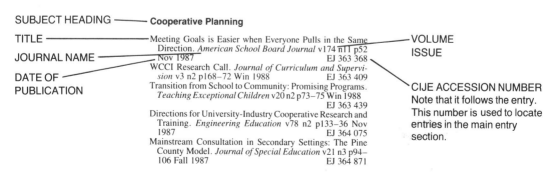

SUBJECT HEADING   **Cooperative Planning**

TITLE   Meeting Goals is Easier when Everyone Pulls in the Same Direction. *American School Board Journal* v174 n11 p52 Nov 1987   EJ 363 368

JOURNAL NAME   WCCI Research Call. *Journal of Curriculum and Supervision* v3 n2 p168–72 Win 1988   EJ 363 409

DATE OF PUBLICATION   Transition from School to Community: Promising Programs. *Teaching Exceptional Children* v20 n2 p73–75 Win 1988   EJ 363 439
                         Directions for University-Industry Cooperative Research and Training. *Engineering Education* v78 n2 p133–36 Nov 1987   EJ 364 075
                         Mainstream Consultation in Secondary Settings: The Pine County Model. *Journal of Special Education* v21 n3 p94–106 Fall 1987   EJ 364 871

VOLUME ISSUE

CIJE ACCESSION NUMBER Note that it follows the entry. This number is used to locate entries in the main entry section.

Figure 11.5 *CIJE* subject entry. (From *CIJE*, 1988, January–June, p. 578)

The steps for using ERIC are

1. Refer to the *Thesaurus of ERIC Descriptors*.
2. Select an appropriate monthly, semiannual, or annual edition of *RIE*.
3. Go to the subject section or author index to locate entries and ED accession numbers.
4. Locate abstracts of the entries in the document resume section.
5. Locate the full text of the document in the microfiche collection.

Here is an example of a manual search of the ERIC system for entries related to the problem area *cooperative learning*.

Since the thesaurus already has been examined, the research consumer goes directly to *RIE*. The entries for *cooperative learning* are found in the subject index of the January–June 1988 semiannual consolidation of *RIE*. These entries are shown in Figure 11.6.

The last entry, "Effects of Cooperative Learning on Achievement in Secondary Schools: A Summary of Research," with the accession number ED 288 853, is noted. In addition, the author index is examined. The entry for "Slavin, R. E." is shown in Figure 11.7.

The noted review of research is located in the document resumes section. The entry for ED 288 853 is shown in Figure 11.8.

Since the information in the abstract indicates that "high quality studies were reviewed," the full text of the document is located in the library's ERIC microfiche collection.

A companion resource to *CIJE* and *RIE* is produced by the ERIC Clearinghouse on Handicapped and Gifted Children. The *Exceptional Child Educational Resources (ECER)* searches over 200 journals dealing with all forms of exceptionality, many of which are not indexed in *CIJE* or *RIE*. The *ECER* indexes documents the same way as *CIJE* and *RIE*; however, it contains information not readily available through the ERIC: commercially published books, nonprint materials, and doctoral dissertations. Entries use an EC-prefixed accession number, and the full documents are not reproduced on microfiche.

Cooperative Learning —————————————————— SUBJECT HEADING
Cooperative Learning Strategies Applied in the Language ————— ENTRY TITLE
Classroom. Reading Around Series No. 1.
                     ED 285 122 ——————— ERIC ACCESSION NUMBER   Note
Cooperative Learning with Limited-English-Proficient   that it follows the entry. This number is
Students.   used to locate entries in the document
                     ED 287 314   resume section.
Effective Classroom Programs for Students at Risk.
                     ED 288 922
Effects of Cooperative Learning on Achievement in Secon-
dary Schools: A Summary of Research.
                     ED 288 853

Figure 11.6 *RIE* subject entry. (From *RIE*, Author Index, 1988, January–June, p. 510)

INTERPRETING EDUCATIONAL RESEARCH

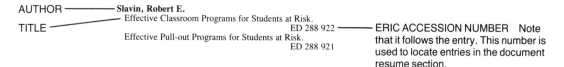

AUTHOR ——————— **Slavin, Robert E.**
————— Effective Classroom Programs for Students at Risk.
TITLE ——————— ED 288 922 ——————— ERIC ACCESSION NUMBER   Note
Effective Pull-out Programs for Students at Risk. that it follows the entry. This number is
ED 288 921 used to locate entries in the document
resume section.

Figure 11.7 *RIE* author entry. (From *RIE*, Author Index, 1988, January–June, p. 510)

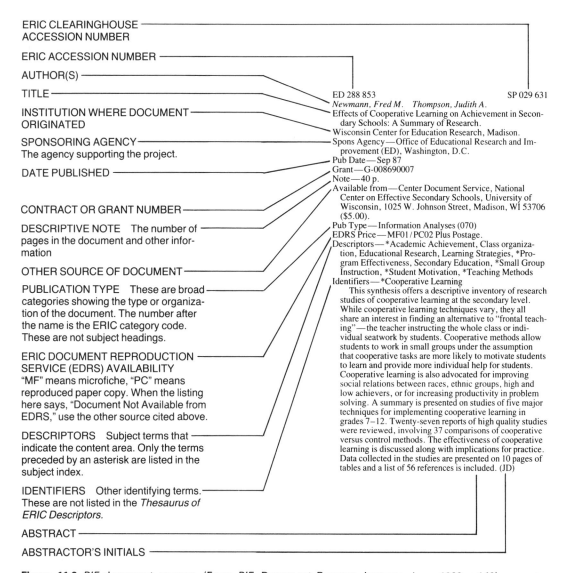

ERIC CLEARINGHOUSE
ACCESSION NUMBER

ERIC ACCESSION NUMBER

AUTHOR(S)

TITLE

INSTITUTION WHERE DOCUMENT
ORIGINATED

SPONSORING AGENCY
The agency supporting the project.

DATE PUBLISHED

CONTRACT OR GRANT NUMBER

DESCRIPTIVE NOTE   The number of
pages in the document and other information

OTHER SOURCE OF DOCUMENT

PUBLICATION TYPE   These are broad
categories showing the type or organization of the document. The number after
the name is the ERIC category code.
These are not subject headings.

ERIC DOCUMENT REPRODUCTION
SERVICE (EDRS) AVAILABILITY
"MF" means microfiche, "PC" means
reproduced paper copy. When the listing
here says, "Document Not Available from
EDRS," use the other source cited above.

DESCRIPTORS   Subject terms that
indicate the content area. Only the terms
preceded by an asterisk are listed in the
subject index.

IDENTIFIERS   Other identifying terms.
These are not listed in the *Thesaurus of
ERIC Descriptors.*

ABSTRACT

ABSTRACTOR'S INITIALS

ED 288 853   SP 029 631
Newmann, Fred M.   Thompson, Judith A.
Effects of Cooperative Learning on Achievement in Secon-
dary Schools: A Summary of Research.
Wisconsin Center for Education Research, Madison.
Spons Agency—Office of Educational Research and Im-
provement (ED), Washington, D.C.
Pub Date—Sep 87
Grant—G-008690007
Note—40 p.
Available from—Center Document Service, National
Center on Effective Secondary Schools, University of
Wisconsin, 1025 W. Johnson Street, Madison, WI 53706
($5.00).
Pub Type—Information Analyses (070)
EDRS Price—MF01/PC02 Plus Postage.
Descriptors—*Academic Achievement, Class organiza-
tion, Educational Research, Learning Strategies, *Pro-
gram Effectiveness, Secondary Education, *Small Group
Instruction, *Student Motivation, *Teaching Methods
Identifiers—*Cooperative Learning
    This synthesis offers a descriptive inventory of research
studies of cooperative learning at the secondary level.
While cooperative learning techniques vary, they all
share an interest in finding an alternative to "frontal teaching"—the teacher instructing the whole class or individual seatwork by students. Cooperative methods allow
students to work in small groups under the assumption
that cooperative tasks are more likely to motivate students
to learn and provide more individual help for students.
Cooperative learning is also advocated for improving
social relations between races, ethnic groups, high and
low achievers, or for increasing productivity in problem
solving. A summary is presented on studies of five major
techniques for implementing cooperative learning in
grades 7–12. Twenty-seven reports of high quality studies
were reviewed, involving 37 comparisons of cooperative
versus control methods. The effectiveness of cooperative
learning is discussed along with implications for practice.
Data collected in the studies are presented on 10 pages of
tables and a list of 56 references is included. (JD)

Figure 11.8 *RIE* document resume. (From *RIE*, Document Resume January–June, 1988, p.140)

There are other, specialized abstracts and indexes (not connected with the ERIC system) that research consumers might wish to examine for information related to educational problems or questions. Each of these abstracts and indexes uses its own formats for subject and author indexes; a full explanation of those systems are in the front of each. Several that might be of most interest to educators are *Sociological Abstracts*, *Psychological Abstracts*, *State Education Journal Index*, *Business Education Index*, *Educational Administration Abstracts*, *Physical Education Index*, and *Child Development Abstracts and Bibliography*.

Dissertation Abstracts International contains abstracts of doctoral dissertations from about 400 participating universities. It is published monthly in two sections: Section A contains dissertations in the humanities and social sciences, which include education. Section B covers the science areas, which include psychology. The dissertations themselves are usually not available, but research consumers should check with reference librarians to see whether copies of selected dissertations are available in the universities' microform section. The abstract's index is arranged alphabetically by key words and alphabetically by titles for key words. The location of abstracts is indicated by page numbers.

LOCATING INFORMATION ABOUT INSTRUMENTS

Information about instruments' format, content, and administration procedures, together with reliability and validity estimates, can be found in yearbooks, handbooks, and professional journals.

Yearbooks and Handbooks

The major source of information on standardized tests are the *Mental Measurements Yearbooks (MMY)*. These have been published since 1938; the most recent are the *Ninth Mental Measurements Yearbook (9thMMY)* (Mitchell, 1985), the *Supplement to the Ninth Mental Measurements Yearbook* (9thMMY-S) (Conoley, Kramer, & Mitchell, 1988), and the *Tenth Mental Measurements Yearbook (10thMMY)* (Conoley & Kramer, 1989). They contain reviews of tests and selected bibliographies of related books and journal articles for each instrument.

The purposes of the latest *MMY*s are to provide (a) factual information on all known new or reviewed tests in the English-speaking world, (b) objective test reviews written specifically for the *MMY*s, and (c) comprehensive bibliographies, for specific tests, of related references from published literature. Each volume of the *MMY*s contains information on tests that have been published or significantly revised since a previous edition.

The *9thMMY*, *9thMMY-S* and *10thMMY* provide six indexes. The index of titles is an alphabetical listing of test titles. The classified subject index lists tests alphabetically under one or more classification headings, for example, Achievement, Intelligence, Mathematics, Personality, Reading. This index is of great help for those wishing to locate tests in a particular curriculum area. The publishers directory and index gives the names and addresses of the publishers of all the tests included in the *MMY*, as well as a list of test numbers for each publisher. The index of names includes the names of test developers and test reviewers, as well as authors of related references. The index of acronyms gives full titles for commonly used abbreviations. For example, someone may not know that DRP stands for Degrees of Reading Power. Each entry also gives the population for which the test is intended. The score index gives the subtest scores and their associated labels for each test. These labels are operational definitions of the tests' variables.

The organization of these *MMYs* is encyclopedic: All the test descriptions and reviews are presented alphabetically by test title. To find a particular test, the reader can go right to it without using any index. All test entries are given index numbers that are used in place of page numbers in all the indexes.

Entries for new or significantly revised tests in the tests and reviews section, the main body of the volume, include information such as title, author (developer), publisher, cost, a brief description, a description of groups for whom the test is intended, norming information, validity and reliability data, whether the test is a group or individual test, time requirements, test references, and critical reviews by qualified reviewers. Among other things, the reviews generally cite any special requirements or problems involved in test administration, scoring, or interpretation.

The classified subject index is a quick way to determine whether an instrument is reviewed within a particular volume of *MMY*. For example, in the classified subject index of *10thMMY* under *achievement* (p. 945), you will find the following entry (among others):

Metropolitan Achievement Tests, Sixth Edition, grades K.0–K.9, K.5–1.9, 1.5–2.9, 2.5–3.9, 3.5–4.9, 5.0–6.9, 7.0–9.9, 10.0–12.9, see 200.

Remember, the 200 means that the description of the Metropolitan Achievement Tests is *entry 200* in the main body of the volume; it does *not* mean that it is on page 200. Page numbers are used only for table of contents purposes.

However, the *Degrees of Reading Power* (DRP) cannot be found in either the achievement section or the reading section in *10thMMY* because it has not been significantly revised since its original publication. It *is* found in the reading section of *9thMMY* as

Degrees of Reading Power, grades 3–14, see 305.

A companion source of information about instruments is *Tests in Print (TIP)*, which contains comprehensive bibliographies of instruments that have been reviewed in *MMYs*. The latest edition, *TIP III*

(Mitchell, 1983) is structured in the same way as the classified subject index of *MMY*. Its value comes not from its reviews of instruments but from its listings of all tests that were in print at the time of publication, the location of test reviews in *MMY*s 1 through 8, and other writings about the instruments.

There are specialized volumes that contain information about instruments in various curriculum areas. These duplicate *MMY* information and reviews; their value comes from having test information for a particular discipline in a single volume. These monographs are:

English Tests and Reviews

Foreign Language Tests and Reviews

Intelligence Tests and Reviews

Mathematics Tests and Reviews

Personality Tests and Reviews

Reading Tests and Reviews

Science Tests and Reviews

Social Studies Tests and Reviews

Vocational Tests and Reviews

Additional specialized sources of test information reviews are:

A Sourcebook for Mental Health Measures

Advances in Psychological Assessment

Assessment in Gifted Children

Assessment Instruments in Bilingual Education

Bilingual Education Resource Guide

CSE Elementary School Test Evaluations

Directory of Unpublished Experimental Mental Measures

Evaluating Classroom Instruction: A Sourcebook of Instruments

Handbook for Measurement and Evaluation in Early Childhood Education

Instruments That Measure Self-Concept

Language Assessment Instruments for Limited English-Speaking Students

Measures for Psychological Assessment: A Guide to 3,000 Sources and Their Applications

Mirrors for Behavior III

Oral Language Tests for Bilingual Students

Preschool Test Descriptions

Psychological Testing and Assessment

Psychological Testing and Assessment of the Mentally Retarded

Reading Tests for Secondary Grades

Review of Tests and Assessments in Early Education

Scales for the Measurement of Attitudes

Screening and Evaluating the Young Child

Socioemotional Measures for Preschool and Kindergarten Children

Sociological Measurement

Tests and Measurements in Child Development

Tests Used with Exceptional Children

Testing Children: A Reference Guide for Effective Clinical and Psychological Assessments

Valuable companions to the *Ninth* and *Tenth MMYs* are *Tests: A Comprehensive Reference for Assessment in Psychology, Education, and Business* and *Tests: A Comprehensive Reference for Assessment in Psychology, Education, and Business—Supplement* (Sweetland & Keyser, 1985; 1984). These volumes contain listings of instruments by specialty areas.

Professional Journals and Textbooks

A number of professional journals and textbooks contain information and reviews of instruments. Journals such as the *Journal of Educational Measurement*, the *Journal of Reading*, and *The Reading Teacher* regularly contain reviews of new and revised instruments. Other journals published by professional associations often contain information about newly published instruments.

Several professional textbooks dealing with educational assessment and evaluation contain information and critiques about various types of instruments. The following contain extensive information about all types of instruments.

Compton, C. (1984). *A guide to 75 tests for special education.* Belmont, CA: Fearon Education/Pitman Learning.

Although the title suggests the book is intended only for special education, this is an excellent reference about instruments commonly used in research for measuring academic areas, perception and memory functions, speech and language areas, bilingual functioning, gross motor areas, and intelligence. Each entry contains basic information about an instrument, sample questions, and discussions of the instrument's strengths and limitations.

McLoughlin, J. A., & Lewis, R. B. (1986). Assessing Special Students (2nd ed.). Columbus, OH: Merrill.

The text contains descriptions of and critical comments about instruments commonly used in research for measuring school performance, learning attributes, classroom behavior, academic areas, and career and vocational interests.

SUMMARY

How is an educational problem defined before primary research reports are located?

After considering an educational problem, research consumers should refer to educational dictionaries for specific technical definitions.

How are integrative reviews and essays about research located?

Research consumers can locate an educational question in educational encyclopedias and journals specializing in publishing only integrative reviews and meta-analyses.

How are primary research reports located?

Primary research reports published in journals are located through the *Education Index (EI)* and the *Current Index to Journals in Education (CIJE)*. EI lists items alphabetically by subject heading. A reference item contains the article's title; the author's name; whether a bibliography is included; and the journal's title and volume number, the article's pages, and the date of publication. *CIJE* contains similar information as well as a brief annotation of the article's contents. Using *CIJE* necessitates several steps: (1) referring to the *Thesaurus of ERIC Descriptors*, (2) using the subject index and the author index to locate accession numbers, and (3) referring to the main entry section. The journals containing the selected articles are then located in the periodicals or microform section of the library. A wide variety of educational documents can be located through *Resources in Education (RIE)*, which is also part of the ERIC system and uses an indexing system identical to that used in *CIJE*. Using *RIE* necessitates several steps: (1) referring to the *Thesaurus of ERIC Descriptors*, (2) using the subject index and the author index to locate accession numbers, and (3) referring to the document resume section. The microfiche containing the documents' full text are filed by accession numbers in libraries' microform section. A companion ERIC resource is *Exceptional Child Education Resources (ECER)*. Other abstracts produced by specialty areas and for doctoral dissertations in education can be examined, too.

Where can information about instruments be located?

Research consumers can find descriptive information and critical reviews about instruments in yearbooks and handbooks, professional journals, and textbooks. The major source of this information are the *Mental Measurement Yearbooks*.

ACTIVITIES

Activity 1

Using the *Ninth Mental Measurements Yearbook* and one or more other sources discussed in the section "Locating Information About Instruments" (pp. 308–311), determine the appropriateness of the following instruments for the indicated research purposes.

Test of Adolescent Language (TOAL) by D. D. Hammill, V. L. Brown, S. C. Larsen, & J. L. Wiederholt (1980).

Purpose: To compare the language proficiency of high school students with and without learning disabilities and to determine the relationship between their language proficiency and reading achievement.

Slosson Intelligence Test for Children and Adults (SIT) by R. L. Slosson (1981).

Purpose: To identify the learning potential and establish profiles of learning strengths and weakness for students with limited English proficiency.

Boehm Test of Basic Concepts by A. E. Boehm (1971).

Purpose: To determine the effect of a special cognitive readiness instructional program on the concept attainment of kindergarten students.

Activity 2

1. Select an education topic related to your teaching situation and locate (a) the definition of at least one key term in an educational

dictionary, (b) one interpretive essay or integrative research reviews, (c) one primary research report in an educational, psychological, or other social science journal, and (d) one primary research report reproduced on microfiche in the ERIC system.

2. Using the questions and criteria for evaluating primary research reports and integrative research reviews or meta-analyses presented in this text (Chapters 3–9), evaluate the selected essays, reviews, and reports.

FEEDBACK

Activity 1

1. TOAL is an appropriate instrument to use in the comparative part of the study. Since the TOAL contains a reading subsection, the correlation with another reading test might be expected. For this part of the study, some other language proficiency test, less dependent on reading, might be more appropriate. Also, the TOAL is a lengthy test and might discriminate against students with learning disabilities.

2. Individuals with limited English proficiency were not part of the norming group for the SIT. Therefore, it would be inappropriate to use the test in this study.

3. The Boehm is appropriate to use with kindergarten students. Some care should be taken in interpreting the results since there may be a learning effect from the pretest to the posttest. That effect can be measured if the researchers use a posttest-only control group. Also, the treatment program should be examined to ensure that specific items similar to the test items on the Boehm are not taught.

Activity 2

Feedback will be provided by your course instructor.

References

Abrami, P. C., Cohen, P. A., & d'Apollonia, S. (1988). Implementation problems in meta-analysis. *Review of Educational Research, 58*, 151–180.

Abramson, M., Willson, V., Yoshida, R. K., & Hagerty, G. (1983). Parents' perceptions of their learning disabled child's educational performance. *Learning Disability Quarterly, 6*, 184–194.

Aksamit, D. L., & Alcorn, D. A. (1988). A preservice mainstream curriculum infusion model: Student teachers' perceptions of program effectiveness. *Teacher Education and Special Education, 11*, 52–58.

Allen, J. D. (1986). Classroom management: Students' perspectives, goals, and strategies. *American Educational Research Journal, 23*, 437–459.

Alvermann, D. E. (1988). Effects of spontaneous and induced lookbacks on self-perceived high- and low-ability comprehenders. *The Journal of Educational Research, 81*, 325–331.

Anderson, R. C., Wilson, P. T., & Fielding, L. G. (1988). Growth in reading and how children spend their time outside of school. *Reading Research Quarterly, 23*, 285–303.

Babad, E., Bernieri, F., & Rosenthal, R. (1987). Nonverbal and verbal behavior of preschool, remedial, and elementary school teachers. *American Educational Research Journal, 24*, 405–415.

Balow, I. H., Farr, R., Hogan, T. P., & Prescott, G. A. (1985). *Metropolitan achievement tests* (6th ed.). Cleveland: Psychological Corporation.

Berliner, D. C. (1987). Knowledge is power: A talk to teachers about a revolution in the teaching profession. In D. C. Berliner & B. V. Rosenshine (Eds.), *Talks to teachers: A festschrift for N. L. Gage* (pp. 3–33). New York: Random House.

Blase, J. J. (1986). A qualitative analysis of sources of teacher stress: Consequences for performance. *American Educational Research Journal, 23*, 13–40.

Blase, J. J. (1987). Dimensions of effective school leadership: The teacher's perspective. *American Educational Research Journal, 24*, 589–610.

Bleakley, M. E., Westerberg, V., & Hopkins, K. D. (1988). The effect of character sex on story interest and comprehension in children. *American Educational Research Journal, 25*, 145–155.

Boehm, A. E. (1971). *Boehm test of basic concepts.* Cleveland: Psychological Corporation.

Bogdan, R. C., & Biklen, S. K. (1982). *Qualitative research for education: An introduction to theory and methods.* Boston: Allyn and Bacon.

Borg, W. R. (1987). *Applying educational research: A practical guide for teachers.* White Plains, NY: Longman.

Borg, W. R. & Gall, M. D. (1983). *Educational research: An Introduction* (4th ed). White Plains, NY: Longman.

Brown, V. L., Hammill, D. D., & Wiederholt, J. L. (1978). 1. Reading Comprehension: A Frame of Reference. *The Test of Reading Comprehension: A Method for Assessing the Understanding of Written Language* (pp. 5–11). Austin, TX: PRO-ED.

Burns, J. M., & Collins, M. D. (1987). Parents' perceptions of factors affecting the reading development of intellectually superior accelerated readers and intellectually superior nonreaders. *Reading Research and Instruction, 26*, 239–246.

Burns, R. B., & Lash, A. A. (1986). A comparison of activity structures during basic skills and problem-solving instruction in seventh-grade mathematics. *American Educational Research Journal, 23*, 393–414.

Bursuck, W. D., & Lesson, E. (1987). A classroom-based model for assessing students with learning disabilities. *Learning Disabilities Focus, 3*, 17–29.

Campbell, D. T. & Stanley, J. C. (1963). *Experimental and quasi-experimental designs for research.* Chicago: Rand McNally.

Carlberg, C. G., Johnson, D. W., Johnson, R., Maruyama, G., Kavale, K., Kulik, C., Kulik, J. A., Lysakowski, R. S., Pflaum, S. W., & Walberg, H. J. (1984). Meta-analysis in education: A reply to Slavin. *Educational Researcher, 13*(8), 16–23.

Clements, D. H., & Nastasi, B. K. (1988). Social and cognitive interactions in educational computer environments. *American Educational Research Journal, 25*, 87–106.

Comprehensive test of basic skills (1988, 4th ed.). New York: CTB/McGraw Hill.

Cooperative learning. (1989–1990). *Educational Leadership, 47*(4).

Cooper, H. M. (1982). Scientific guidelines for conducting integrative research reviews. *Review of Educational Research, 52*, 291–302.

Conoley, J. C., & Kramer, J. J. (Eds.) (1989). *Tenth Mental Measurements Yearbook.* Lincoln, NE: University of Nebraska Press.

Conoley, J. C., Kramer, J. J., & Mitchell, J. V., Jr. (Eds.) (1988). *Supplement to the Ninth Mental Measurements Yearbook.* Lincoln, NE: University of Nebraska Press.

Corno, L. (1987). Teaching and self-regulating learning. In D. C. Berliner & B. V. Rosenshine (Eds.), *Talks to teachers: A* festschrift *for N. L. Gage* (pp. 249–266). New York: Random House.

Crooks, T. J. (1988). The impact of classroom evaluation practices on students. *Review of Educational Research, 58*, 438–481.

Dar, Y., & Resh, N. (1986). Classroom intellectual composition and academic achievement. *American Educational Research Journal, 23*, 357–374.

DeLain, M. T., Pearson, P. D., & Anderson, R. C. (1985). Reading comprehension and creativity in black language use: You stand to gain by playing the sounding game! *American Educational Research Journal, 22*, 155–173.

Duffelmeyer, F. A., & Adamson, S. (1986). Matching students with instructional level materials using the *Degrees of Reading Power* system. *Reading Research and Instruction, 25*, 192–200.

Elley, W. B. (1989). Vocabulary acquisition from listening to stories. *Reading Research Quarterly, 24*, 174–187.

Fagan, W. T. (1988). Concepts of reading and writing among low literate adults. *Reading Research and Instruction, 27*(4), 47–60.

Firestone, W. A. (1987). Meaning in method: The rhetoric of quantitative and qualitative research. *Educational Researcher, 17*(7), 16–21.

Fiske, E. B. (1983). Etzioni wants to shift focus to the students. *The New York Times*, November 1, C1,C9.

Fleisher, B. M. (1988). Oral reading cue strategies of better and poor readers. *Reading Research and Instruction, 27*, 35–60.

Fuchs, D., & Fuchs. L. S. (1986). Test procedure bias: A meta-analysis of examiner familiarity effects. *Review of Educational Research, 56*, 243–262.

Fuchs, D. & Fuchs, L. S. (1989). Effects of examiner familiarity on Black, Caucasian, and Hispanic children: A meta-analysis. *Exceptional Children, 55*, 303–308.

Gay, L. R. (1987). *Educational research: Competencies for analysis and application* (3rd ed.). Columbus, OH: Merrill.

Getsie, R. L., Langer, P., & Glass, G. V (1985). Meta-analysis of the effects of type and combination of feedback on children's discrimination learning. *Review of Educational Research, 55*, 9–22.

Glass, G. V. (1976). Primary, secondary, and meta-analysis of research. *Educational Researcher, 5 (10)*, 3–8.

Good, C. V. (1973). *Dictionary of education* (3rd ed.). New York: McGraw Hill.

Goodwin, L. D., Goodwin, W. L., Nansel, A., & Helm, C. P. (1986). Cognitive and affective effects of various types of microcomputer use by preschoolers. *American Educational Research Journal, 23*, 348–356.

Greenbaum, P. E. (1985). Nonverbal differences in communication style between American Indian and Anglo elementary classrooms. *American Educational Research Journal, 22*, 101–115.

Guthrie, L. F., & Hall, W. S. (1984). Ethnographic approaches to reading research. In P. D. Pearson, R. Barr, M. L. Kamil, & P. Mosenthal (Eds.). *Handbook of reading research* (pp. 91–110). New York: Longman.

Guthrie, L. F., Seifert, M., & Kirsch, I. S. (1986). Effects of education, occupation, and setting on reading practices. *American Educational Research Journal, 23*, 151–160.

Haertel, G. D., Walberg, H. J., Junker, L., & Pascarella, E. T. (1981). Early adolescent sex differences in science learning: Evidence from the National Assessment of Educational Progress. *American Educational Research Journal, 18*, 329–341.

Hallinan, M. T., & Sørensen, A. B. (1985). Ability grouping and student friendships. *American Educational Research Journal, 22*, 485–499.

Harris, T. L., & Hodges, R. E. (Eds.). (1981). *A dictionary of reading and related terms*. Newark, DE: International Reading Association.

Hill, J. W., Seyfarth, J., Banks, P. D., Wehman, P., & Orelove, F. (1987). Parent attitudes about working conditions of their adult mentally retarded sons and daughters. *Exceptional Children, 54*, 9–23.

Hoover-Dempsey, K. V., Bassler, O. C., & Brissie, J. S. (1987). Parent involvement: Contributions of teacher efficacy, school socioeconomic status, and other school characteristics. *American Educational Research Journal, 24*, 417–435.

Howe, K. R. (1988). Against the quantitative–qualitative incompatibility thesis or dogmas die hard. *Educational Researcher, 17*(8), 10–16.

Hughes, C. A., Ruhl, K. L., & Gorman, J. (1987). Preparation of special educators to work with parents: A survey of teachers and teacher educators. *Teacher Education and Special Education, 10*, 81–87.

Hunsucker, P. F., Nelson, R. O., & Clark, R. P. (1986). Standardization and evaluation of the Classroom Adaptive Behavior Checklist for school use. *Exceptional Children, 53,* 69–71.

Jackson, G. B. (1980). Methods for integrative reviews. *Review of Educational Research, 50,* 438–460.

Jacob, E. (1989). Qualitative research: A response to Atkinson, Delamont, and Hammersley. *Review of Educational Research, 59,* 229–235.

Jacob, E. (1987). Qualitative research traditions: A review. *Review of Educational Research, 57,* 1–50.

Jacob, E. (1988). Clarifying qualitative research: A focus on traditions. *Educational Researcher, 17*(1), 16–24.

Joint Committee on Standards for Educational Evaluation (1981). *Standards for evaluation of educational programs, projects, and materials.* New York: McGraw-Hill.

Joyce, B. (1987). A rigorous yet delicate touch: A response to Slavin's proposal for "best-evidence" reviews. *Educational Researcher, 16*(4), 12–14.

Kamil, M. L. Langer, J. A., & Shanahan, T. (1985). *Understanding research in reading and writing.* Boston: Allyn & Bacon.

Kerlinger, F. N. (1973). *Foundations of behavioral research: Education, psychological, and sociological inquiry.* (2nd ed.). New York: Holt, Rinehart & Winston.

Kinzie, M. B., Sullivan, H. J., & Berdel, R. L. (1988). Learner control and achievement in science computer-assisted instruction. *Journal of Educational Psychology, 80,* 299–303.

Konopak, B. C. (1988). Eighth graders' vocabulary learning from inconsiderate and considerate text. *Reading Research and Instruction, 27,* 1–14.

Ladas, H. (1980). Summarizing research: A case study. *Review of Educational Research, 50,* 597–624.

Langer, J. A. (1984). The effects of available information on responses to school writing. *Research in the Teaching of English, 18,* 27–44.

Lass, B. (1984). Do teachers individualize their responses to reading miscues?: A study of feedback during oral reading. *Reading World, 23,* 242–254.

LeCompte, M. D. & Goetz, J. P. (1982). Problems of reliability and validity in ethnographic research. *Review of Educational Research, 52,* 31–60.

Lehr, S. (1988). The child's developing sense of theme as a response to literature. *Reading Research Quarterly, 23,* 337–357.

Leinhardt, G., & Pallay, A. (1982). Restrictive educational settings: Exile or haven? *Review of Educational Research, 52,* 557–578.

Leithwood, K. A., & Montgomery, D. J. (1982). The role of the elementary school principal in program improvement. *Review of Educational Research, 52,* 309–339.

Lincoln, Y. S., & Guba, E. G. (1985). *Naturalistic inquiry.* Beverly Hills, CA: Sage.

McDaniel-Hine, L. C., & Willower, D. J. (1988). Elementary school teachers' work behavior. *Journal of Educational Research, 81,* 274–280.

McKeown, M. G., Beck, I. L., Omanson, R. C., & Pople, M. T. (1985). Some effects of the nature and frequency of vocabulary instruction on the knowledge and use of words. *Reading Research Quarterly, 20,* 522–535.

McKinney, C. W., Larkins, A. G., Ford, M. J., & Davis, J. C. III. (1983). The effectiveness of three methods of teaching social studies concepts to fourth-grade students: An aptitude–treatment interaction study. *American Educational Research Journal, 20,* 663–670.

Madden, N. A., & Slavin, R. E. (1983). Mainstreaming students with mild handicaps: Academic and social outcomes. *Review of Educational Research*, 53, 519–1169.

Maeroff, G. I. (1982). Specific TV shows tied to child's achievement. *The New York Times*, March 30, C9.

Mandoli, M., Mandoli, P., & McLaughlin, T. F. (1982). Effects of same-age peer tutoring on the spelling performance of a mainstreamed elementary LD stdudent. *Learning Disability Quarterly*, 5, 185–189.

Manning, B. H. (1988). Application of cognitive behavior modification: First and third graders' self-management of classroom behaviors. *American Educational Research Journal*, 25, 193–212.

Manning, M., Manning, G., & Cody, C. B. (1988). Reading aloud to young children: Perspectives of parents. *Reading Research and Instruction*, 27, 56–61.

Martineck, T. J., & Butt, K. (1988). An application of an action research model for changing instructional practice. *Journal of Teaching in Physical Education*, 7, 214–220.

Mitchell, J. V. Jr. (Ed.). (1983). *Tests in print III: An index to tests, test reviews, and the literature on specific tests*. Lincoln, NE: University of Nebraska Press.

Mitchell, J. V. Jr. (Ed.). (1985). *The ninth mental measurements yearbook.* Lincoln, NE: University of Nebraska Press.

Morrow, L. M. (1985). Attitudes of teachers, principals, and parents toward promoting voluntary reading in the elementary school. *Reading Research and Instruction*, 25, 116–130.

Morrow, L. M. (1988). Young children's responses to one-to-one story readings in school settings. *Reading Research Quarterly*, 23, 89–107.

Nist, S. L., & Hogrebe, M. C. (1987). The role of underlining and annotating in remembering textual information. *Reading Research and Instruction*, 27, 12–15.

Olson, M. W. (1990). The teacher as researcher: A historical perspective. In M. W. Olson (Ed.). *Opening the door to classroom research* (pp. 1–20). Newark, DE: International Reading Association.

Osborne, S. (1985). Effects of teacher experience and selected temperament variables on coping strategies used with distractible children. *American Educational Research Journal*, 22, 79–86.

Pascarella, E. T., Pflaum, S. W., Bryan, T. H., & Pearl, R. A. (1983). Interaction of internal attribution for effort and teacher response mode in reading instruction: A replication note. *American Educational Research Journal*, 20, 269–276.

Pomplun, M. (1988). Retention: The earlier, the better? *Journal of Educational Research*, 81, 281–286.

Popham, W. J., & Sirotnik, K. A. (1967). *Educational statistics: Use and interpretation* (2nd ed.). New York: Harper & Row.

Radebaugh, M. R. (1983). The effects of pre-organized reading material on the comprehension of fourth and fifth grade readers. *Reading World*, 23, 20–28.

Reinking, D., & Schreiner, R. (1985). The effects of computer mediated text on measures of reading comprehension and reading behavior. *Reading Research Quarterly*, 20, 536–552.

Richgels, D. J. (1986). Grade school children's listening and reading comprehension of complex sentences. *Reading Research and Instruction, 25,* 201–219.

Ross, J. A. (1988). Improving social–environmental studies problem solving through cooperative learning. *American Educational Research Journal, 25,* 573–591.

Rowe, D. W., & Cunningham, P. M. (1983). The effect of two instructional strategies on kindergartners' concept of word. In J. A. Niles & L. A. Harris (Eds.), *Searches for meaning in reading/language processing and instruction* (pp. 226–230). Yearbook of the National Reading Conference.

Rowe, D. W., & Rayford L. (1987). Activating background knowledge in reading comprehension assessment. *Reading Research Quarterly, 22,* 160–176.

Santa, C. M. (1988). Changing teacher behavior in content reading through collaborative research. In S. J. Samuels & P. D. Pearson (Eds.). *Changing school reading programs: Principles and case studies* (pp. 185–204). Newark, DE: International Reading Association.

Schneider, W., & Treiber, B. (1984). Classroom differences in the determination of achievement changes. *American Educational Research Journal, 21,* 195–211.

Scruggs, T. E., Mastropieri, M. A., Levin, J. R., & Gaffney, J. S. (1985). Facilitating the acquisition of science facts in learning disabled students. *American Educational Research Journal, 22,* 575–586.

Shanahan, T., & Kamil, M. (1982). The sensitivity of cloze to passage organization. In J. A. Niles & L. A. Harris (Eds.). *New inquiries in reading research and instruction.* Thirty-first Yearbook of the National Reading Conference, 204–208.

Shapiro, S. (1985). An analysis of poetry teaching procedures in sixth-grade basal manuals. *Reading Research Quarterly, 20,* 368–381.

Slavin, R. E. (1983). *Cooperative learning.* New York: Longman.

Slavin, R. E. (1984a). Meta-analysis in education: How has it been used? *Educational Researcher, 13*(8), 6–15.

Slavin, R. E. (1984b). A rejoinder to Carlberg et al. *Educational Researcher, 13*(8). 24–27.

Slavin, R. E. (1986). Best-evidence synthesis: An alternative to meta-analytic and traditional reviews. *Educational Researcher, 15*(9), 5–11.

Slavin, R. E. (1987a). *Cooperative learning: Student teams.* Washington, D.C.: National Education Association.

Slavin, R. E. (1987b). Best-evidence synthesis: Why less is more. *Educational Researcher, 16*(4), 15–16.

Slavin, R. E. (1987c). Mastery learning reconsidered. *Review of Educational Research, 57,* 175–213.

Smith M. L. (1987). Publishing qualitative research. *American Educational Research Journal, 24,* 173–183.

Smith, J. K., & Heshusius, L. (1986). Closing down the conversation: The end of the quantitative–qualitative debate among educational inquirers. *Educational Researcher, 15*(1), 4–12.

Solomon, D., Watson, M. S., Delucchi, K. L., Schaps, E., & Battistich, V. (1988). Enchancing children's prosocial behavior in the classroom. *American Educational Research Journal, 25,* 527–554.

Sparks, G. M. (1986). The effectiveness of alternative training activities in changing teaching practices. *American Educational Research Journal, 23,* 217–225.

Stahl, S. A., & Clark, C. H. (1987). The effects of participatory expectations in classroom discussion on the learning of science vocabulary. *American Educational Research Journal, 24,* 541–555.

Stahl, S. A., & Fairbanks, M. M. (1986). The effects of vocabulary instruction: A model-based meta-analysis. *Review of Educational Research, 56,* 72–110.

Stock W. A., Okun, M. A., Haring, M. J., Miller, W., Kinney, C., Ceurvost, R. W. (1982). Rigor in data synthesis: A case study of reliability in meta-analysis. *Educational Researcher, 11*(6), 10–14.

Sundbye, N. (1987). Text explicitness and inferential questioning: Effects on story understanding and recall. *Reading Research Quarterly, 22,* 82–98.

Swanson, B. B. (1985). Teacher judgments of first-graders' reading enthusiasm. *Reading Research and Instruction, 25,* 41–36.

Sweetland, R. C., & Keyser, D. J. (1983). *Tests: A comprehensive reference for assessments in psychology, education, and business.* Kansas City, MO: Test Corporation of America.

Sweetland, R. C., & Keyser, D. J. (1984). *Tests: A comprehensive reference for assessments in psychology, education, and business*—Supplement. Kansas City, MO: Test Corporation of America.

Thames, D. G., & Readence, J. E. (1988). Effects of differential vocabulary instruction and lesson frameworks on the reading comprehension of primary children. *Reading Research and Instruction, 27,* 1–12.

Van Maanen, J., Dabbs, J. M. Jr., & Faulkner, R. R. (1982). *Varieties of qualitative research.* Beverly Hills, CA: Sage.

Vukelich, C. (1986). The relationship between peer questions and seven-year-olds' text revisions. In J. A. Niles & R. V. Lalik (Eds.), *Solving problems in literacy: Learners, teachers, and researchers* (pp. 300–305). Thirty-fifth Yearbook of the National Reading Conference.

Webb, N. M., Ender, P., & Lewis, S. (1986). Problem-solving strategies and group processes in small groups learning computer programming. *American Educational Research Journal, 23,* 243–261.

Wechsler, D. (1974). *Wechsler intelligence scale for children—Revised.* Cleveland, OH: Psychological Corporation.

Welch, W. W., Anderson, R. E., & Harris, L. J. (1982). The effects of schooling on mathematics achievement. *American Educational Research Journal, 19,* 145–153.

Wiener, J. (1987). Peer status of learning disabled children and adolescents: A review of the literature. *Learning Disabilities Research, 2,* 62–79.

Wiersma, W. (1986). *Research methods in education: An introduction* (4th ed.). Boston: Allyn & Bacon.

Wilkinson, I. Wardrop, J. L., & Anderson, R. C. (1988). Silent reading reconsidered: Reinterpreting reading instruction and its effects. *American Educational Research Journal, 25,* 127–144.

Willig, A. C. (1985). A meta-analysis of selected studies on the effectiveness of bilingual education. *Review of Educational Research, 55,* 269–317.

Wilson, S. (1977). The use of ethonographic techniques in educational research. *Review of Educational Research, 47,* 245–265.

Wixson, K. K. (1986). Vocabulary instruction and children's comprehension of basal stories. *Reading Research Quarterly, 21,* 317–329.

Woodcock, R. W. (1973). *Woodcock reading mastery tests.* Circle Pines, MN: American Guidance Service.

Yopp, H. K. (1988). The validity and reliability of phonemic awareness tests. *Reading Research Quarterly, 23,* 159–177.

Zutell, J., & Rasinski, T. (1986). Spelling ability and reading fluency. In J. A. Niles & R. V. Lalik (Eds.), *Solving problems in literacy: Learners, teachers, and researchers* (pp. 109–112). Yearbook of the National Reading Conference.

APPENDICES

Appendix A

abstract—a summary of a research report.

accessible populations—groups that are convenient to the researcher and are representative of the target population. Practical considerations that lead to the use of an accessible population include time, money, and physical accessibility.

action research—directed to studying existing educational practice and to producing practical, immediately applicable findings. The questions or problems studied are local in nature (e.g., to a specific class), and generalizability to other educational situations is not important to the researchers. Often action research is a collaboration between classroom teachers without research expertise and trained researchers.

action research reviews—reviews of research produced for local consumption.

analysis of covariance (ANCOVA)—allows researchers to examine differences among the means of groups of subjects as if they were equal from the start. They do this by adjusting the differences in the means to make them hypothetically equal.

analysis of variance (ANOVA)—used to show differences among the means of two or more groups of subjects or two or more variables. It is reported in *F*-ratios. The advantage in using an ANOVA is that several variables as well as several factors can be examined. In its simplest form, ANOVA can be thought of as a multiple *t*-test.

background section—contains (a) an explanation of the researcher's problem area, (b) its educational importance, (c) summaries of other researchers' results that are related to the problem (called a *literature review*), and (d) strengths from the related research that were used and weaknesses or limitations that were changed.

base-line measure—the pretest in single-subject research; it can take the form of one or several measurements.

best evidence—a technique for selecting and reviewing studies for inclusion in research reviews. Studies are selected only if they are specifically related to the topic, are methodologically adequate, and are generalizable to a specific situation.

case study—a form of single-subject research. Case studies are undertaken on the premise that someone who is typical of a target population can be located and studied. In case studies the individual's (a) history within an educational setting can be traced, (b) growth pattern(s) over time can be shown, (c) functioning in one or more situations can be examined, and (d) response(s) to one or more treatments can be measured.

causal–comparative research—establishing causations based on preexisting independent variables. Researchers do not induce differences in an experimental situation; instead they seek to identify one or more preexisting conditions (independent variables) in one group that exist to a lesser degree in the other. When one or more conditions are identified, they can attribute causality. Also called *ex post facto research*.

causative research. See *experimental research*.

central tendency, measure of—the average or middle score in a group of scores. The middle score is called the median; the arithmetical average score is called the mean.

Chi-square test—a nonparametric statistic used to test the significance of group differences when data are reported as frequencies or percentages of a total or as nominal scales.

cluster sampling—when intact groups are selected because of convenience or accessibility. This procedure is especially common in *causal–comparative research*.

coefficient of correlation—the results of an arithmetic computation done as part of a product–moment correlation. It is expressed as r, a decimal between -1.0 and $+1.0$. (See *product-moment correlation* and *Pearson product-moment correlation*.)

comparative research—provides an explanation about the extent of a relationship between two or more variables or examines differences or relationships among several variables. These variables might represent characteristics of the same group of subjects or those of separate groups.

conclusion section—a section of a research report containing the researcher's ideas about the educational implications of the research results.

concurrent validity—extent to which the results show that individuals' scores correlate, or are similar, on two instruments.

construct validity—when an instrument's creator demonstrates the instrument as representing a supportable theory.

content validity—when an instruments' creators demonstrate the specific items or questions represent an accurate sampling of specific bodies of knowledge (i.e., curricula or courses of study).

control group—the group of subjects in experimental research not receiving the experimental condition or treatment. Sometimes called the *comparison group*.

control—procedures used by researchers to limit or account for the possible influence of variables not being studied.

correlation—shows the extent to which two or more variables have a systematic relationship.

counterbalanced design—two or more groups get the same treatment; however, the order of the treatments for each group is different and is usually randomly determined. For this type of design to work, the number of treatments and groups must match. Although the groups may be randomly selected and assigned, researchers often use this design with already existing groups of subjects.

criterion-referenced tests—determine whether an individual or group has achieved a certain level of mastery. A criterion-referenced test is a set of goals representing a set of tasks that students are supposed to master. Scores on these tests show subjects' placement in relation to a set of goals. They do not show subjects' rankings compared to a standardization group, as norm-referenced tests do. A *standardized criterion-referenced test* is one for which the administration and scoring procedures are uniform but the scoring is in relation to the established goals, not to a norm group.

cross validation—when researchers investigate the same purpose, method, and data analysis procedure but use subjects from a different population.

dependent variable—the variable researchers make the acted-upon variable. It is the variable whose value may change as the result of the experimental treatment (the *independent variable*).

descriptive research—provides information about one or more variables. It is used to answer the question "What exists?" This question can be answered in one of two ways: using *quantitative methods* or *qualitative methods*.

descriptors—key words found in the *ERIC Thesaurus* and used in indexing documents such as *Resources in Education* and *Current Journals in Education*.

design—the plan used to study an educational problem or question. Three broad designs categories are descriptive, comparative, and causative.

direct observation—researchers take extensive field notes or use observation forms to record information. They categorize information on forms in response to questions about subjects' actions or categories of actions. Or, researchers tally subjects' actions during a time period within some predetermined categories. *Field notes* consist of written narratives describing subjects' behavior or performance during an instructional activity. These notes are then analyzed and the information categorized for reporting. The analysis can start with predetermined categories and information from the notes is recorded accordingly. Or, the analysis can be open-ended in that the researchers cluster similar information and then create a label for each cluster.

directional hypothesis—used when previous research evidence supports a statement of the specific way one variable will affect another variable (also called a *one-tailed hypothesis*).

ERIC or Educational Resources Information Centers—a national network supported by the Office of Education Research and Improvement of the U.S. Department of Education. The purpose of ERIC is to provide access to current research results and related information in the field of education. It is a decentralized system composed of about sixteen clearinghouses, each specializing in a major education area.

effect sizes—created during meta-analyses. They are standard scores created from a ratio derived from the mean scores of the experimental and control groups and the standard deviations of the control groups. Effect size scores show the size of the differences between the experimental and control groups in relation to the standard deviation.

equivalent forms reliability—(sometimes called *parallel forms reliability*) is determined by correlating the scores from two forms of an instrument given to the same subjects. The instruments differ only in the specific nature of the items.

ethnographic research—term is often used synonymously with *qualitative research method*, but some researchers consider ethnography a subtype of qualitative research.

evaluation research—applying the rigors of research to the judging of the worth or value of educational programs, projects, and instruction. It extends the principle of action research, which is primarily of local interest, so that generalizations may be made to other educational situations. And, although undertaken for different reasons than is experimental research, the quantitative research method used in evaluation research is based on that of experimental research.

experimental condition—how the independent variable is manipulated, varied, or subcategorized in experimental research. Also called *treatment*.

experimental designs—the blueprints that researchers use to decide about causative effects; the plans provide researchers with structures for studying one or more independent variables with one or more groups of subjects. Researchers select designs that best fit their purposes, answer questions about causation, and efficiently control extraneous variables.

experimental group—the group of subjects in experimental research receiving the experimental condition or treatment.

experimental research—answers questions about causation. Researchers wish to attribute the change in one variable to the effect of one or more other variables. The variables causing changes in subjects' responses or performance are the *independent variables*. The variables whose measurements may change are the *dependent variables*. The measurements can be made with any instrument type: survey, test, or observation.

external validity—researchers' assurance that results can be generalized to other persons and other settings.

extraneous variables—variables that might have an unwanted influence, or might change, on dependent variables. Researchers can restrict the influence of extraneous variables by controlling *subject variables* and *situational variables*.

F ratio—ways in which an analysis of variance (ANOVA) and analysis of covariance (ANCOVA) are reported.

face validity—the extent to which an instrument *appears* to measure a specific body of information. In other words, "Does the instrument look as if it would measure what it intends to measure?"

factorial designs—research studies in which there are multiple variables and each is subcategorized into two or more levels, or factors. The simplest factorial design involves two independent variables, each of which has two factors. This is called a 2 × 2 factorial design. Factorial designs can have any combination of variables and factors.

generalizability—when results can be extended to other students or the target population. That means, a research consumer in a different place can have confidence in applying the first researcher's results.

hypothesis—a tentative statement about how two or more variables are related. A hypothesis is the researchers' conjectural statement of the relationship between the research variables and is created after the investigators have examined the related literature but before they undertake their study. It is a tentative explanation for certain behaviors, phenomena, or events that have occurred or will occur.

independent variable—the influencing variable in experimental research; the one to which researchers wish to attribute causation. Sometimes the independent variable is called the *experimental variable*. When the independent variable is an activity of the researcher, it is called a treatment variable.

instruments—denotes a broad range of specific devices and procedures for collecting, sorting, and categorizing information about subjects and research questions.

instruments section—contains a description of the data collection instruments: observation forms, standardized and researcher-made tests, and surveys.

integrative reviews of research—critical examinations of research producers' methods and conclusions and of the generalizability of their combined findings.

internal consistency reliability—determined by comparing the subjects' scores on individual items to their scores on each of the other items and to their scores on the instrument as a whole. Sometimes called rationale equivalence reliability.

internal validity—researchers' assurance that changes to dependent variables can be attributed to independent variables.

interval scales—the most common form of data reporting in educational social science research. Interval scales present data according to preset, equal spans and are identified by continuous measurement scales: raw scores and derived scores such as IQ scores, percentiles, stanines, standard scores, normal curve equivalents. They are the way data from most tests are recorded.

interrater/interjudge reliability. See *scorer reliability*.

interviews—used to obtain structured or open-ended responses from subjects. They differ from questionnaires in that the researcher can modify the data-collection situation to fit the respondent's responses.

inventories—questionnaires that require subjects to respond to statements, questions, or category labels with a "yes" or "no" or ask subjects to check off appropriate information within a category.

Likert-type scale—forced choice procedure used on some scales, for example, "Always," "Sometimes," or "Never." Each response is assigned a value; a value of *1* represents the least positive response.

literature review—contains summaries of related research; in it, researchers indicate strengths from the related research that were used in their study and weaknesses or limitations that were changed.

matched groups design—the experimental and control groups are selected or assigned to groups on the basis of a single subject variable such as reading ability, grade level, ethnicity, or special disabling condition.

mean—the arithmetical average score.

median—the middle score in a group of scores.

meta-analyses of research—ways of critically examining primary research studies in which quantitative data analyses were used. Research reviewers use meta-analyses as analyses of analyses (statistical data analyses of already completed statistical data analyses). In them, they convert the statistical results of the individual studies into a common measurement so they can obtain an overall, combined result.

method section—a section of a research report usually containing three subsections: *subjects, instruments*, and *procedures*.

multiple regression technique—used to examine the relationships among more than two variables. The procedure is interpreted similarly to a single correlation coefficient. It can be used to make predictions. The technique is used frequently in causal—comparative experimental research.

nominal scales—data reported as number of items or as percentages of a total. Data from surveys and observations are often recorded in this way.

nondirectional research hypothesis—a statement used when a researcher has strong evidence from examining previous research that a relationship or effect exists, but the evidence does not provide indications about the direction (positive or negative) of the influence.

nonequivalent control group design—in which the groups have not been randomly selected or assigned and no effort is made to equate them statistically.

nonparametric statistics—used with data that are measured in nominal and ordinal scales. These statistics work on different assumptions than do parametric statistics.

norm-referenced tests—measure individuals' performance compared to a standardization, or norming, group. A *norming group* consists of individuals used in researching the standardization of the tests' administration.

normal distribution curve—represents how human variables can be seen to be distributed among a normal, or typical, population. Other names are the *normal probability curve*, or *bell-shaped curve*.

norming group—the individuals used in researching the standardization of the administration and scoring of norm-referenced tests.

one-tailed hypothesis. See *directional hypothesis*.

operational definition—a definition of a variable that gives the precise way an occurrence of that variable is viewed by researchers.

ordinal scales, or **rankings**—show the order, from highest to lowest, for a variable. There are no indications as to the value or size of differences between or among items in a list; the indications refer only to the relative order of the scores.

parallel forms reliability. See *equivalent forms reliability*.

parametric statistics—statistical procedures used with interval scales and based on certain assumptions, all of which are related to the concept of a normal distribution curve.

participant observer—a qualitative researcher who goes to the particular setting being studied and participates in the activities of the people in that setting. Researchers functioning in this role try to maintain a middle position on a continuum of complete independence as an observer to complete involvement in the people's activities.

Pearson product–moment correlation—the most common correlation coefficient. (See *product-moment correlation* and *coefficient of correlation*.)

pilot study—a limited research project usually with a few subjects that follows the original research plan in every respect. By analyzing the results, research producers can identify potential problems.

population—the group of individuals having at least one characteristic that distinguishes them from other groups. A population can be any size and can include people from any place in the world.

posttest—second and subsequent measurements after a pretest.

posttest-only control group design—the experimental and control groups are not pretested. An example of this design is two or more randomized groups being engaged in comparison activities without being given a pretest.

practical significance—a determination about how useful research results are. To determine this, research consumers need to answer: How effectively can the results be used in my teaching situation?

predictive validity—determined by comparing a sample's results on the instrument to their results after some other activity.

pretest—used to collect initial, or baseline, data.

pretest–posttest control group design—all groups are given the same pretest and posttest (survey, observation, or test).

procedure section—a subsection of the methods section containing a detailed explanation of how researchers conducted their study.

product-moment correlation—refers to the quantified relationship between two sets of scores for the same group of subjects. The result of the arithmetical computation is a coefficient of correlation, which is expressed as r, a decimal between -1.0 and $+1.0$. The most common interval scale correlation coefficient is the Pearson product-moment r. Correlations show whether two or more variables have a systematic relationship of occurrence—that is, whether high scores for one variable occur with high scores of another (a positive relationship) or whether they occur with low scores of that other variable (a negative relationship). A low score for one variable occurring with a low score of another is also an example of a positive relationship. A correlational coefficient of zero (0) indicates that the two variables have no relationship with each other, that is, are independent of each other.

purpose section—contains the specific goal or goals of the research project. These can be expressed as a statement of purpose, as questions, or as hypotheses.

qualitative research method—a term used for a broad range of research strategies that have roots in the field research of anthropology and sociology. It involves collecting data within natural settings, and the key data collection instruments are the researchers themselves. Qualitative research method data are verbal, not numerical. Since qualitative researchers are concerned equally with the process of activities and events as they are with results from those activities or events, they analyze data through inductive reasoning rather than by statistical procedures.

quantitative research method—procedure involving the assignment of numerical values to variables. The most common quantitative descriptive measures researchers use are the *mean*, a measure of central tendency, and the *standard deviation*, a measure of the variability of the data around the mean.

questionnaires—require the respondent to either write or orally provide answers to questions about a topic. The answer form may be structured in that there are fixed choices, or the form may be open-ended in that respondents can use their own words. Fixed-choice questionnaires may be called inventories.

random sampling—or randomization, works on the principle that all members of the target population have an equal chance of being selected for the sample. The subjects that are finally selected should reflect the distribution of relevant variables as found in the target population.

randomization—an unbiased, systematic selection or assignment of subjects. When randomization is used, researchers assume all members of the target population have an equal chance of being selected for the sample and that most human characteristics are evenly distributed among the groups.

ratio scales—show relative relationships among scores, such as half-as-large or three-times-as-tall. In dealing with educational variables, researchers do not have much use for these scales.

rationale equivalence reliability. See *internal consistency reliability*.

reference section—contains an alphabetical listing of the books, journal articles, other research reports, instructional materials, and instruments cited in the report.

reliability—the extent to which an instrument measures a variable consistently; a statistical estimate of the extent to which a test's results can be considered dependable.

reliability coefficient—expressed in decimal form, ranging from .00 to 1.00. The higher the coefficient, the higher the instrument's reliability.

replication—repeating an investigation of a previous study's purpose, question, or hypothesis.

representativeness—when researchers' results are generalizable from samples to target populations, the samples are considered representative.

research hypothesis—a statement of the specific relationship or effect among variables.

research—systematically collecting information about an identified problem or question, analyzing the data, and on the basis of the evidence, confirming or disconfirming a prior prediction or statement.

research designs—the structure for researchers' methods of answering research questions and conducting studies. Three basic research designs are description, comparison, and attribution of causality.

research report—a summary of researchers' activities and findings.

results section—contains the results of the researchers' data analyses; contains not only the numerical results (often presented in tables and charts) but an explanation of the significance of those results.

sample—a representative group of subjects; they are a miniature target population. Ideally, samples have the same distribution of relevant variables as found in the target population.

sampling error—any mismatch between the sample and the target population.

scales—measure variables related to attitudes, interests, and personality and social adjustment. Usually, data are quantified in predetermined categories representing levels of statements or questions showing the degree or intensity of their responses. Unlike data from tests, which are measured in continuous measurements (e.g., stanines 1 through 9, or percentiles 1 through 99), data from scales are discrete measurements. The discrete measurements in scales force respondents to indicate their level of reaction; common forced choices are "Always," "Sometimes," or "Never." This type of data quantification is called a *Likert-type scale.*

scorer or **rater reliability**—determined by comparing the results of two or more scorers, raters, or judges. Scorer reliability is sometimes presented as a percentage of agreement and not as a coefficient. Sometimes called interrater or interjudge reliability.

simple experimental designs—experimental designs with one independent variable or have subject selection procedures that limit the generalizability of their results. (See *experimental designs.*)

single-subject research—any research in which there is only one subject or one group that is treated as a single entity (e.g., when an entire school is studied without regard to individual students' performances). Single-subject research may be descriptive or experimental. Case study is a form of single-subject research.

situational variables—variables related to the experimental condition (that is, variables outside the subjects) that might cause changes in their responses relating to the dependent variable.

Solomon four-group design—Using random selection and random assignment, four groups are formed. All four groups are posttested, but only two groups are pretested. One pretested group and one nonpretested group is then given the experimental condition.

split-half reliability—a form of internal consistency reliability; determined by dividing the instrument in half and statistically comparing the subjects' results on both parts. The most common way to split a test is into odd- and even-numbered items.

standard deviation—a measure of the variability of the data around the mean. It shows how far from the mean most of the scores are. It is the way variability is usually reported.

standardized test—an instrument that has been experimentally constructed. The test constructor uses accepted procedures and researches the test's (a) content, (b) procedures for administering, (c) system for recording and scoring answers, and (d) method of turning the results into a usable form. A standardized test is one for which the methods of administering, recording, scoring, and interpreting have been made uniform. Everything about the test has been standardized so that if all its directions are correctly followed, the results can be interpreted in the same manner, regardless of where in the country the test was given.

statistical regression—the tendency of extreme high and low standardized test scores to move toward the group arithmetic mean.

statistical significance—occurs when results exceed a predetermined chance level. When results are significant, researchers know how confident they can be about the conclusions they can make from their findings.

statistics—numerical ways to describe, analyze, summarize, and interpret data in a manner that conserves time and space. Researchers select statistical procedures after they have determined what research designs and types of data will be appropriate for answering their research questions.

stratified random sample—the subjects are randomly selected by relevant variables in the same proportion as those variables appear in the target population.

subject variables—variables on which humans are naturally different and which might influence their responses in regard to the dependent variable.

subjects—the particular individuals or objects used in the research.

subjects section—contains a description of the individuals or objects included in the study. The section gives general information about age, sex, grade level, intellectual and academic abilities, socioeconomic levels, and so on. It also contains the number of subjects and an account of how the subjects were selected and assigned to groups.

***t*-test**—used when there are two sets of scores and reported as numbers such as $t = 1.6$ or $t = 3.1$. It is used to determine whether the difference between the means of two sets of scores is significant. After determining the value of t, researchers consult a statistical table to determine whether the value is a significant one.

target population—the specific group to which the researchers would like to apply their findings. It is from target populations that researchers select samples, which become the subjects of their studies.

test–retest reliability—determined by administering the same instrument again to the same subjects after a time period has elapsed. It is also referred to as *stability*.

triangulation—a procedure used in qualitative research for cross-validating information. Triangulation is collecting information from several different sources about the same event or behavior.

two-tailed research hypothesis. See *nondirectional research hypothesis.*

validity—the extent that an instrument measures what it is intended to measure.

validity generalization—researchers use the same purpose, method, and data analysis procedure, but they use subjects from a unique population.

variability—the extent to which scores cluster about the mean. The variability of a normal distribution is usually reported as the *standard deviation* (SD).

variable—anything in a research situation that varies and can be measured. It can be human characteristics (of students or teachers) or it can be characteristics of classrooms, groups, schools and school districts, instructional materials, and so on.

volunteer subjects—because of some inherent motivational factor, volunteers by nature are different from nonvolunteers. Results from the use of volunteer subjects might not be directly generalizable to target populations containing seemingly similar, but nonvolunteer, individuals or groups.

Appendix B

RESEARCH REPORTS AND REVIEWS FOR ANALYSIS

Wright, D., & Wiese, M. J. (1988). Teacher judgment in student evaluation: A comparison of grading methods. *Journal of Educational Research, 82,* 10–14. Reprinted with permission of the Helen Dwight Reid Educational Foundation. Published by Heldref Publications, Washington, D.C. Copyright © 1988.

Teacher Judgment in Student Evaluation: A Comparison of Grading Methods

Dan Wright
Ralston Public Schools

Martin J. Wiese
University of Nebraska—Lincoln

ABSTRACT

This validity study compares the *Parent–Teacher Conference Guide* grading system with another system based on teachers' experience. In addition to assigned third-quarter grades, teachers provide alternative ratings of effort and achievement and predict student scores on a standardized group achievement battery. Results indicate that: (a) teachers do discriminate *between* effort and achievement; (b) teachers can make better predictions toward external measures of achievement when they use a standard based on professional experience; and (c) the experience-based ratings offer a better fit with the concept of achievement as an interaction of effort and ability. These results offer encouraging support for the soundness of teacher judgment as a subjective, but necessary, component in any grading system.

Teacher-assigned classroom grades are a traditional and nearly universal means of documenting student achievement in American schools. Aside from serving as a measure of achievement, grades are an important medium for communicating with parents and within the schools, and they form a cumulative record of student progress. For the school psychologist, such records may be useful in determining the nature of a student's difficulties that have resulted in referral. Subsequent guidance decisions also are based on such achievement history.

Yet problems exist with grading practices that suggest caution when using grades for decision making. Among other limitations, Thorndike (1969) observed that grades often lack reliability, which makes meaningful comparisons across classes or schools difficult. Thorndike also suggested that teachers use grades ineffectively and that grades are an inadequate medium of communication. These problems are more evident at the elementary level, where most schools have grading systems that use peer performance as a frame of reference and result in letter or number categories (Hopkins & Stanley, 1981).

Of more interest than the merits or construction of various grading systems is the underlying ability of teachers to make judgments based on normative comparisons. Cronbach (1970) observed that, unless determined mathematically from examination scores, grades are essentially like ratings on simple scales. Most grading systems call for subjective consideration at some level of formulation, which makes the validity and accuracy of teacher judgment an important question. Hopkins and Stanley (1981) contend that the normative performance of previous students is the most meaningful standard in generating grades; however, this standard usually consists of an imprecise, internal standard developed through teacher experience.

The extent to which teachers are able to use a student's peers as a frame of reference also has implications beyond the measurement of school achievement. Teachers must frequently use their judgment to complete behavior rating scales and to make decisions that lead to referrals for consultation or assessment. Such decisions often have important educational outcomes for students. For these reasons, an examination of teacher judgment as an integral component of grading seems appropriate.

An opportunity for inquiry into this topic arose when the school district employing the first author (Wright) sought to revise its grading system at the elementary level. For the preceding 12 years, the district had used a "Parent–Teacher Conference Guide" instead of a traditional report card. The intended function of the reporting tool was to serve as a discussion guide at parent-teacher conferences and to facilitate inquiry, rather than to provide strict categorical ratings. Students, nonetheless, received separate ratings for effort and achievement in each academic area on a 1–3 scale, with 1 representing *excellent*; 2, *satisfactory*; and 3, *needs to improve*.

Teachers initially tried to use this scale in a fashion similar to previous systems with which they were familiar by adding " + " and " − " qualifiers where they felt appropriate (this practice recently was discouraged). Because the basis for comparing students was not specified to teachers, different practices arose among them. Some teachers compared students with all their classmates, some teachers compared them with only instructional-group peers, and other teachers compared students only against individual expectations. Growing teacher dissatisfaction and the observation that some parents were forming erroneous impressions regarding their children's progress precipitated a revision of the grading system.

The present study was conceived to compare the Parent–Teacher Conference Guide system with proposed grading alternatives. Many teachers and parents had requested adoption of a more traditional, 1–5 categorical rating system that created the opportunity to conduct this validity study. Time constraints allowed only single-occasion access to district teachers and student records. Normative ratings on a broad basis of comparison, similar to the internal standards hypothesized by Hopkins and Stanley (1981), were solicited from teachers on a random sample of students. Classroom grades and other available criterion variables also were collected from student records.

METHOD

Subjects

Requests for grades, achievement ratings, effort ratings, and predictions of achievement were distributed to 43 teachers of Grades 3 through 6 in six elementary school buildings. Each teacher was asked to generate information on 5 students from his or her home room group (the 3rd, 6th, 9th, 12th, and 15th students listed on their class rosters). Responses were returned by 39 teachers, a 91% return rate that yielded information on 195 students.

For a variety of reasons nearly one third of the cases were composed of less than complete information. For example, one of the criterion variables (a standardized social studies test) was not available for third graders. Also, a few teachers who were in team-teaching assignments neglected to share their surveys with colleagues. This left some cases without a full complement of information. All subsequent analyses, however, were based on samples of 144 to 190 cases. There was no reason to suspect that selection bias was introduced by any of the missing data encountered.

Procedure

Requests were distributed to the teachers following the third-quarter parent–teacher conferences. The timing of these requests ensured that the teachers had enough experience with the students to be familiar with their academic progress and that the teachers had recently reviewed their students' progress. The time of administration also preceded the return of results from the recently administered SRA Achievement Series (Naslund, Thorpe, & Lefever, 1978). Supplementary data were later collected from conference guides and SRA reports.

MEASURES

For each of 5 selected students, teachers were asked to provide ratings in four academic areas: reading, mathematics, language arts, and social studies. Ratings in each academic area were requested separately for student effort and student achievement on 5-point, Likert-type scales ranging from *very poor* through *average* to *very good*. Also, teachers were asked to predict student performance on comparable areas of the SRA batteries. The following instructions to teachers were intended to encourage a broad frame of reference:

A. For the *effort* ratings, please circle a number that indicates how hard the student tries and how motivated or interested he/she is in that subject area, compared with all other students at this grade level with whom you have ever had experience.

B. For the *achievement* rating, please circle a number that indicates the student's level of accomplishment in that subject, compared with all other students at this grade level with whom you have ever had experience.

C. In the box at the right, please make your best prediction of the national percentile score the student will receive in that area in the upcoming SRA group tests. What do you think the student's score will be?

Besides the ratings requested on the survey, third-quarter conference guides were reviewed and the grades (1–3) in each of the four academic areas were collected for all students. When SRA results were available, national percentile scores for each student also were collected. Additionally, the Educational Ability Series (EAS) score for each student was recorded from SRA results. The EAS is a less academically oriented subtest than the SRA and is purported to be a measure of general ability or academic potential. Although the EAS is limited as an individual measure of ability, it is useful for some types of decision making and should be adequate for research purposes (Wright & Piersel, 1987).

Analyses

A variety of procedures were conducted to explore teachers' abilities to identify student attributes and predict objective measures of achievement, and to compare the current and alternative rating systems. First, a principal components factor analysis procedure was used to determine whether teachers made separate ratings of achievement and effort. Second, teacher predictions of their students' SRA scores were correlated with the students' actual SRA scores to examine the accuracy of the teachers' predictions. Next, correlations between the requested ratings, current grades, and actual SRA scores were obtained. Finally, requested ratings of student effort and EAS scores were used to predict current grades, requested ratings of achievement, and actual SRA scores.

RESULTS

Means and standard deviations for all variables are presented in Table 1.

A factor analysis of these variables was performed to determine whether teachers made independent judgments of effort and achievement. The 1- to 5-point requested ratings, selected because they would provide greater total variance, were subjected to a principal components factor analysis with varimax rotation. The first solution employed a default criterion of eigen-values equal to or greater than 1 for factor extraction and yielded a single factor. Because we expected this result, we decided in advance to examine at least one solution beyond the one at default level.

We performed a two-factor solution to determine if the solution would offer meaningful results. The factor loadings for this solution are presented in Table 2. Although there were moderate cross loadings, effort and achievement scores aligned on reason-ably discrete factors that indicated that teachers responded to different sets of student attributes to make their ratings.

We entered teachers' predictions of students' SRA scores into simple regression procedures with actual SRA scores to determine how accurately teachers predicted external achievement criteria. The Pearson correlation coefficient and standard error of estimate resulting from these procedures in each academic area (reading, mathematics, language arts, and social studies) are presented in Table 3. Teachers' estimates of achievement were highly correlated with actual achievement (SRA) scores. The standard errors of estimate amounted to only 4 or 5 percentile points across areas.

After we examined direct prediction toward an external criterion (SRA scores), we realized the importance of determining whether the teachers' requested ratings of student achievement showed comparable validity. Therefore, teachers' achievement ratings via two methods, current grades and the requested 1- to 5-point ratings, were correlated with actual SRA scores in each academic area. These correlations are presented in Table 4.

Whereas both forms of ratings demonstrated moderate predictive validity, the requested ratings were consistently and

Table 1 Means and Standard Deviations for Variables

	Reading		Math		Language Arts		Social Studies	
	Mean	SD	Mean	SD	Mean	SD	Mean	SD
Current grades								
Effort	1.36	.56	1.45	.57	1.51	.57	.154	.61
Achievement	1.46	.52	1.63	.52	1.65	.52	.173	.57
Requested ratings								
Effort	3.84	1.15	3.70	1.10	3.68	1.11	3.59	1.07
Achievement	3.68	1.06	3.48	1.06	3.56	1.07	3.57	1.06
SRA								
Predicted	72.08	21.67	68.47	23.15	69.04	22.28	64.94	22.48
Actual	68.84	24.17	68.89	25.60	65.62	25.76	68.38	25.64

Note: SRA scores are reported as national percentile scores. Educational Ability Series Mean = 62.19, Standard Deviation = 27.31.

Table 2 Factor Loadings for Requested Ratings of Effort and Achievement Following Varimax Rotation

| Rating | Factors | | |
	1	2	h^2
Reading effort	.80	.40	.80
Reading achievement	.39	.83	.84
Math effort	.74	.44	.74
Math achievement	.43	.73	.72
Language arts effort	.82	.42	.85
Language arts achievement	.43	.79	.81
Social studies effort	.75	.46	.77
Social studies achievement	.45	.70	.69
Eigenvalues	3.15	3.08	
Percentage of h^2	50.56	49.44	100.00
Percentage of total variance	39.38	38.50	77.88

Table 3 Pearson Correlation Coefficients, Standard Estimating Errors from Predictions of Actual SRA Scores

Academic Area	r	SEE
Reading	.82	4.05
Mathematics	.77	4.20
Language arts	.76	4.80
Social studies	.67	5.18

Note: $p < .01$ for all correlations. SEE is expressed in percentile points.

Table 4 Correlations of SRA Scores

Academic Area	Current Grades	Requested Ratings
Reading	.50	.71
Mathematics	.44	.71
Language arts	.58	.70
Social studies	.42	.57

Note: $p < .01$ for all correlations. Current grades ranged from 1 to 3. Requested ratings ranged from 1 to 5.

significantly higher ($p < .01$, one-tailed, in all areas). Comparisons were made in each academic area using Hotelling's (1931) T^2 test for related validity coefficients. Also, the sizes of correlations with the requested ratings of achievement were similar in pattern to teachers' direct predictions toward SRA scores.

A final set of analyses examined the components of variance in some of the achievement measures. We entered requested ratings of student effort and EAS scores into independent stepwise multiple regression procedures predicting current grades, requested ratings of achievement, and SRA scores. We restricted analyses to the areas of reading and math for simplicity in reporting and consideration. Table 5 reports the total amount of variance accounted for in the criterion variables (total R^2), as well as the incremental variance accounted for with the inclusion of each of the predictor variables (R^2 change). Requested ratings of effort and EAS scores together accounted for about one third of the variance in current grades of reading and math, about two thirds of the variance in requested ratings of achievement, and over half of the variance in SRA achievement scores.

Table 5 Variance Accounted for in Measures of Reading and Math Achievement

| | Criterion Variables | | |
	Current Grades	Requested Ratings	SRA Scores
Reading			
R^2 change			
Effort	.286	.495	.196
EAS	.048	.139	.329
Total R^2	.334	.634	.525
Math			
R^2 change			
Effort	.375	.533	.274
EAS	.006	.094	.291
Total R^2	.381	.627	.565

DISCUSSION

We considered teachers' ratings of achievement in Table 1 and found that both current grades and requested ratings show means about half a standard deviation above the "average" points on their scales. This showing may represent some form of generalized positive bias or halo effect or, considering that the level of the SRA group scores is generally commensurate with these ratings, this showing may reflect accurate teacher perceptions. The consistently higher ratings on effort, compared with achievement, are of equal interest. The differences seem to represent a tendency by these teachers to ascribe more effort to their students than is reflected in observed achievement.

We found in this sample that teachers who have been directed for the past several years to differentially rate student effort should have sharpened their awareness of some student attributes other than achievement (i.e., effort). Whether this finding is actually demonstrated in the current study is not clear. A case-by-case review of student ratings revealed that effort and achievement ratings often were similar. Only in a small minority of cases were ratings of achievement and effort markedly divergent.

When we speculated about possible factor structures in an analysis of such ratings, we considered the possibility that no interpretable component factors would be identified or that two or more factors would represent different subject areas. Instead, the solution we reported in Table 2 reflected an effort-achievement distinction that accounted for nearly 78% of the total variance. Teachers apparently were responding to somewhat different sets of student attributes when making these ratings.

However, the moderate cross loadings indicate that these two constructs are similar or redundant to a considerable degree. Most sorely lacking in the present data is any independent measure of motivation to validate effort scores. We also are uncertain whether teachers are able to identify successfully differences in effort within subject areas.

Teachers' ability to predict external achievement criteria received better support. From the simple regression procedures reported in Table 3, we showed that direct predictions of SRA scores were highly correlated with actual scores. Also, standard errors of estimate of only 4 or 5 percentile points indicated that the teachers' predictions were reasonably accurate. The SRA battery apparently represented a frame of reference with which teachers were sufficiently familiar to use in making quick and accurate estimates of student ability.

Teachers' ratings of student achievement on the restricted scales of current grades and requested ratings also demonstrate moderate-to-high criterion-related validity, as indicated in Table 4. The requested ratings are consistently superior for this purpose, although this could be attributed partly to the greater amount of total variance available with a 5-point scale. However, the magnitude of the validity coefficients using requested ratings is closer both absolutely and in pattern to those of direct predictions toward SRA scores.

With validity coefficients in the area of social studies noticeably lower, this pattern could be attributed to differences between SRA test content and district social studies curriculum, as has been observed by district curriculum planners. This pattern, not observed among coefficients involving current grades, suggests a degree of discriminant validity that would be encouraging if further verified.

Table 5 shows that the requested ratings of achievement offer a better match than do current grades with a theoretical definition of achievement. In any measure, if relatively little variance can be explained by effort and ability, then large components of variance other than *achievement* must exist. In academic areas (reading and math), the requested ratings show substantially more variance accounted for by effort and ability. Also, by examining proportions of variance, this comparison negates the likelihood that findings may result from the different metrics of the ratings.

As mentioned above, requested ratings of effort and EAS scores account for about one third of the variance in current grades of reading and math, for about two thirds of the variance in requested ratings of achievement, and for over one half of the variance in SRA achievement scores. In addition to total variance, however, the relative contribution of effort ratings and EAS scores is of particular interest in predicting the latter two criterion variables.

Effort ratings made proportionally greater contributions to requested ratings of achievement, whereas the EAS made proportionally greater contributions to SRA achievement scores, suggesting that each probably shares a considerable amount of variance with its corresponding criterion variable.

If one considered the more conservative contributions (EAS toward requested ratings of achievement and effort ratings toward SRA achievement scores), then a reasonable proposition would be that these predictors could account for about one third of the variance of the *achievement* construct underlying the criterion variables. Therefore, while the analyses support the requested ratings of achievement over current grades, they also reveal much information about the limitations of the predictor variables.

In summary, these data provide useful information about teachers' abilities to judge student achievement and to assign representative ratings. The data suggest that teachers are able to differentiate effort and achievement when assigning ratings, although the validity of the effort ratings remains uncertain. Teachers can make reasonably accurate direct predictions toward external criteria upon request, and can assign ratings that display moderate-to-high criterion-related validity.

The requested ratings of achievement, which incorporate a broader basis for comparison, show higher criterion-related validity than do current grades. The ratings also offer a better theoretical match with the construct of *achievement*, although the predictor variables used appear to have capitalized on variance shared within rating systems to some extent. The ability of these teachers to make accurate judgments based on their own experience and on their knowledge of important external measures suggests that experiential relevance and familiarity are important factors in any grading system that teachers will be able to use successfully. Although not surprising in itself, this inference follows from surprisingly encouraging data.

Further inquiry into the validity of teacher ratings of effort or motivation would be appropriate. Despite the strong positive relationship between teacher-assigned grades and standardized test scores, teacher ratings obviously are not entirely redundant, and further inquiry into the nature of their differences also would be useful. We tentatively suggest that test scores and grades might be more sensitive measures of learning and performance, respectively, thus offering equally useful but complementary information.

REFERENCES

Cronbach, L. J. (1970). *Essentials of psychological testing* (3rd ed.). New York: Harper & Row.

Hopkins, K. D., & Stanley, J. C. (1981). *Educational and psychological measurement and evaluation* (6th ed.). Englewood Cliffs: Prentice-Hall, Inc.

Hotelling, H. (1931). The generalization of Student's ratio. *Annals of mathematical statistics*, 360–378.

Naslund, R. A., Thorpe, L. P., & Lefever, D. W. (1978). *SRA achievement series*. Chicago: Science Research Associates.

Thorndike, R. L. (1969). Marks and marking systems. In R. L. Ebel (Ed.). *Encyclopedia of educational research* (4th ed.). New York: Macmillan.

Wright, D., & Piersel, W. C. (1987). Usefulness of a group-administered ability test for decision making. *Journal of School Psychology*, 25, 63–71.

Freeman, E. B., & Sanders, T. R. (1989). Kindergarten children's emerging concepts of writing functions in the community. *Early Childhood Research Quarterly, 4*, 331–338.

Kindergarten Children's Emerging Concepts of Writing Functions in the Community

Evelyn B. Freeman
The Ohio State University—Newark

Tobie R. Sanders
Capital University

This study explored young children's concepts of the functions of writing in community contexts. Twenty kindergarten children responded to three videotaped vignettes depicting people writing in community settings. The children answered questions regarding who writes, what they write, where they write, and their purposes for writing. Results indicated that kindergarten children can identify a range of writing functions, including memory device, communication with others, learning, and personal expression. They also value writing and describe the negative consequences if people do not write. Results are discussed in terms of the theory and research on emergent literacy. Areas for further study are generated.

Kindergartners, who were not yet proficient writers themselves, responded to a researcher's probes about the reasons why people write with the following: "People write so they won't forget important stuff"; "People write to learn how to read"; "People write because they like to do it"; "So they won't get in trouble with their boss"; "So they can send a message"; "To help people know who they are." These responses indicate that the children's knowledge about written language extended far beyond the range of writing they could produce themselves. The focus of the study reported here is kindergarten children's concepts of the functions served by writing in community settings. It is an extension of a growing body of research on the emergence of literacy.

The beginnings of literacy have been the focus of abundant language development research in the last 10 to 15 years. Researchers from the varied disciplines of anthropology, linguistics, psychology, sociology, and education have pursued information about how it is that young children learn to become literate, the developmental course that learning to be literate follows, the relation-ship between learning to read and learning to write, and the social meaning of literacy in the lives of young children.

Research concerning the emergence of literacy provides compelling evidence that young children, in cultural environments where reading and writing are used, enter into the process of learning to be literate long before they begin literacy instruction in school (Ferreiro & Teberosky, 1982; Goodman, 1986; Harste, Woodward, & Burke, 1984; Sulzby, 1985). Research further indicates that reading and writing develop concurrently and in an interrelated manner (Clay, 1975; Dyson, 1982) as young children engage in literacy events that are deeply embedded in everyday activities (Heath, 1983; Scollon & Scollon, 1981; Taylor, 1983; Teale, 1986).

To date, the study of writing development has focused primarily on features of written products rendered by young children and their own comments concerning their writing (Bissex, 1980; Clay, 1975; Klein, 1985; Read, 1975; Taylor, 1983). While these studies yield a wealth of information about written language development, their focus on product ignores another crucial aspect of writing development, namely, children's knowledge about the functions of writing.

Halliday (1975), who described language learning as a process of "learning how to mean," generated seven functions of oral language that young children acquire. Similarly, Shuy (1981) asserted that function precedes form in the course of language development. Specifically in terms of literacy, Goodman (1983) believes that "children construct a variety of principles about language relevant to their developing literacy" (p. 73). One of these kinds of principles, functional principles, concerns the purposes for which written language is used and values attributed to written language and writing events.

Our knowledge of young children's concepts about writing functions is scant. Yet the significance of functional principles as a foundational component of literacy is likely to be profound, for as Smith (1984) stressed, "Language, whether spoken or written, produced or comprehended, always is related to intentions and purposes . . ." (p. 144). He continued:

> Children are less likely to discover possibilities of written language from their own spontaneous experimentation with writing than they learn about spoken language from their babbling and early speech. They need to see what written language will do for readers or writers. They learn about language, spoken or written, in the process of doing other things for which language can be recruited. . . . Thus, children must be entirely dependent on literate others to lead them into literacy, to show them how written language can be used. (p. 145)

The study reported here represents an effort to examine kindergarten children's concepts of functions served by writing in community contexts in which literate others are using writing. As such, it is a departure from product-oriented investigations of chil-

dren's development as writers and is not dependent on a child's attainment of prerequisite writing skills. Rather, this study enters the process of written language development at a level that focuses on children's awareness of the purposes served by and value attributed to writing and writing events.

The specific research questions of this investigation were twofold:

1. What are kindergarten children's concepts of the functions and value of writing in the community context?
2. Are kindergarten children able to identify who is writing, what is written, and why people write?

METHOD

Subjects

Twenty kindergarten children, 10 boys and 10 girls, participated in the study. At the time of the interview, their ages ranged from 67 months (5 years, 7 months) to 79 months (6 years, 7 months), with a mean age of 73 months (6 years, 1 month). The children attended a public elementary school in a small midwestern city. The school, 1 of 11 elementary schools in the district, was described as middle class by a school administrator. Twenty percent of the school's children qualify for free or reduced lunch.

All of the kindergarten children in the school received parental permission forms inviting them to participate in the study. From the forms that were returned, 10 boys and 10 girls were randomly selected. University procedures dictate that only children with signed permission forms can serve as subjects in the study. Each child was assigned a numerical code to preserve anonymity.

Procedures

The research instrument consisted of six videotaped sequences depicting children and adults engaged in naturally occurring writing instances in a variety of community settings (Freeman & Sanders, 1987). Community settings included a pediatrician's office, a public library, a toy store in a mall, a post office, a family restaurant and ice cream parlor, and an elementary school office. Each child was individually interviewed by a female researcher who had extensive experience working with young children. The interview lasted approximately 20 min. Each child viewed three of the videotaped sequences, which were randomly selected. After viewing each sequence, the child responded to a series of open-ended questions. The session was tape recorded.

The interview questions served as a guide during the interview and had no predetermined or prescribed answers. Additional questions emerged in response to each subject's comments. The guiding interview questions were as follows:

1. Tell me what you saw in the videotape.
2. Who is writing?
3. What do you think they are writing?
4. Where are they writing?
5. Why do you think they are writing?
6. What would happen if they didn't write it down?
7. What will happen to the writing next?

After viewing all three tapes, the child responded to two general summary questions: (a) Why do people write? (b) What would happen if people didn't write?

A total of 60 protocols were transcribed and then analyzed in a descriptive manner. The researcher and two consultants independently reviewed the data to generate categories regarding the functions of writing from the children's perspective. After this inductive analysis was completed and the categories were established and refined, two researchers assigned children's responses to categories and analyzed emerging patterns within the results.

RESULTS

All subjects responded to most of the interview questions. Many children expressed excitement when they recognized familiar community settings. Of the 60 protocols, there were only four instances in which three children failed to recognize that writing had occurred (6.7% of the protocols). In 7 of the 60 protocols, five children responded that they did not know why people were writing (8.8%).

The children were generally able to identify who was writing, where they were writing, and what was written. In addition, they possessed the vocabulary necessary to talk about writing. The children correctly labeled letter, check, homework, list, prescription, and note.

The kindergarten children identified a wide range of writing functions. As Table 1 indicates, 17 of the 20 children identified communicating with others as a function of writing. Within this broad category, several subcategories emerged: writing a letter or sending a personal message to someone; identifying oneself to others; relaying a message from one person to another; making various types of transactions. For example, after a child noted that a man was writing a letter, she answered, when asked why he was writing, "To give it to someone he liked." Another child commented, "He wanted to send it [note] to somebody 'cause it was their birthday."

Writing to communicate with others was perceived as a way to identify oneself to others. This subcategory was exemplified when a child commented, "You have to write the number and your name and your address so they'll know whose it is." Another child noted that we write our name "to sign up for a club or somethin'." Writing also serves as a means to communicate with others when a message is being relayed from someone else. For example, one child felt that the school secretary "was writin' down what the kids' mom and dad was saying so she

Table 1 Functions of Writing Identified by 20 Kindergarten Children

Function	Identified by Number of Children
Communicating with others[a]	17
Letter writing	4
Identifying oneself to others	5
Relay message from someone else	3
Part of a transaction	6
Memory device	13
Individual expression	5
Learning	9

[a]One subject identified two subcategories of communicating with others, that of letter writing and identifying oneself to others.

would tell the kids." Writing to communicate with others is needed to complete various types of transactions, as evidenced in this statement: "If she didn't [write on the paper] she wouldn't get her money back or she wouldn't get the train." If a waitress didn't write down an order "then she wouldn't know what they were gonna eat."

Writing that serves as a memory device was identified by 13 of the kindergartners. When asked why people in the videotapes wrote, the children responded, "So she wouldn't forget" or "So they'll remember." In responding to the waitress writing down the food order, one child said, "She wouldn't remember what they were gonna order." To the same situation, another child remarked, "In case [she] can't remember anything and just look on the thing [little tablet] and then she can fix it." Kindergartners, therefore, recognized that writing serves both to prevent people from forgetting and to help them remember when they do forget. Although children view writing as an adult way to remember, it is not the means by which they themselves remember. Their ability to identify the memory function of writing indicates that these children were able to take the perspective of the adult in the videotape and determine why that individual needed to write.

A function of writing that revolves around its use in learning and school-related tasks was identified by nine children. For example, writing was equated with homework and the need to write in order to complete homework. One child remarked that people write "so they can learn to read." Another child indicated that if the person in the tape didn't write it down, "he wouldn't learn how to do it." Children also pointed out that writing helps us know things. For instance, a child noted that the doctor wrote down "a little girl's name 'cause he wanted to know what her name was."

Five children identified a fourth function of writing that could be termed individual expression. This category includes the identification of writing as a pleasurable activity, something people want to do as a way to express themselves. For example, people write things down " 'cause they want to" or "they might like to write."

Eighteen of the 20 kindergartners evidenced a sense of audience. They recognized that writing will be read by someone else or reread by the writer. Several subjects noted that being the receiver of a written message is a positive and pleasurable event.

Kindergartners placed value on writing and believed it was important, as manifested in their recognition of negative consequences for not writing and their acknowledgment of the superiority of writing over other forms of communication. Examples of negative consequences that occur if a person does not write were "Wouldn't learn to read," "Boss would fire him," "The baby will still be sick," or "He would get in trouble." Writing was deemed superior to other forms of communication, as shown by the child who felt that a person who writes it down instead of just telling someone "wouldn't forget it."

DISCUSSION

As the results of this study indicate, one aspect of emergent literacy involves young children's knowledge about the functions of written language. Kindergarten children evidenced understanding of the value, purposes, and social importance of writing as it is performed in the community. As Goodman (1984) pointed out, children construct important knowledge about the nature and function of print in their daily lives prior to schooling.

Educators have often described writing as "talk written down." However, Smith (1982) pointed out that "writing is not speech written down . . . speech and writing are alternative forms of language" (p. 15). The children in this study understood that writing is not limited to speech written down. Examples in the tapes of the boys doing their homework or the pediatrician writing a prescription demonstrated that writing has an existence apart from oral language. Children in emerging stages of literacy development seem to understand that writing can be generated from various sources, some of which are independent of oral language. This is consistent with Smith's (1984) observation that "children are capable of understanding any use of written language that is demonstrated to them, provided that they themselves understand and share the intention (behind the reading or the writing) of the particular manifestation of written language" (p. 146).

The results can also be interpreted in light of children's knowledge that writing has social meaning. Kindergartners clearly viewed a wide range of purposes as well as the social value and importance of writing in the community in which they lived. Young children recognized that a plurality of literacies exist which, as described by Szwed (1981), are created by five elements: text, context, function, participants, and motivation.

This study explored a new dimension in the area of emergent literacy by focusing on children's understanding of writing functions in a community. It is an initial attempt to provide insight into what Goodman (1984) described as the functional principles of written language. Further research can investigate children's knowledge of writing functions in home and classroom contexts. In addition, further research should involve children from various types of communities (rural, urban, suburban) as well as diverse ethnolinguistic groups.

REFERENCES

Bissex, G. (1980). *Gnys at wok: A child learns to write and read.* Cambridge, MA: Harvard University Press.

Clay, M. (1975). *What did I write?* Exeter, NH: Heinemann.

Dyson, A.H. (1982). Reading, writing, and language: Young children solving the written language puzzle. *Language Arts, 59,* 829–839.

Ferreiro, E., & Teberosky, A. (1982). *Literacy before schooling.* Exeter, NH: Heinemann.

Freeman, E.B., & Sanders, T.R. (1987, April). *Probing children's concepts of writing functions: A developmental research instrument.* Paper presented at the annual meeting of the American Educational Research Association, Washington, DC.

Goodman, Y. (1983). Beginning reading development: Strategies and principles. In R.P. Parker & F.A. Davis (Eds.), *Developing literacy: Young children's use of language.* Newark, DE: The International Reading Association.

Goodman, Y. (1984). The development of initial literacy. In H. Goelman, A.A. Oberg, & F. Smith (Eds.), *Awakening to literacy.* Portsmouth, NH: Heinemann.

Goodman, Y. (1986). Children coming to know literacy. In W.H. Teale & E. Sulzby (Eds.), *Emergent literacy: Reading and writing.* Norwood, NJ: Ablex.

Halliday, M.A.K. (1975). *Learning how to mean—Explorations in the development of language.* London: Edward Arnold Ltd.

Harste, J., Woodward, V., & Burke, C.

(1984). *Language stories and literacy lessons*. Portsmouth, NH: Heinemann.

Heath, S.B. (1983). *Ways with words*. Cambridge, England: Cambridge University Press.

Klein, M. (1985). *The development of writing in children*. Englewood Cliffs, NJ: Prentice-Hall.

Read, C. (1975). *Children's categorization of speech sounds in English*. Urbana, IL: National Council of Teachers of English.

Scollon, R., & Scollon, S.B.K. (1981). *Narrative, literacy and face in interethnic communication*. Norwood, NJ: Ablex.

Shuy, R. (1981). A holistic view of language. *Research in the Teaching of English, 15*, 101–111.

Smith, F. (1982). *Writing and the writer*. New York: Holt, Rinehart & Winston.

Smith, F. (1984). The creative achievement of literacy. In H. Goelman, A.A. Oberg, of literacy. In H. Goelman, A.A. Oberg, & F. Smith (Eds.), *Awakening to literacy*. Portsmouth, NH: Heinemann.

Sulzby, E. (1985). Kindergarteners as writers and readers. In M. Farr (Ed.), *Advances in writing research* (Vol. I). Norwood, NJ: Ablex.

Szwed, J.F. (1981). The ethnography of literacy. In M.F. Whiteman (Ed.), *Writing: The nature, development and teaching of written communication* (Vol. I). Hillsdale, NJ: Erlbaum.

Taylor, D. (1983). *Family literacy: Young children learning to read and write*. Exeter, NH: Heinemann.

Teale, W. (1986). Home background and young children's literacy development. In W. Teale & E. Sulzby (Eds.), *Emergent literacy: Writing and reading*. Norwood, NJ: Ablex.

Knudson, R. E. (1989). Effects of instructional strategies on children's informational writing. *Journal of Educational Research*, 83, 91–96. Reprinted with permission of the Helen Dwight Reid Educational Foundation. Published by Heldref Publications, Washington, D.C. Copyright © 1989.

Effects of Instructional Strategies on Children's Informational Writing

Ruth E. Knudson
University of California—Riverside

ABSTRACT

The purpose of this experiment was to test the effectiveness of four instructional strategies on students' writing. Students were instructed in informational writing through one of the following: (a) presentation of model pieces of writing that focused on the *product* of good writing; (b) presentation of scales, questions, and criteria that focused on the *process* of writing by explicitly stating the criteria for good writing; (c) presentation of both model pieces of writing and scales, questions, and criteria—a combined approach involving both product and process strategies; and (d) free writing, a form of procedural facilitation (external supports) in which students were provided with pictures and asked to write about them. Informational writing was taught to 138 students in Grades 4, 6, and 8 in a school district in southern California. Writing samples were collected after treatment and again 2 weeks following the experiment. Results of nonorthogonal repeated measures analyses of variance indicated significant effects for treatment and reading level with informational writing. The most effective strategy was the presentation of model pieces of writing, followed by free writing. Although above-average readers wrote significantly better than below-average readers, for the free-writing group both above- and below-average readers wrote at about the same level for both writing samples.

General agreement exists that writers vary in their ability to write in different modes of discourse (Braddock Lloyd-Jones, & Schoer, 1963). Knowledge of discourse structure directly relates to a writer's knowledge of discourse schema—narration, description, argumentation, and information. Scardamalia and Bereiter (1986) asserted that a major requirement for competence in writing is learning the essential forms of these schemata. Hillocks (1987), also, asserted that effective writers need at least four types of knowledge, one of which is knowledge of discourse structures.

There are many experimental and descriptive studies of children's writing in different discourse structures (Anderson & Bashaw, 1968; Anthony, 1987; Atkins, 1983; Carlman, 1985; Crowhurst, 1978, 1983; Durst, 1986; Erftmier, 1985; Fitzgerald & Teasley, 1986; Hennelly, 1985; Kroll, 1986; Perron, 1976; Prater, 1982; Prater & Padia, 1983; Quellmalz & Capell, 1979; Veal & Tillman, (1982). Two logical conclusions may be drawn from this research. First, older children tend to write better than younger ones. Second, children's writing competence varies across discourse domains. Some evidence exists that there is a developmental pattern in the acquisition of discourse-schema knowledge.

Scardamalia and Bereiter (1986) asserted that discourse-specific competence depends on the degree of "openness" and "closedness" (Rumelhart, 1980) of the discourse schema, that is, on the writer's ability to access the schema without a conversational partner. In other words, the researchers defined discourse schemata as "open" or "closed," depending on the extent to which social turn-taking provides specific instances of the type of items represented in a given schema. Because there are no social inputs when writing, the student writing alone must depend on closed discourse schemata. By these criteria, the narrative schema is relatively closed; the descriptive and expository schemata are less so; and the persuasive-argumentative schema is the most open. Although inputs from conversational partners may influence the amount of elaboration and style of delivery, the narrative schema contains a system of internal requirements that must be met by the speaker. The conversational partner of the speaker in the expository-descriptive mode may take a more active role for assistance than the partner in narrative oral discourse, but the speaker's own knowledge of the activity determines the elements and their order in instruction and direction giving. Persuasive or argumentative oral discourse is open to the extent that there are inputs from the conversational partner, whereas an argumentative essay is closed—there are no inputs because there is no conversational partner.

Written discourse schemata are closed (Bereiter & Scardamalia, 1982). Children have some oral discourse schemata when they begin learning to write, but the learning process implies that children must develop new, closed schemata to direct their written composition. Researchers have hypothesized that children will adapt their existing oral discourse schemata to writing, most easily for those schemata that are relatively closed and hardest for those that are relatively open. Children have a closed schema for narrative writing and an open discourse schemata for informational and persuasive writing.

Although effective instructional strategies have been identified with respect to narrative writing (Scardamalia & Bereiter, 1986), research efforts have not been as successful in determining the effectiveness of instructional strategies in teaching knowledge of other discourse modes, specifically argumentative-persuasive writing and informational-expository writing. Informational-expository writing and reading are important because they are closely related to the kind of writing and reading that occurs in content areas (e.g., science and social studies). Success with expository writing and reading tasks is important for school success.

PURPOSE

Scardamalia and Bereiter (1986) organized approaches to writing instruction into four basic categories: (a) strategy instruction, which involves presenting writing to students as a cognitive process; (b) procedural facilitation, which involves helping students by providing them with external supports; (c) product-oriented instruction, which helps students gain a clear knowledge of goals to attain; and (d) inquiry learning, which helps students through exploration and guided discovery.

This study focused attention on four methods of teaching children to write: presentation of literary models, which is a form of product-oriented instruction; presentation of scales/questions/criteria to guide writing, which is a form of strategy (process) instruction; presentation of both model pieces of writing and scales/questions/criteria to guide writing, a combined approach involving both product- and process-oriented strategies; and free writing, a form of procedural facilitation in which students are presented with pictures to write about.

The selection of these methods was based, in part, on Hillocks' (1984, 1986) meta-analysis of the effectiveness of instructional strategies in teaching writing. He identified six instructional foci of research studies: grammar, sentence combining, model compositions, scales, and guided revision, inquiry, and free writing. He concluded (1984):

1. The study of traditional school grammar had no effect on raising the quality of student writing.

2. The emphasis on the presentation of good pieces of writing as models was significantly more useful than the study of grammar, but the treatments that used the study of models almost exclusively were less effective than other available techniques.
3. Free writing was more effective than teaching grammar in raising the quality of student writing but less effective than any other focus of instruction.
4. Sentence combining (the practice of building more complex sentences from single ones) was twice as effective as free writing as a means of enhancing the quality of student writing.
5. The use of scales, criteria, and specific questions that students apply to their own or others' writing was 2 times more effective than free-writing techniques.
6. Treatments including inquiry, in which the student's attention was focused on strategies for dealing with sets of data, were nearly 4 times more effective than free writing, and 2½ times more powerful than the traditional study of model pieces of writing.

Although the four instructional strategies were derived in part from Hillocks' (1984) meta-analysis, three of Hillocks' foci of instruction were not included in this study. Two of the three foci (grammar and sentence combining) were directed toward improvement of word and sentence-level skills. I excluded grammar and sentence combining as strategies of instruction because the purpose of the study was to identify effective instructional strategies for global writing competence. Inquiry was not included because it may not be a discrete category. Inquiry training, as defined by Hillocks, may expand the problem-solving ability of the writer by teaching algorithmic and heuristic approaches to composition.

The evidence is convincing that children's knowledge of discourse structure varies. Researchers generally agree that children come to school with an idea of nar-

rative structure. Their knowledge of informational writing is less developed. I conducted the experiment to examine the effects of instructional strategies with respect to informational writing tasks.

METHODS

Subjects

Informational writing was taught to 138 students in District A who lived in a semirural area in southern California. One fourth-grade and one sixth-grade class in one elementary school and three eighth-grade classes in a middle school were subjects for the informational writing experiment. All students could read and write English. Fifty-four percent of the subjects were girls, and 46% were boys. Sixty-eight percent of the subjects were Anglo; 24%, Hispanic; 4%, Black; 2% Oriental; and 2%, other. There were no statistically significant differences in the mean age of the students between or among treatment groups within grade (alpha = .05).

I conducted random assignment to instructional strategy (treatment group) so that students were equally divided by grade into treatment groups. In order that ability was not a confounding variable in the evaluation of the efficacy of the instructional strategies, I specified nonorthogonal analyses of variance to determine statistically significant differences in the number of above- and below-average readers assigned to each treatment group. The total reading score on a standardized test was used as a measure of prior ability. The reading score was taken from the Iowa Test of Basic Skills (ITBS). Students who scored above the 50th percentile were considered above-average readers; students who scored below the 50th percentile were labeled below-average readers. There were no statistically significant differences in the number of above- and below-average readers between or among treatment groups (alpha = .05). (See Table 1 for percentage of above- and below-average readers by treatment groups.)

Table 1 Percentage of Above-Average and Below-Average Readers by Treatment Groups

Treatment Group	Above-Average Readers	Below-Average Readers
1 (Models)	54	46
2 (Scales/questions/criteria)	50	50
3 (Models and scales/questions/criteria)	55	45
4 Free writing	50	50

Treatment Groups

I randomly assigned students to one of four treatment groups, each instructed with a different strategy. Treatment Group 1 was instructed with model pieces of writing; Treatment Group 2, by presentation of scales, questions, and criteria for writing; Treatment Group 3, by presentation of both model pieces of writing and scales, questions, and criteria for writing; and Treatment Group 4, by free writing. Because the random assignment occurred by student and not by classroom, the individual student was the unit of analysis, rather than the classroom or teacher.

Procedures

Students were instructed in writing for 14 days, 20 min per day. At the end of the experiment and again 2 weeks after its completion, I collected writing samples from all the students. These writing samples were written in response to a writing prompt, which was carefully written so that the audience and purpose were clearly expressed in each instance.

Scoring

This assessment included two scoring procedures. The first procedure was holistic, in Cooper's (1977) use of the term "holistic," to mean any procedure that stops short of enumerating linguistic, rhetorical, or informational features of a piece of writing. The holistic score in this study did not require an enumeration of any features. The score was similar to a Primary-Trait Assessment (Lloyd-Jones, 1977), however, in that the purpose for the writing, its audience, and the degree to which the task was addressed were considered in the scoring. Because there were two raters, the summed score for a given essay ranged from 2–12.

Readability Level

Two sets of materials were designed for informational writing. I used one set with fourth- and sixth-grade students and one set with eighth-grade students. The Fry Readability Formula (Fry, 1968) was applied to material given to the students. The reading level of the fourth-sixth grade material was approximately 3.5 to 3.8, with only a few instances of a low fourth-grade readability level. The eighth-grade materials were of approximately fifth-grade reading level (as determined by the Fry Readability Formula). My purpose in controlling the readability level was to ensure that the treatment, not the reading level, influenced the outcome of the study.

Experimental Check

I frequently observed each classroom to verify that the procedures were being implemented appropriately. The results of these observations verified that the experimental conditions were taught suitably.

RESULTS

A nonorthogonal repeated measures analysis of variance was specified for the model. For the informational writing experiment, the model contained two between-subject effects (treatment and reading level) and one within-subjects effect (time of measurement). The four levels of treatment included in the analysis are those presented in Table 2. Level of reading achievement had two levels, one above the 50th percentile and the other below the 50th percentile, both

Table 2 Means and Standard Deviations for the Holistic Score by Treatment by Reading Level, Information Writing

Holistic Test	N	M	SD
Treatment 1 (model pieces of writing)			
Above-average reading level			
1	13	9.23	1.88
2	14	8.50	2.10
Below-average reading level			
1	11	6.18	1.60
2	10	6.40	1.07
Treatment 2 (scales/questions/criteria)			
Above-average reading level			
1	13	7.08	1.50
2	13	7.62	1.85
Below-average reading level			
1	13	6.00	1.47
2	12	5.50	1.31
Treatment 3 (models, scales/questions/criteria)			
Above-average reading level			
1	15	7.66	2.02
2	14	7.00	1.52
Below-average reading level			
1	12	6.17	1.03
2	11	5.09	0.94
Treatment 4 (free writing)			
Above-average reading level			
1	11	8.00	2.72
2	10	7.30	2.06
Below-average reading level			
1	11	6.45	1.75
2	10	7.50	2.61

with total reading score on the Iowa Test of Basic Skills (ITBS). The two levels of the within-subject factor, time of measurement, are the writing sample immediately following treatment and the posttest writing sample, 2 weeks after the conclusion of treatment.

Descriptive statistics for each treatment, by reading level, are displayed in Table 2. There were significant main effects for treatment [$F(3, 80) = 3.04$, $p = .034$] and for reading level [$F(1, 80) = 22.62$, $p = .0001$]. Follow-up of significant main effects for the holistic score using Scheffé tests (alpha = .05) indicated that for the main effect of reading level, above-average readers wrote significantly better than below-average readers for Writing Samples 1 and 2. The interaction for Time × Treatment × Reading Level was significant [$F(3, 80) = 4.53$, $p = .0055$]. The interaction is graphically presented in Figure 1.

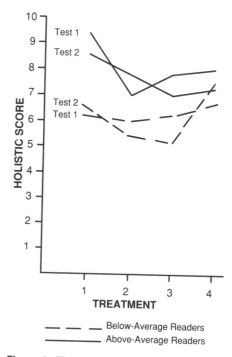

Figure 1. Time x Treatment x Reading Level Interaction, Holistic Scores

DISCUSSION

The most effective instructional strategy for informational writing is the presentation of model pieces of writing, followed by free writing. The success of model pieces of writing as an instructional strategy is borne out, at least in part, by past experience and research. One of the oldest, if not the oldest, ways to teach children to write is by presenting them with model pieces of writing. It is assumed that students will be able to transfer what they see in the model to their own writing. Instruction using model pieces of writing involves connections between reading and writing. Much student learning about writing results from exposure to examples (Smith, 1982). Knowledge is obtained from reading the examples; reading usually gives no clue to the process through which the author works to create the literary work. One assumes that knowledge of writing through reading necessitates a directing of attention, separate from that required to comprehend the text. Little research exists on how students extract literary knowledge from examples, although it is known that students from third grade on can extract knowledge of literary features from model texts (Scardamalia & Bereiter, 1986). Studies finding that presentation of model pieces of writing are effective in improving student composition have several common characteristics and draw similar conclusions. Thibodeau (1964), Pinkham (1969), Andreach (1976), Wood (1978), and Laurencio (1984) all found that teaching with literary models increases students' organization and may result in improvement in the mechanics of writing.

Important questions remain, however. Why do the students in the groups presented with scales/questions/criteria to guide writing and both scales/questions/criteria and model pieces of writing not improve? One explanation is that the students presented with both scales/questions/criteria to guide writing and model pieces of writing are presented with too much information

in too short a period of time. Either the students need more models before being introduced to questions/scales/criteria, or they need more time to write without models. This instructional strategy may be effective if the learner has prior knowledge of the discourse schema. Most of the studies that prove the effectiveness of scales/questions/ criteria in teaching children to write involve narrative, descriptive, or expressive discourse structures, which are thought to be closed earlier than either the persuasive or informational structures. Presumably, once a student has knowledge of the discourse schema, scales/questions/criteria will help him or her plan or revise the composition. In other words, with a more open discourse schema, the presentation of model pieces of writing helps close the schema and the prompt can provide procedure facilitation to access the discourse structure.

Scales, questions, and criteria do not close the schema, but serve as a form of strategy instruction. When the schema is relatively closed, scales/questions/criteria can help students focus on the importance of revision and the characteristics of the writing to be considered during revision.

The free writing in this experiment is a form of procedural facilitation because pictures serve as prompts for the writing. Children report that their problems in composition are mainly problems of finding content for the text that they generate, not of finding language to express the content (Bereiter & Scardamalia, 1982). The picture prompt helps provide the content for the free writing activities; the students develop general fluency in writing and are able to transfer the acquired fluency to a different discourse schema (informational writing).

The effectiveness of free writing as an instructional strategy probably occurs because practice in it increases general fluency in writing. Because free writing is so effective for low readers, important implications exist for permitting these low-achieving students, often grouped into "competency" classes, to practice writing without traditional remedial instruction. Such an opportunity to write may increase their awareness of text production from sentence level to text level.

Students also may benefit from using scales, questions, and criteria to guide writing, but more research needs to be conducted on exactly when this strategy should be introduced into the writing process. Scales, questions, and criteria may be helpful in improving student learning at the revision point in the composing process, but they may not be helpful for learning general organizational components of discourse structure, which is probably the strength of model pieces of writing; or in increasing general fluency, which is the strength of free writing.

This study contains important implications for the teaching of writing and for future research. Efforts should continue to identify effective ways of teaching discourse structures. Also, learning a discourse structure itself is different from the procedural knowledge necessary to manipulate content within a discourse structure. Research efforts need to continue with respect to identifying why effective instructional strategies are effective. Researchers should be made to understand why strategies are or are not effective in terms of understanding how and why learners gain knowledge of content, procedural knowledge to manipulate content, knowledge of discourse structures, and the procedural knowledge to manipulate content within discourse structures.

ACKNOWLEDGMENT

I thank the principal and teachers of Magnolia Elementary School and Central Middle School, Riverside Unified School District, for their participation in this project. I also acknowledge the assistance of principal Hal Ensey and teachers Janelle Krell and George Neuhaus of Ruth Grimes School and principal Patt Ensey and teacher Christy Marin of Terrace Hills Junior High School, Colton Joint Unified School District.

NOTE

A version of this paper was presented at the annual meeting of the American Educational Research Association (AERA) in April 1989, in San Francisco, California. This article was based on research conducted for my dissertation, which earned the Outstanding Dissertation of the Year Award 1988–1989 from AERA. Partial funding for the research was provided by grants from the University of California.

REFERENCES

Anderson, H. E., Jr., & Bashaw, W. L. (1968). An experimental study of first grade theme writing. *American Educational Research Journal, 5*(2), 239–247.

Andreach, J. R. (1976). The use of models to improve organizational techniques in writing. *DAI 36*, 4980-A.

Atkins, C. L. (1983). Examining children's sense of audience on a persuasive writing task: Grades two, four, and six. *DAI 44*(8), 2351-A.

Anthony, P. J. (1987). Examining children's written narratives: The relationship between writing ability and logical thinking during the period between concrete and formal operations. *DAI 48*(1), 68-A.

Bereiter, C., & Scardamalia, M. (1982). From conversation to composition: The role of instruction in a developmental process. In R. Glaser (Ed.), *Advances in instructional psychology, (Vol. 2.)* Hillsdale, NJ: Lawrence Erlbaum Associates.

Braddock, R., Lloyd-Jones, R., & Schoer, L. (1963). *Research in written communication.* Champaign, IL: National Council of Teachers of English.

Carlman, N. (1985). The effects of scoring method, topic, and mode on grade 12 students' writing scores. *DAI 46*(2), 367-A.

Cooper, C. R. (1977). Holistic evaluation of writing. In C. R. Cooper & L. Odell (Eds.), *Evaluating writing.* Urbana, IL: National Council of Teachers of English.

Crowhurst, M. (1978). Syntactic complexity in two modes of discourse at grades 6, 10 and 12. ED168037.

Crowhurst, M. (1983, April). *Persuasive writing at grades 5, 7, and 11: A cognitive-developmental perspective. Paper* presented at the annual meeting of the American Educational Research Association, Montreal, Canada, ED230977.

Durst, R. K. (1986). Cognitive and linguistic dimensions of analytic writing. *DAI 46*(12), 3635-A.

Erftmier, T. A. (1985). Oral and written persuasion: Strategies of fourth-grade students. *DAI 46*(7), 1857A.

Fitzgerald, J., & Teasley, A. B. (1986). Effects of instruction in narrative structure on children's writing. *Journal of Educational Psychology, 78*(96), 424–432.

Fry, E. B. (1968). A readability formula that saves time. *Journal of Reading, 11,* 513–516.

Hennelly, J. M. (1985). A study comparing persuasive and narrative writing at two grade levels across cognitive measures of writing and reading ability. *DAI* 451-A.

Hillocks, G., Jr. (1984). What works in teaching composition: A meta-analysis of experimental treatment studies. *American Journal of Education, 93*(1), 133–169.

Hillocks, G., Jr. (1986). *Research on written composition.* Urbana, IL: National Council of Teachers of English.

Hillocks, G., Jr. (1987). Synthesis of research on teaching writing. *Educational Leadership, 44*(8), 71–82.

Kroll, B. M. (1986). Explaining how to play a game. *Written Communication, 3*(2), 195–218.

Laurencio, D. E. (1984). The effect of using written models on the writing performance of secondary English as a second language student, *DAI 44*(9), 2698-A.

Lloyd-Jones, R. (1977). Primary trait scoring. In C. R. Cooper & L. Odell (Eds.), *Evaluating writing,* Urbana, IL: National Council of Teachers of English.

Perron, J. D. (1976). The impact of mode on written syntactic complexity: Part II —Fourth grade. Report No. 25. Georgia University, Athens, ED126511.

Pinkham, R. G. (1969). The effect on the written expression of fifth grade pupils of a series of lessons emphasizing the characteristics of good writing as exemplified in selected works from the area of children's literature. *DAI 29,* 2613-A.

Prater, D. (1982, February). *The effects of writing task on mastery classification of high school students.* Paper presented at the Annual Meeting of the Southwest Educational Research Association, Austin, TX, ED215367.

Prater, D., & Padia, W. (1983). Effects of mode of discourse on writing performance in grades four and six. *Research in the Teaching of English, 17*(2), 127–134.

Quellmalz, E., & Capell, F. (1979). Defining writing domains: Effects of discourse and response mode. California University, Los Angeles. Center for the Study of Evaluation. ED212861.

Rumelhart, D. E. (1980). Schemata: The building blocks of cognition. In R. Spiro, B. Bruce, & W. Brewer (Eds.), *Theoretical issues in reading comprehension.* Hillsdale, NJ: Lawrence Erlbaum Associates.

Scardamalia, M., & Bereiter, C. (1986). Research on written composition. In M. C. Wittrock (Ed.), *Handbook of research on teaching* (3rd ed.) New York: Macmillan, 778–803.

Smith, F. (1982). *Writing and the writer.* New York: Holt, Rinehart & Winston.

Thibodeau, A. E. (1964). Improving composition writing with grammar and organization exercises utilizing differentiated groups patterns, *DAI 25*: 2389.

Veal, L. R., & Tillman, M. (1971). Mode of discourse variation in the evaluation of children's writing. *Research in the Teaching of English, 5*(1), 37–45.

Wood, B. W. (1978). A structured program for teaching composition in senior high school English classes. *DAI 39,* 2173-A.

Schunk, D. H., & Hanson, A. R. (1989). Self-modeling and children's cognitive skill learning. *Journal of Educational Psychology, 81*, 155–163. Copyright 1989 by the American Psychological Association. Reprinted by permission.

Self-Modeling and Children's Cognitive Skill Learning

Dale H. Schunk

School of Education
University of North Carolina—Chapel Hill

Antoinette R. Hanson

College of Education
University of Houston

We investigated self-modeling among children who had experienced arithmetic difficulties. In Experiment 1, some children observed peer models solve fraction problems. Others were videotaped while solving problems, after which they viewed their tapes. Observing self-model tapes raised achievement outcomes as well as viewing peer models; each treatment was more effective than a videotape control condition. In Experiment 2, children were videotaped solving easier problems or solving more difficult problems, after which they viewed their tapes. The two self-model treatments promoted achievement behaviors equally well and better than the videotape control and instructional control conditions. In Experiment 3, children were videotaped while learning to solve problems or after they had learned to solve the problems. Self-model subjects demonstrated higher achievement outcomes than videotape control children. Collectively, these results show that self-model tapes highlight progress in skill acquisition, which enhances self-efficacy.

Bandura (1982, 1986) contended that psychological procedures change behavior in part by creating and strengthening perceived *self-efficacy*, or personal beliefs about one's performance capabilities in a given domain. Self-efficacy influences choice of activities, effort expended, persistence, and task accomplishments. Individuals acquire information about their self-efficacy through their actual performances, vicarious (observational) experiences, forms of persuasion, and physiological indexes (e.g., heart rate, sweating).

Observation of models is an important vicarious source of efficacy information. The effect on observers depends in part on *perceived similarity* to models (Schunk, 1987). Festinger (1954) hypothesized that, where objective standards of behavior are unclear or unavailable, observers evaluate themselves through social comparisons with others. The most accurate self-evaluations derive from comparisons with those similar in the ability or characteristic being evaluated. Observing similar others succeed raises observers' self-efficacy and motivates them to try the task. Model attributes (e.g., age, perceived competence) often are predictive of performance capabilities (Bandura, 1986). Similarity is especially influential when individuals are uncertain about their capabilities, as when they lack task familiarity and have little information on which to base efficacy judgments or when they have experienced difficulties and possess doubts about performing well.

Given that ability-related behaviors are highly susceptible to peer influence (Davidson & Smith, 1982), an adult's flawlessly modeled demonstration may not promote self-efficacy in students who have experienced learning difficulties and who view the teacher as superior in competence. Peer models who students believe are similar in competence to themselves may better promote students' self-efficacy for learning. Schunk and Hanson (1985) found that children who observed a peer model learn to solve subtraction problems developed higher self-efficacy for learning than did children who observed an adult model learning the same operations.

Model–observer attribute similarity is heightened when one is one's own model (Bandura, 1986). *Self-modeling* refers to behavioral change that derives from observing oneself on videotapes that portray only desired (target) behaviors (Dowrick, 1983; Hosford, 1981). In a typical experiment, subjects are videotaped individually as they perform behaviors, after which they view their own tapes. Tapes can capture existing behaviors by having subjects role play or perform previously learned skills or can portray behaviors created with editing (deleting errors) and illusory techniques (using camera angles that obscure aid from others). Self-modeling has been used to train physical, vocational, communication, teaching, and social-personal skills (Carroll & Bandura, 1982; Davis, 1979; Dowrick & Dove, 1980; Dowrick & Hood, 1981; Dowrick & Raeburn, 1977; Fuller & Manning, 1973; Hosford & Mills, 1983; Miklich, Chida, & Danker-Brown, 1977; Pigott & Gonzales, 1987).

The purpose of the present three experiments was to determine the effects of self-model treatments on children's achievement beliefs and behaviors during mathematical skill learning (fractions). We expected that self-model procedures would raise self-efficacy and achievement behaviors among our subjects, who had encountered mathematical difficulties. Observing a self-model tape allows one to rehearse mentally the skills portrayed. Observing oneself performing well also raises observers' self-efficacy for further learning and leads them to expend effort and persist at the task. Self-modeling is enhanced by increases in self-efficacy even when subjects are given erroneous skills information (Dowrick, 1983).

EXPERIMENT 1

In Experiment 1 we compared self-modeling with the effects of observing peer models. We expected that these treatments would be equally effective in enhancing children's achievement behaviors. Observing peer models solve problems enhances children's self-efficacy for learning, which subsequently is substantiated as children solve problems themselves (Schunk & Hanson, 1985). We believed that children's observations of themselves performing well would enhance their perceptions of progress in learning and their self-efficacy for further learning.

Method

Subjects. The initial subject pool of 54 children from three elementary schools previously had been classified by the school district as working below grade level in mathematics. During the preceding academic year, children had been administered the California Achievement Tests (CTB/McGraw-Hill, 1977). Children were assigned to below-level classes if their mathematics total score was below the 35th percentile and if their previous year's teacher approved. At the time of this study, no subject received special education services.

Six children were excluded: Three were absent and missed some instructional sessions, one was accidentally shown the wrong videotape, and two were randomly excluded from the appropriate cells to equate cell sizes. Ages of the 48 children in the final sample (27 girls, 21 boys) ranged from 9 years, 3 months to 12 years, 11 months ($M = 10.9$ years). Various socioeconomic backgrounds were represented, but children were predominantly middle class. Ethnic composition was 46% White, 42% Black, and 12% Mexican American.

Materials and procedures. The pretest on fractions self-efficacy and skill was administered to children individually by one of four adult testers from outside the school.

The *self-efficacy* test assessed children's perceived capabilities for correctly solving types of problems. The scale ranged in 10-unit intervals from *not sure* (10) to *really sure* (100). The stimulus materials comprised 31 sample pairs of problems. The two problems constituting each pair were similar in form and operations required and corresponded to one problem on the skill test, although they involved different numbers. The reliability of the efficacy test was assessed in conjunction with a previous study (Schunk, Hanson, & Cox, 1987), test-retest $r = .79$.

After receiving practice using the self-efficacy scale, children were shown the 31 pairs of fraction problems (about 2 s for each pair). This brief duration allowed assessment of problem difficulty but not actual solutions; children judged their certainty of solving different types of problems rather than their certainty of solving any particular problem. After privately making each judgment, children covered it with a blank sheet of paper to minimize influence from prior judgments. The 31 scores were summed and averaged.

The *fraction skill* test was administered after the efficacy assessment and comprised 31 problems that tapped addition and subtraction as follows (examples in parentheses): addition, like denominators, no carrying ($\frac{1}{6} + \frac{4}{6}$); addition; like denominators, carrying ($\frac{9}{10} + \frac{5}{10}$); addition, unlike denominators, no carrying ($\frac{5}{16} + \frac{3}{4}$); addition, unlike denominators, carrying ($\frac{11}{15} + \frac{37}{45}$); subtraction, like denominators, no regrouping ($\frac{7}{9} - \frac{3}{9}$); and subtraction, unlike denominators, no regrouping ($\frac{21}{36} - \frac{5}{18}$). Approximately 70% of these problems were similar to those children solved during the instructional sessions; the others were more complex. For example, during the sessions students solved problems with two terms, whereas some skill test problems included three terms ($\frac{1}{3} + \frac{2}{12} + \frac{1}{4}$). Different forms of the skill test were used on the pretest and posttest to eliminate effects due to problem familiarity (parallel forms $r = .90$; Schunk et al., 1987).

The tester presented problems to children one at a time on separate sheets of paper and verbally instructed them to place each page on a completed stack when they finished solving the problem or chose not to work on it any longer. Children were given no feedback on solution accuracy. The measure of skill was the number of problems solved correctly.

After the pretest, children were assigned randomly within sex and school to one of four treatment conditions: peer-model, self-model, peer- + self-model (combined), or videotape control. During a special session prior to the instructional program, peer-model and peer- + self-model subjects viewed a 45-min videotape that presented each of the six fraction skills in 7- to 8-min blocks. The videotape, which ensured standardized presentation across subjects, portrayed a female adult teacher and three peer (child) models ranging in age from 10.0 to 11.1 years ($M = 10.5$ years). Multiple peer models were used to enhance the likelihood of subjects perceiving themselves as similar to at least one of the models and because multiple models promote self-efficacy better than a single model (Schunk et al., 1987; Thelen, Fry, Fehrenbach, & Frautschi, 1979). There were two versions of the tape; they portrayed three male (female) peer models and were shown to male (female) subjects. A female teacher was used because most elementary teachers in the school district were women. Teachers and models were unfamiliar to subjects.

Each videotape initially showed the teacher at a chalkboard explaining and demonstrating how to add fractions with like denominators (no carrying). After this 2- to 3-min demonstration, the teacher wrote a comparable problem on the board for the model to solve. The model worked at an average rate while verbalizing the problem-solving operations. After finishing the problem, the model was told that the solution was correct, after which the teacher erased the work and wrote another problem on the board. The model solved problems for the remainder of the block (5–6 min). The teacher then explained and demonstrated the next fraction skill, gave the model problems to solve, and so on. Each peer model in each of the tapes participated in two of the six blocks.

Children viewed the appropriate videotape in small groups. An adult trainer stated that it showed a teacher and some boys (girls) who were learning to solve fractions but did not comment while children were watching the videotape. On completion of the tape, the trainer administered the *self-efficacy for learning* measure, which was identical to the pretest efficacy assessment except that children judged their certainty of *learning* to solve different types of problems rather than their certainty of being able to solve them. Self-model and videotape control children completed the self-efficacy for learning measure at this time.

All children received the *fractions instructional program* during 45-min sessions on 6 school days. Sessions were conducted by adult trainers from outside the school. For any given child, the same trainer administered all six sessions but had not administered the child's pretest or videotape and was unaware of the child's experimental assignment.

Each of the six sets of instructional material incorporated one of the six fractions operations. In each set, the first page contained an explanation of the relevant operations, along with two examples illustrating their application. Each of the following pages contained several similar problems to be solved using the designated strategy. Students worked on one set during each instructional session. Each set included sufficient problems so that children could not complete all of them during the session.

At the start of each session, children met in small groups with their trainer, who verbally reviewed the explanatory page. After this instructional phase (about 5 min), children solved two practice problems. The trainer stressed the importance of performing the steps as shown on the explanatory

page, seated subjects at desks separated from one another, and moved out of sight. Children solved problems alone during the remainder of the session (about 30 min). If they were baffled about how to solve a problem they could consult the trainer, who reviewed the troublesome operation.[1]

All children were videotaped during a special session following the third session, which gave children experience in working fractions and allowed for potential self-modeling effects in subsequent sessions. Each child was escorted to a private room by an adult who had not served as his or her tester or trainer. Initially, each child practiced solving three problems with corrective instruction as necessary. Once the trainer was satisfied that children could solve the problems, he or she wrote 12 problems on a chalkboard that involved addition of fractions and were similar to those covered during the first three sessions. Children verbalized while solving problems so that verbalizations could serve as self-model cues. They were given no feedback during taping; when they finished a problem they began solving the next one. Children were prompted verbally when they failed to verbalize or when they made a computational error (e.g., "How much is seven times four?"). Taping lasted approximately 15 min per child. No child experienced conceptual difficulties.[2]

---

[1] Of the 48 students in the final sample, 8 (17%) consulted the trainer of various times during the instructional program; they were equally distributed across experimental conditions. Comparable percentages were obtained in Experiments 2 (22%) and 3 (15%).

[2] As Dowrick (1983) observed, between-conditions comparisons of videotape treatments are problematic if the quality of the interaction is not controlled. In the present studies, the trainers present with children during the videotape sessions followed a standard set of instructions. With the exception of the progress self-model treatment of Experiment 3, interactions between the trainers and children were comparable across the various treatments of the three studies.

Each self-model and peer- + self-model subject viewed his or her videotape the next day in a private room. The trainer did not comment until after the tape, when children were administered a measure of perceived progress. This 10-unit scale ranged in 10-unit intervals from *not better* (10) to *a whole lot better* (100). Children were asked to think about their problem solving and judge how they were in working fractions compared with when the project began. Subjects in the other two conditions completed the progress measure at this time but did not view their videotapes until after the posttest.

Children received the posttest (self-efficacy, skill) on the day after the last instructional session. For any given child, the tester was unaware of the child's experimental assignment and performance during the instructional program. Tests and instructional materials were scored by an adult who had not participated in the data collection and was unaware of children's experimental assignments.

Results

Means and standard deviations are shown in Table 1. Preliminary analyses of variance (ANOVAS) yielded no significant between-conditions differences on pretest self-efficacy or skill. There also were no significant differences on any measure due to tester, school, or sex of student.

Self-efficacy and skill. Intracondition changes (pretest to posttest) on each measure were evaluated using the t test for correlated scores (Winer, 1971). All four conditions showed significant increases ($ps < .01$ except videotape control $p < .05$ on self-efficacy).

Posttest self-efficacy and skill were analyzed with a 2 × 2 (Peer-Model: Yes/No × Self-Model: Yes/No) multivariate analysis of covariance (MANCOVA), the corresponding pretest measures were covariates. This analysis yielded significant effects for peer-model, Wilks's lambda = .818, $F(2, 41)$ =

4.56, $p < .05$, and for self-model, lambda = .729, $F(2, 41) = 7.61$, $p < .01$; the peer-model × self-model interaction also was significant, lambda = .746, $F(2, 41) = 7.00$, $p < .01$. Univariate analyses of covariance (ANCOVAS) revealed significant effects on self-efficacy for peer-model, $F(1, 43) = 6.58$, $p < .05$, and for self-model $F(1, 43) = 10.22$, $p < .01$, as well as a significant peer-model × self-model interaction, $F(1, 43) = 8.67$, $p < .01$ ($MS_e = 134.96$). The skill measure yielded a significant effect for self-model, $F(1, 43) = 6.06$, $p < .05$, and a significant interaction, $F(1, 43) = 6.35$, $p < .05$ ($MS_e = 18.09$).

Posttest means were evaluated using Dunn's multiple comparison procedure (Kirk, 1982). The peer-model, self-model, and peer- + self-model conditions did not differ on either measure, but each condition scored higher than the videotape control condition (self-efficacy $ps < .01$; skill $ps < .05$ except $p < .01$ for the self-model/videotape control comparison).

Instructional session measures. A 2 × 2 AN-COVA applied to the self-efficacy for learning measure using pretest efficacy as the covariate yielded a significant peer-model effect, $F(1, 43) = 27.71$, $p < .001$ ($MS_e = 207.28$). The peer-model and the peer- + self-model conditions did not differ, but each condition judged self-efficacy significantly higher than the self-model and videotape control conditions ($ps < .01$ except $p < .05$ for the self-model/peer- + self-model comparison). The self-model and videotape control conditions did not differ.

The progress measure was analyzed with a 2 × 2 ANOVA, which yielded a significant self-model effect, $F(1, 44) = 6.46$, $p < .05$ ($MS_e = 542.24$). Subjects assigned to the self-model and to the peer- + self-model conditions judged perceived progress significantly ($ps < .05$) higher than did videotape control subjects.

The number of problems completed during the instructional sessions was analyzed with a 2 × 2 ANOVA, which yielded a sig-

Table 1 Means and Standard Deviations: Experiment 1

Measure/Phase	Experimental Condition			
	Peer-model	Self-model	Peer- and Self-models	Videotape Control
Self-efficacy[a]				
Pretest				
M	52.0	52.2	46.8	51.2
SD	15.7	14.5	15.8	19.1
Posttest				
M	85.2	87.3	86.2	66.7
SD	11.6	10.2	10.4	13.6
Skill[b]				
Pretest				
M	6.1	5.8	4.8	5.4
SD	5.2	5.5	4.2	3.9
Posttest				
M	14.8	15.3	14.2	9.1
SD	5.4	3.7	4.2	4.9
Self-efficacy for learning[c]				
M	83.3	61.9	80.3	59.8
SD	12.9	17.5	11.3	20.1
Instructional performance[d]				
M	168.2	161.8	150.0	120.7
SD	18.6	25.2	23.2	28.2
Perceived progress[e]				
M	74.2	80.0	78.3	50.0
SD	26.1	26.6	22.5	16.5

Note: N = 48; *n* per condition = 12.
[a]Average judgment per problem; 10 (low) to 100.
[b]Number of correct solutions on 31 problems.
[c]Average judgment per problem; 10 (low) to 100.
[d]Number of problems completed.
[e]10 (*not better*) to 100 (*a whole lot better*).

nificant peer-model effect, $F(1, 44) = 6.63$, $p < .05$, and a significant peer-model $\times$ self-model interaction, $F(1, 44) = 18.21$, $p < .001$ ($MS_e = 578.29$). Peer-model ($p < .01$), self-model ($p < .01$), and peer- + self-model ($p < .05$) children solved significantly more problems than did videotape control subjects. More rapid problem solving was not attained at the expense of accuracy; similar results were obtained using the proportion of problems solved correctly (number correct divided by number completed).

Correlational analyses. Product-moment correlations were computed among self-efficacy for learning, perceived progress, in-structional session performance (number of problems completed), posttest self-efficacy, and skill. All correlations were positive and significant (*ps* < .05 except *p* < .01 for progress/posttest self-efficacy and instructional performance/posttest self-efficacy).

EXPERIMENT 2

In Experiment 2 we investigated the timing of self-model videotaping and tape review —early or later in the instructional program. We expected that exposure to self-model tapes would be more important than timing, despite Dowrick's (1983) suggestion that greater behavioral change occurs from viewing self-model tapes later in an experimental intervention. We thought that observing early successes would enhance children's self-efficacy for continued learning, motivation, and skill development throughout the instructional program. We also believed that the late self-model treatment would result in high task motivation during the remaining instructional sessions, because viewing personal successes on difficult tasks builds a strong sense of efficacy (Bandura, 1986).

Method

Subjects. Subject selection procedures were identical to those of Experiment 1. The final sample included 40 children (24 boys, 16 girls) enrolled in below grade level classes for mathematics in two elementary schools. Ages ranged from 10 years, 0 months to 12 years, 3 months ($M = 11.0$ years). Socioeconomic and ethnic backgrounds of subjects were similar to those in Experiment 1.

Materials and procedure. The pretest, instructional session, self-model videotape session, and posttest materials and procedures of Experiment 1 were used with the following modifications. After pretesting, children were assigned randomly within sex and school to one of four treatments—early self-model, late self-model, videotape control, or instructional control. Children in the first three conditions were videotaped during the experiment. The instructional control condition was included to disentangle effects of being videotaped from those due to receiving instruction. Instructional control children were told that they would be videotaped later (after the posttest). Children value the opportunity to be videotaped, and we did not want these subjects to become discouraged.

The videotaping procedure of Experiment 1 was used with the following modifications. Early self-model subjects were videotaped after the second instructional session, which gave children experience

with fractions but allowed for self-modeling effects in later sessions. Children solved 15 problems (about 15 min) comparable to those included in the first two instructional sessions. Late self-model subjects were videotaped after the fourth session, which permitted self-modeling effects during the two remaining sessions. These children solved 12 problems (about 15 min) comparable to those included in the third and fourth sessions. No child experienced conceptual difficulties while being taped. All subjects privately viewed their tapes on the day after taping and completed the perceived progress and self-efficacy for learning measures. Videotape control subjects were videotaped either after the second or fourth instructional session. They completed the progress and efficacy measures on the day following taping but did not view their tapes until after the posttest. Instructional control subjects completed the progress and efficacy measures either after session two or four.[3]

Results

Means and standard deviations are shown in Table 2. Preliminary ANOVAS yielded nonsignificant results.

Self-efficacy and skill. Each condition demonstrated significant ($ps < .01$) pretest-to-posttest increases in self-efficacy and skill except for instructional control subjects, who showed no change in self-efficacy. Posttest self-efficacy and skill were analyzed with a MANCOVA; the four treatments constituted the treatment factor. This analysis was sig-

---

[3] The self-efficacy for learning measure is not too meaningful for subjects in the late self-model condition, because when these subjects completed this measure they had learned to solve more than half of the problems portrayed. We administered this measure at this point to determine whether exposure to a self-model tape influenced self-efficacy. Self-efficacy for learning was not assessed in Experiment 3 because all subjects were videotaped late in the instructional program.

Table 2 Means and Standard Deviations: Experiment 2

Measure/Phase	Experimental Condition			
	Early Model	Late Model	Videotape Control	Instructional Control
Self-efficacy[a]				
Pretest				
M	43.8	41.0	37.4	44.1
SD	9.9	15.3	16.8	12.3
Posttest				
M	74.8	80.9	52.4	54.8
SD	14.2	15.3	13.9	14.6
Skill[b]				
Pretest				
M	2.8	2.5	2.4	2.8
SD	2.7	2.1	1.8	2.3
Posttest				
M	14.2	14.3	8.4	9.4
SD	2.7	2.5	2.3	2.8
Self-efficacy for learning[c]				
M	75.9	77.9	51.3	58.1
SD	11.7	13.4	15.0	11.9
Instructional performance[d]				
First half				
M	147.2	119.6	123.7	114.8
SD	22.9	45.8	28.5	39.6
Second half				
M	83.2	82.6	57.1	58.4
SD	18.1	11.3	26.0	18.3
Perceived progress[e]				
M	81.0	83.0	54.0	56.0
SD	13.7	8.2	12.6	15.8

Note: $N = 40$; n per condition = 10.
[a]Average judgment per problem; 10 (low) to 100.
[b]Number of correct solutions on 31 problems.
[c]Average judgment per problem; 10 (low) to 100.
[d]Number of problems completed.
[e]10 (*not better*) to 100 (*a whole lot better*).

nificant, $\lambda = .422$, $F(6, 66) = 5.94$, $p <$ .001. There were significant treatment effects on self-efficacy, $F(3, 35) = 9.35$, $p <$ .001 ($MS_e = 215.68$), and skill, $F(3, 35) = 14.51$, $p < .001$ ($MS_e = 6.65$). The early and late self-model conditions did not differ on either measure, but each condition outperformed the videotape and instructional control conditions ($ps < .01$ except $p < .05$ for the early self-model/ videotape control and early self-model/ instructional control comparisons on self-efficacy).

Instructional session measures. The self-efficacy for learning measure yielded a significant treatment effect, $F(3, 35) = 10.03$, $p < .001$ ($MS_e = 173.81$). The early and late self-model conditions did not differ, but each judged self-efficacy higher than the videotape control ($ps < .01$) and instructional control ($ps < .05$) conditions. The progress measure yielded a significant treatment effect, $F(3, 36) = 14.71$, $p < .001$ ($MS_e = 166.11$). Self-model conditions judged progress higher ($ps < .01$) than did the videotape and instructional control conditions.

Experimental conditions did not differ in the number of problems completed during the instructional sessions. To determine whether self-model timing influenced problem solving, we analyzed the number of problems that children completed during the first three instructional sessions and during the second three. First-half performance yielded nonsignificant results. A significant treatment effect was obtained on second-half performance, $F(3, 36) = 4.01$, $p < .05$ ($MS_e = 367.61$). Early and late self-model children completed more problems ($ps < .05$) than did videotape and instructional control subjects. Identical results were obtained using the proportion of problems solved correctly.

Correlational analyses. Correlational results were similar to those of Experiment 1. In addition, second-half performance was positively and significantly related to self-efficacy for learning, first-half performance, perceived progress, posttest self-efficacy, and skill.

EXPERIMENT 3

In Experiment 3 we examined how the content of self-model tapes influenced children's achievement beliefs and behaviors, where the content indicated either progress in skill development or complete mastery. As originally conceptualized, self-model tapes portray no errors (Dowrick, 1983; Hosford, 1981); however, viewing errors exerts beneficial effects on self-perceptions and behaviors when people believe that they have improved their skills or when they receive information on how to perform more productively (Hung & Rosenthal, 1981; Trower & Kiely, 1983). We believed that both the mastery and progress self-model treatments would lead children to believe that they had made progress in skill development and thereby enhance self-efficacy and achievement behaviors.

Method

Subjects. The final sample included 60 children (30 girls, 30 boys) enrolled in below grade level classes in two elementary schools. Ages ranged from 8 years, 7 months to 11 years, 5 months ($M = 10.2$ years). Socioeconomic and ethnic backgrounds were similar to those in Experiment 1.

Materials and procedure. The pretest, instructional session, videotape session, and posttest materials and procedures of the preceding experiments were employed with the following modifications. After pretesting, children were assigned randomly within sex and school to one of three conditions: mastery self-model, progress self-model, or videotape control. All subjects were videotaped on the day following the fourth instructional session. Children participated in a 45-min session during which they worked on addition of mixed numbers with and without carrying (e.g., $5\frac{1}{7} + 7$; $4\frac{5}{8} + \frac{2}{8}$; $5\frac{1}{6} + 1\frac{1}{6}$; $10\frac{6}{9} + 9\frac{7}{9}$). This material was not included in the instructional program, but there were three problems with mixed numbers on the skill test.

Each child was videotaped privately solving 12 problems (about 15 min) involving addition of mixed numbers with carrying (e.g., $7\frac{9}{11} + 3\frac{9}{11}$). The trainer initially solved two problems while verbalizing the steps involved. Children solved their problems at a chalkboard and were asked to verbalize as they proceeded. The trainer prompted children if they failed to verbalize or if they made computational errors. If children were unsure of what to do or made a conceptual error, the trainer responded with a prompt or provided corrective instruction.

Mastery and progress self-model conditions were distinguished by the timing of videotaping. Progress self-model subjects were videotaped during the first half of this instructional session; children were learning how to solve fractions with mixed numbers while they were being videotaped. Mastery self-model subjects were videotaped during the second half of this session; problem solving during videotaping constituted a review because they had solved comparable problems during the first half of the session. Self-model subjects viewed their videotapes the following day and completed the perceived progress measure. Videotape control children were videotaped during either the first or second half of this session. These children completed the progress measure the following day but not view their tapes until after the posttest.

Results

Children's videotapes were scored for conceptual errors by an adult who had not participated in the data collection. Conceptual errors included children not knowing how to solve a problem (e.g., asking the trainer for assistance) or performing an erroneous operation (adding denominators). The criteria for retaining subjects were no conceptual errors for mastery self-model subjects and no conceptual errors during the second half of the problem solving (i.e., last six problems) for progress self-model subjects. The mean numbers of conceptual errors made were 4.1 (progress self-model) and 2.7 (videotape control), which were not significantly different.[4]

Means and standard deviations are presented in Table 3. Preliminary ANOVAS yielded nonsignificant differences on all measures.

Self-efficacy and skill. Each experimental condition showed significant increases in self-efficacy and skill from pretest to posttest

---

[4] From the original sample we dropped 3 students whose problem-solving behaviors did not match their treatment assignments. Two children were dropped from the mastery self-model treatment, and 1 was excluded from the progress self-model condition. The criteria for retaining subjects also were applied to videotape control subjects, but no child in this condition had to be excluded.

($ps < .01$). MANCOVA applied to posttest self-efficacy and skill was significant, lambda = .481, $F(4, 108) = 11.93$, $p < .001$. Univariate ANCOVAS revealed significant treatment effects on self-efficacy, $F(2, 56) = 20.65$, $p < .001$ ($MS_e = 89.56$); and skill, $F(2, 56) = 21.29$, $p < .001$ ($MS_e = 11.49$). The two self-model conditions did not differ, but each condition scored higher on each measure than did the videotape control condition ($ps < .01$).

Instructional session performance. Analysis of the progress measure yielded a significant treatment effect, $F(2, 57) = 7.11$, $p < .01$ ($MS_e = 304.56$). Mastery ($p < .01$) and progress ($p < .05$) self-model subjects judged progress higher than videotape control children; the former two conditions did not differ.

The ANOVA applied to the number of problems completed during the instructional sessions was significant, $F(2, 57) = 8.12$, $p < .01$ ($MS_e = 260.83$). Self-model conditions did not differ, but each completed more problems than did the videotape control condition ($ps < .01$). Similar results were obtained using the proportion of problems solved correctly.

Correlational analyses. Product-moment correlations computed among progress, instructional performance (number of problems completed), posttest self-efficacy, and skill were significant and positive ($ps < .05$ except $p < .01$ for self-efficacy/skill and self-efficacy/progress).

GENERAL DISCUSSION

These studies support the idea that self-model treatments promote children's achievement behaviors during cognitive skill learning. Children who observed their successful problem solving judged their skill acquisition progress greater and demonstrated higher instructional performance, self-efficacy, and skill than did children who

Table 3 Means and Standard Deviations: Experiment 3

Measure/Phase	Experimental Condition		
	Mastery Model	Progress Model	Videotape Control
Self-efficacy[a]			
Pretest			
M	49.5	47.4	49.0
SD	20.2	22.8	18.4
Posttest			
M	85.7	82.1	67.6
SD	9.4	10.4	12.3
Skills[b]			
Pretest			
M	4.8	3.9	4.1
SD	4.0	2.7	2.6
Posttest			
M	15.0	14.1	8.3
SD	4.6	4.3	2.6
Instructional performance[c]			
M	181.4	180.4	158.7
SD	21.1	13.1	12.8
Perceived progress[d]			
M	73.0	68.0	53.0
SD	19.2	16.4	16.6

Note: N = 60; per condition = 20.
[a]Average judgment per problem; 10 (low) to 100.
[b]Number of correct solutions on 31 problems.
[c]Number of problems completed.
[d]10 (*not better*) to 100 (*a whole lot better*).

were videotaped but did not observe their tapes and those who were not videotaped. In Experiment 1 we found that the benefits of observing self-model tapes are comparable to those of videotaped peer models. In Experiment 2 we showed that observing a self-model tape is more important than the timing of the observation. In Experiment 3 we demonstrated that self-model tapes portraying progress in skill acquisition are as effective as tapes portraying mastery.

Children who have learning difficulties often doubt their capabilities and are unsure of how well they are developing skills (Schunk, in press). Videotape feedback showing their skillful performance conveys that they have made progress in skill development and that they can continue to improve their skills. Higher self-efficacy in-

stated by such self-observation enhances motivation and further skill acquisition. In the absence of this efficacy information, children might wonder whether they have improved their skills and whether they possess the requisite learning capability. Such doubts do not instill positive achievement beliefs or behaviors.

Experiment 1 supports the idea that observing peer models promotes children's self-efficacy for learning, which is substantiated later as children successfully solve problems (Schunk et al., 1987). Peer models raise self-efficacy in part through perceived model-observer similarity (Bandura, 1986). By observing similar peers, children may believe that if peers can learn to solve fractions, they, too, can improve their skills. Multiple models increases the likelihood that children will perceive themselves as similar to at least one of the models (Thelen et al., 1979).

In Experiment 2 we found that exposure to a self-model tape was beneficial but that timing made no difference. The effects of timing might depend in part on how difficult the task is for the subjects. Performing difficult tasks builds stronger self-efficacy than does success on easier tasks (Bandura, 1986). Given that our subjects had encountered prior arithmetic difficulties, the skills covered early in the instructional program probably were difficult for them. The timing issue could be investigated further by including tasks of varying difficulty and by determining whether repeated videotaping produces added benefits.

Experiment 3 revealed comparable benefits of mastery and progress self-model tapes. Both of these treatments portrayed successful problem solving, which raises self-efficacy (Bandura, 1986). Progress self-model children viewed some errors, but they judged their progress as high as did mastery self-model subjects. Showing errors, however, is not always desirable. Errors can have deleterious effects on subjects who already possess negative self-beliefs (Hosford & Mills, 1983; Trower & Kiely, 1983). Subjects who perceive little progress in learning are likely to believe that they are not capable of much improvement (Schunk, in press). When errors are portrayed, they need to be used as the basis for progress (i.e., making fewer errors now) or accompanied by information on how to perform more productively (Dowrick, 1983). Observing oneself overcome errors and master a task shows that one is capable of learning, which raises self-efficacy.

Self-model tapes allow one to review skills, but we do not believe that the obtained effects are due to instructional factors. Children in each condition received the same instructional program. Before self-model subjects observed their tapes, their performance did not differ from those of children not assigned to a self-model treatment (videotape or instructional control). The peer- + self-model subjects in Experiment 1 had two extra videotape skill reviews, yet they differed from self-model children only on the self-efficacy for learning measure administered immediately after exposure to peer models. Self-model subjects in Experiments 1 and 2 were videotaped solving problems they learned to solve prior to the taping; videotape review had little, if any, impact on their skill acquisition.

This is not to suggest that instruction is unimportant. Our self-model tapes were employed during a fractions instructional program. Videotaping children while they work on tasks and showing them their tapes will not raise self-efficacy if their skills are not well established and they receive no instruction or feedback. In therapeutic settings, the effectiveness of videotaped feedback depends on the presence of a comprehensive treatment program (Hung & Rosenthal, 1981).

We want to emphasize that the present results were obtained with children who had experienced mathematical difficulties and who had few prior successes with fractions. Many schoolchildren are confident about their learning abilities, including some with learning problems (Licht & Kistner, 1986). Children typically receive multiple cues that indicate they are learning and that raise their efficacy for continued learning (e.g., actual task successes, observation of successful peers, positive teacher feedback). For such children, observing a self-model tape may have no benefit because it would merely confirm what they already know. As a means of building self-efficacy and motivating students, self-model tapes seem most effective with students who typically experience problems or who doubt their capabilities to master skills.

Consistent with previous research (Schunk & Hanson, 1985; Schunk et al., 1987), these studies support the idea that self-efficacy is not merely a reflection of prior performances. In Experiments 1 and 2, for example, self-model and videotape control subjects did not differ in their problem solving prior to or during videotaping, yet observation of the tape raised self-model children's self-efficacy. The perception of progress is an important cue in gauging self-efficacy (Schunk, in press). This research also shows that capability self-perceptions bear an important relation to achievement. Personal expectations for success are viewed as important influences on behavior by various theories (Bandura, 1986; Corno & Mandinach, 1983; Covington & Beery, 1976; Weiner, 1985).

These results have implications for educational practice. Videotaping is common in schools, but it rarely is used to portray cognitive skill acquisition. Teachers have neither the time for videotaping nor the technical and editing skills. The present results suggest a target population for self-model tapes and a way to make tapes that requires little technical skill. Students who have experienced learning difficulties can be taped while they practice a recently acquired skill or while they are learning a skill. Videotapes of students' successful performances can serve as a useful adjunct to a sound instructional program in developing their skills and self-efficacy for applying them.

REFERENCES

Bandura, A. (1982). Self-efficacy mechanism in human agency. *American Psychologist, 37,* 122–147.

Bandura, A. (1986). *Social foundations of thought and action.* Englewood Cliffs, NJ: Prentice-Hall.

Carroll, W. R., & Bandura, A. (1982). The role of visual monitoring in observational learning of action patterns: Making the unobservable observable. *Journal of Motor Behavior, 14,* 153–167.

Corno, L., & Mandinach, E. B. (1983). The role of cognitive engagement in classroom learning and motivation. *Educational Psychologist, 18,* 88–108.

Covington, M. V., & Beery, R. G. (1976). *Self-worth and school learning.* New York: Holt, Rinehart & Winston.

CTB/McGraw-Hill. (1977). *California Achievement Tests.* New York: Author.

Davidson, E. S., & Smith, W. P. (1982). Imitation, social comparison, and self-reward. *Child Development, 53,* 928–932.

Davis, R. A. (1979). The impact of self-modeling on problem behaviors in school-age children. *School Psychology Digest, 8,* 128–132.

Dowrick, P. W. (1983). Self-modeling. In P. W. Dowrick & S. J. Biggs (Eds.), *Using video: Psychological and social applications* (pp. 105–124). Chichester, England: Wiley.

Dowrick, P. W., & Dove, C. (1980). The use of self-modeling to improve the swimming performance of spina bifida children. *Journal of Applied Behavior Analysis, 13,* 51–56.

Dowrick, P. W., & Hood, M. (1981). Comparison of self-modeling and small cash incentives in a sheltered workshop. *Journal of Applied Psychology, 66,* 394–397.

Dowrick, P. W., & Raeburn, J. M. (1977). Video editing and medication to produce a therapeutic self model. *Journal of Consulting and Clinical Psychology, 45,* 1156–1158.

Festinger, L. (1954). A theory of social comparison processes. *Human Relations, 7,* 117–140.

Fuller, F. F., & Manning, B. A. (1973). Self-confrontation reviewed: A conceptualization for video playback in teacher education. *Review of Educational Research, 43,* 469–528.

Hosford, R. E. (1981). Self-as-a-model: A cognitive social learning technique. *The Counseling Psychologist, 9*(1), 45–62.

Hosford, R. E., & Mills, M. E. (1983). Video in social skills training. In P. W. Dowrick & S. J. Biggs (Eds.), *Using video: Psychological and social applications* (pp. 125–150). Chichester, England: Wiley.

Hung, J. H., & Rosenthal, T. L. (1981). Therapeutic videotaped playback. In J. L. Fryrear & B. Fleshman (Eds.), *Videotherapy in mental health* (pp. 5–46). Springfield, IL: Thomas.

Kirk, R. E. (1982). *Experimental design: Procedures for the behavioral sciences* (2nd ed.). Belmont, CA: Brooks/Cole.

Licht, B. G., & Kistner, J. A. (1986). Motivational problems of learning-disabled children: Individual differences and their implications for treatment. In J. K. Torgesen & B. W. L. Wong (Eds.), *Psychological and educational perspectives on learning disabilities* (pp. 225–255). Orlando, FL: Academic Press.

Miklich, D. R., Chida, T. L., & Danker-Brown, P. (1977). Behavior modification by self-modeling without subject awareness. *Journal of Behavior Therapy and Experimental Psychiatry, 8*, 125–130.

Pigott, H. E., & Gonzales, F. P. (1987). Efficacy of videotape self-modeling in treating an electively mute child. *Journal of Clinical Child Psychology, 16*, 106–110.

Schunk, D. H. (1987). Peer models and children's behavioral change. *Review of Educational Research, 57*, 149–174.

Schunk, D. H. (in press). Self-efficacy and cognitive skill learning. In C. Ames & R. E. Ames (Eds.), *Research on motivation in education* (Vol. 3). Orlando, FL: Academic Press.

Schunk, D. H., & Hanson, A. R. (1985). Peer models: Influence on children's self-efficacy and achievement. *Journal of Educational Psychology, 77*, 313–322.

Schunk, D. H., Hanson, A. R., & Cox, P. D. (1987). Peer-model attributes and children's achievement behaviors. *Journal of Educational Psychology, 79*, 54–61.

Thelen, M. H., Fry, R. A., Fehrenbach, P. A., & Frautschi, N. M. (1979). Therapeutic videotape and film modeling: A review. *Psychological Bulletin, 86*, 701–720.

Trower, P., & Kiely, B. (1983). Video feedback: Help or hindrance? A review and analysis. In P. W. Dowrick & S. J. Biggs (Eds.), *Using video: Psychological and social applications* (pp. 181–197). Chichester, England: Wiley.

Weiner, B. (1985). An attributional theory of achievement motivation and emotion. *Psychological Review, 92*, 548–573.

Winer, B. J. (1971). *Statistical principles in experimental design* (2nd ed.). New York: McGraw-Hill.

Hoge, R. D., & Coladarci, T. (1989). Teacher-based judgments of academic achievement: A review of literature. *Review of Educational Research, 59,* 297–313. Copyright 1989 by the American Educational Research Association. Reprinted by permission of the publisher.

Teacher-Based Judgments of Academic Achievement: A Review of Literature

Robert D. Hoge
Carleton University

Theodore Coladarci
University of Maine

The focus of this paper is on data reflecting the match between teacher-based assessments of students' achievement levels and an objective measure of student learning. These data are treated as relevant to the validity or accuracy of the judgmental measures. The paper begins with a discussion of two contexts in which such judgments are relevant: the teacher decision-making and assessment contexts. The second section presents a review of studies in which data are presented on the match between judgments and test scores. Two types of studies are reviewed. The first represents an indirect test of validity in the sense that there is a discrepancy between the judgmental measure (usually a rating of achievement) and the criterion measure (a score on a standardized achievement test). The second provides a more direct test of validity in that teachers are directly asked to estimate the achievement test performance of their students. On the whole, the results revealed high levels of validity for the teacher-judgment measures. The studies revealed, however, some variability across teachers in accuracy levels and suggested the operation of certain other moderator variables. The paper concludes with a set of recommendations for future research on the judgments and a set of recommendations for improvements in the teacher-assessment process.

In this paper we examine the empirical literature on the match between teacher-based assessments of student achievement levels and objective measures of student learning. Our specific concern is with the examination of concurrent relationships: the extent to which a teacher's a priori judgment of a student's achievement corresponds to the student's actual achievement on a measure administered at approximately the same time. These data are treated as reflecting on the validity or accuracy of the teacher-judgment measures. We begin with a discussion of the contexts in which teacher judgment emerges as an important question.

THE CONTEXT OF TEACHER JUDGMENTS

Teacher Cognition

Models of teacher cognition suggest that teachers base their instructional decisions, in part, on judgments they make of student comprehension (e.g., Borko, Cone, Russo, & Shavelson, 1979; Clark & Peterson, 1986; Peterson, 1988; Shavelson & Stern, 1981). In the preinstructional, or preactive, phase of teaching, for example, teachers form judgments about their students' relative reading abilities before making decisions about instructional groupings (Shavelson & Borko, 1979).

There also is evidence that these judgments influence decisions in the interactive phase of teaching. McNair (1978–1979), through stimulated recall interviews, found that teachers' main consideration in making decisions during reading instruction was student achievement. Her 10 teachers "based many of their decisions on *what they surmised* was happening" with each student (p. 32; italics added). Research on "steering groups" further illustrates the role teacher judgments can play in the classroom. Specifically, Dahllof and Lundgren (1970, cited in Clark & Peterson, 1986, p. 256) found that teachers paced whole-class instruction according to whether a reference group of students (the steering group) "seemed to understand what was being presented." If teachers judged sufficient comprehension on the part of the steering group, a new topic was introduced; if not, the pace was slowed.

Through a series of stimulated recall interviews with six teachers, Colker (1984) found that 41% of the teachers' interactive thoughts pertained to student cognition. And 61% of these thoughts were categorized by Colker as "pupil": "The teacher evaluates or questions pupil comprehension, learning, thinking, knowledge, or task performance (e.g., 'I was thinking . . . that they don't understand what they're doing')" (Colker, 1984, Table 3). Indeed, in their review of this literature, Clark and Peterson (1986) reported that the largest proportion of teachers' interactive thoughts pertained to the "learner" (p. 269).

Thus, it is apparent that the decision-making process of teachers, particularly in the interactive context, is influenced by the judgments they make about their students' cognitions. In turn, it seems reasonable to suggest that the decision-making process proceeds differently when based on accurate teacher judgments than when based on inaccurate teacher judgments (cf. Clark & Peterson, 1986; Peterson, 1988). This, then, is the primary context in which the accuracy of teacher judgments surfaces as an important question.

The Assessment Issue

The accuracy of achievement judgments may also be viewed as relevant in an assessment context. We clearly depend on teacher-based assessments of academic achievement in making educational decisions regarding students and for providing feedback to children, parents, and school psychologists (Elliott, Gresham, Freeman, & McCloskey, 1988; Gerber & Semmel, 1984; Hoge, 1983). These judgments probably constitute the primary source of information in such contexts. Similarly, there is a heavy dependence on these achievement judgments in research settings; teacher ratings of performance levels frequently appear as measures in research and evaluation studies (cf. Gresham, 1981; Hoge, 1983).

Often, these teacher-based measures are treated in a very casual way. For example, teachers are often asked to designate the students in their classroom possessing high "gifted potential" without being provided any real guidance in defining the construct (Hoge & Cudmore, 1986). There is, however, an increasing recognition that the judgments and assessments of teachers are being used as psychological measures and that the same psychometric criteria that apply to other measures, such as tests or observation schedules, should apply here as well (Edelbrock, 1983; Gerber & Semmel, 1984; Gresham, 1981; Hoge, 1983, 1984; Hoge & Cudmore, 1986).

There is another sense in which the accuracy issue is important within this assessment context. There seems to be a widespread assumption, particularly among school psychologists, educational researchers, and other professionals, that teachers are generally poor judges of the attributes of their students—that their perceptions are often subject to bias and error. This assumption is rarely given explicit acknowledgment, but it does exist, and it has been discussed in connection with the decision-making literature by Egan and Archer (1985), the expectancy literature by Brophy (1983) and Hoge (1984), and the assessment literature by Hoge (1983) and Hoge and Cudmore (1986). One form of the criticism has been expressed as follows:

> Directly or indirectly, the accuracy of teachers' assessments of student ability is often an issue in educational research. It is commonly argued that commercial tests provide teachers with valuable information about the abilities and deficiencies of their students, from which it follows that teachers who rate their students without such information will often be in error. (Egan & Archer, 1985, p. 25)

Such an assumption represents a rather serious criticism of teachers, and a careful examination of the evidence bearing on it is therefore in order.

REVIEW OF THE RESEARCH
Terms of the Review

The studies reviewed here are ones in which data are presented regarding the relationships between teacher judgments of student achievement and the student's actual performance on an independent criterion of achievement. The studies were located through a search of *Psychological Abstracts* and ERIC databases and a manual search of key journals. With three exceptions, the studies focused on students within regular classrooms. The exceptions are Gresham, Reschly, and Carey, (1987), who included both learning disabled (LD) and non-LD students in their sample; Leinhardt (1983), whose sample solely comprised LD students; and Silverstein, Brownlee, Legutki, and MacMillan (1983), who used only educable mentally retarded (EMR) students.

Three constraints were imposed for selecting studies. First, only studies employing naturalistic data were included; thus, analogue and simulation studies are not represented in the review. Second, the review focuses on cases where judgmental and test data were collected concurrently; thus, expectancy-type studies where teachers were asked to make a prediction of future performance are not included. Third, the review includes only published studies. This last criterion was introduced to ensure that some minimal level of methodological standards was met and that readers have access to original sources. (See Achenbach, McConaughy, & Howell, 1987, for an elaboration of this and related points.)

Methodological Considerations

The 16 studies included in the review have a common focus: the relationship between teachers' judgments of their students' academic performance and the students' actual performance on an achievement criterion. These studies are methodologically similar in some general respects: Each contains a variable representing a teacher's judgment of a student's academic performance and each examined the correspondence between the teacher-judgment measure and student performance on a standardized achievement test.

There are also a number of methodological differences among these 16 studies that affect interpretation of results. These methodological characteristics are summarized in Table 1. A synthesis of the research results follows a discussion of these characteristics.

Direct versus indirect evaluations of teacher judgments. Nine of the studies summarized in Table 1 entailed relating teacher ratings or rankings of achievement levels to standardized achievement test scores. For example, Airasian, Kellaghan, Madaus, and Pedulla (1977) had teachers rate, on a 5-point scale, the performance of their students in English and mathematics and then related those ratings to standardized achievement test scores. These ratings are viewed as indirect evaluations of teacher judgments insofar as teachers were not

Table 1 Methodology Characteristics of the Studies Reviewed

Author	Direct vs. Indirect	Judgment Measure	Reference Group	Accuracy Assessment	Unit of Analysis
Airasian, Kellaghan, Madaus, & Pedulla (1977)	I	Ratings	NR	C	Pooled
Coladarci (1986)	D	IR	PI	C & PA	WC
Doherty & Conolly (1985)	D	GE	NR	C	Pooled
Farr & Roelke (1971)	D	Ratings	NR	C[a]	WC
Gresham, Reschly, & Carey (1987)	—	Ratings	NR	C	Pooled
Helmke & Schrader (1987)	D	NC	PI	C	WC
Hoge & Butcher (1984)	D	GE	NR	C & MR	Pooled[b]
Hopkins, Dobson, & Oldridge (1962)	—	Rankings	NR	C	Pooled
Hopkins, George, & Williams (1985)	—	Ratings	NR	C	WC
Leinhardt (1983)	D	IR	PI	C & PA	Pooled
Luce & Hoge (1978)	—	Rankings	NR	C	Pooled
Oliver & Arnold (1978)	—	GE	NR	C	Pooled
Pedulla, Airasian, & Madaus (1980)	—	Ratings	NR	C	Pooled
Sharpley & Edgar (1986)	—	Ratings	NR	C[a]	Pooled
Silverstein, Brownlee, Legutki, & MacMillan (1983)	—	Ratings	NR	C	Pooled
Wright & Wiese (1988)	I & D	Ratings, GE	NR	C	Pooled

Note: I = indirect, D = direct, IR = item response estimates, GE = grade equivalence or percentile estimates, NC = number correct estimates, NR = norm-referenced estimates, PI = peer-independent estimates, C = correlational analysis, PA = percent agreement, WC = within class.
[a]Complete multitrait-multimethod analysis performed.
[b]Analyses were based on both pooled and within-class data.

asked specifically to estimate achievement test performance.

The direct judgments, in contrast, asked teachers specifically to estimate their students' performance on a concurrently administered achievement test. Helmke and Schrader (1987), for example, had teachers estimate the number of problems on an achievement test that each student would solve correctly. Teacher judgments of this kind represent direct judgments in that there is a stronger logical link between judgment and criterion. Seven of the studies summarized in Table 1 employed direct assessments; Wright and Wiese (1988) included both types.

Judgment specificity. The direct/indirect distinction also has implications for the specificity of the judgment, although the link is not entirely consistent. By definition, indirect measures of teacher judgments are less specific than direct measures in that the former are not explicitly tied to any one criterion in the judgmental process. Nonetheless, the degree of specificity varies among studies employing only indirect measures of teacher judgments. Luce and Hoge (1978), for example, asked teachers to rank order their students on various academic abilities. This kind of judgment, albeit indirect, requires teachers to make finer discriminations among students than those required by a 5-point rating scale.

Similarly, degree of specificity varies among studies involving direct measures of teacher judgments, although these direct measures are, in general, more specific than the indirect. For example, Hoge and Butcher (1984) asked teachers to estimate, in grade-equivalence scores, the likely performance of each of their students on an achievement test administered concurrently. Although direct, this summary index is less specific than the format employed by Coladarci (1986) and Leinhardt (1983), where teachers were asked to make judgments on an item-by-item basis.

Five types of judgment measures were employed in the studies reviewed, and these can be ordered roughly by the level of specificity the judgment entailed: (a) *ratings* (low specificity), where teachers rated each student's academic ability (e.g., "lowest fifth of class" to "highest fifth of class"); (b) *rankings*, where teachers were asked to rank order their students according to academic ability; (c) *grade equivalence*, where teachers estimated, in the grade-equivalent metric, each student's likely performance on a concurrently administered achievement test; (d) *number correct*, where teachers were asked to estimate, for each student, the number of correct responses on an achievement test, administered concurrently; and (e) *item responses* (high specificity), where teachers indicated, for each item on an achievement test administered concurrently to the students, whether they thought the student would respond correctly to the item or had sufficient instruction to respond correctly.

Norm-referenced versus peer-independent judgments. Some teacher-judgment measures had a decidedly norm-referenced flavor, whereas others did not. Regarding the former, for example, 1 and 5 on the 5-point teacher judgment scale in the Airasian et al. (1977) study signified a student in the *lowest fifth* and *highest fifth* of the class, respectively. Rankings, as well as estimates of grade equivalents and instructional levels, also reflect a norm-referenced judgment. In contrast, a peer-independent judgment is called for where, for example, the teacher is asked to estimate the number of test problems a student will solve correctly. This judgment does not require the teacher to compare one student with another.

Assessing the accuracy of teacher judgments. Where teacher judgments were expressed as ratings, rankings, grade equivalents, or total-score estimates, the accuracy of the judgments was assessed by examining the correlation between judgment and criterion. Thus, accuracy is operationally defined as the correspondence between the relative standing of two sets of values: (a) the teachers' judgments of their students and (b) the students' actual performance on a relevant standardized test. Fourteen of the 16 studies reported correlations (or regression coefficients) as the sole index of accuracy.

Offering an alternative operational definition of accuracy, Coladarci (1986) examined the percentage of items for which (a) the teacher reported the student would answer the item correctly and (b) the student, in fact, answered the item correctly. Leinhardt (1983) also obtained item-level judgments: She determined the percentage of items—what she called the "hit rate"—for which (a) the teacher indicated sufficient instruction had been provided for the student to answer the test item correctly and (b) the student, in fact, answered the item correctly. In addition to examining accuracy in this way, both Coladarci and Leinhardt reported correlations between summary measures of teacher judgment and student achievement. That is, a "total" teacher judgment was derived by summing the teacher's item-level judgments, which, in turn, were correlated with the students' total scores on the achievement criterion. (A parallel procedure was followed to construct subscale teacher judgments.)

Unit of analysis. Researchers took one of two general approaches in calculating correlations between judgment and criterion. Some investigators combined K teachers and N students into a single, undifferentiated group. That is, class membership was ignored. Such a procedure can either overestimate or underestimate the judgment/criterion relationship. For example, where teacher judgments are in the form of ratings, judgment/criterion correlations based on a single, undifferentiated group will be attenuated by individual differences among teachers in how each calibrates the rating scale (Hopkins, George, & Williams, 1985).

Irrespective of calibration error, these correlations also will be underestimated

where there is a positive correlation between judgment and criterion when computed for each of the K classes separately, but the scatterplot with all classes combined is considerably less elliptical. This could occur, for example, where there is little variability among class means on either the criterion measure or the judgment measure.

A similar phenomenon can *over*estimate the judgment/criterion relationship. That is, one might obtain a significant correlation when based on a single, undifferentiated group of N students; when computed for each of the K classes separately, however, the correlation is zero. (Imagine a series of circles, sloping upward at a 45° angle.) Thus, within any one class, a teacher's judgments about student knowledge could be quite inaccurate. By determining the relationship across a wide range of classes, however, the investigator artificially inflates the judgment/criterion correlation.

To address these concerns, some investigators have incorporated class membership into their statistical analyses. In three studies, for example, the investigators computed judgment/criterion correlations separately for each of K classes and then, using the r to z transformation, determined the mean within-class correlation (Coladarci, 1986; Farr & Roelke, 1971; Hopkins et al., 1985). Choosing an alternative to this procedure, Helmke and Schrader (1987) simply reported the median of K correlations. Finally, Hoge and Butcher (1984) presented K within-class regression equations, where the dependent variable was a teacher judgment measure and one of the predictors was the student's performance on an achievement test. (Hoge and Butcher also presented the regression equation on the basis of a single, undifferentiated group of N students.)

The Correspondence Between Teacher Judgments and Student Achievement

Table 2 contains a summary of the principal findings of the studies, divided according to

Table 2 Summary of Results

Study	Results	
	Indirect Assessments	
Airasian, Kellaghan, Madaus, & Pedulla (1977)	Reading	$r = .64$
	Math	$r = .62$
Gresham, Reschly, & Carey (1987)	Reading recognition	$r = .62$[a]
		$r = .67$
	Reading comprehension	$r = .64$
		$r = .66$
Hopkins, Dobson, & Oldridge (1962)	Reading	$r = .79$ (Grade 1)
		$r = .74$ (Grade 2)
		$r = .86$ (Grade 3)
		$r = .86$ (Grade 4)
		$r = .85$ (Grade 5)
Hopkins, George, & Williams (1985)	Reading	$r = .73$
	Language arts	$r = .74$
	Math	$r = .72$
	Social studies	$r = .64$
	Science	$r = .60$
Luce & Hoge (1978)	Reading	$r = .41$
	Math problem solving	$r = .28$
	Math concepts	$r = .29$
Oliver & Arnold (1978)	Reading	$r = .74$
Pedulla, Airasian, & Madaus (1980)	Reading	$r = .65$
	Math	$r = .63$
Sharpley & Edgar (1986)	Reading vocabulary	$r = .42$ (boys)
		$r = .44$ (girls)
	Reading comprehension	$r = .50$ (boys)
		$r = .56$ (girls)
	Math	$r = .45$ (boys)
		$r = .38$ (girls)
Silverstein, Brownlee, Legutki, & MacMillan (1983)	Reading	$r = .55$[b]
		$r = .61$
		$r = .48$
	Math	$r = .44$
		$r = .55$
		$r = .37$
Wright & Wiese (1988)	Reading	$r = .71$
	Language arts	$r = .70$
	Math	$r = .71$
	Social studies	$r = .57$
	Direct Assessments	
Coladarci (1986)	Reading vocabulary	$r = .67$ (74%)[c]
	Reading comprehension	$r = .70$ (73%)
	Math concepts	$r = .72$ (70%)
	Math comprehension	$r = .70$ (76%)
Doherty & Conolly (1985)	Math	$r = .67$
	English	$r = .72$
	Reading	$r = .68$

Table 2 Summary of Results (Continued)

Study	Results	
Farr & Roelke (1971)	Reading vocabulary	$r = .92$
	Reading comprehension	$r = .59$
	Reading word analysis	$r = 48$
Helmke & Schrader (1987)	Math	$r = .67$
Hoge & Butcher (1984)	Reading	$\beta = .71$[d]
Leinhardt (1983)	Reading	$r = .67$ (64%)[e]
Wright & Wiese (1988)	Reading	$r = .82$
	Math	$r = .77$
	Language arts	$r = .76$
	Social studies	$r = .67$

[a]Separate ratings were collected for (a) pupils judged relative to classmates and (b) relative to grade-level expectations.
[b]Based on data collected on a group of pupils in each of 3 successive years.
[c]Agreement between teachers' item judgments and students' item responses in parentheses.
[d]Beta based on teacher estimate of performance wtih pupil IQ the other independent variable; multiple $R = .85$.
[e]Agreement between teachers' item judgments regarding sufficiency of instruction and students' item responses in parentheses.

whether they called for direct or indirect teacher judgments of student achievement. Taken as a whole, these studies yielded judgment/criterion correlations ranging from 0.28 to 0.92. The median correlation, 0.66, suggests a moderate to strong correspondence between teacher judgments and student achievement. Instead of reporting a judgment/criterion correlation, Hoge and Butcher (1984) presented the results of a multiple regression analysis in which achievement test, IQ, and gender served as the predictors of teacher judgments. The standardized partial regression coefficient associated with achievement test was 0.71, which, like the correlations above, suggests a strong correspondence between teacher judgments and student achievement.

The percentage-agreement statistics reported by Coladarci (1986) similarly point to the validity of teacher judgments. Teachers, on the average, correctly judged their students' responses to at least 70% of the items on reading and mathematics subtests. Somewhat analogous to this statistic, Leinhardt (1983) found a "hit rate" of 64% on a reading comprehension test. That is, for roughly two thirds of test items, teachers were correct in determining whether sufficient instruc-

tion had been provided for the student to answer the item correctly.

As noted above, however, these 17 studies vary methodologically in several basic ways. Do these methodological differences affect the results of these studies, particularly those involving judgment/criterion correlations? To address this question, we determined the median judgment/criterion correlation for the following methodological groupings: (a) indirect versus direct teacher judgments, (b) levels of judgment specificity, (c) norm-referenced or peer-independent teacher judgments, and (d) statistical analyses based on a single, undifferentiated group versus those that took class membership into account.

Indirect versus direct teacher judgments. Direct teacher judgments entailed an explicit link between criterion and judgment. In contrast, indirect evaluations did not involve an explicit criterion. Instead, the teacher was asked to provide an achievement judgment, but with little guidance as to the nature of the construct. Yet, in both cases, teacher judgments were related to a single criterion: a score on a standardized achievement test.

Insofar as an ambiguous link between judgment and criterion should attenuate resulting correlations, one might expect *indirect* teacher judgments to correlate less with actual achievement than do *direct* teacher judgments. Interestingly, although this was the case, the differences were not dramatic. Among the studies calling for indirect teacher judgments, the judgment/criterion correlations ranged from 0.28 to 0.86; the median correlation was 0.62. In contrast, the studies involving direct assessments of teacher judgments yielded a range of judgment/criterion correlations of 0.48 to 0.92, with a median correlation of 0.69.

Judgment specificity. As indicated above, the operational definitions of teacher judgments in these studies differed in their specificity. For example, ratings required the least specificity: Teachers merely were asked to place each student on a scale ranging from, say, 1 to 5. All other forms of teacher judgments, on the other hand, called for considerably greater specificity. In ranking students, for example, the teacher must consider each student relative to his or her classmates; in predicting a student's actual achievement score, the teacher selects from a full continuum of possible values.

Among studies employing ratings—the predominant form of teacher judgment—the median judgment/criterion correlation was 0.61, with a range from 0.37 to 0.92. In fact, these correlations were generally lower than those associated with ranks (median r = 0.76; range: 0.28 to 0.86), grade equivalents (median r = 0.70; range: 0.67 to 0.74), number correct (single study r = 0.67), and item judgments (median r = 0.70; range: 0.67 to 0.72). The lower correlations associated with ratings probably reflect teachers' disclination to use the full range of rating categories, which reduces the variability among teacher judgments and, consequently, the judgment/criterion correlations (Hopkins et al., 1985). The relative value of these correlations notwithstanding,

there is strong correspondence between teacher judgment and student achievement, irrespective of how the former is operationally defined.

Norm-referenced versus peer independent. Again, some teacher judgments were measured in a norm-referenced fashion (e.g., rankings, grade equivalents); others called for peer-independent judgments (e.g., number correct, item judgments). This distinction, however, did not appreciably affect the judgment/criterion correlations. Among studies employing peer-independent ratings, the median judgment/criterion correlation was 0.68, with a range from 0.67 to 0.72; for norm-referenced judgments, the median correlation was 0.64, with a range from 0.28 to 0.92.

Unit of analysis. Most researchers based their correlational analyses on a single, undifferentiated group. Some, however, took class membership into account by determining the mean (or median) within-class correlation. Interestingly, both kinds of analyses produced similar judgment/criterion correlations. Among studies where the analyses involved a single, undifferentiated group, the median judgment/criterion correlation was 0.64, with a range from 0.28 to 0.86; for within-class analyses, the median correlation was 0.70, with a range from 0.48 to 0.92.

Moderator Variables

Some researchers explored the possible effects of additional variables on the accuracy of teacher judgments.

Differences among teachers. Research on teacher decision making has pointed to the hazards of pooling data across teachers in reporting summary statistics such as correlations or regression coefficients. Specifically, such a practice fails to recognize individual differences among teachers in their cognitions and instructional strategies (e.g., Borko & Cadwell, 1982; Clark & Peterson, 1986; Shavelson, Webb, & Burstein, 1986).

Although most of the studies in our review pooled data across teachers, there were some exceptions. For studies solely reporting judgment/criterion correlations, these exceptions entailed the separate calculation of K correlations, where K corresponds to the number of teachers. Variability among the K correlations, of course, speaks to the question of individual differences among teachers in the accuracy of their judgments.

In short, these data suggest that teachers do, in fact, differ in how accurately they judge their students' achievement. For example, Hopkins et al. (1985) obtained a range of within-class correlations of 0.44 to 0.88 across their 42 teachers. Even greater variability among teachers was found by Helmke and Schrader (1987), who reported within-class correlations ranging from .03 to .90 ($K = 31$). Finally, Hoge and Butcher (1984) also uncovered individual differences among teachers in judgment accuracy. As shown above, these researchers estimated separate within-class multiple regression equations, where the dependent variable was teacher judgment and the predictor variables were IQ, achievement test, and gender. Hoge and Butcher reported standardized partial regression coefficients for achievement test ranging from 0.40 to 0.87 ($K = 12$).

Finally, Coladarci (1986) investigated teacher effects on his percentage-agreement index by treating "teacher" as the independent variable in an analysis of variance; the dependent variable, percentage agreement, was the mean percentage of items for which the teacher correctly judged the student's item-level responses. A significant teacher effect was found for one of the four achievement areas: mathematics concepts.

Although the 16 studies generally point to the validity of teacher-based achievement judgments, the results of the four studies just discussed are important insofar as they demonstrate that not all teachers are equally

adept at making these judgments. "Teacher judgment accuracy," then, appears to be an individual-difference variable that is worthy of further examination in research on teaching.

Student gender. In all three studies examining it, student gender failed to show a significant effect on the judgment/criterion relation (Doherty & Conolly, 1985; Hoge & Butcher, 1984; Sharpley & Edgar, 1986). These essentially negative results are consistent with the general findings within the teacher-judgment literature. Thus, although Dusek and Joseph (1983) concluded that teachers hold differential social-behavioral expectations for boys and girls, their meta-analysis yielded no significant gender differences in expectations for academic performance (also see Brophy & Good, 1974.)

Subject matter differences. Although a number of researchers reported analyses separately by subject matter, in only two cases was this variable systematically analyzed. Hopkins et al. (1985) found that judgment/criterion correlations for achievement in social studies and science were significantly lower than for achievement in language arts, reading, and math. However, the magnitude of correlations in all five content areas was appreciable.

Coladarci (1986) calculated his percentage-agreement index separately for four subtests: reading vocabulary, reading comprehension, mathematics concepts, and mathematics computation. An analysis of variance resulted in a significant effect of subject matter: Teachers were considerably more accurate in judging performance in mathematics computation than in mathematics concepts. He saw this difference as due, in part, to the greater amount of direct instruction involved in teaching computation skills compared with mathematics concepts.

Student ability. Student ability, broadly conceived, was explored as a potential moderator variable in two studies. Although Leinhardt (1983) did not report detailed data on the issue, she did indicate that her "hit rate" index correlated $r = 0.39$ with actual achievement. That is, teachers of the learning disabled were somewhat more accurate in judging the sufficiency of instruction for higher-achieving than for lower-achieving students.

Coladarci (1986) found substantial correlations between his percentage-agreement index and student ability: rs ranged from 0.78 to 0.89, depending on the subject matter. Across all items on the four subtests, the mean percentage agreement was roughly 60% for students in the lowest quartile and 88% for students in the highest quartile. Clearly, these eight teachers were less able to judge the performance of their lower-achieving students.

Student IQ was explored as a moderator of the judgment/criterion relation in one study. Because they included student IQ as a predictor variable in their study, Hoge and Butcher (1984) were able to separate the effect of student "intelligence" from student "achievement" in predicting teacher judgments of the latter. With 12 teachers pooled, IQ made a significant contribution to the prediction of the achievement judgments ($\beta = 0.18$), although the magnitude of the contribution was far less than that of the achievement test scores ($\beta = 0.71$). It is interesting to observe, however, that the extent of the independent contribution of IQ scores to the achievement judgments varied widely across the 12 teachers. This is evident both from the separate within-class multiple regression analyses and from an analysis of residual scores in which it was revealed that 4 of the 12 teachers displayed a tendency to overestimate the performance of high-IQ students.

There is, then, a relatively strong suggestion from these four studies that students' academic ability may influence the accuracy with which teachers judge student achievement. Coladarci (1986) suggested that the higher levels of accuracy observed for high-performance pupils may arise from a response set that operates with the achievement judgments; however, as he admitted, the whole issue requires further exploration.

DISCUSSION

The 16 studies reviewed in the previous section yielded data indicating generally high levels of agreement between the judgmental measures and the standardized achievement test scores. The range of correlations for the indirect comparisons was 0.28 to 0.86, with a median correlation of 0.62, whereas the direct tests yielded a range of correlations from 0.48 to 0.92, with a median of 0.69. In our view, these data support the validity of the teacher judgments of academic achievement. The correlations certainly exceed the convergent and concurrent validity coefficients normally reported for psychological tests, and it is encouraging that the correlations remain strong irrespective of methodological distinctions among the studies. Finally, it is worth noting that the levels of association between teacher judgment measures and the criterion measures uncovered in this review were similar to those reported in teacher expectation studies (cf. Brophy, 1983).

This overall positive conclusion regarding the accuracy of these judgments must, as we have shown, be interpreted in light of some methodological considerations and the operation of moderator variables. (These considerations are dealt with in the following sections detailing research and practical implications.) Still, the conclusion that these achievement judgments are generally veridical has important implications for the teacher decision-making and assessment contexts discussed at the beginning of our review.

Teacher cognitions about student attributes and performance levels constitute only one element in the teacher decision-making process. It can be argued, however, that they are critical elements in the process: Other things being equal, decisions based on accurate assessments of student attributes will be more functional than those based on inaccurate assessments. Our conclusion that the achievement judgments are generally veridical is an encouraging one in this context, but it also highlights the importance of considering this aspect of the decision-making process in future analyses.

Our conclusion that the performance judgments are, by and large, valid also has important implications for the practical use of teacher-based assessments. In particular, it speaks to members of the public and to educational professionals (e.g., university-based researchers, school psychologists) who express doubts regarding the quality of teacher-based assessments of students. Although the studies in our review by no means provide a final evaluation of the accuracy of achievement judgments or any evidence that the judgments are without error, this literature does not support the total rejection of teacher judgments that one sometimes encounters.

Implications for Research

The first recommendation is that research be guided by more explicit statements of the achievement construct. Much of the research has entailed global achievement judgments being assessed against scores from standardized achievement tests that are sometimes of questionable construct validity (Linn, 1986; Sattler, 1988; Snow, 1980). It is, therefore, not always clear in this research just what aspect of student performance is being assessed.

A related point is that, in developing this achievement construct, efforts should be made to ensure that the construct is one relevant to the teaching process. There are several aspects to this issue. First, questions can be raised about the extent to which the definition of achievement represented in standardized achievement tests corresponds to the learning objectives of a particular classroom. Second, questions can be raised about the meaningfulness of the global

achievement judgments collected in many of the studies reviewed. As Coladarci (1986) noted in his study. "Because of the summary nature of such teacher judgments, little is disclosed about the teacher's specific knowledge of what the student has and has not mastered in some domain" (p. 142). Future research should probably employ specific rather than global judgment indices.

A second recommendation for future research in this area is that closer attention be paid to the match between judgment and criterion. Although our analysis did not reveal major differences in the outcomes of direct and indirect tests of validity, the use of parallel judgment/criterion dimensions facilitates a less equivocal interpretation of findings. A related suggestion is that the measurement scales underlying judgment and criterion should correspond (Egan & Archer, 1985).

Third, we recommend that both convergent and discriminant validity of teacher judgments be examined. We have seen that most of the validity evaluations focused on convergent validity. The two cases using complete multitrait-multimethod matrices, Farr and Roelke (1971) and Silverstein et al. (1983), found support for convergent validity but reported less impressive levels of discriminant validity. Evaluations focusing on both convergent and discriminant validity actually have two advantages. First, they provide us with more complete validity evaluations of the judgmental measure and, second, they encourage a more thorough exploration of the achievement construct.

A fourth recommendation is that further attention be paid to the operation of moderator variables in the judgment/criterion relation. For example, rather strong suggestions were obtained in this literature to the effect that student ability and achievement levels might be functioning as moderators and that teachers might be more accurate at assessing achievement in high- than low-performing students (Coladarci, 1986; Hoge & Butcher, 1984; Leinhardt, 1983). Unfortunately, in no case were variables that might be associated with this effect investigated, and it certainly merits further exploration. It should be noted, however, that there are nagging methodological problems with analyses of this kind that make these findings difficult to interpret (cf. Gage & Cronbach, 1955; Kenny & Albright, 1987).

The most convincing evidence for the operation of a moderator was in connection with the teacher variable; Coladarci (1986), Helmke and Schrader (1987), Hoge and Butcher (1984), and Hopkins et al. (1985) all presented evidence of individual differences among teachers in judgmental accuracy. Unfortunately, the research included in the review provides few clues as to whether these differences arise from characteristics of teachers (e.g., experience, training, teaching philosophy, measurement policy), the composition of the class, or some other variable. It is worth noting, however, that useful information regarding individual differences in teacher judgments can be found in the teacher expectancy (e.g., Babad, Inbar, & Rosenthal, 1982; Tom, Cooper, & McGraw, 1984) and teacher cognition (e.g., Carpenter, Fennema, Peterson, & Carey, 1988; Carpenter, Fennema, Peterson, Chiang, & Loef, in press; Peterson, Carpenter, & Fennema, in press) literatures. The latter studies are especially interesting in that they are able to link individual differences among teachers in cognitions about pupils to differences in teacher effectiveness.

Implications for Teaching

The achievement judgments revealed themselves to be generally accurate. Still, there was clearly some degree of error operating, and, further, levels of accuracy varied across teachers. There is, therefore, room for improvement.

There are several directions these efforts might take. First, greater efforts should be made to sensitize teachers to the extent and importance of the assessment role in the teaching process (Hoge, 1983; Hoge & Cudmore, 1986). Second, more intensive ex-

perience with the basic principles of measurement and assessment should be provided. Third, teachers should be familiarized with the interpretation of different types of assessment devices, including norm-referenced tests, observational procedures, and judgmental measures. Fourth, improved judgmental tools should be developed and made available to teachers. Finally, recently developed programs of the sort described by Carpenter et al. (in press) and Peterson et al. (in press) for enhancing teachers' abilities at diagnosing cognitions and knowledge states in children should be expanded and encouraged.

In summary, parents, researchers, school psychologists, and others depend very heavily on the assessments of achievement provided by teachers. Further, these assessments constitute important elements in the teaching process. It is time that we began giving these measures the same attention accorded other types of measuring instruments.

REFERENCES

Achenbach, T. M., McConaughy, S. H., & Howell, C. T. (1987). Child/adolescent behavioral and emotional problems: Implications of cross-informant correlations for situational specificity. *Psychological Bulletin, 101,* 213–232.

Airasian, P. W., Kellaghan, T., Madaus, G. F., & Pedulla, J. J. (1977). Proportion and direction of teacher rating changes of pupils' progress attributable to standardized test information. *Journal of Educational Psychology, 69,* 668–678.

Babad, E., Inbar, J., & Rosenthal, R. (1982). Pygmalion, Galatea, and the Golem: Investigations of biased and unbiased teachers. *Journal of Educational Psychology, 74,* 459–474.

Borko, H., & Cadwell, J. (1982). Individual differences in teachers' decision strategies: An investigation of classroom organization and management decisions.

Journal of Educational Psychology, 74, 598–610.

Borko, H., Cone, R., Russo, N. A., & Shavelson, R. J. (1979). Teachers' decision making. In P. L. Peterson & H. J. Walberg (Eds.), *Research on teaching: Concepts, findings, and implications* (pp. 136–160). Berkeley, CA: McCutchan.

Brophy, J. E. (1983). Research on the self-fulfilling prophecy and teacher expectations. *Journal of Educational Psychology, 75,* 631–661.

Brophy, J. E., & Good, T. L. (1974). *Teacher-student relationships: Causes and consequences.* New York: Holt, Rinehart and Winston.

Carpenter, T. P., Fennema, E., Peterson, P. L., & Carey, D. A. (1988). Teachers' pedagogical content knowledge of students' problem solving in elementary arithmetic. *Journal for Research in Mathematics Education, 19,* 385–401.

Carpenter, T. P., Fennema, E., Peterson, P. L., Chiang, C., & Loef, M. (in press). Using knowledge of children's mathematics thinking in classroom teaching: An experimental study. *American Educational Research Journal.*

Clark, C. M., & Peterson, P. L. (1986). Teachers' thought processes. In M. C. Wittrock (Ed.). *Third handbook of research on teaching* (pp. 255–296). New York: Macmillan.

Coladarci, T. (1986). Accuracy of teacher judgments of student responses to standardized test items. *Journal of Educational Psychology, 78,* 141–146.

Colker, L. (1984, April). *Teachers' interactive thoughts about pupil cognition.* Paper presented at the annual meeting of the American Educational Research Association, Chicago.

Doherty, J., & Conolly, M. (1985). How accurately can primary school teachers predict the scores of their pupils in standardised tests of attainment? A study of some non-cognitive factors that influence specific judgments. *Educational Studies, 11,* 41–60.

Dusek, J. B., & Joseph, G. (1983). The bases of teacher expectancies: A meta-analysis. *Journal of Educational Psychology, 75,* 327–346.

Edelbrock, C. (1983). Problems and issues in using rating scales to assess child personality and psychopathology. *School Psychology Review, 12,* 293–299.

Egan, O., & Archer, P. (1985). The accuracy of teachers' ratings of ability: A regression model. *American Educational Research Journal, 22,* 25–34.

Elliott, S. N., Gresham, F. M., Freeman, T., & McCloskey, G. (1988). Teacher and observer ratings of children's social skills: Validation of the Social Skills Rating Scales. *Journal of Psychoeducational Assessment, 6,* 152–161.

Farr, R., & Roelke, P. (1971). Measuring subskills of reading: Intercorrelations between standardized reading tests, teachers' ratings, and reading specialists' ratings. *Journal of Educational Measurement, 8,* 27–32.

Gage, N. L., & Cronbach, L. J. (1955). Conceptual and methodological problems in interpersonal perception. *Psychological Review, 62,* 411–422.

Gerber, M. M., & Semmel, M. I. (1984). Teacher as imperfect test: Reconceptualizing the referral process. *Educational Psychologist, 19,* 137–148.

Gresham, F. M. (1981). Social skills training with handicapped children: A review. *Review of Educational Research, 51,* 139–176.

Gresham, F. M., Reschly, D. J., & Carey, M. P. (1987). Teachers as "tests": Classification accuracy and concurrent validation in the identification of learning disabled children. *School Psychology Review, 16,* 543–553.

Helmke, A., & Schrader, F-W. (1987). Interactional effects of instructional quality and teacher judgment accuracy on achievement. *Teaching and Teacher Education, 3,* 91–98.

Hoge, R. D. (1983). Psychometric properties of teacher-judgment measures of pupil aptitudes, classroom behaviors, and achievement levels. *Journal of Special Education, 17,* 401–429.

Hoge, R. D. (1984). The definition and measurement of teacher expectations: Problems and prospects. *Canadian Journal of Education, 9,* 213–228.

Hoge, R. D., & Butcher, R. (1984). Analysis of teacher judgments of pupil achievement levels. *Journal of Educational Psychology, 76,* 777–781.

Hoge, R. D., & Cudmore, L. (1986). The use of teacher-judgment measures in the identification of gifted pupils. *Teaching and Teacher Education, 2,* 181–195.

Hopkins, K. D., Dobson, J. C., & Oldridge, O. A. (1962). The concurrent and congruent validities of the Wide Range Achievement Test. *Educational and Psychological Measurement, 22,* 791–793.

Hopkins, K. D., George, C. A., & Williams, D. D. (1985). The concurrent validity of standardized achievement tests by content area using teachers' ratings as criteria. *Journal of Educational Measurement, 22,* 177–182.

Kenny, D. A., & Albright, L. (1987). Accuracy in interpersonal perception: A social-relations analysis. *Psychological Bulletin, 102,* 390–402.

Leinhardt, G. (1983). Novice and expert knowledge of individual student's achievement. *Educational Psychologist, 18,* 165–179.

Linn, R. L. (1986). Educational testing and assessment: Research needs and policy issues. *American Psychologist, 41,* 1153–1160.

Luce, S. R., & Hoge, R. D. (1978). Relations among teacher rankings, pupil-teacher interactions, and academic achievement: A test of the teacher expectancy hypothesis. *American Educational Research Journal, 15,* 489–500.

McNair, K. (1978–1979). Capturing inflight decisions: Thoughts while teaching. *Educational Research Quarterly, 3,* 26–42.

Oliver, J. E., & Arnold, R. D. (1978). Comparing a standardized test, an informal inventory and teacher judgment on third grade reading. *Reading Improvement, 15,* 56–59.

Pedulla, J. J., Airasian, P. W., & Madaus, G. F. (1980). Do teacher ratings and standardized test results of students yield the same information? *American Educational Research Journal, 17,* 303–307.

Peterson, P. L. (1988). Teachers' and students' cognitional knowledge for classroom teaching and learning. *Educational Researcher, 17*(5), 5–14.

Peterson, P. L., Carpenter, T., & Fennema, E. (in press). Teachers' knowledge of students' knowledge in mathematics problem solving: Correlation and case analysis. *Journal of Educational Psychology.*

Sattler, J. M. (1988). *Assessment of children* (3rd ed.). San Diego, CA: Sattler Publishing Co.

Sharpley, C. F., & Edgar, E. (1986). Teachers' ratings vs standardized tests: An empirical investigation of agreement between two indices of achievement. *Psychology in the Schools, 23,* 106–111.

Shavelson, R. J., & Borko, H. (1979). Research on teachers' decisions in planning instruction. *Educational Horizons, 57,* 183–189.

Shavelson, R. J., & Stern, P. (1981). Research on teachers' pedagogical thoughts, judgments, decisions, and behavior. *Review of Educational Research, 51,* 455–498.

Shavelson, R. J., Webb, N. M., & Burstein, L. (1986). Measurement of teaching. In M. C. Wittrock (Ed.), *Third handbook of research on teaching* (pp. 50–91). New York: Macmillan.

Silverstein, A. B., Brownlee, L., Legutki, G., & MacMillan, D. L. (1983). Convergent and discriminant validation of two methods of assessing three academic traits. *Journal of Special Education, 17,* 63–68.

Snow, R. E. (1980). Aptitude and achievement. In W. B. Schrader (Ed.), *Measur-*

ing achievement: Progress over a decade (pp. 39–59). San Francisco: Jossey-Bass.

Tom, D. Y. H., Cooper, H., & McGraw, M. (1984). Influences of student background and teacher authoritarianism on teacher expectations. *Journal of Educational Psychology, 76*, 259–265.

Wright, D., & Wiese, M. J. (1988). Teacher judgment in student evaluation: A comparison of grading methods. *Journal of Educational Research, 82*, 10–14.

AUTHORS

ROBERT D. HOGE is Professor, Department of Psychology, Carleton University, Ottawa, Ontario, KIS 5B6, Canada. He specializes in educational psychology and psychological assessment.

THEODORE COLADARCI is Associate Professor, College of Education, University of Maine, Orono, ME 04469. He specializes in educational psychology.

Name Index

Rowe, D. W., 50, 158, 202
Ruhl, K. L., 126

Santa, C. M., 3
Schneider, W., 114
Schreiner, R., 95
Scruggs, T. E., 104–107
Seifert, M., 42
Seyfarth, J., 130
Shanahan, T., 29, 155
Shapiro, S., 92
Siefert, 137
Slavin, R. E., 2, 3, 255, 264, 299
Smith, J. K., 30
Smith, M. L., 30
Solomon, D., 228
Sørensen, A. B., 102–103, 106–107
Sparks, G. M., 138
Stahl, S. A., 36, 37, 258, 259
Stock, W. A., 255
Sullivan, H. J., 180, 223
Sundbye, N., 36
Swanson, B. B., 111
Sweetland, R. C., 311

Thames, D. G., 46
Treiber, B., 114

Van Maanen, J., 30, 195
Vukelich, C., 149, 199

Walberg, H. J., 113
Wardrop, J. L., 94
Watson, M. S., 228
Webb, N. M., 138
Wechsler, D., 25
Welch, W. W., 168, 208
Westerberg, V., 36, 37
Wiederholt, J. L., 131
Wiener, J., 272
Wiersma, W., 155, 195
Wilkinson, I., 94
Willig, A. C., 261
Willower, D. J., 178, 237
Willson, V., 26
Wilson, P. T., 116
Wilson, S., 30, 195
Wixson, K. K., 50, 55
Woodcock, R. W., 25

Yopp, H. K., 136
Yoshida, R. K., 26

Zutell, J., 150, 201, 229

Subject Index

Interviews, 26
Inventories, 125

Likert-type scale, 128
Literature review, 90, 241

Matched group design, 158
Mean, 28, 188
Median, 28
Meta-analyses of research, 255, 261,
    269
Method sections, 45
Microfiche, 305
Multiple correlation, 194
Multiple regression (*see* Multiple
    correlation)

Nominal scales, 188
Nonequivalent control group, 158
Nonparametric statistics, 194
Norm, 188
Normal distribution curve, 188, 213
Normal probability curve (*see*
    Normal distribution curve)
Norm-referenced tests, 25, 121

Operational definition, 125

Parametric statistics, 191
Participant observation, 30
Pilot study, 146
Population, 10, 109
    accessible, 111
    sample, 109
    target, 109, 110
Practical significance, 191
Procedure section, 47
Product-moment correlation, 192
Purpose, statement of, 10
    (*See also* Hypothesis)
Purpose section, 44

Qualitative method, 30, 34, 186
    descriptive research, 29
Quantitative data, 212

Quantitative method, 26, 186, 212
    descriptive research, 26
Question, research, 10
Questionnaires, 26, 125
    interviews, 125
    inventories, 125
    open-ended, 125
    structured, 125

Randomization, 37
    assignment, 166
    sample, stratified, 113
    sampling, 112
    selection, 166
Reading plan, 58
Reference section, 58
Reliability, 130
    coefficient, 134
    Cronbach alpha, 135
    equivalent forms, 134
    interjudge, 134
    internal consistency, 134
    interrater, 134
    Kuder–Richardson formula, 135
    parallel forms, 134
    rater, 134
    scorer, 134
    split-half, 134
    test–retest, 134
Replication, 93
Research, 2
    action, 171
    attrition, 152
    baseline measure, 168
    causal–comparative experimental
        design, 166
    causal–comparative research, 37
    causation, 25
    causative, 9
    comparative, 9, 25
    comparison group, 155
    control group, 155
    counterbalanced design, 159
    current events, 152
    descriptive, 9, 25, 26, 146
    ethnographic, 30
    evaluation, 175
    experimental, 9, 25
    experimental designs, 154
    experimental group, 155